Anti-Catholicism in the Mexican Revolution, 1913–1940

Diálogos Series
Kris Lane, Series Editor

Understanding Latin America demands dialogue, deep exploration, and frank discussion of key topics. Founded by Lyman L. Johnson in 1992 and edited since 2013 by Kris Lane, the Diálogos Series focuses on innovative scholarship in Latin American history and related fields. The series, the most successful of its type, includes specialist works accessible to a wide readership and a variety of thematic titles, all ideally suited for classroom adoption by university and college teachers.

Also available in the Diálogos Series:

The Struggle for Natural Resources: Findings from Bolivian History edited by Carmen Soliz and Rossana Barragán
Viceroy Güemes's Mexico: Rituals, Religion, and Revenue by Christoph Rosenmüller
At the Heart of the Borderlands: Africans and Afro-Descendants on the Edges of Colonial Spanish America edited by Cameron D. Jones and Jay T. Harrison
The Age of Dissent: Revolution and the Power of Communication in Chile, 1780–1833 by Martín Bowen
From Sea-Bathing to Beach-Going: A Social History of the Beach in Rio de Janeiro, Brazil by B. J. Barickman
Gamboa's World: Justice, Silver Mining, and Imperial Reform in New Spain by Christopher Albi
The Conquest of the Desert: Argentina's Indigenous Peoples and the Battle for History edited by Carolyne R. Larson
From the Galleons to the Highlands: Slave Trade Routes in the Spanish Americas edited by Alex Borucki, David Eltis, and David Wheat
A Troubled Marriage: Indigenous Elites of the Colonial Americas by Sean F. McEnroe
Staging Frontiers: The Making of Modern Popular Culture in Argentina and Uruguay by William Garrett Acree Jr.

For additional titles in the Diálogos Series, please visit unmpress.com.

ANTI-CATHOLICISM in the MEXICAN REVOLUTION, 1913-1940

Edited by **JÜRGEN BUCHENAU**

and **DAVID S. DALTON**

© 2024 by the University of New Mexico Press
All rights reserved. Published 2024
Printed in the United States of America

ISBN 978-0-8263-6690-0 (cloth)
ISBN 978-0-8263-6691-7 (paper)
ISBN 978-0-8263-6692-4 (ePub)
ISBN 978-0-8263-6693-1 (pdf)

Library of Congress Cataloging-in-Publication data is on file with the Library of Congress.

Founded in 1889, the University of New Mexico sits on the traditional homelands of the Pueblo of Sandia. The original peoples of New Mexico—Pueblo, Navajo, and Apache—since time immemorial have deep connections to the land and have made significant contributions to the broader community statewide. We honor the land itself and those who remain stewards of this land throughout the generations and also acknowledge our committed relationship to Indigenous peoples. We gratefully recognize our history.

Cover illustration: adapted from political cartoon published ca. 1930
Designed by Isaac Morris
Composed in Impact and Scala Pro

Contents

vii	LIST OF ILLUSTRATIONS
viii	TIMELINE OF EVENTS
xii	ACKNOWLEDGMENTS
1	INTRODUCTION. The Role of Anti-Catholicism in the Mexican Revolution JÜRGEN BUCHENAU AND DAVID S. DALTON

SECTION I. Anti-Catholicism in Government

21	CHAPTER ONE. Plutarco Elías Calles: Patriarch of Revolutionary Anti-Catholicism JÜRGEN BUCHENAU
48	CHAPTER TWO. Lawyers, Guns, and Money: Revolution, Religion, and Authoritarianism in Tabasco, Mexico, 1920–1936 SARAH OSTEN
77	CHAPTER THREE. Educating Anti-Catholicism: Manuel Gamio, Indigenismo, and Secular Redemption DAVID S. DALTON

SECTION II. Popular Anti-Catholicism

99	CHAPTER FOUR. A Gendered Anticlericalism: Feminist Intellectuals, Sexuality, and the Mexican Revolution ELISSA J. RASHKIN
126	CHAPTER FIVE. "Desfanatizar y Desalcoholizar la Población": The Interrelated Anti-Catholic and Anti-Alcohol Campaigns GRETCHEN PIERCE

SECTION III. Alternatives to Catholicism

157   CHAPTER SIX. The Germ of Fanaticism: Anti-Catholicism, Scientism, and Tabasconization, ca. 1925–1935
BEN FALLAW

191   CHAPTER SEVEN. From Heaven to Earth: Rivera, Siqueiros, and the Mexican Muralist Project
HÉCTOR JAIMES

213   CHAPTER EIGHT. Immigrant Religious Communities in an Anti-Catholic Context: Mormons and Mennonites Petition the Mexican State, 1928–1936
REBECCA JANZEN

236   AFTERWORD. The Ever-Cooling Worlds of Mexican Anti-Catholicism
MATTHEW BUTLER

257   GLOSSARY
259   LIST OF CONTRIBUTORS
262   INDEX

Illustrations

24	FIGURE 1. Plutarco Elías Calles
32	FIGURE 2. Anti-Catholics in the Council of Ministers: Morones, Calles, Obregón, and Tejeda, 1925
38	FIGURE 3. Hortensia Elías Calles Chacón on the day of her religious wedding, 1923
76	FIGURE 4. Manuel Gamio, 1924
130	FIGURE 5. Unifying the Anti-Alcohol Campaign
132	FIGURE 6. Red Saturdays, Bourgeois Saturdays
160	FIGURE 7. Tomás Garrido Canabal, 1923
196	FIGURE 8. Diego Rivera, Symbols of the New Regime
202	FIGURE 9. David Alfaro Siqueiros, The Devil in the Church

Timeline of Events

1856–1857	Culminating in the 1857 Constitution, a series of Liberal laws restrict the Catholic Church by installing lay public education, eliminating Church influence in political matters, and nationalizing its landholdings.
1857–1861	Reform War between Liberals and Conservatives ends in a Liberal victory under President Benito Juárez and additional strictures on the Church.
1864–1867	Following the French occupation of Mexico, Conservatives crown Habsburg Prince Maximilian emperor, hoping that he will restore Church property and privileges.
1876–1910	Era of General Porfirio Díaz features a dictatorship and mutual toleration between church and state despite the provisions of the 1857 Constitution.
1910 (Nov. 20)	Francisco I. Madero issues a manifesto to overthrow Díaz and restore democracy in Mexico, thus beginning the first phase of the Mexican Revolution.
1911 (May)	Díaz resigns, paving the way to Madero's election in October.
1911 (Oct.)	Madero elected president; the Mexican Catholic Party gains seats in the federal Congress.
1913 (Feb. 19)	General Victoriano Huerta's coup d'état leads to Madero's resignation, followed by his assassination three days later. Anti-Catholics blame the Church for the coup.
1913–1914	Second phase of the Mexican Revolution: the war against the Huerta dictatorship. Four major revolutionary factions formulate social and economic goals in addition to calling for the removal of the dictator.

1914 (Jan. 11)	The Mexican episcopate consecrates Mexico to Christ the King. Beginning of first wave of revolutionary anti-Catholicism, resulting in anticlerical laws in areas where anti-Huerta insurgents control state and local governments.
1914 (July 15)	Huerta's resignation paves the way for the third phase of the revolution, the War of the Winners, among the victorious factions.
1915 (Feb.)	Obregón's general summons of Mexico City clergy to the National Palace on pain of death (foreign priests subsequently deported; nationals detained, fined, expelled, and given medical exams to identify STDs).
1915 (summer)	Triumph of Venustiano Carranza's and Álvaro Obregón's Constitutionalist alliance over Pancho Villa and Emiliano Zapata's Conventionist coalition.
1916	Two Feminist Congresses held in Yucatán, convoked by the state government of Salvador Alvarado. Some participants express anticlerical positions regarding issues such as marriage and family planning.
1917 (Feb. 5)	Promulgation of Constitution of 1917. Episcopate rejects the new constitution and particularly its anticlerical provisions. President Venustiano Carranza ignores these new provisions.
1920–1924	Presidency of Álvaro Obregón begins the era of reconstruction. His government does not implement the anticlerical provisions of the constitution.
1924–1928	Presidency of Plutarco Elías Calles, characterized by growing conflict with the Church.
1925 (Feb. 21)	Soledad incident in Mexico City inaugurates schismatic Iglesia Católica Apostólica Mexicana (ICAM); Roman Catholics mobilize in protest.

1926 (Feb. 5)	*El Universal* publishes old declarations of the Mexico City archbishop to the effect that Catholics should combat the Constitution of 1917; repression of the Church ensues. Second wave of revolutionary anti-Catholicism begins.
1926 (June 14)	A reform of the penal code, the Calles Law criminalizes routine activities of ministry.
1926 (July 31)	Mexican clergy suspend all public religious ceremonies.
1926–1929	The Cristero War (Cristiada) features a large-scale uprising in central and western Mexico.
1928 (July 17)	President-elect Obregón assassinated by a devout Catholic.
1928–1935	Obregón's assassination leads to Calles's informal political role as *jefe máximo* (supreme chief) of the revolution.
1929 (June 21)	Brokered by US Ambassador Dwight Morrow, an agreement between the episcopate and President Emilio Portes Gil ends the Cristiada without addressing the root causes of the conflict.
1930	Beginning of third wave of revolutionary anti-Catholicism, featuring repression of the Church at the state level and then the promulgation of socialist education at the federal level.
1932–1937	So-called Second Cristiada characterized by sporadic violence in the countryside, particularly in western and central Mexico.
1934 (July 20)	Calles's *grito de Guadalajara* calls for a psychological revolution against "eternal enemies of the Revolution," especially Catholicism.

1934 (Dec. 13)	Publication of the amendment to the constitutional article 3, introducing socialist education to "combat fanaticism."
1934–1940	President Lázaro Cárdenas pays lip service to anti-Catholicism but slowly de-escalates the conflict.
1940 (Sept. 30)	Incoming President Manuel Ávila Camacho declares "yo soy creyente" (I am a believer), signaling the fact that his government will not continue anti-Catholic policies.

Acknowledgments

This volume started like many others, with a conversation at a conference. In March 2017, the two editors—faculty members in different departments at UNC Charlotte—discussed this idea at a beer garden during a meeting of the Southeastern Council of Latin American Studies in Chapel Hill. Over the next year, we were lucky enough to find six authors who were as interested as we were in exploring anti-Catholicism in the Mexican Revolution.

The book would not have been possible without collaboration and support. To begin with, we wish to thank our contributing authors, who diligently worked with us throughout the process from the initial idea through several drafts, a book proposal, and the publication process. Scholarly publications almost always take more time than anticipated, and we appreciate the team's patience, especially as we navigated the interdisciplinary nature of our project. A special word of thanks to Matthew Butler for authoring a thought-provoking afterword to round out the book and for providing valuable suggestions to the rest of us in the process.

We consider ourselves very lucky to have this book included in the highly regarded *Diálogos* series published by the University of New Mexico Press. Thank you to Michael Millman, the press's Senior Acquisitions Editor, for his support of the project. Series editor Kris Lane provided valuable suggestions for improvement. The manuscript also benefited from the sage advice of Jason Dormady and one anonymous reader. Financial support for this project, and specifically for the images and the index, came from the Office of Interdisciplinary Studies and the Dowd chair endowment at UNC Charlotte.

Introduction

The Role of Anti-Catholicism in the Mexican Revolution

JÜRGEN BUCHENAU AND DAVID S. DALTON

In 1919 the medic and philosopher Eduardo Urzaiz Rodríguez (1876–1955) published his only novel, *Eugenia: esbozo novelesco de costumbres futuras*. Born in Cuba, Urzaiz had followed his family to Mérida in the southeastern Mexican state of Yucatán at the age of fourteen. There, he experienced the Mexican Revolution, which began in 1910 with the aim of overthrowing the longtime dictator General Porfirio Díaz (1830–1915) but acquired wide-ranging economic, social, and cultural aims as it progressed. Urzaiz set his novel in a distant-future Mérida rebaptized as Villautopía, and he espoused revolutionary ideals by imagining a utopian society where men and women enjoyed equal rights to work and own property. The novel fits within a corpus of literary, utopian Mexican texts that imagined different paths toward modernity through a combination of eugenics and social revolution, along with Manuel Gamio's *Forjando patria* (1916) and José Vasconcelos's *La raza cósmica* (1925).[1] *Eugenia* stands out through its premise that the late-1910s socialist experiments in revolutionary Yucatán could only succeed by means of the removal of the Catholic Church—and religion in general—from the national consciousness.[2] Indeed, the novel imagines a future society, now free from the Catholic Church that had dominated Mexico since the Spanish conquest, where the people enjoy free love, the socialist dissolution of the family unit (a necessary step in abolishing the inheritance system that kept capital in the hands of powerful families), and a radical reimagining of gender roles.

In contrast to other revolutionary intellectuals (like Vasconcelos, Gamio, or even Alfonso Caso), Urzaiz has been largely forgotten. While his prominence at the Universidad Autónoma de Yucatán ensured occasional reprints of his novel, most critics either ignored it or referred to it as little more than a pioneering work of the science fiction traditions of Mexico and Latin America.[3] In a larger sense, Urzaiz's relative marginalization reflects the fact that few scholars have studied revolutionary anti-Catholicism with the kind of keen interest that has characterized the historiography of the dominant Roman Catholic Church in Mexico or even popular religion.[4]

This book addresses the need for a deeper interrogation of anti-Catholicism in revolutionary Mexico. It employs a multidisciplinary framework to discuss anti-Catholic scholars, political leaders, activists, religious minorities, and social movements during the revolution. Drawing on precedents going back to the Bourbon reforms of the eighteenth century, Mexican anti-Catholics navigated what one might call an "hour of unbelief" that began with the resistance to General Victoriano Huerta's coup d´état in 1913 and ended in 1940 when the incoming President Manuel Ávila Camacho proclaimed "yo soy creyente" (I am a believer).[5] Anti-Catholicism appeared across all social strata, from presidents to middle-class intellectuals to agrarian and labor activists. This assessment complicates Jean Meyer's classic contrast of "elite" anticlericalism versus "popular" Catholicism.[6] The country could only truly move past the violence triggered by the revolution after the reconciliation between Catholics and anti-Catholics.[7]

Not frequently used in the historical literature on Mexico, anti-Catholicism is an overarching category that connects Mexico's faith history to those of other nations. A phenomenon as ancient as the Church itself, anti-Catholicism includes all beliefs and measures opposed to the worldview, doctrine, and practices of the Roman Catholic Church, its clergy, and its faithful. One early popular manifestation of anti-Catholicism came in the Pueblo Revolt (1680), whose leader, Popé, proclaimed the death of the Christian god once his Indigenous forces had temporarily expelled the Spaniards from the province of Santa Fe de Nuevo México. Some anti-Catholics are irreligious. Others subscribe to Protestant and Restorationist faith traditions.

Anticlericalism is a narrower term than anti-Catholicism. Anticlericalism opposes religious authority in political or social matters and particularly focuses on the clergy. Its wellspring is the charge that the Catholic clergy take their orders from the papacy based in Rome. As early as the 1520s, the Italian philosopher Niccolò Machiavelli asserted that the Church would usurp power from any head of state who granted it too many privileges.[8] Since then, anticlericalism has reared its head on numerous occasions in Mexican and world history. In the eighteenth century, for example, Bourbon reformers assailed the Roman Catholic clergy as a state within the state—a hierarchy disloyal to the colonial government. These charges contributed to the expulsion of the Jesuits from the Spanish Empire in 1767. Many anticlericals, however, were religious—even Catholic—in private. Some supported other Catholicisms like the Iglesia Católica Apostólica Mexicana (ICAM), or Mexican Catholic Apostolic Church.[9]

A sketch of Mexican anti-Catholicism since independence will outline the significance of this topic. In the first decades after independence, a coalition of reformers—known first as Federalists and later as Liberals—sought to limit the wealth and political influence of the Catholic Church. At the time, the Church owned half of the nation's arable land and enjoyed special legal protection, including a provision in the Constitution of 1824 that identified Mexico as a Catholic nation. In 1855 a Liberal coalition came to power bent on breaking the Church's influence following examples from France and the United States. Under the leadership of Benito Juárez—Mexico's only Indigenous president thus far—Liberal laws and the Constitution of 1857 stripped the Church of most of its land and virtual monopoly over education. These measures led to the devastating Reform War. Allied with the Church, the Conservatives ousted the Liberals from Mexico City, leading to Juárez's subsequent *Leyes de Reforma* (Reform Laws) that nationalized most Church property, suppressed convents and monasteries, and instituted civil marriage. In the opinion of the historian David Gilbert, it was the "end of Catholic Mexico."[10]

The Liberals triumphed in the war, but in 1863 a French invasion army occupied Mexico in collaboration with the Conservatives. The following year, the coalition installed a Habsburg emperor, Maximilian, who did not repeal the Liberal laws, much to the chagrin of the Church hierarchy. The conflict abated after Juárez's return to power following Maximilian's execution in 1867. After 1876 the Church enjoyed a mutually beneficial relationship with the longtime dictator Porfirio Díaz, who did not enforce the anticlerical clauses in the constitution. In return, the episcopate did not openly challenge the language of the Liberal legislation still on the books.

Initially, this policy of mutual toleration did not change when the revolution led by Francisco I. Madero overthrew Díaz in May 1911. Madero had called for effective suffrage and parliamentary democracy, not measures to be taken against the Church. Likewise, the landless poor allied with Madero wanted land from landowners who had usurped their holdings before and during the Díaz dictatorship. While the opposition to the Díaz regime had included anarchists such as the Flores Magón brothers, who assailed the Church as part of an oligarchy in cahoots with large landowners and foreign mining companies that repressed the poor majority, Madero's program did not target Catholicism. The Church thus lent him tepid support, and Madero's parliamentary democracy—limited as it was—featured the emergence of the Partido Católico Nacional (National Catholic Party) in the federal and several state legislatures and that party's dominance in the state of Jalisco. But the Church withdrew its support when Madero demanded that the clergy respect the limitations of its power as decreed in the constitution.

In February 1913, the establishment of the Huerta dictatorship after the brutal murders of Madero and Vice President José María Pino Suárez helped seed revolutionary anti-Catholicism. Like many of Madero's former allies, the Church chose to cooperate with Huerta, angering the factions who revolted against this new dictatorship. Anti-Catholicism played an important role in the diverse cast of revolutionary factions that rose up against this illegitimate government.[11] By then, the northern factions led by Venustiano Carranza, Álvaro Obregón, and Pancho Villa had turned against a Church that, in their estimation, had enabled Huerta's usurpation of power and hence, indirectly, the deaths of Madero and Pino Suárez. The anti-Catholic sentiments among the revolutionaries reached a boiling point in January 1914 when the Church consecrated Mexico to Christ the King. That act implied its stamp of approval of Huerta's government.

Examples abound during what the historian Adrian Bantjes called the first wave of revolutionary anticlericalism from 1914 to 1917.[12] During the war against Huerta, Villa's troops in Chihuahua and other northern states made headlines by murdering foreign priests. In Jalisco, the Sonoran general Obregón and his ally, Manuel M. Diéguez, ousted the ruling National Catholic Party and declared the Church their primary enemy. In the ensuing War of the Winners, which pitted Carranza's and Obregón's "Constitutionalists" against Villa and Emiliano Zapata's "Conventionists," anti-Catholicism became the hallmark of the Constitutionalist faction. Constitutionalist state governors such as Diéguez, Plutarco Elías Calles, and Yucatán's Salvador Alvarado made anticlericalism official policy.[13] State-level policies then influenced the negotiation of a new constitution in the city of Querétaro (1916–1917). Addressing the social causes such as landlessness and miserable working conditions that had motivated ordinary Mexicans to take up arms during the revolution, this constitution was the first such document on the world stage that guaranteed social rights while also enunciating a stringently anticlerical code.[14]

Some scholars have identified the ratification of a new constitution as the end of the revolution. Others have signaled the Plan of Agua Prieta of 1920 as the moment that marked the beginning of the postrevolutionary period due to its status as the final successful coup d'état in Mexican history. These dates are clearly important because they heralded a change in regime that set the framework for reconstruction. That said, the insistence on such a clean transition ignores the fact that the passage of the constitution and the triumph of the Sonoran Dynasty in 1920 did not eliminate conflict or bring in a stable new order. Rather, its sweeping provisions regarding education, land tenure, labor, the rights of foreigners, and public health placed it in conflict with different stakeholders throughout the nation.[15] State, local, and federal governments implemented these provisions, but they did so haltingly and, in some cases, not at all. The chapters in this book do not seek to resolve the issue of when, exactly, the revolution ended and gave way to a postrevolutionary phase. Instead, we focus on the fact that the new constitution, far from reconciling a war-torn public, established the conditions for the next phase of the conflict.

In terms of its strictures on the Catholic Church, the new document went far beyond the provisions of the 1857 Constitution, at least in theory. The new constitution featured a radical separation of church and state and, arguably, the repression of Catholic believers and the clergy. Article 3 prohibited the teaching of religion in any schools, public or private. Article 5 denounced religious vows, equating them with slavery. Article 13 stripped religious organizations of their legal status. Article 24 restricted the exercise of worship to Church and private property; article 33 threatened foreign residents (including priests) with expulsion at the discretion of the federal executive, and article 130 denied citizenship rights to the clergy and allowed the state to regulate the practice of religion.[16]

The promulgation of the revolutionary constitution set the tone for the church-state conflict in the 1920s. The episcopate never accepted the new constitution, and some archbishops rejected it in its entirety. In turn, unlike the administrations of Porfirio Díaz, the revolutionary governments viewed the task of reining in the Church as key to their own legitimacy. As such, they took steps to put anticlerical provisions into practice. For example, the Obregón administration (1920–1924) sent to the countryside federally trained teachers who attempted to instill nationalist and anti-Catholic values among the nation's rural population. Over the next two decades, the zeal of federal teachers to "defanaticize" rural Mexicans via scientific education led many Catholic leaders to cast them as agents of the devil.[17] Defined as an effort to reduce what anti-Catholics saw as fanatical religious fervor, "defanatization" became a flashpoint of conflict as Catholics interpreted it as an effort to wipe out their religion. Violent clashes became the norm, and, according to the historian Jean Meyer, a "second Revolution" enveloped the nation.[18] Religious and anti-Catholic activists squared off in the cultural, economic, political, and social arenas, as Catholic lay mobilization clashed with government restrictions on religious practice.[19]

After 1924, President Plutarco Elías Calles directed the apex of the anti-Catholic momentum. He was the archetype of the enemies of the Church: a believer in economic development, scientific progress, public education, and public health; a nationalist resentful of both US and "ultramontane" papal interference; disdainful of both the Church hierarchy and popular Catholicism; and willing to use authoritarian methods to achieve political and cultural objectives. Calles's attempt to enforce the anticlerical policies in the constitution via a reform of the penal code led to a violent conflict known as the Cristiada (1926–1929). The war ended with a ceasefire that saw the Catholic Church disavow the Cristeros in exchange for a respite from the enforcement of the anticlerical Calles Law. There were also "defanaticization campaigns" that included the profanation of Catholic churches and religious symbols. No other issue during these years excited popular opinion as much as the conflict between church and state. After the end of Calles's presidential term, when the strongman continued to play a significant political role as *jefe máximo* (or supreme chief), a revolutionary regime that had run out of steam in its reform drive kept up the flames of anti-Catholicism. Finally, President Lázaro Cárdenas (1934–1940) rekindled the movement for social reform while gradually dialing down the confrontation with the Church. Of course, Ávila Camacho's profession of faith in 1940 did not end anti-Catholicism in Mexico, which has continued to exist to this day, but it did signal the twilight of the revolutionary anti-Catholic moment analyzed in this book.

In the end, the Church stood strong despite these challenges.[20] In contrast to the Central American countries, where Protestantism has made major inroads, for example, Mexico remains primarily Catholic. According to the Pew Research Center, 81 percent of Mexico's population in 2014 identified itself as Catholic, as opposed to only 50 percent in Guatemala.[21] The Catholic Church in Mexico owes much of its resilience to its ability to weather the serious attacks of the revolutionary period. Another reason for its success lies in the fact that women's lay organizations served as a primary vehicle of Catholic mobilization since the 1850s, strengthening Catholic resistance against its adversaries.[22]

The foes of Roman Catholicism may have never claimed the hearts and minds of the majority of the Mexican population, but they strove to achieve just that through their combative stance toward both the Church and popular manifestations of Catholic faith. These actors left a palpable effect on the country at large. While the Church would regain much of the prominence it had enjoyed before the conflict, the state had also secured primacy in education and establishing itself as the sole legal arbiter of marital unions. Revolutionary anti-Catholics furthered the cause of separation of church and state.

In that regard, Mexican anti-Catholics shared striking similarities with an array of actors throughout the world who similarly confronted ecclesiastical authorities in the period between the world wars (1918–1939). In the United States, for example, anti-Catholicism manifested in numerous forms, running the gamut from discrimination against Irish and Italian immigrants to the Prohibition movement, which chastised Catholics for their supposed abuse of alcoholic beverages, and all the way to the Ku Klux Klan. In a completely different context, the Nazi party in Germany embraced anti-Catholicism along with its murderous anti-Semitism, even though its fanatical leader, Adolf Hitler, was born in a Catholic household. Indeed, one could argue that anti-Catholicism in this context allowed for the construction of a pliant Protestant Reich Church.[23]

Mexican revolutionary anti-Catholicism was therefore but one movement opposed to dominant religious traditions. The Bolshevik Revolution in deeply Orthodox Russia (1917) and the founding of the Republic of Turkey out of the remnants of the Islamic-dominated Ottoman Empire (1923) stand out. The Bolshevik leader, Vladimir I. Lenin, engaged in a hot conflict with the Russian Orthodox Church, a state religion supporting the Czarist monarchy and, hence, opposed to the Bolshevik cause. During the years 1917–1918, Lenin referred to Patriarch Tikhon as "a leader of the counterrevolutionary clergy," a fact that explicitly tied the state church to subversive and antirevolutionary causes.[24] In a similar vein, Kemal Atatürk's Turkey found itself embroiled in a conflict with an Islamic caliphate that bore striking similarities to Mexico's own Cristero Wars.[25] In each of these cases, revolutionary governments ultimately achieved secular hegemony within their borders only after violent conflict with organized religions and their followers. While the Soviet and Turkish governments weakened state-supported faith traditions, neither antireligious regime succeeded in exorcising religion from the national psyche. Against this global historical backdrop, religion and the role of the Catholic Church served as flashpoints from the earliest days of the Mexican Revolution. Anti-Catholic thinkers, politicians, and actors espoused an array of worldviews. In some cases, one of their only points of agreement was a deep antipathy toward the Catholic Church, an entity they blamed for Mexico's perpetual underdevelopment.[26]

In focusing on anti-Catholicism, this book builds on Matthew Butler's edited volume *Faith and Impiety in Revolutionary Mexico*. Butler took issue with the scholarship's "tendency to view religion in rather *causal* terms—what else can it explain?—and thus to argue it away as intangible or commonplace in comparison to more tangible factors."[27] The author team of this volume posits that one could argue the same for anti-Catholicism, which sat at the fore of the revolutionary struggle as many leaders saw the objective of weakening the Church as a commendable end in and of itself. Just as state leaders "appropriated religious ideas" into public projects, they also explicitly built on irreligious and anti-Catholic ideals.[28] In that way, *Anti-Catholicism in the Mexican Revolution* builds on Butler's groundbreaking work while signaling the need for a deeper interrogation of anti-Catholic thought.

The Many Faces of Anti-Catholicism

Although irreligious Mexicans sought to escape the realm of the faith, they built their ideological world within the imagery and language of a predominantly Catholic culture. As Butler has argued, "enlightened unbelief" featured "scattered theological motifs"[29] expressing a Manichaean struggle between rationalist light and Catholic darkness, carried forward with almost messianic fervor. With good reason, Meyer has called irreligion a "religion of incredulity."[30]

Revolutionary leaders had to weigh their reaction to an array of Catholicisms—and other religions—existing throughout the country. Perhaps the most important division was that between institutional and popular Catholicism. The former referred to the beliefs and practices of the Vatican-based Church, which included sacraments like Communion as well as the Church's infallibility in decreeing doctrine. Popular or folk Catholicism referred to popular religious practices as a way of life.[31] While ostensibly based on Catholic doctrine, popular Catholicism often deviated from the ways of the institutionalized Church by mixing with Indigenous cosmologies. Anti-Catholics often disagreed about how to engage with both institutional and popular Catholicism. Many conflated popular manifestations of personal faith with the institutional reach of the Church. Others, like the famed Golden Age director Emilio "El Indio" Fernández, expressed skepticism in the clergy even as they exalted popular Catholic faith as a positive manifestation of a mestizo nation.

After 1917, national leaders turned to the new constitution to justify their anti-Catholic policies. For example, they used state resources to punish Catholic worship in public outdoor spaces and Catholic-sponsored education, but they often pragmatically supported other faith traditions in an attempt to siphon support away from the Roman Catholic Church. Tending to avoid attacks on religion and belief more generally, revolutionary leaders saw adherents of non-Roman Catholic faiths as potential allies in countering the institutional Catholic Church's hegemony within the country. This held especially true as church and state gradually headed toward conflict in the period 1920–1926.[32]

Sometimes, doing so meant embracing Catholicisms at variance with the Roman Catholic one. Indeed, the schismatic ICAM is a great example of a minority faith that embraced Catholic doctrine but opposed the hierarchy. Anticlerical leaders lent that church support in an attempt to suppress the Holy See's influence in the country by uniting the people under a religious banner that supported the statist ideals of the revolution. Several especially visible cases of state support for the institution came in the 1920s, when anticlerical governors like Tomás Garrido Canabal (Tabasco) and José María Elizalde (Aguascalientes) seized local Catholic churches and handed them over to the ICAM. Anticlerical plans to move the Mexican population to this schismatic church largely failed as the ICAM struggled to convince people to abandon one Catholic Church for another. Local presses in the Bajío region accused the ICAM's founder, José Joaquín Pérez Budar, of seizing churches (even in specific instances where this was not true) and violating the sanctity of the Virgin of Guadalupe, Mexico's patron saint. The irony of such a sensationalist claim was the fact that the ICAM itself identified Guadalupanism as a central tenet of the doctrine of salvation. Indeed, as the historian Matthew Butler shows in his recent work, the ICAM promoted an array of popular manifestations of folk belief dressed in an appropriately revolutionary and anti-Vatican manner. Contrary to the long-standing belief that the ICAM was nothing more than a creation of Mexico's official labor union of the time, the Confederación Regional Obrera Mexicana (CROM, or Mexican Regional Workers' Confederation) became a dissenting voice within Catholicism, a church with "Mexicanized" religious practices. Its constituency was heavily Indigenous. At its peak, there were hundreds of ICAM congregations in the East and Southeast.[33]

The rise of Protestantism in Mexico also represented a particularly potent challenge to Catholicism that continues into the present. This played out in both local contexts and nationally.[34] In September 1923, Aarón Sáenz became the first prominent Protestant in the national government when Álvaro Obregón appointed him as secretary of foreign relations. At the end of the following year, his brother Moisés, a Presbyterian minister, became under-secretary of public education.[35] Protestant and restorationist denominations provided a more radical break with the Roman Catholic Church than did the ICAM.[36] These faith traditions opposed many manifestations of folk Catholicism. To this day, for example, most of these religions employ literalist readings of Exodus 20:4—which forbids worshipping "graven images"—to cast devotion to the Virgin of Guadalupe as sinful. Viewed in this light, it should come as no surprise that revolutionary leaders viewed Protestants and Restorationists as potential allies in their drive against the Catholic Church. Even as the state pushed for greater separation of (Catholic) church and state, then, it built alliances with other faith traditions. Non-Catholic religions could leverage their opposition to Roman Catholicism as a way to build favor with governing bodies throughout the country.

Anti-Catholic discourse also appeared in the nation's cultural production, much of which contributed to debates about the characteristics of a secular society. Few media allowed for a more wide-ranging discussion about church and state than the nation's walls. Héctor Jaimes's chapter explores how the muralists ultimately muted religious discourse through anti-Catholic imagery that foregrounded their support for a Marxist order. Each of the muralists had a different set of personal politics, and each afforded the Church and religion a very different place in their thought.[37] Diego Rivera depicted the Church itself as a colonizing agent that stripped Indigenous societies of their heritage. At the same time, he tended to view pre-Columbian religions and popular, syncretic manifestations of religious devotion in a positive light. The central images of many of his most interesting *indigenista* murals include Indigenous deities as the central image.[38] His Marxist formation notwithstanding, then, Rivera was not so much irreligious as anti-Catholic. He viewed autochthonous manifestations of religious practice—even when done through a Christian referent—as empowering.[39] He himself likely did not ascribe deistic powers to the figures that he depicted, but he *did* recognize and celebrate their social resonance with people throughout the country.

Rivera's positive depictions of pre-Columbian religions resound all the more as we compare them to the decidedly irreligious artistic production of his colleague, José Clemente Orozco, who tended to depict religious figures of all stripes in a negative light. His *Hombre en llamas* series at Hospicio Cabañas in Guadalajara explicitly ties the Roman Catholic Church to genocide and conquest, while his *Historia de las Américas* series at Dartmouth College depict human sacrifice and other pre-Columbian religious practices as the barbaric rituals of a defeated civilization. Whereas Rivera promoted and even celebrated popular religion, Orozco saw religion in all of its forms as degrading and corrupting. Orozco thus blamed religion in general—both Christian and pre-Columbian—for many of the greatest problems facing the country.

The Chapters

Anti-Catholicism in the Mexican Revolution consists of eight chapters organized into three sections, plus an afterword. Section I, Anti-Catholicism in Government, consists of three chapters. The section looks specifically at anti-Catholic government officials. Beyond a focus on elected federal officials, this section also discusses key individuals who held roles in state government or as unelected bureaucrats. Section II, Popular Anti-Catholicism, consists of two chapters that discuss popular cases of anti-Catholic movements that took place in Mexico during these years. Finally, Section III, Alternatives to Catholicism, considers anti-Catholicism among different groups who, themselves, employed utopian and even religious discourses. These include studies on Marxists, scientists, and foreign religious minority groups within the country. While the editors have made these organizational divisions to achieve a level of cohesiveness in the volume, we also recognize that many of the chapters reflect elements of more than one section. Far from a weakness, we argue that this overlap demonstrates the extent of the interconnectedness among the different anti-Catholic currents of the revolutionary period.

We begin our volume with discussions of political leaders because these actors played an outsized role in laying out the conditions under which anti-Catholic activism and policy could flourish. Chapter 1, by Jürgen Buchenau, discusses General and President Plutarco Elías Calles (1877–1945), often considered to be the primary anticlerical in revolutionary Mexico. The chapter argues that Calles's policies stemmed from the political coalitions that sustained him more so than his personal beliefs. Calles's personal aversion to the Catholic religion played an important but secondary role in the Cristiada. Rather, an array of political interests aligned against one another with Calles at the head. Chapter 2, by Sarah Osten, considers the role of state-level leaders in carrying out anti-Catholic projects through an analysis of Tomás Garrido Canabal, Mexico's most virulently anticlerical state governor. First elected in 1922 and later in 1930, Garrido became one of the most powerful regional politicians in Mexico. Anticlericalism became a centerpiece of Garridismo's uncompromising approach, thus situating it within a larger regional socialist movement in the Southeast in those years. Chapter 3, by David S. Dalton, focuses on the influential indigenista intellectual and anthropologist Manuel Gamio. His seminal text, *Forjando patria* (1916), advocated for the modernization of Indigenous communities through science, hygiene, and education. Deeply suspicious of the clergy's continued insistence on influencing national politics, Gamio advocated for a strict separation of church and state. Nevertheless, he also turned to religious vocabulary in articulating the "redemptive" potential of racial miscegenation on the Indigenous masses, a type of secular redemption that depended on religious imaginaries even as it eschewed religious actions and ideals in the public sphere.

The second section focuses on the role of popular movements in implementing anti-Catholic causes. Chapter 4, by Elissa J. Rashkin, explores manifestations of irreligion and anticlericalism in the thought of a group of influential feminists, including Hermila Galindo, Elvia Carrillo Puerto, Esperanza Velázquez Bringas, and Belén de Sárraga, and relates them to debates around sexuality that arose within feminism during the revolutionary period. The affinity of many feminists with Carrancismo or with anarchist, socialist, and communist currents predisposed them toward an opposition to religious institutions and dogma. Furthermore, the struggle for women's rights, especially regarding their bodies and sexuality, meant confrontation with the Church. Chapter 5, by Gretchen Pierce, focuses on the link between anticlericalism and campaigns against alcohol use. Creating citizens who were both sober and secular was essential to the government's goal of forming modern men, women, and children, and indeed, the stability of the revolution. However, many popular reformers also argued that Catholic festivals led to intemperate consumption or that priests allied with exploitative landowners who plied their peons with drink to keep them impoverished. In addition, these individuals often focused on alcohol's effects—like poor health, indolence, and indigence—many of which overlapped with problems supposedly caused by "fanaticism." As a result, average citizens of a variety of racial, class, and gender identities worked toward simultaneously achieving the goals of both movements.

The final section discusses alternatives to the institutional Catholic Church. Some of these alternatives "sought to repair and remodel the ideational worlds of Catholic Mexico";[40] others were irreligious; and yet others, Protestant. The chapters discuss different discourses that cast themselves as ideological, philosophical, and even cosmological alternatives to Catholicism. Chapter 6, by Ben Fallaw, returns to Garridismo to analyze how irreligious políticos, teachers, soldiers, and intellectuals frequently justified harsh measures against the Catholic Church in the name of science. The chapter shows the national scope of scientistic Garridistas, as they sent reams of propaganda and legions of well-trained teachers and technicians across Mexico. Although the state largely abandoned radical anticlericalism after the mid-1930s, it continued to invoke science to legitimize its intervention in everyday life and stifle Catholic challenges to its authority. Chapter 7, by Héctor Jaimes, explores how many muralists' commitment to the Communist cause rapidly changed the religious themes in the early murals to a more politically and socially committed, Marxist aesthetic. The ideals of the Communist revolution—as a continuation of the Mexican revolution—and the representation of its symbols impacted the imagery of the Mexican muralist movement, thus giving way to a notion of a political art, beyond religion and mysticism. Chapter 8, by Rebecca Janzen, examines anti-Catholicism through the relationship between the government and North American religious immigrants, both Mennonites and Mormons. The government—which held minimal power in northern parts of the country—sought to build a secular nation, for which it needed loyal subjects. Mormons and Mennonites were willing to accede to some state demands, and they enjoyed significant privileges—particularly in the areas of public worship and Church-sponsored education—that their Catholic peers did not have. Practitioners of these faiths enjoyed certain privileges as non-Catholic religious traditions even as they faced hurdles as both foreign entities and religious institutions.

Finally, Matthew Butler, from whom we have all drawn inspiration and insights as a collective of scholars, provides an afterword that brings the discussion to a close. Aside from weaving together the themes from this collection of essays, the afterword suggests that anti-Catholicism did not disappear with President Ávila Camacho's 1940 affirmation that he was a believer. Rather, today's transnational drug wars have revitalized Mexican anti-Catholicism, this time without the support of the Mexican state.

Anti-Catholicism in the Mexican Revolution does not aim to provide an authoritative history of the conflict between church and state in twentieth-century Mexico. Rather, it brings together historiographical and cultural studies essays in an attempt to shed light on the irreligious and anticlerical debates that raged across the country during the early part of the twentieth century. In so doing, it challenges a body of scholarship that has foregrounded the preeminence of the Church, thus providing a more complete vision of the political, cultural, and societal dimensions of the time period. Certainly, Guadalupanism played an integral role in many representations of *mexicanidad*, with both popular and institutional Catholicism contributing to constructs of official mestizaje and national reconciliation.[41] The book does not deny the importance of these discourses in national(ist) debates; rather, it attempts to rescue political and cultural currents that challenged those of the Church but that have, in many cases, been relegated to the periphery. Anti-Catholicism permeated revolutionary society. Representing a wide array of different interests, many postrevolutionary Mexicans recognized a common enemy in a politically active Roman Catholic Church.

Notes

1. For a discussion of the utopian essay as it relates to Vasconcelos and, to an extent, Gamio, see Sánchez Prado, "El mestizaje en el corazón de la utopía: *La raza cósmica* entre Aztlán y América Latina," 2009.
2. See Haywood Ferreira, *Emergence*, 69.
3. For studies that cast the novel as one of science fiction, see Dziubinskyj, "Eduardo Urzaiz's *Eugenia*," 463–72; Haywood Ferreira, *Emergence*. It was not until 2021 that Mexicanist scholarship inscribed Urzaiz's thought into (post)revolutionary Mexico. See Antebi, *Embodied Archive*, chap. 1.
4. Certainly, Matthew Butler's edited volume *Faith and Impiety in Revolutionary Mexico* significantly engages with anticlericals and other "impious" actors. See Butler, *Faith and Impiety*.
5. The term is a play on Stepan, *"Hour of Eugenics."*
6. Meyer, *La cristiada*.
7. See Monsiváis, *El Estado laico y sus malquerientes*, 130.
8. Indeed, Machiavelli chided King Louis of France, stating, "The French do not understand the state, because if they understood, they would not have let the Church come to such greatness." Machiavelli, *The Prince*, 16.
9. Butler, *Mexico's Spiritual Reconquest*.
10. Gilbert, *The End of Catholic Mexico*.
11. Ohan, "Role of the Catholic Church," 56–57; Quirk, *Mexican Revolution*, 40–78.
12. Bantjes, "Regional Dynamics," 113–30.
13. Curley, *Citizens and Believers*, chap. 3; Buchenau, *Sonoran Dynasty*, chaps. 2–3.
14. Garcíadiego, "¿Cuándo, cómo, por qué, y quiénes hicieron la Constitución de 1917?" 1183–270.
15. Buchenau, *Sonoran Dynasty*.

16. Meyer, "An Idea of Mexico," 283.
17. Fallaw, *Religion and State Formation*, 76–82.
18. Meyer, "An Idea of Mexico," 283–91.
19. Curley, *Citizens and Believers*, chap. 2, chap. 4.
20. As Pamela Voekel has demonstrated, in Mexico and the rest of the Spanish-speaking world, the discourse of the Age of Revolution (1776–1848) occurred within a Catholic framework, with reformers pitted against traditionalists. The power of the Church remained after the Wars of Independence (1810–1821) and, in the cultural, political, and social realms, even the *Reforma*. See Voekel, *For God and Liberty*.
21. "Religion in Latin America."
22. Chowning, *Catholic Women*.
23. See, for example, Davies, *Rising Road*; and Steigmann-Gall, *The Holy Reich*.
24. Pochoshajew, "Perspectives," 23.
25. Martínez Assad, "Prólogo," 14.
26. Many of their criticisms had existed long before the revolutionary "hour of unbelief." See also the discussion above.
27. Butler, "Revolution in Spirit," 3.
28. Butler, 5.
29. Butler, 1, 4–10.
30. Meyer, *La cristiada*, 2:111.
31. Buchenau, *Plutarco Elías Calles*, 125.
32. A good discussion of the escalating conflict is in Quirk, *Mexican Revolution*, 113–44.
33. Butler, *Mexico's Spiritual Reconquest*; Ramírez Rancaño, *El patriarca Pérez*, 171.
34. See McIntyre, *Protestantism and State Formation*.
35. Bastian, "Protestantismo y política en México," 1985.
36. See Dormady, *Primitive Revolution*; Janzen, *Liminal Sovereignty*, xvii.
37. For a discussion of the tension among the muralists' representations of the proper nature of a national mestizaje, see Dalton, *Mestizo Modernity*, chap. 2.
38. David S. Dalton discusses numerous murals that favor pre-Columbian deities in Rivera's oeuvre. See Dalton, *Mestizo Modernity*, 81–98.
39. An excellent example of this is his mural, *Vaccination*, in Detroit, which adapts common symbols from the nativity scene to the vaccination against smallpox. See McKeekin, *Science and* Creativity, 25.
40. Butler, "Revolution in Spirit," 5.
41. For studies that discuss how Catholic symbols like the Virgin of Guadalupe facilitated racial and ethnic reconciliation and thus nation-building, see Feder, "Engendering the Nation," 244–46; Noble, *Mexican National Cinema*, 82; Oleszkiewicz, "Los cultos marianos nacionales en América," 241–46.

Works Cited

Antebi, Susan. *Embodied Archive: Disability in Post-Revolutionary Mexican Cultural Production*. Ann Arbor: University of Michigan Press, 2021.

Bantjes, Adrian A. "The Regional Dynamics of Anticlericalism and Defanatization in Revolutionary Mexico." In *Faith and Impiety in Revolutionary Mexico*, edited by Matthew Butler, 111–30. New York: Palgrave Macmillan, 2007.

Bastian, Jean-Pierre. "Protestantismo y política en México." *Revista Mexicana de Sociología* 43 (1981): 1947–66.

Brading, David. "Manuel Gamio and Official Indigenismo in Mexico." *Bulletin of Latin American Research* 7, no. 1 (1988): 75–89.

Buchenau, Jürgen. *Plutarco Elías Calles and the Mexican Revolution*. Lanham, MD: Rowman & Littlefield, 2007.

———. *The Sonoran Dynasty in Mexico: Revolution, Reform, and Repression* Lincoln: University of Nebraska Press, 2023.

Butler, Matthew. "Introduction: A Revolution in Spirit? Mexico, 1910–40." In Butler, *Faith and Impiety in Revolutionary Mexico*, 1–20.

———. *Mexico's Spiritual Reconquest: Indigenous Catholics and Father Pérez's Revolutionary Church*. Albuquerque: University of New Mexico Press, 2023.

———, ed. *Faith and Impiety in Revolutionary Mexico*. New York: Palgrave Macmillan, 2007.

Chowning, Margaret. *Catholic Women and Mexican Politics, 1750–1940*. Princeton, NJ: Princeton University Press, 2023.

Curley, Robert. *Citizens and Believers: Religion and Politics in Revolutionary Jalisco, 1900–1930*. Albuquerque: University of New Mexico Press, 2018.

Dalton, David S. *Mestizo Modernity: Race, Technology, and the Body in Postrevolutionary Mexico*. Gainesville: University of Florida Press, 2018.

———. "Science and the (Meta)physical Body: A Critique of Positivism in the Vasconcelian Utopian." *Revista Canadiense de Estudios Hispánicos* 40, no. 3 (2016): 535–59.

Davies, Sharon. *Rising Road: A True Tale of Love, Race, and Religion in America*. New York: Oxford University Press, 2010.

Dormady, Jason. *Primitive Revolution: Restorationist Religion and the Idea of the Mexican Revolution, 1940–1968*. Albuquerque: University of New Mexico Press, 2011.

Dziubinskyj, Aaron. "Eduardo Urzaiz's *Eugenia*: Eugenics, Gender, and Dystopian Society in Twenty-Third-Century Mexico." *Science Fiction Studies* 34, no. 3 (2007): 463–72.

Fallaw, Ben. *Religion and State Formation in Postrevolutionary Mexico*. Durham, NC: Duke University Press, 2013.

Feder, Elena. "Engendering the Nation, Nationalizing the Sacred: Guadalupismo and the Cinematic (Re)Formation of Mexican Consciousness." In *National Identities and Sociopolitical Changes in Latin America*, edited by Mercedes F. Durán-Cogan and Antonio Gómez-Moriana, 229–68. New York: Routledge, 2001.

Gamio, Manuel. *Forjando patria. Pro nacionalismo*. Mexico City: Porrúa, 1916.

———. *Mexican Immigration to the United States: A Study of Human Migration and Adjustment*. Chicago: University of Chicago Press, 1930.

Garcíadiego, Javier. "¿Cuándo, cómo, por qué, y quiénes hicieron la Constitución de 1917?" *Historia Mexicana* 66, no. 3 (2017): 1183–270.

Gilbert, David. *The End of Catholic Mexico: Causes and Consequences of the Mexican Reforma, 1855-1861*. Nashville, TN: Vanderbilt University Press, 2024.

Haywood Ferreira, Rachel. *The Emergence of Latin American Science Fiction*. Middletown, CT: Wesleyan University Press, 2011.

Hernández Berrones, Jethro. "Healers and Doctors: A History of the Healing Occupations in Mexico." In *Healthcare in Latin America: History, Society, Culture*, edited by David S. Dalton and Douglas J. Weatherford, 19–39. Gainesville: University of Florida Press, 2022.

Hoeg, Jerry. *Science, Technology, and Latin American Narrative in the Twentieth Century and Beyond*. Bethlehem, PA: Lehigh University Press, 2000.

Janzen, Rebecca. *Liminal Sovereignty: Mennonites and Mormons in Mexican Culture*. Albany: State University of New York Press, 2018.

Machiavelli, Niccolò. *The Prince*. 2nd ed. Translated by Harvey C. Mansfield. Chicago: University of Chicago Press, 1998.

Martínez Assad, Carlos. "Prólogo." In *Calles y Atatürk: Revolución en México y Turquía* by Andrés Orgaz Martínez. Mexico City: FCE, 2021.

McIntyre, Kathleen M. *Protestantism and State Formation in Postrevolutionary Oaxaca*. Albuquerque: University of New Mexico Press, 2019.

McKeekin, Dorothy. *Science and Creativity in the Detroit Murals/Ciencia y creatividad en los murales de Detroit*. East Lansing: Michigan State University Press, 1985.

Meyer, Jean. "An Idea of Mexico: Catholics and the Revolution." In *The Eagle and the Virgin: Nation and Cultural Revolution in Mexico, 1920–1940*, edited by Mary Kay Vaughan and Stephen E. Lewis, 281–96. Durham, NC: Duke University Press, 2006.

———. *La Cristiada*. 3 vols. Mexico City: Siglo XXI Editores, 1973–1975.

Monsiváis, Carlos. *El Estado laico y sus malquerientes*. Mexico City: UNAM, 2008.

Noble, Andrea. *Mexican National Cinema*. New York: Routledge, 2005.

Ohan, Christopher. "The Role of the Catholic Church in the Mexican Revolution." *Voices of Mexico* (2001): 53–62.

Oleszkiewicz, Malgorzata. "Los cultos marianos nacionales en América: Guadalupe/Tonantzin y Aprecida/Iemanjá." *Revista Iberoamericana* 64, no. 182–83 (1998): 241–52.

Orgaz Martínez, Andrés. *Calles y Atatürk: Revolución en México y Turquía*. Mexico City: FCE, 2021.

Pierce, Gretchen. "Fighting Bacteria, the Bible, and the Bottle: Projects to Create New Men, Women, and Children, 1910–1940." In *A Companion to Mexican History and Culture*, edited by William H. Beezley, 505–17. Oxford: Blackwell Press, 2011.

Pochoshajew, Igor. "Perspectives on the Russian Orthodox Church in Soviet Times." *Occasional Papers on Religion in Eastern Europe* 27, no. 1 (2007): 20–34.

Quirk, Robert. *The Mexican Revolution and the Catholic Church, 1910–1929*. Bloomington: Indiana University Press, 1973.

Ramírez Rancaño, Mario. *El patriarca Pérez: La Iglesia católica apostólica mexicana*. Mexico City: UNAM, 2006.

"Religion in Latin America." Pew Research Center. Accessed May 31, 2024 https://www.pewresearch.org/religion/2014/11/13/religion-in-latin-america/.

Sánchez Prado, Ignacio M. "El mestizaje en el corazón de la utopía: *La raza cósmica* entre Aztlán y América Latina." *Revista Canadiense de Estudios Hispánicos* 33, no. 2 (2009): 381–404.

———. *Naciones intelectuales: Las fundaciones de la modernidad literaria mexicana (1917–1959)*. West Lafayette, IN: Purdue University Press, 2009.

———. *Screening Neoliberalism: Transforming Mexican Cinema, 1988–2012*. Nashville: Vanderbilt University Press, 2014.

Schuler, Friedrich E. "Mexico and the Outside World." In *The Oxford History of Mexico*, edited by William H. Beezley and Michael C. Meyer, 488–94. Oxford: Oxford University Press, 2010.

Spitta, Silvia. "Of Brown Buffaloes, Cockroaches and Others: *Mestizaje* North and South of the Río Bravo." *Revista de Estudios Hispánicos* 35, no. 2 (2001): 333–47.

Steigmann-Gall, Richard. *The Holy Reich: Nazi Conceptions of Christianity, 1919–1945*. New York: Cambridge University Press, 2003.

Voekel, Pamela. *For God and Liberty: Catholicism and Revolution in the Atlantic World, 1790–1861*. New York: Oxford University Press, 2023.

Yankelevich, Pablo. *Los otros: raza, normas y corrupción en la gestión de la extranjería en México, 1900–1950*. Mexico City: El Colegio de México, 2019.

SECTION I

ANTI-CATHOLICISM in GOVERNMENT

CHAPTER ONE

Plutarco Elías Calles

Patriarch of Revolutionary Anti-Catholicism

JÜRGEN BUCHENAU

This chapter examines anti-Catholicism through the lens of a political leader whom Matthew Butler once called Mexico's "arch-clerophobe:"[1] General and President Plutarco Elías Calles (1877–1945). Although he only served as president from 1924 to 1928, Calles exemplified anti-Catholicism throughout his long and deeply influential political career. That said, his policies primarily corresponded to his reading of the political landscape. Specifically, the culmination of the revolutionary government's conflict with the Catholic Church beginning in 1926 coincided with a moment when anti-Catholics held significant power in the governing Council of Ministers (Consejo de Ministros). A triumvirate that included Luis Napoleón Morones, secretary of industry, commerce, and labor; Adalberto Tejeda, secretary of the interior (Gobernación); and General Joaquín Amaro, secretary of war and the navy, played important roles in promulgating and enforcing anti-Catholic policies.[2] These included the Calles Law, a reform to the penal code that imposed a strict registration requirement on the clergy and criminalized many of their routine duties. The law precipitated a national Catholic strike and ultimately touched off the devastating Cristero Rebellion. The government's intelligence operations kept Calles and his allies up to date about Catholic efforts to gather support in the neighboring United States. This information reinforced their quest to vanquish the Church. More than anything, these leaders' policies confronted a resilient and determined Church and particularly its burgeoning mass organizations.

    Calles's personal opposition to organized religion directly influenced his anti-Catholic policies. Calles was irreligious but welcomed the growth of Protestantism in Mexico as a counterweight to the Catholic Church.[3] Hard on the Church as he was, his world view was not altogether different from the religion that he tried to escape. Within the cultural context of a largely Catholic and also deeply spiritual nation, it formed within Manichaean opposites in which rationalism and secularism represented light, science, and progress; and Roman Catholicism, darkness, superstition, and a burdensome colonial legacy.[4] Late in life, Calles's stance softened.

A Natural-Born Clerophobe?

The historical record of Calles's early years reveals little about his attitude regarding the Catholic Church. Plutarco Elías Campuzano was born to a poor single mother in the port city of Guaymas on the Sea of Cortez in the northwestern state of Sonora. His father, an alcoholic, came from a wealthy family but had frittered away his share of the clan's fortune—and true to form, he did not look after his son. Plutarco was not baptized until he was fifteen months old. After the death of his mother when he was just four years old, his maternal uncle, Juan Bautista Calles, took him in, leading him to add "Calles" to his name.[5] The elder Calles and his wife raised their nephew in the Catholic tradition, but Plutarco later recalled these early encounters with the Church thus: "When I was an altar boy . . . I stole alms in order to buy candy."[6] He was certainly insubordinate as a child: the historian Carlos Macías has called Calles a "nightmare in the classroom."[7] After his formal schooling ended, Calles tried his luck in various professions, including schoolteacher, hotel manager, mill operator, and farmer. Alcoholism and failed efforts to reclaim the high social status of his forebears plagued his early adulthood.[8]

Calles grew up in a frontier society with minimal ecclesiastical infrastructure. Only some thirty priests served in the entire state, and it was common for children not to receive baptism. A large number of households included many children born outside matrimony; single parents and unmarried couples were typical. Northern religiosity was heterodox: witness, for example, the influence of Teresa Urrea (1873–1906). A native of Sinaloa, Urrea was a folk saint (the "Santa de Cábora") and insurgent, calling for a direct relationship with God and inspiring the 1891 Tomóchic rebellion in Chihuahua.[9]

In this rough-and-tumble world, the formal Roman Catholic hierarchy and its values mattered little. Growing up out of wedlock in Sonora therefore did not feature the kind of stigma that would have attached to Calles in central Mexico. The historian Enrique Krauze's unproven hypothesis that the twin stigmas of an out-of-wedlock birth and belated baptism forged a lifelong opposition to the Catholic Church superimposes the values and structures of central Mexico upon the borderlands.[10] Similarly, the psychoanalysis utilized by the historian Michael Monteón is of limited use in explaining Calles's opposition to religion. Monteón suggested that his motherless childhood was "traumatic" and helped shape a personality marked by introversion, a lack of flexibility, and an inability to trust others.[11] But many devout Catholics could look back at similar childhoods.

In a common anti-Semitic trope, Calles's Catholic opponents frequently maintained that he was of Jewish origin and attributed his anticlerical policies to that fact. There is no evidence for that assertion. True, "Elías" can be a Hebrew surname. But the first Elías in Mexico, Francisco Elías González, was a Catholic from La Rioja in northern Castile and arrived in northeastern Sonora in the 1720s. In the course of the next five generations, the Elíases became one of the state's notable families, allied after independence with the powerful Pesqueira clan of Benito Juárez's Liberal Party. At the height of his influence, Plutarco's paternal grandfather owned more than 120,000 acres.[12] Even Héctor Aguilar Camín, a highly respected historian of revolutionary Sonora, insisted that the Elías clan was Jewish and perhaps of immediate Levantine descent.[13] This legend—coupled with the fact that Calles had a somewhat darker complexion than his patron, Obregón—contributed to the moniker "el turco" (the Turk), a label that denoted Middle Eastern origin more so than a specific religion or ethnicity (see fig. 1). In truth, both Obregón and Calles were from Spanish Creole families and from a state in which 43 percent of the population classified itself as White in the 1921 census.[14]

Calles's status as a Freemason is another unsatisfactory explanatory angle. Calles was a member of the Helios Lodge in his hometown of Guaymas. At the height of the church-state conflict, Freemasons all over the world sent Calles congratulatory telegrams and letters, and the Scottish Rite in Mexico City awarded him a medal of merit for his anti-Catholic work. Although the Holy See forbade Catholics to affiliate with Masonic societies, the association between Freemasonry and anti-Catholicism is overblown. According to the historian Karen Racine, most presidents in the century following independence were Freemasons—for example, Antonio López de Santa Anna, Benito Juárez, Porfirio Díaz, Francisco I. Madero, Victoriano Huerta, and Venustiano Carranza.[15] Of those, only Juárez deserves the anti-Catholic label. In addition, Calles's extensive private archive contains only a few documents dealing with Freemasonry, and none suggesting that

FIGURE 1. Plutarco Elías Calles. FAPECFT. Fototeca Colección de Álbumes Fotográficos de los Archivos Plutarco Elías Calles y Fernando Torreblanca. (AAPECFT), Fondo Fernando Torreblanca (FAFFFT), álbum 2: *Historia Política de México 1913–1920. Volumen II.* Fotografía: 459, inventario: 72.

his Masonic affiliations affected his political ideas. Given the rumors of Calles's Jewish origins, the supposed causal link between Calles the Mason and Calles the anti-Catholic was part and parcel of the early twentieth-century Catholic trope of a Judeo-Masonic conspiracy supposedly bent on the destruction of Christianity and Western civilization.[16]

These stories matter principally because they illustrate the retroactive invention of a natural-born clerophobe or priest hater. The historical documentation of Calles's early years, and even his stints in Sonoran municipal governments (1906–1909) and as police chief of the small border town of Agua Prieta (1911–1913), do not support this notion. The Church simply did not matter to this itinerant descendant from a notable family seeking to rebuild his clan's status in a frontier society. As a young schoolteacher in the 1890s, Calles taught the positivist curriculum common in Porfirian public schools. As police chief in the early 1910s, Calles was an unflinching and repressive modernizer. While he fought for "moralization" by criminalizing public inebriation and punishing outspoken critics of the Madero administration, Calles did not distinguish himself as an enemy of the Catholic Church; there was not even a priest in Agua Prieta.[17] It does appear, however, that Calles may have had good reason to resent the bishop of Sonora, Ignacio Valdespino y Díaz (1861–1928). In 1916, a representative of the Holy See reported that "several years ago, a priest from Hermosillo seduced Calles's niece. . . . Was he punished? No, Valdespino rewarded him with a promotion as rector of the cathedral in Hermosillo. Later, he seduced another girl in San Miguel."[18]

Whatever the case may be, Calles's opposition to the Catholic clergy first manifested itself during what Adrian Bantjes identified as the first wave of anticlericalism in the early Constitutionalist era (1914–1915).[19] This wave occurred in a dialectic with Catholic supporters of the Huerta dictatorship that the revolutionaries had just defeated. In Porfirian Mexico, the call for social Catholicism in the papal letter or encyclical *Rerum Novarum* (1890) had found but weak echoes among the Catholic hierarchy, which had allied firmly with large landowners. As the historian Alan Knight has observed, Catholic Conservatives "represented an ideological inclination toward order, hierarchy, property, and stability; a preferential option for the well-to-do, one might say."[20] Robert Curley and other historians have traced a stronger echo of this encyclical in the Partido Católico Nacional (National Catholic Party), which emerged during the Madero administration, remained a dominant force in the state of Jalisco until the Constitutionalist victory in the summer of 1915, and (once outlawed in the 1917 Constitution) helped inspire the Catholic social organizations of the 1920s.[21]

In August 1915, First Chief Venustiano Carranza appointed Calles governor and military commander of Sonora. In March 1916, Calles ordered the expulsion of all priests—a grand total of thirty-five—labeling them "bad elements" that had colluded with the Huerta dictatorship.[22] Two years later, Sonora's interim governor Cesáreo Soriano reported the closure of eighty-three churches and religious institutions over the previous three years and their conversion into hospitals, schools, and public offices. But Calles had only served as governor for less than half of this period. For example, his friend and ally, Adolfo de la Huerta, had presided over the state as interim governor between March 1916 and June 1917. Also a future president of Mexico, Governor de la Huerta continued his friend's secularization campaign.[23] Meanwhile, from exile in the United States, Valdespino—now the Bishop of Aguascalientes—hinted at supporting a conspiracy that would remove the Constitutionalist state government.[24]

Calles's opposition to the Church as governor might seem drastic in isolation, but it was not particularly radical in comparison with other Carrancista military proconsuls. Examples of anticlerical governors in the mid-1910s include Manuel M. Diéguez of Jalisco, Salvador Alvarado of Yucatán, Francisco Coss of Puebla, and Antonio Villarreal of Nuevo León—all northerners except Diéguez, who had moved to Sonora as a young adult.[25] This northern flavor of Constitutionalist anti-Catholicism contributed to José Vasconcelos's sarcastic characterization of the "men from the northern frontier, carriers of civilization."[26] Witness the systematic profanation and iconoclasm perpetrated by troops operating in states with powerful and sizable Catholic hierarchies, and three archbishops, to boot.[27] For example, Diéguez expelled the archbishop of Guadalajara, confiscated gold found in churches, suppressed religious holidays, and imprisoned 120 priests, whom he characterized as "those who, clothed as sheep, deceive the people."[28]

In addition, the national policy of the Constitutionalists was anticlerical. In April 1916, the secretary of the interior ordered state governments to take actions against the "sedition of the clergy."[29] Witness the attitude of the erstwhile Constitutionalist commander, General Álvaro Obregón, secretary of war and the navy until May 1, 1917. According to Obregón, religious "fanaticism" or blind devotion to the Church made citizens willing accomplices of tyranny. "It atrophies the brain, because it disavows the right to investigation and discussion, and it withers civic-mindedness because it establishes the unconditional submission to its priests."[30]

During the Constitutionalist era, Calles therefore displayed a repressive leadership style, but the evidence suggests he was not radically opposed to religion in general. Consider Calles's single-minded determination to expand primary education in Sonora, his successful effort to extract production taxes from the state's copper companies, his bloody quest to extirpate the Yaqui indigenous community in Sonora, or even his attempt to ban alcohol (see Gretchen Pierce's chapter on the connection between anticlericalism and abstinence campaigns). Ultimately, Calles displayed pragmatism in allowing priests to return to their posts, at first intermittently for no more than four days at a time. The governor's rule was uncompromising, even bulldozing, but the distinguishing feature of Calles's authoritarian rule as governor was the determination to wipe out the Yaqui rather than his anticlerical acts, which resembled those of several other governors and formed part of the Constitutionalist playbook at the state level.[31]

The first wave of Mexican anticlericalism fed directly into the Constitutional Convention in Querétaro (1916–1917), where the so-called Jacobins coalesced around the cause of removing the Church from public life. This constitution set up the next phase of anticlericalism in pitting the Church against the official document of the revolution. Not surprisingly, the episcopate asked Catholics to disobey the anticlerical articles, but the Archbishop of Mexico City, José Mora y del Río, did not stop there. In a letter to the Holy See written from exile, the archbishop branded the entire constitution "illegitimate."[32] The furor over the constitution soon died down, however, as President Carranza and Congress did not enforce the offending articles.

In this context, Calles's track record in three positions in the national cabinet did not presage the rabid anti-Catholicism that was to come during his presidency. These included brief stints as secretary of industry, commerce, and labor (1919, under Carranza) and war and the navy (1920, under Adolfo de la Huerta) as well as a three-year term as interior secretary (1920–1923) under Obregón. The latter position included control of the federal police as well as relations with state governments and involved Calles directly in Obregón's efforts to strike a balance between secularizing laws and the segment of the population that supported such laws on one side and the growing influence of Catholic popular organizations on the other.

It was a difficult balancing act indeed. In Mexico City, Calles's first year as secretary of the interior featured bomb attacks against Mora y del Río and the Basilica of Our Lady of Guadalupe, respectively.[33] Who tossed these bombs is unknown, but at the state level, and especially in the Southeast, new radical movements with genuine popular support had emerged. These movements targeted the Catholic Church. Witness the self-described

"Socialist" movements such as those headed by Felipe Carrillo Puerto (Yucatán) and especially Tomás Garrido Canabal (Tabasco)—the latter discussed in Sarah Osten's and Ben Fallaw's chapters. Fallaw has argued elsewhere that "revolutionary anticlericalism was not just orchestrated from above."[34] Between the North and the Southeast, anti-Catholic movements had a broad regional base.

On the other side, Catholics also took to grassroots organizing. Excluded from formal political participation under the new constitution, they founded associations such as the Gran Confederación Nacional Católica de Trabajo (Great National Catholic Labor Confederation), the Unión de Damas Católicas Mexicanas (Union of Mexican Catholic Ladies), and the Asociación Católica de la Juventud Mexicana (Catholic Association of Mexican Youth). In 1922, the first encyclical of the new Pope, Pius XI, *Ubi Arcano Dei Consilio* (By the Inscrutable Counsel of God), gave these associations even more energy. Reflecting on the carnage of World War I, the encyclical reminded Catholics to live in the peace of Christ in the kingdom of Christ—a strong critique of secular governments.

Calles formed part of an administration that mended fences with the Holy See while also cracking down on Catholic outdoor worship. In 1922, the Obregón administration and the new pope reestablished diplomatic relations. The new papal delegate in Mexico, Ernesto Filippi, pointed out that Obregón's government had "never committed an act that might be considered hostile toward the Church."[35] That quickly changed, however, when Catholics commenced construction of a "Christ the King" shrine on Cubilete Hill in Guanajuato. On January 11, 1923, a crowd of 50,000 witnessed Filippi laying the first stone and the officiating bishop proclaiming Jesus Christ the "king of Mexico." Obregón and Calles invoked Article 24 to halt construction of the shrine and expelled Filippi, actions that provoked widespread Catholic outcry.[36] In a collective letter, the Mexican episcopate lamented: "So long as there are so many laws in existence that abridge the rights of Catholics, there will be a religious question."[37]

While this conflict was unfolding, Calles emerged as a leading presidential candidate, thanks in large part to Obregón's support. Ever the pragmatist, he struck a conciliatory tone toward the Church. He went further in this direction after the de la Huerta Rebellion (1923–1924) threatened the government and his candidacy. Calles could ill afford to add more enemies to the rebel coalition, which included a majority of the army units and featured four different geographic theaters. Consider the following speech given in Morelia, Michoacán:

> My enemies say that I am an enemy of the religions and faiths, and that I do not respect religious beliefs. I ... understand and approve all religious beliefs because I consider them beneficial for the moral program they encompass. I am an enemy of the caste of priests that sees in its position a privilege rather than an evangelical mission. I am the enemy of the political priest, the scheming priest, the priest as exploiter, the priest who intends to keep our people in ignorance, the priest who allies with the hacendado to exploit the campesino, and the priest allied with the industrialist to exploit the worker.[38]

The papal chargé, Tito Crespi, considered this a "very moderate" address.[39] Indeed, Crespi favored Calles over de la Huerta, a leader widely considered more friendly to Roman Catholicism. He thought he could work with Calles, whose discourses "have not contained any aggressive note against the Church or the clergy." Crespi considered de la Huerta "hypocritical" and added: "Without character or principles, ... he does not know how to do either good or bad, but he will let both good and bad things happen."[40]

Notwithstanding this moderate stance, as Sarah Osten also explains in the chapter that follows, the de la Huerta Rebellion contributed to the anti-Catholic stance of Calles's ensuing presidency. Obregón's and Calles's enemies had come close to extinguishing their regime and had failed only because of their lack of unity and US support for the government. The Church numbered among those enemies, and despite Crespi's sense that de la Huerta's triumph would not have helped the Church, many devout Catholics supported the rebellion; among them, the mastermind of the uprising, the congressional delegate Jorge Prieto Laurens. In a larger sense, the rebellion increased Calles's and Obregón's fear of their enemies, both domestic and foreign, and contributed to the building of a repressive state apparatus.

Soon after Calles took office as president, the foundation of a schismatic church brought anticlericalism to the fore. On February 21, 1925, a throng that included so-called Knights of Guadalupe burst into the Iglesia Soledad de Santa Cruz in eastern Mexico City and drove out the priest. The "Knights of Guadalupe" were at the beck and call of Morones, the secretary of industry, commerce, and labor. When the crowd installed Juan Joaquín Pérez Budar as patriarch of the Iglesia Católica Apostólica Mexicana (ICAM, or Mexican Catholic Apostolic Church), a protest of more than one thousand Catholics interrupted his first Eucharist. Unwilling to confront either Morones or the Catholic Church, Calles ordered Pérez to vacate Soledad and instead officiate in the Corpus Christi church at Alameda Park, a much more central location and a church already closed to Catholic religious services.[41]

The Catholic hierarchy interpreted Calles's order as an open challenge. Soon thereafter, Catholics founded the Liga Nacional de la Defensa Religiosa (National League for Religious Defense), which quickly grew to more than 30,000 members. As Matthew Butler has demonstrated, however, the ICAM was far from a puppet for an anticlerical government but rather a dissenting, nationalist, agrarian, and often Indigenous Catholic voice. Hundreds of ICAM communities took root in central and southern states such as México, Puebla, Veracruz, Oaxaca, and Chiapas.[42]

Symbolic acts added to formal and popular Catholic opposition to Calles. For example, the new administration transferred the remains of independence heroes such as Miguel Hidalgo, José María Morelos, and Vicente Guerrero (the first two of them, Catholic priests) from the Mexico City cathedral to a mausoleum underneath the famed Porfirian-era Angel of Independence on the Paseo de la Reforma. By contrast, the remains of Emperor Agustín Iturbide (1821–1823), who represented the union of the nation and the Church in the minds of many Mexicans, were left at the cathedral. As Calles explained to US journalist Ernest Gruening: "I left Iturbide there, among his kind, where he belongs."[43] Calles's actions and words suggested that there were two kinds of independence fighters: secular patriots and Catholic sell-outs.

The Apex of Anti-Catholicism

The road from these symbolic confrontations to the full-blown conflict with the Church that made Calles famous as a clerophobe passed through the second major wave of revolutionary anticlericalism—one that originated in Mexico's south and center rather than the north and that had significant popular support, even if it remained a minority position. This second wave was as diverse as its adherents, including *agraristas* (advocates for land reform), workers, students, and teachers, and it also included many Mexicans outside identifiable "anticlerical" or "clerical" camps.

But anti-Catholicism was particularly important in Calles's Council of Ministers, or cabinet (see fig. 2). The most influential cabinet member on the religious question was Luis N. Morones, the instigator of the Soledad incident. In August 1925, the irreligious former governor of Veracruz,

Adalberto Tejeda, became interior secretary, replacing the moderate Gilberto Valenzuela. Tejeda was at least as anti-Catholic as Calles, if not more so. Finally, Secretary of War and the Navy General Joaquín Amaro had a reputation as a ruthless opponent of the Catholic Church. He was nicknamed "the whip of God." Amaro's enemies feared his uncompromising methods.[44] This governing trio not only held the key to the enforcement of central authority but (through Morones) also the control over Mexico's largest labor organization, the CROM. In a cabinet in which Obregón—still Mexico's undisputed caudillo or charismatic leader—wielded some influence from behind the scenes, these three anti-Catholic ministers constituted Calles's base of support, with Morones the most powerful among them.

The president initially kept up his messaging, stressing the need for social and economic reconstruction and indicating that "clericalism now signifies no danger at all."[45] But as Obregón planned a comeback despite the constitutional ban on reelection, Calles increasingly relied on the radicals in his cabinet for support. And none was more important to him than Morones, the architect of legislation implementing national control over Mexico's oil reserves. This legislation provoked a serious crisis with US Ambassador James R. Sheffield, a corrupt diplomat in cahoots with the oil industry who resented his post and Mexicans in general, and Secretary of State Frank B. Kellogg, who on June 12, 1925, declared Mexico to be "on trial before the world" for its failure to meet its obligations to US capitalists and implied that his government might not come to Calles's assistance the next time a rebellion broke out.[46]

On the Church's side was an aging episcopate, especially Archbishops Mora y del Río of Mexico City and José Francisco Orozco y Jiménez of Guadalajara. These Porfirian aristocrats opposed not only the anticlerical articles but the revolution in general. Ernest Lagarde, the French chargé d'affaires, did not mince words in his contempt for the high clergy. He called the episcopate "indiscreet, restricted in vision, intransigent, vain, and thoroughly disunited" and Mora y del Río, "a decrepit old man, an opportunist without will-power, a believer in political intrigue."[47] Of course, the lower clergy were another matter, let alone ordinary Catholics, but the episcopate was the Church's interlocutor for the Mexican national government. Only later on would it become clear that other Church leaders, including Villahermosa's Pascual Díaz y Barreto and Morelia's Leopoldo Ruiz y Flores, were more flexible in dealing with an anti-Catholic administration.

With these problematic and belligerent personalities, the state's conflict with the Catholic Church came to a head in early 1926. The spark

FIGURE 2. Anti-Catholics in the Council of Ministers: Morones, Calles, Obregón, and Tejeda, 1925. APECFT. Fototeca. Archivo Fernando Torreblanca (AFFT), Fondo Plutarco Elías Calles, Oficial: (FFPECO), serie: *Presidencia de la República, 1924–1928*. Mfn: 873, imagen: 34, inventario: 299.

that ignited the conflict was a February 4 newspaper story in *El Universal* that quoted Archbishop Mora y del Río as saying, in reference to the 1917 Constitution: "The Episcopate, Clergy, and Catholics do not recognize and will combat Articles 3, 5, 27, and 130."[48] As many scholars have pointed out, *El Universal* had not published new news. Instead, it had quoted a statement released immediately after the promulgation of the constitution in 1917, almost a decade earlier. But the archbishop had made a similar comment regarding state-level regulations just two weeks prior. On February 8, *El Universal* published another article that quoted the episcopate as opposing the entire constitution for violating "the most sacred rights of the Catholic Church, Mexican society, and Christian individuals."[49] The new apostolic delegate, George Caruana, did not approve of this position: in his words, the Church "ought to use the utmost caution" with regard to the revolutionary program, "praising what there is to praise and repudiating the rest."[50]

Tejeda, initially served as the government's point person in the controversy. The interior secretary referred the statement to the Attorney General's office as a criminal offense: "The state . . . cannot permit the Church to ignore or combat the constitutional laws."[51] When the archbishop pointed out that his words were from 1917, the office dropped the criminal proceedings.[52] On February 17, Tejeda announced that Article 130 would be strictly enforced, even in the absence of enabling legislation required to put each constitutional article into practice. He ordered the closure of all monasteries and convents and forbade the ministry of foreign clerics. These measures gave the episcopate's opposition to the constitution more legitimacy, as they showed the imposition of unprecedented restrictions on the practice of Catholicism. Not until February 23, 1926, did Calles get in on the act. Blaming lax enforcement of the constitution under Carranza and Obregón for the conflict, he ordered state governors to enforce anticlerical provisions. Three weeks later, the measures had led to the closure of one hundred religious schools and eighty-three monasteries and convents as well as the expulsion of two hundred foreign-born priests.[53]

The Church mounted a counterattack. Caruana created an Episcopal Committee that included the archbishops of Guadalajara, Morelia, Mexico City, and Puebla, among others. The National League for Religious Defense became the Liga Nacional Defensora de la Libertad Religiosa (National League for the Defense of Religious Liberty, or LNDLR). For these efforts, Caruana found himself expelled.[54] A letter from the Episcopal Committee warned Calles: "If the goal of the repeated expulsions of

Apostolic delegates is to relax and sever . . . the traditional links of the Mexican Church with Rome, Mr. President, know that every new instance of pain is a new connection of love and union."[55] But Calles, now fully committed to the fight, promised to "use all necessary energy to ensure" that the Church complied with Mexican laws.[56]

The "Calles Law" of July 2, 1926 amounted to the ultimate confrontation. In a reform of the penal code, the government mandated that the priests register with local authorities while reiterating constitutional strictures on Church activities. This included shuttering all religious schools, monasteries, and convents. The episcopate immediately objected that the registration requirement amounted to giving the state the power to decide who could exercise ministry. Incensed, the LNDLR announced an economic boycott. The Episcopal Committee ordered the suspension of religious ceremonies on July 31, when the Calles Law took effect. But Calles expressed his delight, telling Lagarde that this step would cost the Catholic hierarchy approximately 2 percent of its followers each week.[57]

When the episcopate requested negotiations, Calles thus assumed that the archbishops operated from a weak position. Asked for a full retreat from the Calles Law and, indeed, the anticlerical articles of the constitution, the president asserted that the clergy fomented "open revolts . . . to the end of abolishing or reforming the Constitution." He also asked the archbishops to take up their concerns with Congress as the sole body that could implement revisions to the constitution.[58] At an August 21 meeting with Díaz and Ruiz y Flores, Calles appeared to soften his stance when he stated that the registration requirement only served statistical purposes.[59] A few days later, however, an article in *El Universal* quoted Calles as saying that the negotiations had not led to any progress. Congress rejected the entreaties to amend the constitution.[60]

Catholics then took matters into their own hands. Their boycott crippled the economy in the heartland. On November 26, 1926, LNDLR leader René Capistrán Garza called for Calles's overthrow. Soon thereafter, *campesinos* in Jalisco, Michoacán, and other states in the center-west rose up in rebellion. *La Cristiada* (or the Cristero Revolt) devastated agricultural production in Mexico's breadbasket and pushed the Calles government to the brink. The Cristiada lasted until 1929.

In July 1928, Obregón's assassination at the hands of the devout Catholic José de León Toral gave fresh ammunition to Calles's anti-Catholicism. According to one of his allies, Calles exclaimed: "This time they really screwed us! We will need to unite to resist the force of reaction."[61] Although Obregón had endeavored to resolve the church-state conflict, leading many to believe that the assassin had targeted the wrong leader, he, too, was irreligious. Obregón's last will stipulated that his burial "not be desecrated by any religious ceremony."[62] In a perceptive analysis, the historian Robert Weis has argued that León Toral killed Obregón because he was a tyrant, in the belief that tyrannicide would confer martyrdom upon him.[63] The assassination also paved the way for the creation of a national ruling party under Calles's aegis. The Partido Nacional Revolucionario (National Revolutionary Party, PNR) embraced anticlericalism along with all other precepts of the 1917 Constitution.

Why did Calles and his team pick a fight with the Church that still appears today as a singular political mistake? The most convincing explanation is that Calles, Morones, Tejeda, and Amaro believed that (1) anti-Catholicism was broadly popular with their base; and (2) the Catholic clergy and burgeoning social organizations mounted a challenge to the authority of the state that they directed. They saw the Church as an enemy that did not accept the supremacy of the law. In Lagarde's words, the Church had "here more than elsewhere to form a state within the state and not to accept from the civil power any regulation, any law."[64] This observation recalled the rationale for the expulsion of the Jesuits in 1767 provided by Spain's Bourbon rulers.

Calles was also less willing than Obregón to sacrifice his priorities for political expediency and saw himself as the guardian of the constitution that he had sworn to protect. Even as he was uninterested in implementing all of its provisions, the president would not tolerate an overt challenge to state authority such as the one that the prelates had issued. In his words, "So long as I am President of the Republic, the Constitution of 1917 will be obeyed."[65] Motivating Catholic opposition, the December 1925 papal encyclical, *Quas Primas* (In the First), also bears mention. *Quas Primas* introduced the Feast of Christ the King, a direct challenge to secular nationalism in its celebration of Jesus Christ as the "true" king of all of humanity. Calles may also have been aware of the dissension between the episcopate and grassroots believers and particularly the fact that the diplomats of the Holy See were distracted with other matters. The papacy had begun negotiating with the Italian state regarding the future of Vatican City—a future ultimately settled by means of the 1929 Lateran Pacts. It is difficult to know for sure how much of this figured into the president's calculations. What is clear, however, is that the opposition to the Catholic hierarchy was multifaceted and complex. If Calles was Mexico's arch-clerophobe, it was because he—and not Morones, Tejeda, or Amaro—was the man in the presidential chair.

The Denouement

On November 30, 1928, Calles handed off the presidency to interim President Emilio Portes Gil. Sojourning in Paris, he was therefore not directly involved in the efforts to bring the Cristero Rebellion to an end. In June 1929, with the help of US Ambassador Dwight Morrow, Portes Gil and the episcopate concluded an agreement that offered an amnesty for the Cristeros and resumed Church services. But neither the LNDLR nor the Cristeros were part of these negotiations, and the agreement had not solved the conflict from their point of view, because the anticlerical constitutional articles remained on the books. Thus, Catholics redoubled their efforts at mobilization under the auspices of the Acción Católica Mexicana (Mexican Catholic Action) that ultimately grew to 365,088 members.[66]

Despite Calles's absence from these negotiations, he remained the center of the Mexican political scene, dubbed the *jefe máximo* of the revolution—the power behind the scenes. He keenly made his presence felt in the administration of Portes Gil's successor, Pascual Ortiz Rubio, the candidate of the official revolutionary party that Calles had helped to create (the PNR). Backed by Calles, Ortiz Rubio had waged a hotly contested campaign against José Vasconcelos, who had appealed to Catholic voters during his campaign. Marred by fraud and violence against Vasconcelos supporters, the election ended in Ortiz Rubio's victory.[67]

Ortiz Rubio's administration coincided with a third and final wave of revolutionary anticlericalism. States limited the ratio of priests to inhabitants. In Chiapas, it was 1:60,000; in Michoacán, 1:33,000; and in Veracruz, 1:100,000.[68] "Defanaticization" campaigns spread beyond Veracruz and Tabasco to Sonora, where Calles's son, Rodolfo, served as governor. Ten states decreed the expulsion of all of their priests or allowed only one or two to remain. In one instance, the one priest was required to be fifty years old and married, an apparently sarcastic gesture. Although the decrees often lacked enforcement, they sent a clear message.[69] Mexican Catholics responded with a "Segunda Cristiada," or Second Cristero Revolt, based on guerrilla warfare rather than open military conflict.

The jefe máximo's responsibility for these state-level policies—let alone local-level defanaticization, iconoclastic campaigns, and plain antireligious violence—remains unclear, with the obvious exception of Calles's home state of Sonora. Historiography has often overstated the ex-president's influence during the Maximato (1928–1935), unwittingly contributing to a "great man" vision of the power behind the scenes.[70] This view supposes that the jefe máximo played politicians and movements like puppets on strings instead of recognizing that anti-Catholicism boasted at least some popular support in many regions. This anticlerical third wave had many architects and participants, including agrarians and labor movements other than the CROM, which disappeared from national prominence during the first half of the 1930s. And the PNR, Calles's party, was not particularly anti-Catholic in its program or practice.

Nonetheless, Calles's influence in the national debate remained obvious as per his most radical statement regarding the Catholic Church, made in Guadalajara on July 20, 1934:

> The revolution is not over. . . . We have to . . . take possession of the conscience of children and youths, because they belong . . . to the revolution. . . . We cannot let the future of the country and the revolution fall into the hands of the enemies. With great deception, the reactionaries declare that the child belongs to the home and the youth belongs to the community. [The revolution must] uproot the prejudices and form the new national soul.[71]

This speech, which conflated Catholics with reactionaries, anticipated action at the national level. In October 1934, Congress tightened the anticlerical provisions of Article 3 and added a requirement of socialist education. The speech displayed Calles's continuing commitment to anti-Catholicism at a time when his personal political views had turned to the right in other areas, including agrarian reform, the rights of workers, and US-Mexican relations.[72] Calles's speech likely aimed to weigh in on the congressional debates on socialist education when his close friend and ally, Abelardo L. Rodríguez, served as substitute president. In addition, Calles might have also been practicing some virtue-signaling to the Garrido wing of the PNR. Was Calles also trying to hamstring the incoming president, Lázaro Cárdenas, known to be more committed to the revolutionary principles as enshrined in the constitution than Calles, by fanning the flames of the church-state conflict? Or was he trying to weigh in on the raging debate about "socialist education"?

Whereas Calles's anti-Catholicism remained on display, his personal approach to religion paints a more nuanced picture. As his health declined, Calles came to trust religious institutions in the area of health care, especially outside Mexico. In 1927, his ailing wife traveled to a

FIGURE 3. Hortensia Elías Calles Chacón on the Day of Her Religious Wedding, 1922. FAPECFT. Fototeca Colección de Álbumes Fotográficos de los Archivos Plutarco Elías Calles y Fernando Torreblanca (AAPECFT), Fondo Fernando Torreblanca (FAFFFT), álbum 2: *Historia Política de México 1920–1928. Volumen III.* Fotografía: 634, inventario: 73.

Lutheran hospital in Los Angeles for treatment, where she died. In 1935, Calles visited a Catholic hospital in that same city for gall bladder surgery. Calles also visited a faith healer known as El Niño Fidencio. On February 8, 1928, with the Cristiada in full swing, Calles visited the town of Espinazo (Nuevo León) aboard the presidential train to get help for a skin condition. He joined thousands of Fidencio's followers there and was impressed enough that he exempted the faith healer from legislation proscribing the practice of popular medicine. It is unlikely that the president actually consulted with Fidencio on his condition. Even though the visit was of a private rather than official nature, it suggested that the exponent of anti-Catholicism had a spiritual side after all.[73] Was this Calles the politician or Calles the believer? Or both?

Other anecdotes suggest an appreciation for Catholic traditions in a man who had missed the Catholic wedding of his eldest daughter, Hortensia (see fig. 3). Once out of the public eye after a five-year exile, Calles enjoyed annual celebrations in honor of his Saint's Day organized by an association of affluent women in Cuernavaca, Morelos, complete with Sonoran-style barbeque prepared by Calles himself.[74] He and his second wife, Leonor Llorente, had their eldest son baptized in a Catholic church. Calles served as *padrino* (godfather) to one of his grandchildren, and his two youngest sons attended St. Catherine's Military School in Anaheim, California.[75]

Perhaps the most fascinating aspect of Calles's personal spiritual life is his participation in Spiritist séances in the last four years of his life (1941–1945), following in the footsteps of earlier Mexican Spiritists such as Francisco I. Madero.[76] Sharing a belief in an eternal spirit with the monotheistic faith traditions, Spiritists gather for the purpose of communicating with other spirits across time (including the dead) and space. At first a skeptic, what Calles remembered as the caresses of an apparition convinced him to give Spiritism a try.[77] To Calles, Spiritism appeared an alternative to the Catholic Church that did not jettison the idea of an afterlife that appeared so important to so many (and that he himself shared). His Spiritist circle had a long-deceased guiding spirit, a physician from the nineteenth century particularly interested in sharing suggestions about health. According to Calles, "the recommendations of the maestro are full of wisdom, . . . and I hope they will prolong my life."[78] Over time, other politicians joined Calles in his circle, including those near the end of their careers (like Morones) and future President Miguel Alemán Valdés. Opposition to the Cárdenas administration that had just ended united these politicians. Women were also part of the circle, including four members of Calles's immediate family: three daughters and one daughter-in-law.[79]

The session minutes documenting interactions with the media (the spirits with which a participant reportedly interacted) contain valuable insights about Calles's late-life reflections. One of these media was Carlos Randall, the last Conventionist governor of Sonora and a longtime rival. Randall's medium enjoined Calles: "I am leaving ... with the advice not to remember your political past. It is not worth worrying about a world like ours full of Kaffirs [sic]. Devote your last years to leading a comfortable life. ..."[80] The spirit then sent a more explicit political message that reflected Calles's rightward turn after his presidency. "That Agrarian Law and that Labor Law [are] two knives that are killing the nation. ... Let those work the land who are able, those who are willing, and [let these farmers have] the acreage that they can manage. ... The Ley de Trabajo should have been named Law for the Encouragement of Vagrancy."[81] The spirit added: "Plutarco Elías Calles was and continues to be a patriot. He has never been as well prepared as he is now. Day by day, the hour draws near in which our poor and unfortunate fatherland will turn to his experience and wisdom. No one could help the fatherland better than this man of strong character, perfected by his years, without selfishness and vanity."[82] After Calles died from post-surgery complications on 19 October 1945, Rodolfo communicated with his father in the realm of the spirits, reporting Calles as saying: "I am consoled by the fact that I no longer feel the pain that tormented me in my last days. It is necessary for you to forget my death, and not to comment on the cause of my leave-taking. All suppositions are useless. It was destiny that marked my end."[83]

Calles was inarguably the chief patriarch of anti-Catholicism in postrevolutionary Mexico, a title enhanced by his exalted political role as president and kingmaker. But there is plenty of evidence to suggest that Calles was not the revolutionary Mexican leader most fervent in his clerophobia. Yes, Calles was by far the most powerful clerophobe, yet the intensity of this opposition to the Catholic Church was not consistent throughout his life and career. When the end approached, the man who was once at the center of Mexican politics accepted the fact that he lived in a predominantly Catholic country. As he reportedly told his housekeeper every morning in retirement: "Luz, if you are going to mass, please bring me my spearmint tea."[84]

Notes

1. Butler, "Introduction," 1.
2. This chapter draws on my previous work on Calles and the other members of the Sonoran Dynasty in *Plutarco Elías Calles, The Last Caudillo,* and *The Sonoran Dynasty in Mexico.*
3. Blancarte, "Closing Comment," 589–90.
4. Butler, "Introduction," 1.
5. Macías Richard, *Vida y temperamento,* 35–44; Buchenau, *Calles,* chap. 1.
6. Quoted in Krauze, *Reformar desde el origen,* 12.
7. Macías, *Vida y temperamento,* 45.
8. Macías, 45–49.
9. Vanderwood, *Power of God.*
10. Krauze, *Reformar,* 12.
11. Monteón, "Child Is Father," 43–61.
12. Macías, *Vida y temperamento,* 19–31; Voss, *On the Periphery,* 148–60.
13. Aguilar Camín, *La frontera nómada,* 180.
14. Buchenau, *Sonoran Dynasty,* 26.
15. Racine, "Freemasonry," 1:538–40.
16. On Freemasonry in the revolution, see Smith, "Anticlericalism, Freemasonry, and Politics," 559–88. On the Judeo-Masonic trope, see Williford, "Armando los espíritus."
17. Buchenau, *Calles and the Mexican Revolution,* chap. 1.
18. Apostolic Delegation, Mexico City, to Gaetano de Lai, 15 Oct. 1916, Archivio della Sacra Congregazione degli Affari Ecclesiastici Straordinari, Vatican City (hereafter ASCAES), Terzo Periodo (hereafter TP), fasc. 31, pos. 106, 49–55.
19. Bantjes, "Regional Dynamics," 112.
20. Knight, "Mentality," 28.
21. Curley, *Citizens and Believers.*
22. Calles to Moreno, Hermosillo, 19 Mar. 1916, Archivo Histórico General del Estado de Sonora, Hermosillo, vol. 3129.
23. Macías, *La fuerza del destino,* 197–98.
24. Macías, 203.
25. Fallaw, "Varieties," 488–89; Curley, *Citizens;* Aldana, *Manuel M. Diéguez y la Revolución Mexicana;* and Osten, *Mexican Revolution's Wake.*
26. Vasconcelos, *La Tormenta,* 57.
27. Fallaw, "Varieties," 488–89.

28. Quoted in Aldana, *Diéguez*, 140.
29. Quoted in Macías, *La fuerza del destino*, 107.
30. Quoted in Castro, *Álvaro Obregón*, 126–27.
31. Macías, *La fuerza del destino*, 202.
32. Mora y del Río to Gasparri, San Antonio, TX, 25 July 1917, ASCAES, TP, fasc. 138, pos. 769.
33. Dulles, *Yesterday in Mexico*, 298.
34. Fallaw, *Religion and State*, 17.
35. Filippi to Obregón, Mexico City, 3 June 1922, Archivo General de la Nación, Mexico City, Fondo Presidentes, Obregón-Calles, 438-F-1.
36. "No se efectuará el homenaje a Cristo Rey," *El Universal*, 11 Jan. 1923; "Entronización de Cristo Rey en el Cubilete," *El Universal*, 12 Jan. 1923; "La ceremonia religiosa en el Cerro de Cubilete," *El Universal*, 13 Jan. 1923; "Expulsión de Mons. Filippi, Delegado Apostólico en México," *El Universal*, 14 Jan. 1923; "Monseñor Ernesto Filippi, Delegado Apostólico, saldrá de México mañana," *El Universal*, 15 Jan. 1923; "El Vaticano y el gobierno de México tratan el caso de Mons. Filippi," *El Universal*, 17 Jan. 1923.
37. "El clero mexicano se dirige al presidente," *Excélsior*, 7 Feb. 1923.
38. "Discurso," 14 May 1924, in Elías Calles, *Pensamiento político y social*, 122.
39. Tito Crespi to Gasparri, Mexico City, 22 May 1924, ASCAES, Quarto Periodo (hereafter QP), fasc. 16, pos. 493.
40. Crespi to Segreteria di Stato, Mexico City, 7 June 1923, 16 Nov. 1923, and 8 Feb. 1924, ASCAES, QP, fasc. 16, pos. 493.
41. Bailey, *¡Viva Cristo Rey!*, 50–53.
42. Butler, *Mexico's Spiritual Reconquest*.
43. Quoted in Henderson, *Mexican Wars*, 216.
44. Buford, "Biography of Luis N. Morones"; Wood, "Adalberto Tejeda of Veracruz," 77–94; Loyo Camacho, *Joaquín Amaro y el proceso de institucionalización del ejército mexicano*.
45. Quoted in Dulles, *Yesterday in Mexico*, 301.
46. Buchenau, *Sonoran Dynasty*, 195.
47. "The Religious Crisis in Mexico," enclosed in Morrow to secretary, 27 Feb. 1928, National Archives, College Park, MD, RG 59: General Records of the Department of State, 812.404/867 (hereafter "Lagarde memorandum"), 4.
48. Quoted in Bailey, *¡Viva Cristo Rey!*, 62.
49. "Habla el episcopado," *El Universal*, Feb. 8, 1926.
50. Caruana to Pietro Fumasoni-Biondi, Mexico City, 30 Mar. 1926, ASCAES, QP, fasc. 29, pos. 505.
51. Quoted in George Russell, "Mexico: Political," 8 Feb. 1926, NA, Record Group 165: Army and General Staffs, Military Intelligence Division, box 1664, 2657-G-616.

52. Bailey, ¡Viva Cristo Rey!, 63.
53. Bailey, 64–66.
54. Memorandum by Caruana, 16 May 1926, Yale University, New Haven, CT, James Rockwell Sheffield Papers, series I, box 5, folder 50; "Lagarde Memorandum," 40–42.
55. Collective letter to Calles, unsigned, Mexico City, 18 May 1926, FAPEC, Fondo Fernando Torreblanca (hereafter FFT), ser. 010215, exp. 22, inv. 1254, "Mora y del Río, José."
56. Calles to Mora y del Río, Mexico City, 22 May 1926, FAPEC, FFT, ser. 010215, exp. 22, inv. 1254, "Mora y del Río, José."
57. "Lagarde Memorandum," 3–4.
58. Calles to Mora y del Río and Díaz, Mexico City, 19 Aug. 1926, FAPEC, FFT, ser. 010215, exp. 22, inv. 1254, "Mora y del Río, José."
59. "Entrevista del presidente Calles con los obispos Leopoldo Ruiz y Pascual Díaz," 21 Aug. 1926, FAPEC, APEC, gav. 3, exp. 147, "Arzobispos."
60. Morrow, "Memorandum of conversation with Lic. Mestre," 8 Mar. 1929, Amherst College Library, Amherst, MA, Dwight W. Morrow Papers, series X, reel 17; Bailey, ¡Viva Cristo Rey!, 91–93; "Laymen of Mexico Plead for Church," *New York Times*, 13 Oct. 1926.
61. León, *Crónica del poder*, 272.
62. Almada Bay, "De regidores porfiristas a presidentes de la república en el periodo revolucionario," 768.
63. Weis, *For Christ and Country*, 2–6.
64. "Lagarde Memorandum," 5.
65. Quoted in Bailey, ¡Viva Cristo Rey!, 65.
66. Bantjes, "Regional Dynamics," 115.
67. Buchenau, *Sonoran Dynasty*, chap. 9.
68. "San Angel se Denominará Villa Obregón," *El Universal*, 19 Dec. 1931.
69. Bantjes, *Jesus Walked on Earth*, 10–11; Reich, *Mexico's Hidden Revolution*, 36–39.
70. Buchenau, *Plutarco Elías Calles*, chap. 6.
71. Quoted in Meyer et al. *Historia de la Revolución Mexicana*, 178.
72. See interview with Emilio Portes Gil in Wilkie and Monzón de Wilkie, *México visto en el siglo XX*, 540–41.
73. "Memorias del General Juan Andreu Almazán," *El Universal*, 17 Nov. 1958.
74. Interview with Plutarco Elías Calles Llorente, Mexico City, 31 May 2004.
75. Interview with Norma Torreblanca de Mereles, Mexico City, 1 June 2004; FAPEC, FPEC, serie 010901, exp. 59, inv. 694 "Elías Calles Llorente, Plutarco José."
76. *Una ventana al mundo invisible: protocolos del IMIS* (Mexico City: Ediciones Antorcha, 1960).
77. Interview with Plutarco Elías Calles Llorente, Mexico City, 31 May 2004; *Ventana al mundo invisible*, 105–6.

78. Minutes, 15 Feb. 1944, Calles to Rodolfo Elías Calles Chacón, Cuernavaca, 29 Apr. 1944, FAPEC, FPEC, serie 011100, gav. 72, exp. 145 "Elías Calles Chacón, Rodolfo."
79. FAPEC, FPEC, serie 011100, gav. 71, exp. 86 "Castillo, Enrique del. Mtro. Sesiones espiritistas;" *Ventana al mundo invisible*, 81–85.
80. "Sesión en que trabajaron el Sr. Rodolfo Elías Calles y su Sra., en Cuernavaca, Morelos, el 28 de septiembre de 1944," FAPEC, FPEC, serie 011100, gav. 71, exp. 86 "Castillo, Enrique del. Mtro. Sesiones espiritistas."
81. Ibid.
82. Quoted in Krauze, *Mexico: Biography of Power*, 436–37.
83. Rodolfo Elías Calles, minutes, 25 Oct. 1945, FAPEC, FPEC, serie 011100, gav. 71, exp. 86 "Castillo, Enrique del. Mtro. Sesiones espiritistas."
84. Quoted in Macías Richard, "La fuerza del destino," 417.

Works Cited

Archives

Amherst College Library, Amherst, MA, Dwight W. Morrow Papers.
Archivio della Sacra Congregazione degli Affari Ecclesiastici Straordinari, Vatican City.
Archivo General de la Nación, Mexico City.
Archivo Histórico General del Estado de Sonora, Hermosillo.
Fideicomiso Archivo Plutarco Elías Calles y Fernando Torreblanca, Mexico City.
National Archives, College Park, MD.
Yale University, New Haven, CT, James Rockwell Sheffield Papers.

Periodicals

Excelsior
El Universal
New York Times

Primary Sources

Elías Calles, Plutarco. *Pensamiento político y social: Antología, 1913–1936*. Edited by Carlos Macías Richard. Mexico City: Fondo de Cultura Económica, 1988.
León, Luis L. *Crónica del poder: En los recuerdos de un político en el México revolucionario*. Mexico City: Fondo de Cultura Económica, 1987.
Una ventana al mundo invisible: protocolos del IMIS. Mexico City: Ediciones Antorcha, 1960.

Vasconcelos, José. *La Tormenta*. Mexico City: Trillas, 2000.
Wilkie, James W., and Edna Monzón de Wilkie. *México visto en el siglo XX: Entrevistas de historia oral*. Mexico City: Instituto Mexicano de Investigaciones Económicas, 1969.

Secondary Sources

Aguilar Camín, Héctor. *La frontera nómada: Sonora y la revolución mexicana*. Mexico City: Siglo XXI Editores, 1977.
Aldana Rendón, Mario. *Manuel M. Diéguez y la Revolución Mexicana*. Zapopan: El Colegio de Jalisco, 2006.
Almada Bay, Ignacio. "De regidores porfiristas a presidentes de la república en el periodo revolucionario: explorando el ascenso y la caída del 'sonorismo.'" *Historia Mexicana* 60, no. 2 (2010): 729–89.
Bailey, David C. *¡Viva Cristo Rey! The Cristero Rebellion and the Church-State Conflict in Mexico*. Austin: University of Texas Press, 1974.
Bantjes, Adrian. *As If Jesus Walked on Earth: Cardenismo, Sonora, and the Mexican Revolution*. Wilmington, DE: Scholarly Resources, 1998.
———. "The Regional Dynamics of Anticlericalism and Defanatization in Revolutionary Mexico." In *Faith and Impiety in Revolutionary Mexico*, edited by Matthew Butler, 111–30. London: Palgrave, 2007.
Blancarte, Roberto "Closing Comment: 'Personal Enemies of God:' Anticlericals and Anticlericalism in Revolutionary Mexico, 1915–1940." *The Americas* 65, no. 4 (2009), 589–99.
Buchenau, Jürgen. *The Last Caudillo: Álvaro Obregón and the Mexican Revolution*. Chichester, UK: Wiley-Blackwell, 2011.
———. *Plutarco Elías Calles and the Mexican Revolution*. Lanham, MD: Rowman & Littlefield, 2007.
———. *The Sonoran Dynasty in Mexico: Revolution, Reform, and Repression*. Lincoln: University of Nebraska Press, 2023.
Buford, Camile Nick. "A Biography of Luis N. Morones, Mexican Labor and Political Leader." PhD diss., Louisiana State University, 1972.
Butler, Matthew. "Introduction: A Revolution in Spirit? Mexico, 1910–40." In Butler, *Faith and Impiety in Revolutionary Mexico*. New York: Palgrave Macmillan, 2007.
———. *Mexico's Spiritual Reconquest: Indigenous Catholics and Father Pérez's Revolutionary Church*. Albuquerque: University of New Mexico Press, 2023.
Butler, Matthew, ed. *Faith and Impiety in Revolutionary Mexico*. New York: Palgrave Macmillan, 2007.
Castro, Pedro. *Álvaro Obregón: Fuego y cenizas de la Revolución Mexicana*. Mexico City: Ediciones Era, 2009.

Curley, Robert. *Citizens and Believers: Religion and Politics in Revolutionary Jalisco, 1900–1930.* Albuquerque: University of New Mexico Press, 2018.

Dulles, John W. F. *Yesterday in Mexico: A Chronicle of the Revolution, 1919–1936.* Austin: University of Texas Press, 1961.

Fallaw, Ben. *Religion and State Formation in Postrevolutionary Mexico.* Durham, NC: Duke University Press, 2013.

———. "Varieties of Mexican Revolutionary Anticlericalism: Radicalism, Iconoclasm, and Otherwise, 1914–1935." *The Americas* 65, no. 4 (2009): 481–509.

Henderson, Timothy J. *The Mexican Wars for Independence.* New York: Hill and Wang, 2009.

Knight, Alan. "The Mentality and Modus Operandi of Revolutionary Anticlericalism." In *Faith and Impiety in Revolutionary Mexico*, edited by Matthew Butler, 21–56. London: Palgrave, 2007.

Krauze, Enrique. *Mexico: Biography of Power.* Translated by Hank Heifetz. New York: Harper Collins, 1997.

———. *Reformar desde el origen: Plutarco Elías Calles.* Mexico City: Fondo de Cultura Económica, 1987.

Loyo Camacho, Martha Beatriz. *Joaquín Amaro y el proceso de institucionalización del ejército mexicano, 1917–1931.* Mexico City: UNAM, 2003.

Macías Richard, Carlos. "La fuerza del destino: una biografía de Plutarco Elías Calles." Doctoral diss., El Colegio de México, 1994.

———. *Vida y temperamento: Plutarco Elías Calles, 1877–1920.* Mexico City: Fondo de Cultura Económica, 1995.

Meyer, Lorenzo, Rafael Segovia, and Alejandra Lajous. *Historia de la Revolución Mexicana, 1928–1934: Los inicios de la institucionalización.* Mexico City: Colegio de México, 1978.

Monteón, Michael C. "The Child Is Father of the Man: Personality and Politics in Revolutionary Mexico." *Journal of Iberian and Latin American Studies* 10, no. 1 (2004): 43–61.

Osten, Sarah. *The Mexican Revolution's Wake: The Making of a Political System.* Cambridge: Cambridge University Press, 2018.

Racine, Karen. "Freemasonry." In *Encyclopedia of Mexico: History, Society, and Culture*, edited by Michael S. Werner, 538–40. Chicago: Fitzroy Dearborn, 1997.

Reich, Peter L. *Mexico's Hidden Revolution: The Catholic Church in Law and Politics since 1929.* South Bend, IN: University of Notre Dame Press, 1995.

Smith, Benjamin. "Anticlericalism, Freemasonry, and Politics in Mexico, 1915–1940." *The Americas* 65, no. 4 (2009): 559–88.

Vanderwood, Paul. *The Power of God Against the Guns of Government: Religious Upheaval in Mexico at the Turn of the Nineteenth Century.* Stanford, CA: Stanford University Press, 1998.

Voss, Stuart F. *On the Periphery of Nineteenth-Century Mexico: Sonora and Sinaloa, 1810–1877.* Tucson: University of Arizona Press, 1982.

Weis, Robert. *For Christ and Country: Militant Catholic Youth in Post-Revolutionary Mexico.* Cambridge: Cambridge University Press, 2019.

Williford, Thomas J. "Armando los espíritus: Political Rhetoric in Colombia on the Eve of La Violencia, 1930–1945." PhD diss., Vanderbilt University, 2005.

Wood, Andrew G. "Adalberto Tejeda of Veracruz: Radicalism and Reaction." In *State Governors in the Mexican Revolution, 1910–1952,* edited by Jürgen Buchenau and William H. Beezley, 77–94. Lanham, MD: Rowman and Littlefield, 2009.

CHAPTER TWO

Lawyers, Guns, and Money

Revolution, Religion, and Authoritarianism in Tabasco, Mexico, 1920–1936

SARAH OSTEN

In March 1935, the Mexican Minister of Agriculture, Tomás Garrido Canabal, gave a lengthy interview to the socialist newspaper *The Milwaukee Leader*. In it, he proudly described his achievements as governor of his home state of Tabasco: "Whatever my errors, the true situation is this: in Tabasco there are 593 schools for a population of 220,000 inhabitants; there is not one single church, not a clergyman, not an idler, neither a pickpocket; and Tabasco is the only place in the world where not a drop of alcohol is consumed."[1] This was not merely a highlight reel of Garrido Canabal's greatest accomplishments in his own estimation: all of these were related, integral elements of a larger, long-term political project over the course of the 1920s and early 1930s in which the government was both socialist and militantly secular, and so was the moral code that it relentlessly labored to enforce. While Garrido Canabal is best known and most notorious for his radical anti-Catholicism, it was just one constituent piece of a political program led by someone who often regarded politics as a zero-sum game in which fewer churches very directly meant more schools; if someone was not a friend or ally, they were likely an enemy; and any forgiveness shown to the disloyal was folly.[2] Garrido Canabal lived his life under the assumption that his enemies were trying to kill him and that the Catholic Church and its allies would take any opportunity afforded them to destroy all of the hard-won revolutionary reforms he had overseen in Tabasco.[3]

This essay explores why this was, and with what political consequences, via examination of two related elements of Garridismo as a political movement that each provides greater context for Garrido Canabal's well-known, fervent antipathy toward the Catholic Church and its believers: first, the larger regional context of southeastern socialism of which

Garrido Canabal's political project in Tabasco formed a part, and second, his deepened mistrust of the Church as one of the long-term consequences of the de la Huerta Rebellion of 1923–1924. I argue that the former was what initially inspired Garrido Canabal's embrace of anti-Catholicism as one of the core elements of his political program and that the latter served as fuel to a proverbial fire that already had been set over the preceding years. Effectively, for Garrido Canabal the rebellion was proof positive that the Church was one of the most dangerous enemies of Socialist reform.

Garrido Canabal was more passionate and unrelenting in his anticlericalism and iconoclasm than even Plutarco Elías Calles, but the roots and driving causes of this zeal are relatively little explored.[4] This is not an in-depth study of Garridista anti-Catholicism (and along with it, anticlericalism), a topic that has been well covered by other scholars elsewhere, but rather a much-needed contextualization of it.[5] My first objective is to provide a better frame of reference for understanding Garrido Canabal's broader political project not as a radical outlier of postrevolutionary politics and reformism, although it inarguably was that in some respects, but as one manifestation of a larger political movement in the Southeast, and one that had significant national influence by the end of the 1920s. My second aim is to demonstrate that the notorious anti-Catholicism of the Tabasco Socialists (organized in the Partido Socialista Radical Tabasqueño, or Tabasco Radical Socialist Party) was not purely or even principally ideological. Rather, it was understood by its protagonists, and by Garrido Canabal himself, as a logical, strategic, and ultimately pragmatic response to the political circumstances they faced as they understood them, based on recent, bitter experience.[6] As Robert Curley and Adrian Bantjes have both argued, ideology informed Mexican postrevolutionary anti-Catholicism and anticlericalism even when it was deployed for politically pragmatic and strategic reasons.[7] Thus, we may better understand Garridista socialism, including its extreme anti-Catholicism, not as an isolated regional political aberration but as a manifestation of larger, national political trends, including the little-understood and profound long-term political consequences of a rebellion that has often been described as principally personalist and military.

Both of these elements together are necessary considerations to interpret Garrido Canabal's more authoritarian innovations on the southeastern socialist model of leftist corporatism, as most vividly and infamously illustrated by his extreme restrictions on religious practice and institutions.[8] Garridista socialism combined ambitious promises of reform with economic nationalism, an ambivalent approach to democracy while nevertheless insisting on the necessity of elections, the empowerment but also the profound cooptation of its grassroots base and most particularly of organized labor, and extreme concentration of power in the executive branch of government. It was intended to remake politics but also society: the role of the state was to be transformed but so were the behaviors and beliefs of its citizens. It also blurred the lines between the state government and the not-officially official party of the state and embraced authoritarian solutions to organized challenges to its dominance, with its commitment to revolutionary principles, including anti-Catholicism, as the justification for its systematic debilitation of individual political rights.[9]

Garrido Canabal's Socialism

Socialism is a notoriously diverse political brand that is nearly impossible to define, even just in the Mexican context and even just in Mexico in the early twentieth century. Southeastern postrevolutionary socialism (defined here as the family of variants that took root in the states of Campeche, Chiapas, Tabasco, and Yucatán in the 1910s and 1920s) was an idiosyncratic mix of Marxism, anarchosyndicalism, and US progressivism, among other influences, including Mexico's own homegrown brands of revolutionary politics, particularly Zapatismo, Magonismo, and several varieties of Constitutionalism, as well as older influences such as Liberalism and positivism. Southeastern socialists themselves only very rarely explicitly described what they meant by "socialism." Even General Salvador Alvarado, who wrote a multi-volume exegesis of his political beliefs and founded one of Mexico's first Socialist parties, rarely used the word "socialist," never mind delved into concretely defining it. In the few cases in which the self-described Socialists of the Southeast did attempt to define their politics, they often invoked modernity and social and economic justice in the name of a vaguely defined set of revolutionary ideals, always nationalist and nearly always defined in part by its direct, incessant confrontation with counter-revolutionaries of various stripes but particularly the Catholic Church, parasitical capitalists, wealthy landowners, and sometimes also foreigners (whether priests, capitalists, or landowners). As Ivonne Meza Huacuja has emphasized, Garrido's brand of socialism was always presented in Tabasco as "the only way to achieve the objectives of the Mexican Revolution."[10]

Thus, Garrido Canabal's 1935 interview with the US socialist newspaper *The Milwaukee Leader*, in which he described his version of socialism at some length, is of particular value, including for better understanding the ways in which elements of southeastern-style regional socialism had influenced national politics by the 1930s. It is even more so for my specific purposes here, because in the interview he also discussed in some depth how anticlericalism and his antipathy toward both the Catholic Church and religion in general fit into his larger political program and indeed, into his political career—which, unbeknownst to him, was just a little more than a year from its end. At the time of the interview in March 1935, Garrido Canabal was just a few months into his service as President Lázaro Cárdenas's minister of agriculture and was sent into exile by Cárdenas the following May. The first sentence introducing the three-part interview with Garrido Canabal was "Is the present government of Mexico Socialist?" and the second sentence was "What purposes lie behind the severe restrictive laws passed against the Church which may invoke an investigation by the congress of the United States?"

Garrido Canabal submitted his answers to all of the newspaper's questions in writing in English. When asked specifically "Is Mexico Socialist?" he replied:

> There are several concepts and numerous definitions. But my personal opinion is that Socialism is a movement of economic and social adjustment which leads, fundamentally, to raise the level in the standard of living of the working people. I understand that the mission of the true Socialist is not to destroy the nation's resources, but, on the contrary, to facilitate its development and to struggle for a more fair distribution of the profits attainted. Socialism, in opposition to what its enemies affirm, is not a chaotic doctrine of social disjoining; on the contrary, it is aimed to unify and to direct the producing energies, within an ample concept of distributing justice [. . .] our desire is to improve as much as we can the economic conditions of the working people. But very far from promoting conflicts between capital and labor, we are trying to balance both producing factors, so they be identified with the contemporary reality of our nation. The Mexican revolution fights against the absorbing capitalist—that one who is an extortioner and intransigent to the right demands of the workers; but the capitalist who recognizes in the working man a true and necessary ally for their social function, instead of being annoyed, will be fully guaranteed opportunities for the widest development.[11]

Garrido Canabal's main purpose in this interview was to explain the PNR's Six Year Plan for Cárdenas's presidency to a US (socialist) audience, but much of it also amounted to an explanation of his own political program in Tabasco, including the role of anticlerical laws and regulations. For Garrido Canabal, explaining Cardenista land reform and redistribution in the mid-1930s, one of the benefits of this program was to keep campesinos "away from all vices, and from the oppressive authority of the Church, so the products of the land do not vanish in the barroom, neither in the clergyman's purse."[12]

Garrido Canabal was a singular figure but also very much a man of his generation in many respects, as one of the leaders of a broader regional socialist movement in southeastern Mexico in the mid-1910s into the 1930s. All of the Socialist regimes in Campeche, Chiapas, Tabasco, and Yucatán included many of the same elements he described in his *Milwaukee Leader* interview in their particular, localized implementations of a brand of socialism that was pioneered and first tested in practice in Yucatán under Salvador Alvarado as the Constitutionalist proconsul there in 1915–1918 and then by Felipe Carrillo Puerto in the same state in the years that followed. Carrillo Puerto took it in a more radical direction than Alvarado, but one also more tailored to local realities in Yucatán. All over the southeast, Socialist governors argued for a more just relationship between labor and capital, overseen by the state to ensure workers' rights, rather than for an overthrow of capitalism. All generally sought the greater political enfranchisement of the urban and rural working classes and of women and indigenous people. All undertook land and particularly labor reforms as a means of pursuing an unprecedented degree of social and economic justice. And all pursued each of these projects via their corporatist political parties and, in all cases other than in Chiapas, via systems of *"ligas de resistencia,"* the local organizations that comprised the grassroots base of statewide Socialist political parties to which they belonged.

At the same time, all of the Socialist governments of the Southeast adapted to local circumstances and challenges, and the results were quite different in different states as a result. Socialism in Yucatán was the most radical and the most activist; by the time of his assassination in 1924, Carrillo Puerto was actively seeking to spread Yucatecan-style socialism to other states across Mexico. Socialism in Chiapas was moderated by a more daunting set of logistic and political challenges, including that it faced one of the most tenacious local counterrevolutions of the revolutionary period. Socialism in Tabasco shared many of the characteristics of its counterparts elsewhere in the region but was the most radical in its implementation of reform in some respects, as well as most authoritarian in its approach to both local and national politics.[13]

Of all of the Socialist parties of the Southeast, Tabasco had the most complex, most hierarchical, and most highly disciplined system of ligas de resistencia, and the Liga Central, which coordinated all of the state's ligas, was a powerful political institution in its own right. Ligas typically acted as branch offices of the Socialist parties, as well as syndicates and mutual aid organizations. In Tabasco the ligas additionally operated in practice in ways similar to the Committees for the Defense of the Revolution in communist Cuba in later years, serving as mechanisms of accountability, peer pressure, and surveillance of members, by members. Tabasco's ligas were therefore critical sites of political engagement and participation, including their management of elections at the local level, but they also served as instruments of political disenfranchisement of people who were perceived by their friends, neighbors, and coworkers to have transgressed Socialist principles or standards of behavior, including sympathies with the Catholic Church.

Anti-Catholicism and the anticlerical prescriptions that came along with it were another characteristic feature of all of the southeastern Socialist parties and the governments they controlled across the region, principally during the 1920s.[14] The letterhead of the Socialist Party of the Southeast of Yucatán in the late 1910s included advice to its members to "flee from religions, and particularly the Catholic one, as from plagues," among a list of principles and prescriptions otherwise dedicated to questions of labor rights.[15] As Ben Fallaw has underscored, scholarship on this subject has made clear that anticlericalism was revolutionary but also built on a longer-term legacy that predated the Mexican Revolution; Alan Knight likewise emphasizes a history of anticlericalism in Mexico that extends all the way back to the Bourbon Reforms.[16] Nevertheless, revolutionary anticlericalism had its own forms and manifestations that were specific to the 1910s–1930s, and Tabasco's particular rendition was the most notorious, with good reason.

Tomás Garrido Canabal first assumed the governorship of Tabasco in 1921 at the age of 30, clawing his way to power, with the help of national patrons, in a state that had long been mired in bitter infighting between rival factions and which posed a nearly intractable political challenge for the Constitutionalists who sought to pacify and reform it in the mid-late 1910s. Garrido Canabal was a lawyer and ambitious professional bureaucrat who had served during the Mexican Revolution in several southeastern Constitutionalist military governments of the 1910s, including briefly working under Alvarado in his government in Yucatán.[17] Garrido Canabal was also inspired, along with many other reform-minded politicians of his generation, by what Carrillo Puerto was able to achieve in that state with the groundbreaking Socialist Party of the Southeast in terms of popular organizing, land and labor reform, and political institutionalization. Garrido Canabal took power in Tabasco in several stints as interim governor in 1919–1921, supported by the rising Sonoran faction in Mexico City, and then for his first elected term in 1922. By that time, he already had an ambitious reform agenda planned for his state and was determined to pacify it after years of turmoil and political instability.

Unlike his Socialist governor counterparts Carrillo Puerto in Yucatán, Ramón Félix Flores in Campeche, and Carlos A. Vidal in Chiapas, Garrido Canabal also worked as a bureaucrat under the more radical General Francisco Múgica, who was stationed in Tabasco as its Constitutionalist proconsul in 1915–1916. Múgica's influence is plainly evident on Garrido Canabal's political formation and subsequent career. His work for Múgica's administration included the revision of state legal codes and his likely drafting of an anti-alcohol statute for Tabasco in 1915–1916.[18] While other southeastern Socialists also conducted anti-alcohol campaigns, including Carrillo Puerto in Yucatán, this was a prohibitionist fervor that Garrido Canabal either already shared with Múgica or wholeheartedly adopted and which became one of his particularly fervent reformist signatures and moralistic dogmas throughout his own time in power.[19]

As Gretchen Pierce shows in her piece in this volume, by the late 1920s and into the late 1930s, anti-alcohol campaigns at the national level in Mexico were justified as necessary for the "defanaticization" of the nation as part of both postrevolutionary state-building and identity formation; both priests and alcohol were presented by various policymakers as dangerously corrosive to these projects.[20] As Pierce emphasizes, this linking of temperance and anti-Catholicism by that time was already well established in Tabasco, inspired in part by precedents established in Socialist Yucatán. Indeed, anti "vice" campaigns were an integral element of the Garridista revolutionary project into the 1930s.[21] Politics was a matter of morality more generally because a characteristic, distinguishing feature of Garridista socialism much more than anywhere else in the Southeast, but this was a particular, socialist morality that was specifically defined in contrast to religiosity of any kind, but above all to the Catholic Church.[22] As

Ben Fallaw has shown in his study of anticlerical campaigns against confession, a particular brand of Mexican revolutionary morality was explicitly constructed in opposition to Catholicism, with Garrido Canabal himself as a principal promoter of this dogma at the national level.[23]

All of these features already existed within Tabasqueño socialism and had begun to be institutionalized within the Tabasco Radical Socialist Party by 1923, by which time Garrido Canabal had been in power as the state's elected governor for less than a year. That was a watershed year for both Tabasco and the nation, as both were rocked by the de la Huerta Rebellion that lasted from December 1923 to July of the following year. When Garrido Canabal finally retook power in the summer of 1924 after being briefly overthrown by rebel forces, he blended many of the influences of Alvarado and Múgica with his new determination to ensure he never repeated that experience; thereafter, Garridismo was permanently on the offense to avoid ever again being on the defense. This produced what Carlos Martínez Assad has aptly described as an exaggeration of the radical proconsuls' reformist programs.[24] This included Garrido Canabal's iconoclasm and implementation of anticlericalism—not just the prohibitions against religious practice, exiling of priests, burning of saints, seizing of Church buildings, and theatrical lampooning of Catholicism and its practitioners that have made Garrido Canabal notorious but also efforts to systematically politically disenfranchise the faithful as enemies of both the socialist state government and the nation as a whole.

Anti-delahuertismo in Tabasco

In 1923, Adolfo de la Huerta, former interim president (1920) and minister of finance under President Álvaro Obregón since then, resigned from that post and launched a presidential bid in protest of Obregón's choice of Minister of Government Plutarco Elías Calles to succeed him in the presidency. This episode has been thoroughly examined elsewhere, but for the purposes of this essay, a few basic points about the rebellion merit revisiting.[25] While de la Huerta's bruised feelings over this slight were certainly a factor, this was far more than a personal spat that became a bitter political schism, as a very large portion of the political class and at least half of the military supported de la Huerta's opposition presidential candidacy. By November 1923, this political conflict boiled over into an armed insurrection against Obregón's government. Almost none of the support de la Huerta enjoyed was inspired by his actual political platform (other than his opposition to Calles' succession to the presidency), which he was still scrambling to articulate after the rebellion in his name was already well underway. It was largely led by generals discontented with Obregón's choice of Calles, some who feared Calles's relative radicalism and others who resented the imposition of a successor by an incumbent, and it was supported by heterogeneous factions and groups across Mexico that similarly opposed Sonoran hegemony in the presidency for a variety of reasons. Catholics were certainly among these, particularly given Calles's fervent anticlericalism, and likely facilitated by Adolfo de la Huerta's lack of fervency on the issue. Most notably, Jorge Prieto Laurens, leader of the National Cooperatist Party and arguably the political mastermind behind the rebellion, had close, long-standing ties to Catholic activist groups.[26]

Given the scale of the conflict, the federal government's victory over the rebels was relatively quick, but it was also hard fought; Obregón and Calles did not emerge unscathed, even while realizing their succession plans. One of their most significant, single losses was the assassination by rebel forces of Calles's close ally Carrillo Puerto, who was the most important political figure in the Southeast at that time. It is temptingly easy to interpret the de la Huerta Rebellion as a relatively major military conflict that ultimately amounted to a relatively minor bump in an ongoing process of consolidation of Mexico's postrevolutionary political system, but its consequences were profound and far reaching. In particular, the rebellion was formative to Obregón and Calles's responses to political mutinies that followed and contributed to the substantial diminishment of their tolerance for organized dissent.[27] The rebellion also left deep political scars on the states of the Southeast and on Tabasco in particular.

The Southeast was the final battleground of the rebellion. Adolfo de la Huerta himself fled into exile in the United States in March 1924, as did Prieto Laurens. Even after the federal army retook rebel strongholds in Jalisco, Oaxaca, and Veracruz, the rebellion wore on in Tabasco and Chiapas, as rebel leaders fled southward as a last resort in a war they had effectively already lost. This included Salvador Alvarado, the godfather of southeastern socialism, who returned to Mexico from exile in the United States and Canada, convinced by de la Huerta to lead a new military confrontation with Álvaro Obregón, with whom he had long-standing political differences. Garrido Canabal had helped to lead the defense of Villahermosa in December himself during a siege of more than a month that was led by a well-armed rebel brigade named for the Virgin of Guadalupe.[28]

When this finally failed, Garrido Canabal was driven into hiding and then out of the state under the threat of death, and he was only able to return as federal troops finally recaptured the state capital in June 1924.[29]

Garrido Canabal survived, but it was a close scrape by all accounts, including his own. He was well aware that he easily could have met the same grim fate as Carrillo Puerto, whom he regarded as "a martyr of socialism," and he said so on multiple occasions in the following years.[30] As Garrido Canabal understood it, socialism had come under dire threat from a coalition of reactionary forces, including outside forces such as the Catholic Church but also perennial dissident factions within Tabasco that had opportunistically supported de la Huerta, whose shared goal was to rid southeastern Mexico of reformers like him—even by murdering them. He would never be shaken in this belief, even once the rebellion was in the distant past, and he understood all future attacks against him as part of this same long-term, incessant threat.[31]

This was not political histrionics by a politician with an evident taste for controversy and a flair for the dramatic (although he had both): for Garrido Canabal, politics became quite literally a matter of life and death, and the several documented assassination attempts against him suggest that he was not wrong to see things in that light. After one of these in December 1926, Garrido Canabal wrote to President Calles that the people who had attempted to kill him planned to try again and that he feared that the military chief of Tabasco, General Juan José Rios, had been influenced by smears against him by Bishop Pascual Díaz y Barreto and other reactionaries who wished to rid Mexico of another prominent socialist politician. He also underscored what was at stake for the national government, writing to Calles that "I am sorry to bother you, but after that happened to me, I believe it is prudent to make you aware of it so that the clergy-reactionaries don't have the pleasure of assassinating men who with all good faith and loyalty collaborate with you."[32]

That summer, the ligas de resistencia of Villahermosa wrote a collective protest to federal authorities, similarly connecting all of these dots, referring to "individuals of disqualified backgrounds, in the service of the reaction, the clergy and capitalism, combined with all delahuertista elements" who had first attempted to overthrow the government of Obregón and deprive the Mexican people of the vote to elect Calles (during the rebellion) and now attempted to kill Garrido Canabal, "the representative of southeastern Socialism."[33] It bears underscoring that this was a title he could only reasonably claim once Carrillo Puerto was dead, killed by the same alleged coalition of reactionary forces.

Garrido Canabal blamed Bishop Díaz y Barreto for having conspired with the delahuertistas to overthrow his state government.[34] It was not a Catholic rebellion, although many religious Catholics assuredly would have welcomed Calles's political defeat in 1924, and both de la Huerta and Prieto Laurens were allied with conservative Mexican Catholic groups and former Cristeros while in exile in the United States in the years that followed, including in conspiracies against the Mexican government.[35] That said, Mexican socialists were certainly not wrong to perceive Catholic conservative opposition to their radical reform project, what Knight describes as "a profound suspicion of radical movements and a lingering suspicion of liberal democracy" by Catholic conservatives of the period.[36] Jürgen Buchenau has underscored that Calles, once president, feared that the Church might support an insurrection against his government, particularly given Catholic support for the de la Huerta Rebellion in Veracruz.[37] The association of the rebellion with Catholicism was therefore not a Garridista invention by any means, but the conflation of the two was particularly enduring and politically significant in socialist Tabasco. Garrido Canabal, in typical form, went on the offensive. In his first state of the state address after the rebellion, he reiterated that the clergy were among the "enemies of the people" and that henceforth his government would be a "reaction to the reaction."[38]

The attack against Garrido Canabal's state government during the de la Huerta Rebellion clearly felt personal to him, but his response was eminently political: in short, he organized his political party and the government it controlled around preventing any such attacks again and preemptively guarding against any of the forces and individuals he blamed for the rebellion gaining any political ground. Martínez Assad has argued that the rebellion ultimately meant that Garrido Canabal's power in Tabasco increased once he returned to the governorship, given a relatively free hand by Mexico City after having shown his fierce loyalty to Obregón and Calles.[39] But another of the reasons for this was Garrido Canabal's careful, rigorous, and tireless efforts to root out any and all sources of support for the rebellion in the state, for years on end. Like many elements of Garridismo post-1924, this impulse predated the rebellion; as early as 1919, Tabasco Socialists discussed the disenfranchisement of counterrevolutionaries as a necessary part of their own consolidation of power in a state that had long been bitterly riven by violent partisan factionalism.[40] But like so many other parts of their political program, this was much more extensively developed as political practice once the socialists retook power in the state in the summer of 1924.

Anti-delahuertismo was just as zealous within the Tabasco Radical Socialist Party and the ligas de resistencia post-1924 as anti-Catholicism was; to be either Catholic or associated in any way with the de la Huerta Rebellion in Tabasco in those years was political poison. It was also usually career suicide, as people who were purged out of ligas de resistencia were often unable to work in the state because they were no longer liga members, which was effectively mandatory by the late 1920s. In November 1925, a man named José Ochoa wrote to Garrido Canabal, after getting fired from his job as Minister of Education, for allegations of delahuertismo: "I respectfully finish my position as a disciplined employee considering that my services are no longer needed but I beg of you, allow me to protest the qualifier delahuertista, because I never was, I am not, nor will I be. I have my Socialist criteria well defined."[41] As Curley has argued in his case study of anticlericalism in Jalisco, one of the principal political consequences of the de la Huerta Rebellion was a markedly decreased tolerance for political opposition by Calles and others and, in practice in Jalisco, the strategic wielding of radical anticlericalism as a means of marginalizing political Catholics.[42] This same phenomenon was evident in Tabasco. Indeed, Garrido Canabal briefly hoped to isolate former delahuertistas from society entirely, proposing to President Obregón in July 1924 that they be forced to live in a labor camp he planned to create (Obregón responded that this was unnecessary but that rebel leaders who provoked disturbances could be banished to Mexico City).[43]

Both Catholics and former de la Huerta associates and sympathizers were described by the Tabasco Socialists, over and over, as ceaselessly seeking to turn back revolutionary reform in the state and undermine the well-being and socioeconomic advances of working people. The word that was commonly used to describe such people in Socialist correspondence was "dissolvent": their presence in the state was construed in terms of a chemical reaction that could destroy whatever or whomever it touched. This terminology was not unique to Tabasco, and its usage predated the de la Huerta Rebellion, but it was used there with particular frequency and urgency as part of a larger, paranoiac politics in the state post-1924. Not just individuals but also political ideas were also sometimes described as "dissolvent" and therefore potentially destructive to the Socialist Party's institutions and achievements. People suspected of being "dissolvent elements," including because of any known or suspected participation in the de la Huerta Rebellion, were effectively blacklisted by the Tabasco Radical Socialist Party and its ligas de resistencia.

That was not a passing concern in the months and years following the defeat of the rebellion. Garrido Canabal believed that Tabasco remained under constant threat from both within and without, which required correspondingly constant vigilance, including armed, preemptive responses. A full year after the final military defeat of the rebellion, he wrote to Calles requesting a shipment of arms, ammunition, and other supplies to combat "150 or 160 chronic rebels" in the Chontalpa region of the state.[44] Accusations and fears about rebels incessantly scheming against the state government, often with the support of larger, outside forces, endured for years. It is impossible to verify the accuracy, or lack thereof, of most of the accusations made against people alleged to be delahuertistas, but by 1926 or so, it had become an epithet that was effectively synonymous with anti-Socialist, or anti-Garrido Canabal more specifically.[45] The Tabasco state government maintained lists of former rebels, their accomplices, or rebel sympathizers across the state, organized by place of residence.[46] In 1926, Garrido Canabal worried to Calles regarding rumors he had read about in a Texas newspaper that Adolfo de la Huerta himself was scheming to invade Mexico and accept the leadership of a new revolutionary movement.[47] In another report to Calles in 1928, Garrido Canabal reported rumors of a possible invasion of Tabasco from Guatemala by ex-delahuertista rebels: "The former rebels do not give up the hope of organizing missions against the current government," he wrote, adding that the Tabasco Socialists were ready as ever to defend their state and the nation.[48] In Garrido Canabal's own words, regarding preemptive organizing against another rumored attack against Tabasco by former delahuertista rebels in 1926: "We only want to be in good conditions to not be victims."[49]

From there, it was a relatively smooth transition within Tabasco's politics to construing political opponents as "rebels" against the Socialist government in a more general sense, although delahuertismo was also still frequently cited as a more specific threat.[50] Belisario Carrillo and Arturo Jiménez de Lara, two opposition gubernatorial candidates who challenged Garrido Canabal's handpicked successor Ausencio Cruz in 1926, were described by Tabasco's socialists as delahuertistas and reactionaries who would "disorganize" the workers of the state—that is to say, they would undo the work of the Radical Socialist Party to organize workers into its hierarchy of ligas de resistencia.[51] One complainant went further, reporting to Garrido Canabal that the reactionaries that supported Jiménez de Lara and Carrillo planned "to assassinate unionized workers to avenge the defeat they had as [delahuertista] traitors."[52] This kind of language was in addition to various other forms of delegitimizing the candidates who opposed Cruz's election. Garrido Canabal himself referred to Carrillo as a "pseudo-candidate," who was only supported by paid partisans from Campeche, foreigners, and national reactionaries (from outside of Tabasco).[53] In a less measured message to a supporter of Carrillo, Garrido Canabal described the opposition candidate as "the servant of all usurpations" and called on "the enemies of organized labor who secretly work for the disunity of the worker to exploit him in isolation and to take these strong organizations from President Calles" to unmask themselves and openly confront the Tabasco Socialists in "the final fight" between slave owners and the Tabasco proletariat.[54] Supporters of Jiménez de Lara who attended a protest in November 1926 were described by the president of the Tabasco Radical Socialist Party as "in their majority Catholic ladies, Knights of Columbus, Spanish and Arab merchants, as well as all retrograde elements and reactionaries of lineage, and a large contingent of delahuertista rebels."[55]

For Garrido Canabal and the Tabasco Socialists, delahuertismo was just one element of a larger, dangerous concurrence of counterrevolutionary forces that were not just aligned against them but also actively and constantly conspiring against the nation as a whole; this included delahuertistas but also the Catholic Church and its supporters and foreign businesspeople, among others. In at least one instance, ligas de resistencia were directed by the Liga Central to write to national politicians, including the president, repeating allegations against Garrido Canabal's political enemies including delahuertista associations, which were pre-prepared and circulated to them for that purpose.[56] The objective, always, was to ensure that what had been achieved by the Socialist Party and the ligas would never be undone; as one socialist partisan described it in 1926, the Tabasco Radical Socialist Party "has known how to interpret the ideals of national reconstruction initiated by the men of the revolution, whose blood watered the soil of our nation, and won't permit that those who yesterday were the tormentor of the humble classes, today be their directors."[57] In Garrido Canabal's own words: "It is true that I am implacable with those individuals who as my enemies are also enemies of the federal government, as well as longtime reactionaries who, goaded by their old, backward ideas, try at any given moment to oppose the socialists and legal institutions of the Republic."[58]

Garridista Anti-Catholicism and Authoritarianism

Tomás Garrido Canabal's efforts to secularize Tabasco included the arrest and banishment of priests, systematic replacement (and displacement) of religious events with cultural ones, often with required attendance by liga members, and more generally the use of the ligas de resistencia as mechanisms of enforcement and surveillance of their members for any religious sympathies or activities.[59] But Garrido Canabal's anti-Catholicism was just one facet of his larger, stated goal of liberating Tabasqueños from numerous forms of oppression. Another related, well-known central element of Garrido Canabal's plans to modernize Tabasco's society was his continued emphasis on public education. Like his attacks on the Catholic Church in Tabasco, Garrido Canabal was even more passionately dedicated to education reform than the radicals and progressives who so strongly influenced him.[60] Churches were routinely seized and transformed into state-run "rational" schools, but, as Fallaw has shown, this was just the most literal manifestation of a larger program to replace religion wholesale with socialist humanism.[61] And as he shows in his chapter in this volume, science and medicine were similarly heralded by Tabasco Socialists as pathways to a less superstitious and more healthful, rational, and modern future, a project undertaken in part in the rationalist schools.

In Tabasco this was another case of socialism being understood as a zero-sum game: fewer churches very directly meant more schools, and less religiosity correspondingly meant more social and economic justice, with education as a fundamental component of the broader liberation of workers in the state. Indeed, as José Alberto Moreno Chávez has shown, students in Tabasco's new schools were taught that "socialism" was a liberating future for the whole world.[62] As Fallaw shows in this volume, Tabasco's schoolchildren were taught about science in the Garridista curriculum as part of this liberatory project to free them from all irrational beliefs (and thereby exploitation by the Church), just as they were to be freed by the socialist state from equally anti-modern political and economic forms of exploitation.

At the local level, the work of eventually converting seventy-eight churches to schools was done by the ligas de resistencia, along with Socialist-controlled municipal governments.[63] As one liga president wrote to Garrido Canabal in 1927: "We will put all of our efforts working, even personally, so that [. . .] temples that were once the refuge of the scoundrels of the dreadful cassock are converted to centers of teaching."[64] As Knight has argued, the repressive nature of Mexican anticlericalism was paired with a constructive project that included schools but also new traditions.[65] Thus, the conversion of Church buildings into public schools was not only a symbolic act but also a practical one to achieve the same goal: defeating a force that undermined the progression of revolutionary reforms of politics, the economy, and society alike.

This was easier said than done, as these efforts inevitably came up against resistance from the Tabasqueño faithful, including Socialists who were ultimately reluctant to give up Catholic beliefs and habits.[66] Municipal president Crispín Pech of Villahermosa wrote with evident frustration to the Liga Central in 1927 that "the city council has tried by all possible means to see that the places where previously evil was preached by the poorly disguised false goodness of the acolytes of the Tyrant of Rome, be converted to Temples of Knowledge."[67] There were numerous incidents reported to Garrido Canabal and Socialist Party and Liga Central authorities of challenges that Socialists faced in taking possession of churches, in some cases revealing that even deep within the Socialist party machine, religion and anticlericalism were sometimes divisive issues in a country that remained overwhelmingly Catholic. In Comalcalco in 1927, a liga president named Eugenio Graniel denounced another local liga for attempting to block the transfer of a church to the Socialists, provoking a confrontation in front of the contested building. Graniel reported that when he invoked the name of Garrido Canabal to try to reestablish order, the members of the opposing liga shouted that they supported Garrido Canabal but not attacks against faith and pleaded with the woman in possession of the key to the church door not to hand it over. Graniel had to request help from the municipal president, who in turn requested federal military assistance to disperse the protesters and gain access to the building. Graniel later requested that the pro-Church liga be expelled from the Liga Central.[68] However, this report by Graniel appears to have been part of a larger, long-term power struggle between competing Socialist factions in Comalcalco in which Garrido Canabal had already sided with Graniel; the president of the liga accused of defending the Church retorted that it was an utterly fabricated report designed to discredit his liga and protested that his faction was unequivocally loyal to Garrido Canabal.[69]

In 1928, the director of a school in Frontera described a dramatic incident at a school theater in a former church building. She had already been warned that parents of her students were angered that the scenery for a performance in commemoration of the birthday of Benito Juárez had been installed on the former high altar and that no one would attend and thereby contribute to profaning a sacred place. These initial challenges eventually overcome, on the day of the performance, in front of an enthusiastic, full house, someone in the crowd saw a slight movement of hanging lightbulbs and shouted "earthquake!" inciting a mass panic. Many of the frightened occupants of the former church, there to mark the legendarily anticlerical Juárez's birthday, immediately recurred to practices of Catholic faith. The director of the school recounted: "It caused panic among the timid, the sanctimonious and the fanatical old ladies, who suddenly fled from the building to go light their little candles in atonement for the SIN committed" (emphasis original). Undeterred, the director planned various upcoming evening events in the building "with the objective that the ideology of this place is transformed, and that they look with indifference and naturalness at these beautiful festivities in the ex-temple."[70] The vanquishment of Catholicism by socialist education was clearly still understood to be a work in progress, even by a dedicated standard-bearer of that project; to borrow from the director's words, irreligion was not yet naturalized in Tabasco, even in Frontera, one of the centers of Socialist popular organizing in the state, and even after seven years of resolute Garridista efforts to that end.

This incident is just one particularly vivid illustration of a larger phenomenon that was of constant worry to the Tabasco Socialists, that Tabasqueños might either backslide into religiosity or continue to practice religion in secret. As Massimo de Giuseppe has shown in his case study of Gabriel García, a Chontal catechist, this was something that did happen in rural indigenous communities, where sacred objects were hidden away from prying socialist view and religious practices were maintained.[71] But Socialists also actively worried about clandestine religiosity within their own ranks. One group of Socialists in Comalcalco in 1927 complained of people who "take the stand to combat fanaticism and in their homes implore and beg on their knees [. . .] at their altars for miracles of employment and undeserved triumphs" and contrasted that behavior with their own efforts to tirelessly and incessantly combat "the reaction," closely follow Garrido Canabal's instructions, and always fight for his principles as "the first socialist of our state."[72] Like delahuertismo, religious fanaticism was perceived by the Tabasco Socialists as a persistent threat that existed covertly within their state, their communities, and their coworkers' and neighbors' homes, which required constant vigilance and defensive action to protect Socialism from its corrosive harms.

For Tabasco's Socialists, the Catholic Church was the most problematic institution it confronted because of its historical role and its present prominence, but it was only one manifestation of a broader, corrosive effect on society of religion in general. In Garrido Canabal's own words:

> Religions have only weakened the human mind, delaying its normal development. They have been the most powerful weapon used by the capitalistic system. The exploitation of the man never would have reached to such an extraordinary proportion had it not been by the ominous influence of the religions. Therefore, during my term as governor in the state of Tabasco, I initiated a strong fight against clergymen and religious frauds, thinking that so long as man adores divinities and believes in tortures and a life beyond, he will be mentally chained and will be an enemy of his own liberation.[73]

Garrido Canabal's construction of the role and purpose of anti-Catholicism and anticlericalism was therefore as core elements of a much larger project to achieve greater social and economic justice through revolutionary reform, effectively inseparable from the larger goal of liberating workers within a more modern and just society. Capitalism and the clergy were commonly listed together by Tabasco Socialists as the greatest threats not just against them but also against the national government and Mexico as a whole.[74] For Garrido Canabal, socialism itself was a new, more moral conception of the world and of the individual person's rights than any religion; religious practice was therefore not just unwelcome within socialism; religion itself, all religion, was anathema to it:

> In order to substantiate behavior characteristics framed by religion, which are inspired on a hypocritical and selfish sentiment of untrue fraternity, we must erect a new moral doctrine which embodies radical changes in man's philosophy and behavior, doing the right thing just because it ought to be done, with a deep sense of justice and with a high concept of solidarity. Morals instead of religion; work, instead of liturgy and all other forms of prayer; self confidence instead of hope in "divinity."[75]

As in several instances described above, the attitudes and behaviors of the ligas de resistencia in Tabasco in the 1920s bear this out. Religious practice was viewed by Socialists with immense suspicion because religion was understood to be corrosive to the fabric of the society (and its economy) that the ligas were intended to build, maintain, and protect for the good of their state but also for that of the nation.

Tabasco was often described by the Socialists there as both ground zero and a bulwark against reactionary conspiracies and attacks against the nation. In Garrido Canabal's own words: "My enemies see in me examples of loyalty and therefore a hindrance to carry out their perfidious machinations against the national government."[76] This perception of things appears to have hardened with time, rather than lessened, even as the Socialists of Tabasco succeeded in achieving political hegemony in the state to an unprecedented degree following the defeat of the de la Huerta Rebellion. Subsequent, incontrovertible threats and attacks against them inevitably served to reinforce this mentality. It is hard to fault Garrido Canabal for his constant fretting about rumored plots to kill him when his enemies did make several attempts, but other perceived threats against Tabasco's Socialists were much more subjective, and in some cases fears were self-fulfilling, as when Socialists sometimes made committed enemies via false or poorly substantiated accusations of religiosity, moral failure, or dubious political associations.

Garridista anti-Catholicism therefore had ideological roots but was not principally ideological in practice. As far as the Tabasco Socialists were concerned, to enact the Mexican Revolution and maintain its achievements in practice very fundamentally required keeping the Catholic Church at bay as part of a broader effort to permanently reform both politics and society. This was not just Garrido Canabal's perspective, but a generalized, widely accepted view among Tabasco Socialists of the national, regional, and local political contexts in which they lived and worked.

Conclusions

The Milwaukee Leader wrote in 1935: "Garrido Canabal is directing measures which he hopes will make impossible a successful counterrevolutionary movement, built on religious prejudice, in Mexico."[77] This was perhaps as good a summary as any of the core objective of Garrido Canabal's anti-Catholicism as part of his larger political program: above all, to protect the hard-won revolutionary progress he and his allies had achieved. It was the de la Huerta Rebellion that most vividly illustrated for Garrido Canabal and other members of the Radical Socialist Party of Tabasco what was at stake: they saw, firsthand, that given the opportunity, the forces that opposed them politically, which they believed prominently included the Catholic clergy and faithful, would not only attempt to violently overthrow their state government and destroy their political party but would also try to kill them. Surely the ongoing Cristero War of 1926–1929 also decisively informed this view, but the assassination of Felipe Carrillo Puerto during the de la Huerta Rebellion was the single most seminal event for Garrido Canabal in cementing his understandings of what was at stake, as his repeated references over the years that followed his Yucatecan counterpart's murder demonstrate.

Anti-Catholicism as an ideological position was deeply embedded in the foundations of southeastern Socialism in the 1920s, thanks in particular to the influences of both outsider proconsuls Salvador Alvarado and Francisco Múgica in the mid-late 1910s, homegrown revolutionary antipathies among toward the Catholic Church in the region, as well as the close alignment of all of the southeastern Socialists with Calles in the years that followed.[78] In practice, however, it was just the most notorious manifestation of a larger, core characteristic of Garridista Socialism that is best described as active, sometimes preemptive vigilance against a cabal of forces that Garrido Canabal and his allies believed to be menacingly aligned against them. Critically, they also perceived this unrelenting threat to be against Mexico as a whole and its national leaders and against Calles and Obregón more specifically; Garrido Canabal's impassioned, early support for Álvaro Obregón's presidential reelection in 1928 must therefore be understood as just one more part of his ongoing, long-term response to the threat against both Tabasco and the nation during the de la Huerta Rebellion, particularly given his consistent (albeit inaccurate) conflation of anti-reelectionists and delahuertistas as indistinguishable enemies of the state.

Tomás Garrido Canabal was an unapologetic atheist firebrand with a relentless grudge against the Catholic Church, its allies, and its faithful, who spent years amassing power in one corner of Mexico and jealously guarding against any threat to it. But his significance went far beyond the borders of Tabasco, something that often has been overlooked or misunderstood within a highly regionalized historiography. Garrido Canabal's downfall is well known: after a decade and a half of dominating Tabasco's politics, his attempted translation of his brash and uncompromising style to the national stage as Cárdenas's minister of agriculture, including the violent unleashing of his Red Shirt brigades on Mexico City, was a legendary fiasco that precipitated his exile shortly thereafter as part of a larger purge by Cárdenas of the old Callista guard (including Calles himself).[79] But all of the most notorious features of Garrido Canabal's political career have overshadowed what is ironically the quieter fact that he was also one of the most important architects of Mexico's postrevolutionary political system as the pioneer of an idiosyncratic, influential blend of postrevolutionary reformism, mass politics, and corporatist authoritarianism overseen by a de facto official party with a highly co-opted popular base. In his study of the consolidation of Mexico's so-called dictablanda (soft authoritarianism) in the two decades that followed, Paul Gillingham describes a convoluted evolution from postrevolutionary to "unrevolutionary" politics as "a key transition period, during which a party leadership of authoritarian ambition coexisted with an eclectic membership and a powerful tradition of popular mobilization."[80] Garrido Canabal and his collaborators in Tabasco (and the larger Socialist Southeast) had helped to push Mexico toward that transition in the previous period by setting a similar precedent at the state level, including by enshrining (co-opted and/or state sponsored) popular mobilization as part of political practice, often by identifying enemies shared by the state and allied popular forces. Anti-Catholicism was a centerpiece of this political project but because it was a means to a larger and much further-reaching end.

Indeed, while in the 1930s "socialist" became effectively synonymous with anti-Catholicism at the national level, particularly in terms of public "socialist" education, the most enduring long-term lessons that national politicians took from Tabasco's "laboratory of revolution" ultimately did not include radical anti-Catholicism.[81] Knight argues that "the state enjoyed least success when it sought to create the progressive, secular, scientific "new" Mexican envisioned in the 1930s socialist blueprints," while Bantjes underscores that the Cristero war of 1926–1929 exhausted the nation, ultimately with very little to show for it and very high human costs.[82]

As Gillingham puts it, by the 1940s, the Mexican state "aspired to control rather than to fundamentally change Mexicans."[83] The national anti-Catholic project was largely abandoned by 1940, but the political structures and practices designed to implement the larger project to which it belonged, pioneered in the Southeast, remained embedded in the post-revolutionary political system moving forward. Southeastern Socialism, including the Garridista implementation, was designed to be democratic in the sense that it leveled the economic and playing field substantially from what had existed before the Mexican Revolution by radically expanding workers' rights, and it encouraged active political participation by previously disenfranchised and underrepresented sectors within its parties and ligas de resistencia. Yet it was also designed to be hegemonic, and particularly in Tabasco, where there was little pretense of a fair electoral fight between the Socialist Party and its opponents. Because it was a system that offered a great deal to its subscribers and very little to those who declined to participate, to purposefully remain outside the system was regarded by Tabasco Socialists as an act of repudiation of their party and of their politics more broadly; thus, Socialists frequently construed their political opponents not just as enemies but also often as rebels against the Socialist government and all that it stood for. Groups that would never be convinced to participate in the Socialist party, particularly Catholics, and priests above all but also business people and elite landowners, were inherently antagonistic forces to be combated. Radical anti-Catholicism was therefore a logical extension and constituent piece of a political system that was markedly intolerant of all recusant elements.

Tabasco's Socialism forged an influential paradigm of semi-authoritarian single-party hegemony in Mexico that, like the Partido Revolucionario Institucional in subsequent decades, included no elegant strategy for dealing with dissident factions that could or would not be co-opted into the system. In a state of less than a quarter million, it was conceivable that these political irritants could simply be either threatened into quiescence, politically quarantined via various suppressive mechanisms, or purged from the body politic, as the bishop Pascual Díaz y Barreto literally was by Tabasco Socialists in 1927, when he was marched on foot out of Tabasco and dumped over the Guatemalan border.[84] That was exponentially more difficult at the national level: indeed, Díaz y Barreto was soon back, elevated to Archbishop of Mexico City, and helped negotiate the 1929 accord that ended the Cristero War, as apt a metaphor as any for the long-term unsustainability of Garridista anti-Catholicism in practice. Yet Garrido Canabal's authoritarian precedents and influence unmistakably remained.

Notes

1. "Revolutionary Mexico Pledges to Safeguard Foreign Money." *The Milwaukee Leader* (Milwaukee, WI), 23 Mar. 1935, 2.
2. Consonant with other authors in this volume, I have elected to describe Garrido Canabal's campaign against the Catholic Church as "anti-Catholicism," a broader umbrella term and therefore a more accurate one in this context than "anticlericalism," which I use here more narrowly to refer to opposition to and restrictions on the Church and its personnel and in cases where I am citing the work of authors who use that term to refer to the larger anti-Catholic phenomenon.
3. Kristin A. Harper has underscored that Garrido Canabal's polarizing politics continue to haunt the historiography in a way she compares to the polemical nature of histories of Peronism and scholarly interpretations of Perón's legacy. Indeed, she has felt it necessary to underscore in published work that her recognition of Garrido Canabal's accomplishments should not be misunderstood as her being an apologist for Garridismo but rather part of her recognition of the "moral ambiguities of Mexican revolutionary reformism," particularly in Garrido Canabal's authoritarian populist regime. See Harper, "Tomás Garrido," 109–10; 18.
4. On Garrido Canabal as an outlier even among radical anti-Catholics and iconoclasts of his generation, see Fallaw, "Varieties."
5. On Garridista Tabasco, see in particular Harper, "Revolutionary Tabasco"; Martínez Assad, *El laboratorio de la revolución*; Canudas, *Trópico rojo*. On Garrido Canabal's anticlericalism, see in particular Domingo Méndez Moreno, *El anticlericalismo en Tabasco*.
6. On the ideological roots of postrevolutionary anticlericalism (and the very great challenges in its implementation), see Knight, "Mentality."
7. Curley, "Anticlericalism," 511–13; Bantjes, "Regional Dynamics," 125.
8. I have done this at much greater length elsewhere as part of a study of the national influence of southeastern Socialism in the 1920s. Some of the broader points I make throughout this essay about the significance of Garridista Socialism are drawn from that work. Osten, *Mexican Revolution's Wake*.
9. Buchenau has argued that Calles's war against the Catholic Church similarly contributed to "the authoritarian aspects of Callista rule [prevailing] over the reform drive" that characterized Plutarco Elías Calles's presidency, pre-Cristiada. Buchenau, *Plutarco Elías Calles*, 130.
10. Meza Huacuja, "Entre libros y fusiles," 25.
11. "Mexican 6-Yr. Plan to Change Social Set-Up." *The Milwaukee Leader* (Milwaukee, WI), 21 Mar. 1935, 4.
12. "Mexican 6-Yr. Plan," 4.
13. Osten, *Mexican Revolution's Wake*, 8–11.

14. On Alvarado's anticlericalism in Yucatán, see Fallaw, "Varieties," 496.
15. Fideicomiso Archivos Plutarco Elías Calles y Fernando Torreblanca (hereafter FAPECFT), Fondo Alvaro Obregón (hereafter FAO), expediente: C-7114: CARRILLO PUERTO, Felipe, legajo: 1, fojas 1–3, inventario 1181. Carrillo Puerto to Obregón, 3 June 1919.
16. Fallaw, "Varieties," 486; Knight, "Mentality," 22–25.
17. On Alvarado's influence on Garrido Canabal, see Martínez Assad, *El laboratorio de la revolución*, 165–66.
18. A hand-edited copy of Múgica's 1916 anti-alcohol decree was among Garrido's personal papers. Archivo General de la Nación de México, Fondo Tomás Garrido Canabal (hereafter AGN-TGC), c. 1, exp. 8. For a more in-depth discussion of Múgica's influence on Garrido Canabal, prohibitionism included, see Osten, *Mexican Revolution's Wake*, 65–66; Harper, "Revolutionary Tabasco," 51–52.
19. On an anti-alcohol campaign in socialist Yucatán in the 1920s, see FAPECFT, Fondo Plutarco Elías Calles (hereafter PEC), expediente: 25, CARRILLO PUERTO, Felipe, legajo 3/7, fojas 151–55, inventario 830. Carrillo Puerto to Calles, April 3, 1922. Alvarado regarded criminality to be a direct result of alcohol consumption: Alvarado, *La reconstrucción de México*, 12–13.
20. Gretchen Pierce, "'Desfanatizar y Desalcoholizar la Población': the Interrelated Anticlerical and Anti-Alcohol Campaigns," this volume.
21. See various related points made by Meza: Meza Huacuja, "Entre libros y fusiles."
22. On this feature of Garridismo, see De Giuseppe, "'El Indio Gabriel,'" 226.
23. Fallaw, "Seduction of Revolution."
24. Martínez Assad, *Laboratorio*, 29.
25. On the de la Huerta Rebellion in the Southeast, see chapter 3 of Osten, *Mexican Revolution's Wake*. For recent work on the rebellion's critically important political aftermath at the national level, see Buchenau, *Sonoran Dynasty*, 182–89. On the rebellion more generally, see in particular José Valenzuela, "La rebelión delahuertista"; Castro Martínez, *Adolfo de la Huerta*; Plasencia de la Parra, *Personajes y escenarios de la rebelión delahuertista*; Castro Martínez, *Adolfo de la Huerta y la Revolución Mexicana*; Capetillo, *La rebelión sin cabeza*.
26. Young, *Mexican Exodus*, 54–55. On Prieto Laurens's role in leading the rebellion, see Osten, "Trials by Fire."
27. On this point, see also chapter 6 of Osten, *Mexican Revolution's Wake*; Osten, "Out of the Shadows."
28. Canudas, *Trópico rojo*, Volume 1, 122.
29. For a more detailed account of the rebellion in Tabasco and Garrido Canabal's own role, as well as Alvarado's, see Osten, *Mexican Revolution's Wake*, 124–29.
30. AGN-TGC, c. 7, exp. 9. Garrido Canabal to Román Sabas Flores, 12 May 1925.

31. De Giuseppe underscores the importance of Garrido's loyalty to the federal government (and the Sonorans) during the rebellion as critical to his "unprecedented strength" as governor afterwards. De Giuseppe, "'El Indio Gabriel,'" 226.
32. FAPECFT, Fondo Fernando Torreblanca (hereafter FFT), expediente "9"/114, GARRIDO CANABAL, Tomás (Lic.), legajo 1, foja 2, inventario 565. Garrido Canabal to Calles, 30 Dec. 1926.
33. AGN-TGC, c. 114, exp. 10, fojas 34–36. Ausencio Cruz to Garrido Canabal, 19 Aug. 1926.
34. De Giuseppe, "'El Indio Gabriel,'" 227.
35. Young, *Mexican Exodus*, 57, 88–89, 91.
36. Knight, "Mentality," 28.
37. Buchenau, *Plutarco Elías Calles*, 126–27. In his most recent work, Buchenau has also underscored that in the lead-up to the Cristero war, Calles critically "underestimated the ability of Catholics to undercut his government via mass action." Buchenau, *Sonoran Dynasty*, 208.
38. Canudas, *Trópico rojo, Volume 1*, 130–31.
39. Martínez Assad, *Laboratorio*, 161.
40. AGN-TGC, c. 1, exp. 11. Felipe Bueno to Garrido Canabal, 7 Mar. 1919.
41. AGN-TGC, c.7, exp. 5. José Ochoa L. to Garrido Canabal, 27 Nov. 1925.
42. Curley, "Anticlericalism," 512, 32–33.
43. AGN, Fondo Presidentes, Obregón-Calles (hereafter OC), c. 200, exp. 707-T-48. Garrido Canabal to Obregón, 21 July 1924.
44. AGN-TGC, c. 8, exp. 2. Garrido Canabal to Calles, 7 July 1925.
45. On this point, see also Harper, "Revolutionary Tabasco," 4.
46. AGN-TGC, c.8, exp. 9.
47. FAPECFT-PEC, expediente: 140, Garrido Canabal, Tomás (Lic.), legajo 3/7, fojas 174–75, inventario: 2312. Garrido Canabal to Soledad González, 19 Nov. 1926. De la Huerta clearly was involved in conspiracies against Calles's government in this period. See Young, *Mexican Exodus*, 88–89.
48. FAPECFT-PEC, expediente: 140, Garrido Canabal, Tomás (Lic.), legajo 3/7, fojas 204–5, inventario 2312. Garrido Canabal to Calles, 17 Aug. 1928.
49. FAPECFT-PEC, expediente: 140, Garrido Canabal, Tomás (Lic.), legajo 2/7, foja 160, inventario: 2312. Garrido Canabal to Soledad González, 13 Jan. 1926.
50. AGN-TGC, c. 114, exp. 7. Juan Lugo to Garrido Canabal, 18 Sept. 1926.
51. For a more in-depth discussion of this election, see Osten, *Mexican Revolution's Wake*, 151–59.
52. AGN-TGC, c. 114, exp. 6, fojas 41–43. C. A. Manuel to Garrido Canabal, 30 Sept. 1926.
53. AGN-TGC, c. 114, exp. 8, foja 131. Garrido Canabal to Crescencio A. Manuel, 3 Sept. 1926.

54. AGN-TGC, c. 114, exp. 8, foja 143. Garrido Canabal to Vicente Melo, 28 Sept. 1926.
55. FAPECFT-PEC, expediente: 1, Partidos Varios, legajo 7/17, fojas 335–36, inventario: 4344. Francisco Ortiz to Soledad González, 20 Nov. 1926.
56. See, for example, AGN-TGC, c9-5-1 (scanned) Homero Margalli to liga president(s), 2 Feb. 1926.
57. AGN-TGC, c. 11, exp. 3. Unsigned letter, 10 Sept. 1926.
58. AGN-TGC, c. 11, exp. 5. Garrido Canabal to Fernando Aguirre, 21 May 1926.
59. AGN-TGC, c. 114, exp. 4. Unsigned telegram to Homero Margalli, 28 Oct. 1925; Harper, "Revolutionary Tabasco," 141.
60. On the intertwining of anticlericalism and education with other elements of Garridista reform, see Vaughan, *Cultural Politics*, 30.
61. Fallaw, "Varieties," 490–91.
62. Moreno Chávez, "Quemando santos para iluminar conciencias," 64.
63. On the numbers of church closures and conversions, see De Giuseppe, "'El Indio Gabriel,'" 228.
64. AGN-TGC, c. 115, exp. 9. S. Contreras O. to Garrido Canabal, 2 Dec. 1927.
65. Knight, "Mentality," 26.
66. On resistance to the cultural elements of Garridismo, including anticlericalism, see in particular Moreno Chávez, "Quemando santos para iluminar conciencias."
67. AGN-TGC, c. 115, exp. 7, foja 34. Crispín Pech G. to J. Medardo Rosado, 2 Dec. 1927.
68. AGN-TGC, c. 115, exp. 10, fojas 37–38. E. Graniel to Garrido Canabal, 26 Dec. 1927.
69. AGN-TGC, TGC, c. 115, exp. 6, foja 15. Garrido Canabal to Presidente de la Liga de Nagateros, 22 Oct. 1927; AGN-TGC, c. 116, exp. 3, fojas 38–9. Heriberto Falconi et al. to Garrido Canabal, 30 Dec. 1927.
70. AGN-TGC, c. 116, exp. 7, fojas 49–50. María R. Franco de L. to Garrido Canabal, 22 Mar. 1928.
71. De Giuseppe, "'El Indio Gabriel.'"
72. AGN-TGC, c. 116, exp. 3, fojas 36–37. José Fernández M. et al. to Garrido Canabal, 28 Dec. 1927.
73. "Religion Most Powerful Capitalist Weapon—Canabal." *The Milwaukee Leader* (Milwaukee, WI), 22 Mar. 1935, 4.
74. AGN-TGC, c. 7, exp. 6. Alcides Caparrozo to Garrido, 9 Jan. 1925.
75. "Religion Most Powerful Capitalist Weapon—Canabal." *The Milwaukee Leader* (Milwaukee, WI), 22 Mar. 1935, 4.
76. AGN-TGC, c. 9, exp. 6. Garrido Canabal to Luis León, 19 Aug. 1926.
77. "Religion Most Powerful Capitalist Weapon—Canabal." *The Milwaukee Leader* (Milwaukee, WI), 22 Mar. 1935, 4.
78. In the case of Tabasco, Bantjes points to the Jacobinism of Carlos Greene as an example of homegrown anticlerical radicalism. Bantjes, "Regional Dynamics," 112.

79. On the Camisas Rojas (formally known as the Bloque de Jóvenes Revolucionarios [BJR]), see in particular Meza Huacuja, "Entre libros y fusiles."
80. Gillingham, *Unrevolutionary Mexico*, 137.
81. On "Socialism" as antireligious, see Bantjes, "Regional Dynamics," 118.
82. Knight, "Mentality," 40; Bantjes, "Regional Dynamics," 114–16.
83. Gillingham, *Unrevolutionary Mexico*, 243.
84. Canudas, *Trópico rojo*, Volume 1, 144.

Works Cited

Alvarado, Salvador. *La reconstrucción de México: un mensaje a los pueblos de America, Volume 2*. México, D.F.: Partido Revolucionario Institucional (PRI), 1919, 1982.

Bantjes, Adrian. "The Regional Dynamics of Anticlericalism and Defanaticization in Revolutionary Mexico." In *Faith and Impiety in Revolutionary Mexico*, edited by Matthew Butler, 111–30. New York: Palgrave Macmillan, 2007.

Buchenau, Jürgen. *Plutarco Elías Calles and the Mexican Revolution*. Lanham, MD: Rowman & Littlefield, 2007.

———. *The Sonoran Dynasty in Mexico: Revolution, Reform, and Repression*. Lincoln, NE: University of Nebraska Press, 2023.

Canudas, Enrique. *Trópico rojo: historia politica y social de Tabasco los años garridistas, 1919–1934*. 2 vols. Villahermosa, México: Gobierno del Estado de Tabasco, Instituto de Cultura de Tabasco, 1989.

Capetillo, Alonso. *La rebelión sin cabeza: génesis y desarrollo del movimiento delahuertista*. México, D.F.: Imprenta Botas, 1925.

Castro Martínez, Pedro. *Adolfo de la Huerta y la Revolución Mexicana*. México, D.F.: Instituto Nacional de Estudios Históricos de la Revolución Mexicana y la Universidad Autónoma Metropolitana Unidad Iztapalapa, 1992.

———. *Adolfo de la Huerta: la integridad como arma de la revolución*. México, D.F.: Universidad Autónoma Metropolitana Iztapalapa, Siglo Veintiuno Editores, 1998.

Curley, Robert. "Anticlericalism and Public Space in Revolutionary Jalisco." *The Americas* 65, no. 4 (2009): 511–33.

De Giuseppe, Massimo. "'El Indio Gabriel': New Religious Perspectives among the Indigenous in Garrido Canabal's Tabasco (1927–30)." In *Faith and Impiety in Revolutionary Mexico*, edited by Matthew Butler, 225–42. New York: Palgrave Macmillan, 2007.

Domingo Méndez Moreno, Carlos. *El anticlericalismo en Tabasco: Entre prácticas, símbolos y representaciones*. Morelia, México: Universidad de San Nicolás de Hidalgo, 2016.

Fallaw, Ben. "Varieties of Mexican Revolutionary Anticlericalism: Radicalism, Iconoclasm, and Otherwise, 1914–1935." *The Americas* 65, no. 4 (2009): 481–509.

———. "The Seduction of Revolution: Anticlerical Campaigns against Confession in Mexico, 1914–1935." *Journal of Latin American Studies* 45, no. 1 (2013): 91–120.

Gillingham, Paul. *Unrevolutionary Mexico: The Birth of a Strange Dictatorship.* New Haven, CT: Yale University Press, 2021.

Harper, Kristin A. "Revolutionary Tabasco in the Time of Tomás Garrido Canabal, 1922—1935: A Mexican House Divided." PhD diss., University of Massachusetts Amherst, 2004.

———. "Tomás Garrido Canabal of Tabasco: Road Building and Revolutionary Reform." In *State Governors in the Mexican Revolution, 1910–1952: Portraits in Conflict, Courage, and Corruption*, edited by Jürgen Buchenau and William H. Beezley, 109–21. Lanham, MD: Rowman & Littlefield Publishers, 2009.

José Valenzuela, Georgette. "La rebelión delahuertista: sus orígenes y consecuencias políticas, económicas y sociales." In *El ejército mexicano*, edited by Javier Garciadiego, 213–70. México, DF: El Colegio de Mexico, 2014.

Knight, Alan. "The Mentality and Modus Operandi of Revolutionary Anticlericalism." In *Faith and Impiety in Revolutionary Mexico*, edited by Matthew Butler, 21–56. New York: Palgrave Macmillan, 2007.

Martínez Assad, Carlos R. *El laboratorio de la revolución: el Tabasco garridista.* 5th ed. México, DF: Siglo Veintiuno Editores, 2004.

Meza Huacuja, Ivonne. "Entre libros y fusiles: la formación ideológica de la juventud garridista y los 'Camisas Rojas' en Tabasco, 1922–1935." *Secuencia* 105 (2019).

Moreno Chávez, José Alberto. "Quemando santos para iluminar conciencias: Desfanatización y resistencia al proyecto cultural garridista, 1924–1935." *Estudios de Historia Moderna y Contemporánea de México* no. 42 (2011): 37–74.

Osten, Sarah. "Trials by Fire: National Political Lessons from Failed State Elections in Post-Revolutionary Mexico, 1920–1925." *Mexican Studies/Estudios Mexicanos* 29, no. 1 (2013): 238–79.

———. *The Mexican Revolution's Wake: The Making of a Political System, 1920–1929.* Cambridge: Cambridge University Press, 2018.

———. "Out of the Shadows: Violence and State Consolidation in Postrevolutionary Mexico, 1927–1940." *The Latin Americanist* 64, no. 2 (2020): 169–99.

Plasencia de la Parra, Enrique. *Personajes y escenarios de la rebelión delahuertista.* México, DF: Instituto de Investigaciones Históricas, UNAM, 1998.

Vaughan, Mary Kay. *Cultural Politics in Revolution: Teachers, Peasants, and Schools in Mexico, 1930–1940.* Tucson: University of Arizona Press, 1997.

Young, Julia G. *Mexican Exodus: Emigrants, Exiles, and Refugees of the Cristero War.* New York: Oxford University Press, 2015.

FIGURE 4. Manuel Gamio. Manuel Gamio, 1924, Library of Congress; https://www.loc.gov/pictures/item/2016837317/ (accessed Apr. 3, 2023).

CHAPTER THREE

Educating Anti-Catholicism

Manuel Gamio, Indigenismo, and Secular Redemption

DAVID S. DALTON

Perhaps no thinker contributed more directly to concepts of modernization and *indigenismo* in postrevolutionary Mexico than the anthropologist Manuel Gamio (1883–1960).[1] He oversaw the excavation of Teotihuacán, the ancient temple complex just outside Mexico City from 1917 to 1925.[2] Beyond uncovering the archaeological ruins, he also engaged with the local Indigenous populations, educating them on how to assimilate culturally and linguistically to the mestizo nation. He called for the "modernization" of the Amerindian through improved diet, health care, and education, all of which he understood through Westernized paradigms.[3] The *letrado* prophesied of a national mestizaje that would redeem Mexico's Indigenous populations and supply a proletariat necessary for the country's incipient industrialization.[4] A (neo)positivist to the core,[5] Gamio defined indigenismo and his ensuing understanding of mestizo nationalism through a scientific—and particularly anthropological—framework.[6] The thinker's focus on science explains his skepticism of religious fanaticism, particularly among Mexico's Catholics. That said, the anthropologist did not support the aggressive antagonization of the Catholic Church. Rather, he asserted that the state should patiently and paternalistically inculcate a secular mindset into its population through public, scientific education. This practice would challenge the Church's historical position of power in two ways: first, in banning the clergy from the classroom, the country would avoid the radicalization the nation's youth; second, a secular education would cause many Mexicans to question dogmatic truth claims through critical thinking about their faith.[7] Gamio also believed that such an education program would combat the superstitions that continued to exist throughout the population well into the twentieth century.[8] Education would thus play a key role in producing a more moderate Catholic population. This, in turn, would quell religion-based violence.

Throughout his long career, Gamio sought a political middle path that consisted of a type of pragmatic anti-Catholicism that set him apart from the militant anticlericalism that would culminate with the Cristiada (1926–1929) on the one hand and José Vasconcelos's aesthetic education that reified the Church on the other. He thus posited scientific education as the antidote to the different struggles confronting his country. The intellectual demonstrated pragmatic savvy through his ability and willingness to work for an array of leaders. His career began during the twilight of the Porfiriato, and he worried that his career opportunities would fade away upon realizing that none of the secretaries in Francisco Madero's cabinet knew or cared about his work.[9] He secured a paid position within the government of Victoriano Huerta, but he began to voice his sympathy for the revolutionary factions—particularly those of Carranza and Zapata—as it became evident that they would seize power.[10] As an academic in need of funding, Gamio sought to remain in the good graces of whomever held power in order to ensure that his research could continue. He wrote the essay *Forjando patria (pro nacionalismo)*—roughly translated as *Forging a Fatherland (Pro Nationalism)*—in 1916 with the hope that it would appeal both to the incoming revolutionary government and to Mexicans at large.[11] Claiming that Mexico was not yet a nation due to its significant ethnic divisions, the book called for a national homogenization through mestizaje that would lead Mexico toward twentieth-century modernity.[12]

Given Gamio's prominence in Mexican government, thought, and society, it is surprising that his work has, for the most part, faded into the recesses of national memory. *Forjando patria* has taken a backseat to José Vasconcelos's *La raza cósmica* (1925) in classrooms despite the fact that Gamio's indigenismo was more in line with statist projects of modernization than were Vasconcelos's aesthetics.[13] When academics do mention Gamio, they tend to cite *Forjando patria* to explain *indigenista* projects of health and hygiene from the 1920s through at least the 1940s; however, they rarely approach his writings as literary texts worthy of critical analysis in and of themselves. Most discussions of Gamio's cultural anthropology place him in binary opposition to Vasconcelos.[14] The two men ran concurrent education programs in many rural communities, and they often prioritized different, even contradictory objectives for national schools.[15] Kelly R. Swarthout identifies Vasconcelos's sympathetic views toward the Church and Gamio's anti-Catholicism as one key reason for their mutual antagonism.[16] Such characterizations may overstate the degree to which

Gamio and Vasconcelos disagreed. We should not forget, for example, that they coauthored the book *Aspects of Mexican Culture* in 1926, and they often presented papers together at conferences on Mexican culture, particularly during their time of shared exile during the Maximato.[17] Both men curried the favor of Venustiano Carranza and Álvaro Obregón before falling out with Plutarco Elías Calles.[18] These shared experiences suggest a degree of camaraderie that many critics—myself included—have largely overlooked.

Scholars who overemphasize the schisms between Vasconcelos and Gamio run the risk of mischaracterizing the anthropologist's thought by conflating him with militaristic anticlericalism. We should certainly note David A. Brading's assertion that "beneath the stern mask of the social scientist there lurked [in Gamio] an unregenerate anti-clerical liberal."[19] Gamio viewed the Church as the primary obstacle—along with "the enduring, isolated backwardness of the Indian peasantry"—to achieving mestizo modernity.[20] Similar to most letrados from the time period, he viewed the state as an important check on the influence of the Catholic Church, both institutional and popular.[21] That said, his training as an anthropologist led him to view frontal assaults against the Church as unreasonable and likely counterproductive. As such, he held that the state should enact "commonsense" regulations on the Church.[22] For example, he suggested that the state decree strict limits on ecclesiastical fees for marriage and other sacraments.[23] He further argued that the state should defanaticize the nation by decreeing secular education for all.

Gamio viewed Mexican Catholicism as particularly corrupt, comparing it unfavorably to the US Catholic Church when he wrote, "The Mexican clergy has usually fought for riches and power, holding only secondary its evangelical duties, whereas the American clergy has not meddled in dangerous politics, nor exploited the people, devoting itself to satisfying their spiritual necessities."[24] Though he remained skeptical of religion in general throughout his writings, Gamio could tolerate it if both ecclesiastical and secular authorities recognized and respected each other's purviews. The anthropologist sought ways to dampen religious fanaticism and belief through a variety of means, even identifying US Protestantism as one particularly interesting—and perhaps unexpected—source of defanaticizing discourse.[25] He expressed some concerns that such religions coerced Mexican-born practitioners toward "foreignization," but he spoke favorably about how they identified the flaws of Catholicism when addressing Mexican members.[26] Gamio believed that, because Mexicans by and large could not identify culturally with the evangelical message, Protestantism pushed them to agnosticism and atheism rather than fanaticism.[27] Viewed in this light, Gamio's anti-Catholicism—and particularly his distrust of the clergy—reflected his experience with the Catholic Church in Mexico, which he hoped would recognize its jurisdictional limits by allowing the state to engage in scientific education without Church interference.

The anthropologist understood that a constructive relationship with believers would help the country to modernize scientifically while avoiding violent conflict. *Forjando patria* includes a section that attempts to classify Mexico's Catholics to gauge their potential for contributing to a modern nation. This ambitious endeavor certainly leads to caricatures of a diverse religious scene, but it also shows how he understood the Church's influence in the country. He divided the nation's believers into three general groups: pagan Catholics, true Catholics, and utilitarian Catholics. First, he discussed a group that he referred to as pagan Catholics, a demographic that ignorantly fused Christian beliefs with pre-Columbian rituals and worship.[28] He followed with a discussion of the true Catholics, a segment of the population that lived by the precept "'render unto Caesar what is Caesar's'" and "'my reign is not of this world.'"[29] Gamio's citation of these Biblical passages evinced a certain familiarity with scripture while allowing him to argue for greater separations between church and state.[30] Perhaps most important for Gamio, true Catholics would "take science as science and religion as religion."[31] As an anthropologist, Gamio understood how personal beliefs shaped subjectivity.[32] Nevertheless, his positivist leanings led him to demand that religious people cede questions of science to experts like himself.[33] While somewhat tautological, Gamio's true Catholics understood the give and take between science and religion, and they never advocated for the Church to overstep its bounds.

This stood in direct opposition to the so-called utilitarian Catholics, a term that Gamio used to refer to those who utilized religion to create a political structure that favored the institutional church's ability to impose its will on society at large. Gamio deplored this group, lamenting how they stifled scientific collaboration with true Catholics:

> But what is most revolting and inspires the most indignation is that when one of these men sees his dirty dealings destroyed or attacked before all of the other Mexican Catholics, he hides

among them. The Utilitarian Catholics set the True Catholics before themselves like a bulwark or trench to resist the first blow—or all of them if possible! Because of this, it is unlikely that the True Catholics, the respectable and worthy ones, will remain unharmed when the pernicious and utilitarian ones are persecuted. It is very unfortunate that the pastoral of the Archbishop of Quito, Ecuador, Sr. D. Federico González Suárez [sic], published in the Mexican press some years ago and in which the bishop hurls anathemas at the Utilitarian Catholics, did not become more popular in our country.[34]

Gamio's allusion to the Ecuadorian archbishop highlights the fact that not all clergy were party to the abuse of religion for political ends. That said, his quote leaves implicit the idea that most Catholic leaders in Mexico lacked the virtue of their Ecuadorian counterpart. This, of course, presented serious challenges for the country since any direct attempt to scale back the Church's influence would foster feelings of victimhood that would potentially radicalize the clergy and their followers, thus leading to violence. Due to their penchant for couching conflict within a framework of religious discrimination, utilitarian Catholics could foreseeably convert others—including true Catholics—to their cause.

Faced with this reality, Gamio advocated for a program of scientific education that would frustrate the most egregious attempts by utilitarian Catholics to project power across the nation. Once instructed, the people themselves would hold the Church in check. Gamio thus advocated for an order where the state would handle secular issues and the Roman Catholic Church would, like its US counterpart, restrict itself to spiritual salvation.[35] Gamio's musings on religion suggest that he understood the drive to establish a secular state as a battle for the support of true Catholics and perhaps pagan Catholics against the utilitarian Catholics. Scientifically minded individuals would need the blessing of the true Catholics as they entered rural communities and educated pagan Catholics out of their superstitions. This same group of believers would provide an invaluable buffer against utilitarian Catholics. The role of the Church in temporal issues would naturally diminish as a newly educated society came of age. Equally important, a rise in education and its accompanying increase in scientific competence would drive utilitarian Catholics to the periphery.

Official Mestizaje and the Church: The Vasconcelos/Gamio Dialectic

Unlike Manuel Gamio, who viewed indigenismo as a political and economic strategy for redeeming Amerindians and assimilating them to a modernizing state, José Vasconcelos viewed a modern, national identity in primarily aesthetic terms that largely ignored utilitarian justifications.[36] Both men embraced the eugenicist beliefs of the day, which held that education and hygiene would play a key role in eugenically perfecting the country, but they imagined very different roles for the national school in this endeavor.[37] Gamio's eugenics led him to advocate education programs tailored to the needs of Indigenous communities with the goal of assimilating them into the mestizo majority. Vasconcelos, however, argued for a form of selective eugenics where people of Indigenous and African descent would choose to breed themselves out of existence by intermarrying with European peoples and producing a mestizo national body.[38] Of course, Vasconcelos's plans depended on Mexico's Indigenous and Black populations learning, internalizing, and accepting his paradigm of racial aesthetics through an aggressive project of public education.[39] Despite the thinkers' competing conceptualizations of mestizo eugenics, the state itself came to conflate their visions in its own articulations of official mestizaje because "one functioned in practice and the other as a philosophical and ideological explanation of national character."[40] Rather than appeal to abstract numbers and figures to quantify (mestizo) modernity—as Gamio did in works like *Hacia un México nuevo* (*Toward a New Mexico*)—Vasconcelos simply imbued mestizaje with a triumphalist, quasi-religious aura by making racial hybridity an aesthetic end in and of itself.[41]

Gamio's attempts to leverage science to improve the nation represented the legacy of the system of scientific politics of the Porfirian era.[42] Based on the writings of the French thinker Auguste Comte, nineteenth-century Mexican positivism had aimed to strengthen society by aggressively employing (social) scientific projects to modernize all of Mexico. The movement's proponents credited this intellectual tradition with catalyzing the Mexican Revolution and emancipating the nation.[43] Critics, however, argued that this intellectual tradition had produced a quasi-religious, secular dogma that exalted positivism while marginalizing other intellectual disciplines.[44] Many anti-positivist intellectuals (like José Vasconcelos) argued that, while these attitudes were clearly born during the Porfiriato, they had also survived the Revolution.

This historical and cultural backdrop proves especially interesting in light of Kelly R. Swarthout's assertion that Gamio and his indigenista colleagues "placed their *faith* in science [. . .] because scientific analyses had helped them to disprove the innate inferiority of the Indian and assert the legitimacy of New World civilizations."[45] Swarthout's invocation of the terms "faith" and "science" alongside one another is especially interesting given these terms' apparent oppositionality. While often conflated with theism, the term *faith* ultimately refers to a belief in something without clear, tangible evidence because such a belief provides some sort of hope to the believer. Science consists of falsifiable observations that observers systematically organize into paradigms.[46] Despite a clear distinction between faith and science, some slippage emerges when we attempt to definitively separate these two concepts one from another, particularly in the realm of policy. Not only do many people express an often uninformed and irrational trust in "science," but many scientific observers' biases can color how they (and even society) interpret their observations. This, in turn, leads to scientific paradigms that reflect social attitudes at least as much as observed reality.[47] The reification of science toward a specific end—national reconciliation and modernization through official mestizaje in the case of Gamio—lent itself to precisely this sort of analytical impasse.

Forjando patria reflects early twentieth-century neopositivist thought, particularly as it asserts that Mexico's Amerindian populations can redeem themselves through education in the social sciences. Gamio begins by arguing that, if the conquest had not interrupted the creation of Indigenous nation-states, these would have established rich societies on par with those of Japan and China.[48] Nevertheless, the colonial period fractured Indigenous societies and destroyed their glorious potential while it existed in embryonic form. The anthropologist also believed that the time had come for Indigenous populations to redeem themselves and enter a truly modern world order. Ironically, this could only happen through mestizaje, a process that would improve the "largely unsatisfactory [culture]" ("cultura [. . .] poco satisfactorio") that, he claimed, continued to inhabit Mexico and the Americas well into the twentieth century.[49] Gamio understood Indigenous society to exist in a state of perdition; Amerindians could only achieve their true potential if they left their ethnic identities behind. Viewed in this light, it should come as no surprise that *Forjando patria* challenged the overt dehumanization of Amerindians by comparing them to the non-Western civilizations of East Asia. On the one hand, this questioned the prevailing views that characterized Indigenous Mexicans as lazy and less human than their European counterparts; on the other hand, however, the very decision to juxtapose them with Far Eastern civilizations showcased Gamio's discomfort with placing Indigenous societies fully on par with the West.

A close reading of Gamio's work suggests that, while Amerindians enjoyed biological equality to their European and mestizo counterparts, he believed they would need to adopt modern (read: Western) culture and (especially) technology if they truly wanted to enter modern society. The redemptive discourse inherent to this strain of thought underscored the quasi-religious tenor of his neopositivist leanings. There were certain problems with Gamio's understanding of race and ethnicity in Mexico. While he understood Mexican character as either Iberian, Indigenous, or mestizo, the country actually boasted greater diversity. For example, it had small but culturally significant immigrant populations from Asia and non-Hispanic European countries, particularly Germany. Gamio's reification of mestizophilia in public discourse almost certainly contributed to statist attempts to regulate the mobility of migrant bodies in the country during the early twentieth century.[50] Furthermore, Gamio has also come under fire in recent years from scholars like Theodore Cohen, who charge him with focusing on Indigenous Mexico to the exclusion of Afro-Mexicans.[51] This critique, while valid, ignores much of the historical referent within which Gamio operated. National understandings of enthnoracial identity remained in their infancy during these years, and Gamio led the charge of an applied anthropology that would integrate Mexico's majority-Indigenous population to the modern state under the umbrella of official mestizaje.[52] Cohen is thus correct to observe Gamio's general ignorance of Afro-Mexican populations, but the criticism ignores the trailblazing work that the anthropologist put toward rehabilitating the image of Indigenous populations throughout his life.

Indeed, Gamio's language took on an evangelical tenor when he alluded to an Indigenous awakening that would, conveniently, only happen when "friendly hearts" ("corazones amigos"), like his own, worked to "redeem" them.[53] This would happen not with the teaching of a new religion but with the profession of a secular order that would wean rural Indigenous communities from their dependence on the Church.[54] Gamio believed that indigenistas necessarily had to learn the languages and cultures of the people that they wished to redeem. Only by this means could they carry out competent education campaigns that would reach the Amerindian. As Gamio noted, "Once the Indian finds himself exempt from this 'contribution for living' and finds himself to be a man, once he has confidence, he will begin to attend school."[55] This assertion underscored his belief that the state could not simply install a school if it wished to redeem its Indigenous population. Rather, it first had to create the infrastructure and framework necessary to convince Amerindians that they would benefit from receiving an education. Given the utilitarian focus of Gamio's approach to education, Swarthout argues that "this practice was not so very different from that of the Catholic missionaries of the sixteenth century who learned Nahuatl with the principal intent of converting the natives to Christianity."[56] Unlike the conquistadores, of course, Gamio advocated for a secular sociopolitical order and an (eventual) Indigenous equality. Nevertheless, he framed his ideals in a millenarian discourse that borrowed heavily from the religious imaginaries that had defined paradigms of conquest for centuries, and he ultimately favored Western culture over the Indigenous. Under Gamio's indigenista education system, teachers would tailor their instruction to the needs and understandings of their rural, Indigenous pupils to strengthen their scientific knowledge, temper their religious beliefs, and assimilate them to the modern state.

The postrevolutionary government, and particularly the Secretaría de Educación Pública (Secretariat of Public Education [SEP]), seemed to endorse these views when Vasconcelos, in his capacity as secretary of public education, commissioned "Apostles of culture" to serve "cultural missions"—both terms with strong religious connotations—in Indigenous areas with the express intent of spreading mestizo modernity.[57] Both Gamio and Vasconcelos concurred with the popular slogan "to educate is to redeem," but they differed on *how* to achieve this end.[58] Their biggest disagreements centered on whom to educate and what to teach. For Vasconcelos, "a common language (Spanish) and religion (Catholicism) would unite its diverse peoples."[59] This support for the Church reverberated with his aesthetics insofar as it reflected his desire to build a mestizo nation predicated on Western values and cosmologies. The inculcation of Catholicism did not represent the spiritual salvation of the Amerindian so much as a means through which they could assimilate to a European, mestizo mold. Gamio rejected this approach on two fronts: first, he believed that educators should teach their Indigenous students in their native languages; second, as his notion of pagan Catholics makes clear, he recognized that the Church had spent centuries within and among these communities. Not only had the Church failed to modernize these populations, but it had brought about much of the segregation between Indigenous and mestizo worlds that plagued the nation. As he explained throughout his writings, Mexico's native populations could only overcome their supposed vices through scientific education.

Gamio's distrust of religion extended beyond the Catholic Church. Indeed, he blamed religion in general for Indigenous Mexico's historical suffering when he stated:

> Poor and pained race! You were oppressed for centuries by a doubly tyrannical yoke. First, there was the pagan fanaticism with which you deified your ancient king-priests. Second, the brutal egoism of the conquerors that always drowned the aspirations of the inferior class. You will not awaken spontaneously, however healthy and elevated you might be. It will be essential that friendly hearts work for your redemption.[60]

Gamio's words indicate that Amerindians have long suffered from a religious fanaticism that began in pre-Columbian times, millennia before the arrival of the Church. At the same time, any charges of religious fanaticism in early twentieth-century Mexico necessarily invoked tensions with the Church, whose clergy and members resisted secularization and the separation of church and state.[61] Any attempt to uplift the Amerindian needed to bypass a Church that had contributed to their subjugation for more than four centuries. The stakes of the tension between the approaches of Gamio and Vasconcelos gained steam through the first half of the 1920s. As Catholic activists organized throughout much of the country in the 1920s, the need to contain the Church's fanaticism became especially pressing.[62] Gamio did not want to antagonize the Church, but his education programs would mitigate its power over the hearts and minds of the people. Gamio and Vasconcelos ultimately compromised on certain points of their educational agendas to ensure an adequate education for all.[63]

Gamio and Scientific Education in Times of Calles

The election of Plutarco Elías Calles in 1924 disrupted the delicate balance between the SEP and the Departamento de Antropología's competing yet complementary education mandates in many ways. Both Manuel Gamio and José Vasconcelos saw their influence wane after that fateful election. Perhaps most obviously, Calles's election resulted in a change in secretaries of public education. José Vasconcelos resigned from his role as secretary of public education in June, before Calles's inauguration, over political disagreements with the incoming president.⁶⁴ Bernardo J. Gastélum served in an interim role through the end of Obregón's presidency. Shortly after taking office, Calles disbanded the Departamento de Antropología, which Gamio headed, and subordinated it to the SEP. The president then invited Gamio to continue his work, particularly his educational activities, under Manuel Puig Casauranc, the new secretary of public education.⁶⁵ Despite some misgivings, the anthropologist accepted the appointment. It is likely that he did so in large part because he believed that a government position would better enable him to carry out his research on applied anthropology, which he would have hoped to leverage toward further archaeological funding and research. Under Calles and Puig Casauranc, the SEP engaged in projects that supported the scientific education for which Gamio had advocated for years. With regard to the agency's approach to the Church, the SEP was more explicitly anti-Catholic under Casauranc than it had been under Vasconcelos.⁶⁶ At least in this regard, then, the SEP adopted Gamio's more anticlerical positions as they related to public education.

Nevertheless, Gamio's influence in the Mexican government diminished quickly amid growing disagreements between Gamio and the Calles administration. This discord seems to have had less to do with policy than with personality clashes. For example, Beatriz Urías Horcasitas has noted that Gamio became increasingly disillusioned with Calles when the president would not reward his loyalty with further funding for anthropological research.⁶⁷ Tensions came to a head when Gamio requested permission from the president to investigate what he suspected to be corruption on the part of Puig Casauranc.⁶⁸ When Calles expressed his confidence in his secretary of public education, Gamio resigned from his position and left for exile in the United States.⁶⁹

Upon realizing that he would not return to Mexico for some time, Gamio decided to embark on new academic projects that he could carry out from beyond Mexico's borders. Shortly after fleeing to the United States, he decided to travel to Guatemala, where he assisted with the excavation of Kaminal Juyú.⁷⁰ This opportunity allowed him to continue to do research on prehistoric Mesoamerican cultures in a more politically safe environment. The anthropologist left his mark on that country as well. His particular brand of applied anthropology would later catch on in Guatemala when the country's revolutionary governments embarked on their own projects of modernization.⁷¹ Afterward, Gamio went to the United States, where he decided to do ethnographic research on Mexican migrants in the United

States. He had to temper his indigenista discourse because the populations of his study were no longer Amerindians. At the same time, however, he continued to criticize the Church for its role in ongoing instability in his country.[72] Viewed in this light, Gamio proves especially interesting when we situate Mexican anti-Catholicism within a global context. Clearly, his is a case where the reverberations of Mexican anti-Catholicism reached far beyond the country's borders.

Conclusion

As this chapter has shown, Gamio was a key contributor to anti-Catholic thought both in Mexico and throughout the world. Throughout his career he advocated for a middle path that would use education as the primary tool of an applied anthropology that aimed to defanaticize and de-Catholicize the Indigenous populations. The anthropologist's focus on scientific education distanced him from Vasconcelian approaches to education. Where Vasconcelos viewed Catholicism as a key plank of a Hispanicized education program, Gamio saw the Church as a principal cause of Mexico's continued relegation to the periphery. Interestingly, while Vasconcelos is often heralded as the father of Mexican education—an assertion bolstered by the fact that he served as the first secretary of public education—Gamio's anticlerical thrust in rural education was, in many ways, the defining element of public education in the country until at least 1940. Gamio's moderate anti-Catholicism aimed to convince individuals to abandon their religious fanaticism. Public schools thus provided a unique opportunity to redeem Indigenous Mexicans for multiple reasons. On the one hand, they provided their students with the skills necessary to contribute to a quickly industrializing society.[73] On the other hand, secular, scientific institutions served as a bulwark against what he viewed as the backwardness of the Church. Gamio cemented his role as a key figure of the revolutionary landscape by creating the infrastructure that could make this a reality. Mexico certainly remains predominantly Catholic, but Gamio's so-called utilitarian Catholics are now few and far between. The anthropologist's educational projects aided in bringing about this reality by ensuring a scientific curriculum that would defanaticize the nation.

Notes

1. For a discussion of Gamio's storied career, see Matos Moctezuma, "Manuel Gamio."
2. Schávelzon, "La primera excavación arqueológica de América," 128–29.
3. Ironically, in recent years, "modernized," Western diets in Mexico have been linked to increased cases of diabetes in the country. See Gálvez, *Eating NAFTA*, chap. 6.
4. The term *letrado* refers to a common type of actor in Latin America who uses writing to access political power and privilege. See Rama, *Lettered City*.
5. Ignacio Sánchez Prado situates Gamio within a neopositivist paradigm, thus considering him as an heir to the *científicos* movement of the nineteenth century. Sánchez Prado, "El mestizaje en el corazón de la utopía," 386. Similar to the positivist científicos before him, Gamio referred to anthropology and archaeology as decidedly "scientific" disciplines throughout his career. This, of course, was due to the rigorous application of the scientific method in his work and research. For a discussion of social scientifism, see Villegas, *Autognosis*, 11.
6. The term *indigenismo* refers to a political and intellectual movement that on the one hand celebrates Indigenous cultures and their influence in Mexico while on the other hand attempting to assimilate them to a Western and mestizo paradigm. For a discussion of indigenismo's ties to official mestizaje—an ideology that Gamio helped to construct—see Lomnitz, *Exits*, 277–80; Janzen, *National Body*, 88. Walter Mignolo has criticized indigenismo as merely a conversation among mestizo elites about Indigenous actors, where "the Indians themselves did not have any role to play or anything to say." See Mignolo, *Idea of Latin America*, 102; Díaz Polanco, *Indigenous Peoples*, 23.
7. Castillo Ramírez, "Hacia un México nuevo," 86.
8. For a discussion of different superstitions that Gamio ascribed to the populations of Teotihuacán, see Gamio, *La población del valle de Teotihuacán*, 298–99.
9. de la Peña, "Nacionales y extranjeros," 50–51.
10. de la Peña, 55.
11. Fernando Armstrong-Fumero notes that Gamio wrote the text in a middlebrow register to increase its appeal to all educated Mexicans. Armstrong-Fumero, "Translator's Introduction," 5.
12. Rivermar Pérez, "En el marasmo de una rebellion cataclísmica (1911–1920)," 118.
13. For a discussion of official mestizaje as a political and economic project, see Lund, *Mestizo State*; Dalton, *Mestizo Modernity*. For a discussion of Vasconcelos's more philosophical approach to mestizaje—especially when compared to Gamio—see Arreola Martínez, "José Vasconcelos," 4.

14. Swarthout, *"Assimilating the Primitive,"* chap. 3; Sánchez Prado, "El corazón de la utopía," 386–87; Castillo Ramírez, "Hacia un México nuevo," 85; Dalton, *Mestizo Modernity*, 37. For a study that shows the convergences between Vasconcelos and Gamio, see Noyola Rocha, "La visión integral," 144–46.
15. Following the thought of Agustín Basave Benítez—who argues that postrevolutionary Mexican intellectuals could only agree that they favored some form of mestizaje—one could argue that Vasconcelos and Gamio only concurred on the fact that the imposition of a mestizo order would benefit their country. That said, they could not agree on the nature of said order. See Basave Benítez, *México mestizo*, 141. For a discussion of Vasconcelos's rural education programs, see Fell, *José Vasconcelos los años del águila (1920–1925)*, chap. 4.
16. Swarthout, *"Assimilating the Primitive,"* 119–20.
17. The Maximato refers to the years 1928–1934, which directly followed the presidency of Plutarco Elías Calles. While Calles was no longer president, the period is characterized by Calles's continued exercise of significant influence in national politics. González Gamio, *Manuel Gamio*, 117; Noyola Rocha, "La visión integral," 147.
18. Indeed, Carranza created the Departamento de Antropología specifically so that Gamio could direct it. See Armstrong-Fumero, "Translator's Introduction," 5. Gamio ensured the prominence of the Departamento de Antropología by supporting major projects and publications. See Noyola Rocha, "La visión integral," 144. Despite writing *Forjando patria* specifically to get Carranza's attention, Gamio ultimately expressed disappointment in all of the northern presidents, none of whom he believed upheld the values of the revolution. See Castillo Ramírez, "Hacia un México nuevo," 81.
19. Brading, "Manuel Gamio," 85.
20. Brading, 76.
21. Brading, 76, 85–86.
22. Brading, 86.
23. Gamio constantly decried the financial demands of the Church on its adherents. See Gamio, *Mexican Immigration*, 116–18.
24. Gamio, 113.
25. See Rebecca Janzen's chapter in this book.
26. For a discussion of Protestantism and how this forced Catholic clergy to rethink their ministry to (particularly poor) members of their flock in Latin America, see Gill, *Rendering unto Caesar*, chap. 4.
27. Gamio, *Mexican Immigration*, 115–16. The assertion that Protestantism would lead to defanatization sounds surprising in a twenty-first-century context where evangelicalism has influenced the political processes of numerous countries, including Mexico. See da Costa Farias et al., "Entre lo religioso y lo político," 83–95.

28. Gamio, *Forjando patria*, 93–94. Gamio identified an exact number of pagan Catholics in Teotihuacán in his dissertation, placing it at 3,469, which he placed against 4,816 nonsyncretic Catholics. See Gamio, *Traduction*, xxxi. For a deeper discussion of pagan Catholicism in practice, see Gamio, *La población del valle de Teotihuacúan*, xxxi–xxxvii.
29. Here I am citing Fernando Armstrong-Fumero's translation of *Forjando patria*. The biblical citation "my reign is not of this world" would probably more appropriately be rendered as "my kingdom is not of this world," which is how it generally appears in English translations of the Bible. See Gamio, *Forjando patria*, 94. Interestingly, Gamio would refer to the "True Catholics" as Conscientious Catholics in his own English-language scholarship. See Gamio, *Mexican Immigration*, 113.
30. Gamio, *Forjando patria*, 94.
31. Gamio, 94.
32. Gamio, *Mexican Immigration*, 108.
33. Certainly, Gamio's neopositivism differed from that of Porfirian positivists in that he believed in a more complete integration of Amerindians into the national body, which he claimed had been impossible under the Porfiriato. See Urías Horcasitas, "Las ciencias sociales," 102–3; Castillo Ramírez, "Hacia un México nuevo," 83–85.
34. Gamio, *Forjando patria*, 95. Gamio referred here to Federico González Suárez, an Ecuadorian historian, politician, and moderate cleric who often criticized the Church when he felt it merited it. At the time of Gamio's writing, he was Ecuador's most famous historian.
35. Gamio, *Mexican Immigration*, 113.
36. Dalton, *Mestizo Modernity*, 33–34.
37. Urías Horcasitas, "Las ciencias sociales," 104–5; Dalton, *Mestizo Modernity*, 12–15.
38. Vasconcelos, *La raza cósmica*, 27; Hernández, "'Afro-Mexican' and the Revolution," 70–74; Varner, *La raza cosmética*, 8.
39. Certainly, the Calles administration—and particularly Vasconcelos's successor, Manuel Puig Causaranc—transformed the rural education apparatus in an explicitly anticlerical institution as it became the face of postrevolutionary socialist programs.
40. Dalton, *Mestizo Modernity*, 33.
41. Romanell, "Bergson in Mexico," 503–8.
42. Hale, *Transformation*, 260.
43. Zea, *El positivismo en México*, 12–14.
44. Villegas, *Autognosis*, 11.
45. Swarthout, *"Assimilating the Primitive,"* 95.
46. Kuhn, *Structure*, 10–11.
47. Kuhn, 4. For a discussion of how cultural attitudes informed racial and eugenicist attitudes in Latin America and Mexico, see Stepan, *"Hour of Eugenics"*; Antebi, *Embodied Archive*. Dalton, *Mestizo Modernity*, 14–27.

48. Gamio, *Forjando patria*, 23.
49. Gamio, *Hacia un México Nuevo*, 27.
50. For a discussion of mestizaje as Hispanicization and the role that this played in the creation of xenophobic immigration laws, see Buchenau, "Limits of the Cosmic Race"; Yankelevich, *Los otros*, 23–68.
51. Cohen, *Finding Afro-Mexico*, 47–48. Cohen also exalts Vasconcelos as a more Black-friendly postrevolutionary thinker, a fact that Hernández contested in his own writing some two decades prior. See Hernández, "'Afro-Mexican.'"
52. Certainly, Indigenous and Afro-Mexican communities knew of their own identities, but Gamio's work helped the state to understand more about the Indigenous communities that made up its population. For a discussion on Gamio's pioneering role in race and ethnicity studies in Mexico, see Portal Ariosa and Ramírez, *Pensamiento antropológico en México*, chap. 5.
53. Gamio, *Hacia un México nuevo*, 27; Gamio, *Forjando patria*, 37.
54. Throughout the 1930s, Gamio spent a considerable amount of time interrogating the itersections of race, class, education, and religious fanaticism. See Urías Horcasitas, "Las ciencias sociales," 116–17.
55. Gamio, *Forjando patria*, 37.
56. Swarthout, *"Assimilating the Primitive,"* 104.
57. Lewis, "Education," 180–82; Palou, *El fracaso del mestizo*, 16–20; Fell, *José Vasconcelos*, 219–38, 254–69.
58. See Benjamin, "Rebuilding the Nation," 450.
59. Swarthout, *"Assimilating the Primitive,"* 108.
60. Gamio, *Forjando patria*, 37.
61. For a discussion of Church attempts to insert themselves into policymaking debates during the Porfiriato, the revolution, and the postrevolutionary periods, see Curley, *Citizens and Believers*, chap. 2, chap. 3.
62. Andes, *Vatican and Catholic Activism*, chap. 2.
63. Swarthout, *"Assimilating the Primitive,"* 119–20.
64. For a discussion of Vasconcelos's penchant for creating political enemies, see Skirius, *José Vasconcelos y la cruzada de 1929*, 92–109.
65. de la Peña, "Nacionales y extranjeros," 62.
66. For a discussion of anticlericalism in rural education, see Pierce, "Fighting Bacteria."
67. Urías Horcasitas, "Las ciencias sociales," 107.
68. Urías Horcasitas notes that SEP funds had been used to pay for personal automobiles, furniture, and other things of that sort. See Urías Horcasitas, "Las ciencias sociales," 109–10.
69. Armstrong-Fumero, "Translator's Introduction," 6; González Gamio, *Manuel Gamio*, 107–10.

70. Kidder, "Archaeological Investigations," 561. Indeed, Gamio's work in Guatemala laid the groundwork for indigenista projects that would play out in that country during its own revolutionary period.
71. See Foss, *On Our Own Terms*, 27.
72. See Gamio, *Mexican Immigration*, 116–18.
73. Dalton, "Educating Cohesion."

Works Cited

Andes, Stephen J. C. *The Vatican and Catholic Activism in Mexico and Chile: The Politics of Transnational Catholicism, 1920–1940*. Oxford: Oxford University Press, 2014.

Antebi, Susan. *Embodied Archive: Disability in Post-Revolutionary Mexican Cultural Production*. Ann Arbor: University of Michigan Press, 2021.

Armstrong-Fumero, Fernando. "Translator's Introduction: Manuel Gamio and *Forjando Patria* [sic]: Anthropology in Times of Revolution." In *Forjando Patria: Pro-nacionalismo (Forging a Homeland)*, by Manuel Gamio, translated by Fernando Armstrong-Fumero, 1–20. Boulder: University Press of Colorado, 2010.

Arreola Martínez, Betsabé. "Jose Vasconcelos: El caudillo cultural de la nación." *Casa del Tiempo* 25 (2010): 4–10.

Basave Benítez, Agustín F. *México mestizo*. Mexico City: FCE, 1992.

Benjamin, Thomas. "Rebuilding the Nation." In *The Oxford History of Mexico*, edited by William H. Beezley and Michael C. Meyer, 438–70. Oxford: Oxford University Press.

Brading, David. "Manuel Gamio and Official Indigenismo in Mexico." *Bulletin of Latin American Research* 7, no. 1 (1988): 75–89.

Buchenau, Jürgen. "The Limits of the Cosmic Race: Immigrant and Nation in Mexico, 1850–1950." In *Immigration and National Identities in Latin America*, edited by Nicola Foote and Michael Goebel, 66–90. Gainesville: University Press of Florida, 2014.

Castillo Ramírez, Guillermo. "Hacia un México nuevo: la geneología indigenista de Gamio a inicios del cardenismo." *Alteridades* 23, no. 46 (2013): 79–95.

Cohen, Theodore W. *Finding Afro-Mexico: Race and Nation after the Revolution*. Cambridge: Cambridge University Press, 2020.

Curley, Robert. *Citizens and Believers: Religion and Politics in Revolutionary Jalisco, 1900–1930*. Albuquerque: University of New Mexico Press, 2018.

da Costa Farias, Deuziane, Franco Galichini, Rosalba Mora Sierra, and Santiago Vanderstichel. "Entre lo religios y lo politico: Presencia evangélica en los procesos politicos de Brasil y México." *Observatorio Latinoamericano y Caribeño* 5, no. 1 (2021): 75–95.

Dalton, David S. "Educating Cohesion: The Teacher as an Agent of the Postrevolutionary State." In *Modern Mexican Culture: Critical Foundations*, edited by Stuart A. Day, 107–22. Tucson: University of Arizona Press.

———. *Mestizo Modernity: Race, Technology, and the Body in Postrevolutionary Mexico*. Gainesville: University of Florida Press, 2018.

de la Peña, Guillermo. "Nacionales y extranjeros en la historia de la antropología mexicana." In *La historia de la antropología en México*, edited by Metchthild Trusch, 41–81. Mexico City: Plaza y Valdez, 1996.

Díaz Polanco, Héctor. *Indigenous Peoples in Latin America: The Quest for Self-Determination*. Translated by Lucia Rayas. Boulder, CO: Westview Press, 1997.

Fell, Claude. *José Vasconcelos. Los años del águila (1920–1925). Educación, cultura e iberoamericanismo en el México posrevolucionario*. Mexico City: Universidad Autónoma de México, 1989.

Foss, Sarah. *On Our Own Terms: Development and Indigeneity in Cold War Guatemala*. Chapel Hill: University of North Carolina Press, 2022.

Gálvez, Alyshia. *Eating NAFTA: Trade, Food Policies, and the Destruction of Mexico*. Berkeley: University of California Press, 2018.

Gamio, Manuel. *Forjando patria: Pro nacionalismo (Forging a Nation)*, translated by Fernando Armstrong-Fumero. Boulder: University Press of Colorado, 2010.

———. *Hacia un México Nuevo: Problemas sociales*. Mexico City: México, 1935.

———. *La población del valle de Teotihuacúan. Edición fascimilar*. Instituto Nacional Indigenista, 1979.

———. *La población del valle de Teotihuacán. Edición facsimilar. Folk-lore*. Mexico City: Instituto Nacional Indigenista, 1979.

———. *Mexican Immigration to the United States: A Study of Human Migration and Adjustment*. Chicago: University of Chicago Press, 1930.

———. *The Mexican Immigrant: His Life Story: Autobiographic Documents*. Chicago: University of Chicago Press, 1931.

———. *Traduction of the Introduction, Synthesis and Conclusions of the Work The Population of the Valley of Teotihuacán*. Mexico City: Talleres Gráficos de la Nación, 1922.

Gill, Anthony. *Rendering unto Caesar: The Catholic Church and the State in Latin America*. Chicago: University of Chicago Press, 1998.

González Gamio, Angeles. *Manuel Gamio: una lucha sin final*. Mexico City: Universidad Nacional Autónoma de México, 2003.

Hale, Charles A. *The Transformation of Liberalism in Nineteenth-Century Mexico*. Princeton, NJ: Princeton University Press, 1989.

Hernández, Marco Polo. "The 'Afro-Mexican' and the Revolution: Making Afro-Mexicans Invisible through the Ideology of *Mestizaje* in *La raza cósmica*." PALARA 4, no. 4 (2000): 59–83.

Janzen, Rebecca. *The National Body in Mexican Literature: Collective Challenges to Biopolitical Control.* New York: Palgrave Macmillan, 2015.
Kidder, Alfred V. "Archaeological Investigations at Kaminaljuyu, Guatemala." *Proceedings of the American Philosophical Society* 150, no. 6 (1961), 559–70.
Kuhn, Thomas S. *The Structure of Scientific Revolutions.* 3rd ed. Chicago: University of Chicago Press, 1996.
Lewis, Stephen E. "Education and the 'Indian Problem' in Mexico, 1920–1940." In *The Eagle and the Virgin: Nation and Cultural Revolution in Mexico, 1920–1940,* edited by Mary Kay Vaughan and Stephen E. Lewis, 180–82. Durham, NC: Duke University Press, 2006.
Lomnitz, Claudio. *Exits from the Labyrinth: Culture and Ideology in the Mexican National Space.* Berkeley: University of California Press, 1992.
Lund, Joshua. *The Mestizo State: Reading Race in Modern Mexico.* Minneapolis: University of Minnesota Press, 2012.
Matos Moctezuma, Eduardo. "Manuel Gamio." In *La población del valle de Teotihuacán. Edición facsimilar,* by Manuel Gamio, vii–xxiv. Mexico City: Instituto Nacional Indigenista, 1981.
Mignolo, Walter D. *The Idea of Latin America.* Malden, MA: Blackwell Publishing, 2005.
Noyola Rocha, Jaime. "La visión integral de la Sociedad Nacional." In *La Antropología en México: Panorama Histórico 2. Los hechos y los dichos (1880–1986),* edited by Carlos García Mora, 133–222. Mexico City: INAH, 1987.
Palou, Pedro Ángel. *El fracaso del mestizo.* Mexico City: Paidós, 2014.
Pierce, Gretchen. "Fighting Bacteria, the Bible, and the Bottle: Projects to Create New Men, Women, and Children, 1910–1940." In *A Companion to Mexican History and Culture,* edited by William H. Beazley, 505–17. Oxford: Blackwell Press, 2011.
Portal Ariosa, María Ana and Xóchitl Ramírez. *Pensamiento antropológico en México: un recorrido histórico.* Mexico City: Universidad Autónoma Metropolitana, 1995.
Rama, Ángel. *The Lettered City.* Translated by John Charles Chasteen. Durham, NC: Duke University Press, 1996.
Rivermar Pérez, Leticia. "En el marasmo de una rebellion cataclísmica (1911–1920)." In *La antropología en México. Panorama histórico. 2. Los hechos y los dichos (1880–1986),* edited by Carlos García Mora, 89–132. Mexico City: INAH, 1987.
Romanell, Patrick. "Bergson in Mexico: A Tribute to José Vasconcelos." *Philosophy and Phenomenological Research* 21, no. 4 (1961): 503–8.
Sánchez Prado, Ignacio M. "El mestizaje en el corazón de la utopía: *La raza cósmica* entre Aztlán y América Latina." *Revista Canadiense de Estudios Hispánicos* 33, no. 2 (2009): 381–404.
Schávelzon, Daniel. "La primera excavación arqueológica de America: Teotihuacan en 1676." *Anales de antropología* 20, no. 1 (1983): 121–34.

Skirius, John. *José Vasconcelos y la cruzada de 1929*. Mexico City: Siglo Veintiuno Editores, 1982.
Stepan, Nancy Leys. *"The Hour of Eugenics": Race, Gender, and Nation in Latin America*. Ithaca: Cornell University Press, 1991.
Swarthout, Kelly R. *"Assimilating the Primitive": Parallel Dialogue on Racial Miscegenation in Revolutionary Mexico*. New York: Peter Lang, 2004.
Urías Horcasitas, Beatriz. "Las ciencias sociales en la encrucijada del poder: Manuel Gamio (1920–1940). *Revista Mexicana de sociología* 64, no. 3 (2002): 93–121.
Varner, Natasha. *La raza cosmética: Beauty, Identity, and Settler Colonialism in Postrevolutionary Mexico*. Tucson: University of Arizona Press, 2020.
Vasconcelos, José. *La raza cósmica*. Mexico City: Porrúa, 2010.
Vasconcelos, José and Manuel Gamio. *Aspects of Mexican Civilization*. Chicago: University of Chicago Press, 1926.
Villegas, Abelardo. *Autognosis: El pensamiento mexicano en el siglo XX*. Mexico City: Instituto Panamericano de Geografía e Historia, 1985.
Yankelevich, Pablo. *Los otros. Raza, normas y corrupción en la gestión de la extranjería en México, 1900–1950*. Mexico City: El Colegio de México, 2019.
Zea, Leopoldo. *El positivismo en México: Nacimiento, apogeo y decadencia*. Mexico City: FCE, 1968.

SECTION II

POPULAR ANTI-CATHOLICISM

CHAPTER FOUR

A Gendered Anticlericalism

Feminist Intellectuals, Sexuality, and the Mexican Revolution

ELISSA J. RASHKIN

In the first decades of the twentieth century in Mexico, feminist theories and praxis emerged in diverse ideological contexts and were neither uniformly nor explicitly anti-Catholic or anticlerical. Nevertheless, despite this diversity, anti-Catholicism and anticlericalism were key elements of much feminist activism. The affinity of many feminists with Carrancismo or with anarchist, socialist, and communist currents undoubtedly predisposed them toward an opposition to religious institutions and dogma. Moreover, many feminists were teachers, active in the defense of public education as a rational, secular enterprise.

On an even more fundamental level, the very struggle for women's rights, in particular with respect to their bodies and sexuality, meant confrontation with the Church and its privileged position in the hearts and minds of the nation. Controversial proposals in favor of free love and the use of contraceptives, within or outside of marriage, went hand in hand with secular and anti-Catholic concepts of society and of gender roles therein; and the notion of reproductive freedom that would liberate women from the role euphemistically known as "ángel del hogar" (angel of the home), but that feminists considered to be domestic slavery, implied defiance of Catholic ideology.[1]

The present chapter explores manifestations of irreligion, anticlericalism, and anti-Catholicism in the thought of a group of influential feminists. It also examines the debates around sexuality that arose in feminist congresses and publications during the Revolution and the immediate postrevolutionary period. First, I consider the ideas of Carrancista spokeswoman Hermila Galindo and her circle, especially her intervention in the two feminist congresses held in Yucatán in 1916. Next, I examine the ideas of feminist leaders such as Elvia Carrillo Puerto in Yucatán and Mexico City in their dialogues with representatives of the US-based American

Birth Control League in 1923. Third, I treat the views of educator, lawyer, and journalist Esperanza Velázquez Bringas in an address to teachers and feminists in Mérida in 1922. Last, as a brief counterpoint, I turn to Mexican perceptions of Spanish anarchist Belén de Sárraga, who traveled throughout the Americas but was particularly important as an anticlerical activist in Mexico in the early 1920s.

This handful of voices represents no more than the tip of the iceberg in terms of collective action carried out by women in the first decades of the twentieth century.[2] In approaching these women from the standpoint of intellectual history and a focus on specific issues, I seek to show how their ideas and activism point toward what we may call a gendered anticlericalism that interfaced nicely with the anti-Catholic projects of the time. This, in turn, enabled public discussion of matters related to female bodies, women's civil and human rights, and the taboo subject of feminine sexuality.

Hermila Galindo, Carrancismo, and the First Feminist Congress, 1916

When Anna Macías published her pioneering study *Against All Odds: The Feminist Movement in Mexico to 1940* (1982), she wrote that Hermila Galindo, as the best-known female participant in the revolutionary struggle between 1915 and 1919, had received more attention from scholars than other important women of the period.[3] Indeed, Galindo's extraordinary political trajectory continues to generate scholarship and a level of (relative) public recognition experienced by few of her feminist peers. Though aware of this historiographical imbalance, I nevertheless begin my discussion with Galindo, since her affiliation with Venustiano Carranza and his followers, the most clearly anti-Catholic faction in this stage of the Revolution, facilitates the introduction of preliminary ideas regarding sexuality and irreligion as intertwined aspects of revolutionary feminist thought.

Born in the state of Durango in 1896, Galindo was a talented young woman who, early on, joined the Liberal cause. Her address to the Liberal Abraham González Club in Mexico City drew the attention of First Chief Carranza, who invited her to collaborate as his secretary.[4] Pushed from the capital by Zapata's and Villa's armies, Carranza's Constitutionalist forces were at the time based in Veracruz, which became a dynamic center of Carrancista propaganda. Galindo participated as editor of *La Mujer Moderna*

("Modern Woman," later *Mujer Moderna*), a magazine that was at once feminist and Carrancista; the cover of its first issue utilized a feminine, Art Nouveau–style design that contrasted starkly with the featured portrait of Carranza, whose military uniform accentuated the image of a strongman of the Revolution.

Carranza's strategic openness to women's participation in the revolutionary movement is interesting and little studied. In this same period, for example, he met the young photographers Dolores and Adriana Ehlers at an event in the port of Veracruz. Impressed by their activity, he awarded them a scholarship to study film in the United States and later incorporated them into his government as heads of the departments of cinema and censorship. Given the political and military strength of the Zapatista and Villista forces, Constitutionalist leaders needed to draw on all possible support in order to attract sympathizers from progressive sectors. The agrarian reform law of January 6, 1915, can be seen as a result of this political need and so can those policies that, without being wholly feminist in nature, expanded women's possibilities in terms of their rights within the family by partially modifying their status as the equivalent of minors, dependent on their husbands and other male relatives.

In essence, the attitudes of Carranza and his circle toward women were closely related to their battle against the power of the Church. The Carrancista ideologues, like many intellectuals, believed that women (and male campesinos such as those who followed Zapata) were particularly susceptible to Catholic indoctrination and the power of the priests, thus constituting an impediment to progress. The revolutionary newspaper *La Vanguardia*, edited by Dr. Atl in Orizaba and contemporary of Galindo's *La Mujer Moderna*—yet in which women collaborators and feminism were notably absent—thus included in its inaugural manifesto the following objective:

> XI. BRING TO THE CONSCIENCE OF THE MEXICAN WOMAN THE CONVICTION OF HER DUTY IN THIS HISTORIC MOMENT—we may obtain all of the conquests imaginable, but if we fail to conquer the intelligence of woman, we will always have an enemy inside our own house.[5]

The proposal is interesting in that, on the one hand, it recognizes that women possess "conscience" and "intelligence" and are a social subject with agency—potentially negative—in the domestic sphere. Yet on the other hand, it is wildly exclusionary; for despite nominally directing their words at "the people," the author or authors of the text, that is, Dr. Atl and his team of artists and intellectuals, assume a masculine "we," frame the consciousness-raising of women as a task for men for their own benefit, and also define this *concientización* or "consciousness-raising" only in terms of a "duty" rather than a liberation.

Like the "redemption" of Indigenous people mentioned in another point of the program, what is involved is an ambiguous *other*, whom the Revolution should take into account but who cannot be counted as an integral part, at least not in terms of political and intellectual leadership. The urgent need, also mentioned in the program, to combat the Church's noxious influence in the country is understood as an intellectual struggle featuring white or mestizo men charged with redeeming the rest of the population. In this view, the masses are easily manipulated due to the ignorance imposed by historical conditions but also by their essentially passive nature and tendency toward superstition.

There is no doubt that Galindo and the other women writers of *La Mujer Moderna* shared the Carranza camp's anticlericalism. In her first editorial, titled "¡Laboremos!" (Let's get to work!), Galindo referred to woman as "man's companion and his equal" (compañera del hombre, y su igual) and called for women's active participation in the transformation of the country: not however, to "usurp or invade the rights of the [male] citizen" (usurpar o invadir los derechos del ciudadano) but rather from the proper and fertile terrain of the home.[6] As Rosa María Valles Ruiz points out, Galindo would quickly change her position in this respect, becoming a vocal promotor of women's political rights. She even ran for a seat in the national congress in Mexico City in 1917, a campaign that she lost but with a respectable number of votes in her favor, including those of many women, despite the fact that female suffrage would not be legally recognized for another three and a half decades.[7]

This turn toward the political sphere emerged organically from the experience of Galindo and her collaborators, as it became clear that women's education, though fundamental, would not be a sufficient route to liberation as long as women remained under the legal custody of their husbands or fathers and ideologically under that of the clergy. On September 30, 1915, Galindo wrote in *La Mujer Moderna*: "Liberation from the harsh clerical tutelage that is the most opprobrious and cruel, since the priest dominates [woman] morally and physically, that is, deadens her and numbs her faculties, all with the calculated weapon of faith, the false admonition of 'believe and you will be saved' or the tremendous one of 'believe or I'll kill you.'"[8]

Here, although Galindo does not deviate noticeably from the position of *La Vanguardia* and other Carrancista ideologues, what is striking is the way in which she understands religious, particularly Catholic, domination: as violent biopower imposed on the bodies and minds of women, a kind of persistent Inquisition using fear to maintain its hegemony and, in doing so, to justify its own moral hypocrisy. That is, if the Church takes advantage of women to assure its own ideological, economic, and social power, it is not because women are *naturally* more susceptible than men but rather because they are much more vulnerable due to the lack of autonomy both in the home and the formal political sphere. It is in this order of ideas where we find what today are called reproductive rights or the lack thereof: the control over women's bodies exercised jointly by Church and state in the integrated context that we may call, also in today's language, heteropatriarchy.

In another important example of Carrancista interest in women's affairs, in 1916, Yucatán governor Salvador Alvarado called for the first Feminist Congress to be held in Mérida during January 13–16. Galindo, Carranza's secretary at the time as well as editor of *Mujer Moderna*, collaborated closely in the organization of the congress in which more than 600 women from Yucatán and the rest of the country would ultimately participate. The agenda contained four predetermined points of discussion, the first of which was implicitly irreligious and even anti-Catholic: "What are the social means that should be used to liberate women from the yoke of traditions?"[9] Galindo was unable to attend in person, but she sent a speech titled "La mujer en el porvenir" (Woman in the Future) that was read aloud by the male representative of the state education department, César González, and caused an uproar among the crowd due to its unvarnished defense of female sexuality.[10]

Galindo presents a condensed narrative of Western history in this document, describing the progression from a state in which brute force has determined social power to the point in which "the sweet and comforting doctrine of the Nazarene" (la dulce y apacible doctrina del Nazareno) has arrived to predicate a form of equality between the sexes that society unfortunately chose to ignore.[11] Galindo thus invokes Christianity in support of her thesis only to develop a crushing argument against its institutions and, particularly, the Catholic Church.[12] Roman law, she continues, began to grant women certain dignity by recognizing their juridical existence and a few rights within the domestic sphere; yet these rights, such as the guardianship of small children, depended on marriage, a contract to which not all subjects had equal access.

It is at this point that the speech becomes racy for early twentieth-century ears. "Though it may be sad to admit it," says Galindo, "man is born an animal and woman, a female animal!"[13] Arguing that both "animals" share the goal of reproduction of the species, she goes on to exalt maternal love as the most sublime of feelings; yet unlike most celebrations of motherhood in this and other epochs, she refuses to ignore the process by which, physiologically, one becomes a mother. On the contrary, Galindo associates the reproductive drive with the sexual one, writing: "The fact is that the sexual instinct prevails so strongly in woman and through such irresistible ruses, that no hypocritical artifice is capable of destroying, modifying or detaining it."[14]

Galindo does not stigmatize this sexual impulse but rather laments the circumstances that lead women to fall into the arms of unscrupulous male lovers who, as a result of the same instinctual act, are cheered on by society as Don Juans, while the female part is "relegated to social contempt, her future cut short and thrown into the abyss of desperation, misery, madness, or suicide."[15] This unhappy outcome does *not* ensue because woman is more animal or less rational than man; for Galindo, is it the result of a sexual double standard, exacerbated by such factors as educational disparities, ignorance about anatomy and physiology (itself the result of inadequate education), and the many barriers that prevent women from earning a dignified living, with or without the marriage contract.

In short, Galindo proposes the existence of a sexual instinct in women that is perverted by legal and educational shortfalls, which, she also proposes, must be addressed. For example: "Generally, women are pushed to develop what is called the life of the heart and the soul, while the development of her reason is ignored and omitted. As a result, she suffers from a hypertrophied intellectual and spiritual life, and is [thus] more susceptible to all the religious beliefs."[16] On this point, Galindo's argument seems to coincide with the Carrancista line: women, due to their lack of education and intellectual development, are easy prey for the manipulations of the Church and reactionary tendencies. However, what sets her thinking apart is the concept of women as social actors, tied down by patriarchal laws and moralism, and whose role in the Revolution is precisely that of overthrowing what she calls "idolatrous prejudices" (idolátricos prejuicios).[17] The Revolution has the *obligation* to create the structural conditions for this to happen by reforming legal codes, granting women equal access to education, and preparing them to work in well-remunerated jobs to meet their economic needs. At the same time, Galindo's message to the Feminist Congress is that women, as bearers of truth, can and must fight for their own emancipation.[18]

The negative reception of this message among many of the feminists gathered in Mérida is legendary.[19] "The mere mention of women's sexuality," writes Stephanie J. Smith, "let alone the idea that women's sexual needs were the same as men's, ran contrary to the positions held by most congress delegates, who viewed women and men as fundamentally different in their biology, behaviors, and social roles."[20] Some members of the audience went so far as to call for the destruction of Galindo's text; in the end, organizers agreed to leave it without comment and move on with discussion of the remaining topics on the agenda. Many of these had to do with rational and secular education, implicitly or explicitly as a means of countering religious influence; from the Congress's radical wing came calls for woman suffrage, and, as a concrete result, a proposal was drawn up for the reform of the discriminatory provisions of the Civil Code of 1884. Yet few participants had the interest or the courage to speak with Galindo's frankness and demand equality in the terrain of sexuality.

The scandalized reaction to "La mujer en el porvenir" was not, however, unanimous. As mentioned above, the Feminist Congress's first discussion topic was "What are the social means that should be used to liberate women from the yoke of traditions?" The commission assigned to this task, a radical trio composed of Porfiria Ávila de Rosado, Clara Steger Loge, and Elena Osorio, expressed ideas similar to those of Galindo regarding the need for *desfanatización* as well as for sex education. These delegates saw Church ideology as the obstacle that had most stood in the way of women's knowledge of their own bodies and biological processes; they called for science and art to replace the willful ignorance imposed by religions like the Catholic Church.

Furthermore, along with consciousness-raising, the committee declared that "an essential or indispensable requisite for women to be able to put an end to the traditions that weigh upon them is that they be free."[21] This definition of freedom was clearly linked to knowledge as well as legal rights, and in particular, to scientific understanding of human biology. The statement avoided inflammatory terms like "sexual instinct" but nevertheless shows that feminists at the congress besides Galindo favored teaching women about the body and sexuality as a tool toward liberation from the yoke of the Church as well as from the barriers established by custom, secular authorities, and the state. Unlike the male ideologues of *La Vanguardia* who sought to inculcate anticlericalism in women as a means of safeguarding revolutionary gains, these feminists considered religion as an institution to be overthrown on women's own behalf because of its fundamental role in obstructing women's intellectual, physical, and sexual freedom.[22]

Reproductive Rights versus the Church

The Yucatán government convened a Second Feminist Congress in November 1916. Once again, Galindo was unable to attend and sent a written address to the assembly, defending the position that had, in January, "stirred up against me a tempest that would be difficult to exaggerate, raining over my humble person a storm of insults and arrows poisoned in the wellsprings of a prudish virtue and a refined Jesuitical hypocrisy"[23] Confronting head-on the accusations of immorality leveled at her by feminists and anti-feminists alike, Galindo quotes Sor Juana Inés de la Cruz's well-known verses beginning "Hombres necios que culpáis a la mujer sin razón ...," commenting that the illustrious poet's defense of women prostitutes[24] had not raised nearly the commotion that her own words had during and after the congress. She also notes that many of the offending words were "literally copied" from works by "illustrious" sociologists, and thus the calls for censorship had targeted not only a feminist thinker but also science itself. To her credit, however, she does not shield herself with male scientists and philosophers. Rather, she expands on her previous argument with an even more forceful anticlerical bent and also cites like-minded feminists in her lengthy defense of women's right to knowledge of and control over their own bodies, as well as freedom from religious-based hypocrisy.[25]

Galindo's crusade came to an end with the Agua Prieta rebellion of 1920. That year, although relations with Carranza were strained by her support for General Pablo González[26] as his successor and *Mujer Moderna* had ceased publication the year before, she continued to collaborate with the president. Her book *La Doctrina Carranza y el acercamiento indolatino* had been published in September, and in May 1920, she was set to embark on a cultural commission to Europe and South America when the uprising put an end to these plans.[27] For Galindo, Carranza's overthrow and death constituted a personal as well as political upset. Condemning the self-serving silence with which other political figures received the change of regime, she was unable to reconcile with Obregón's group and opted to withdraw from political activity.[28]

Other feminists, however, continued to struggle not only for political and educational equality but also, more radically, for reproductive rights. Since the influence of the Church dominated all things sexual, this radical feminism was, as Galindo and her collaborators had argued in *Mujer Moderna*, necessarily anticlerical.[29] During the next few years, with the arrival in Mexico of family planning crusaders associated with Margaret Sanger and the global circulation of diverse theories regarding eugenic social engineering, the "sexual instinct" would reemerge as a crucial topic of debate, in which the worst enemy of rationalist feminist thought was the control that the Catholic Church retained over public discourse and, as a result, public policy. Sanger, of humble Irish American origins, had observed in her own family and community, and later in her work as a nurse, the precarious situation suffered by poor women as the result of numerous pregnancies and births as well as the effort to care for their abundant offspring without sufficient resources. Many women begged her for professional advice on how to avoid conception; but, since the topic of birth control was prohibited, Sanger could offer little to assuage their profound desperation.

Leaving nursing behind, Sanger took on the fight for reproductive rights, challenging the law first with the publication of the magazine *The Woman Rebel* in 1914—quickly prohibited on grounds of obscenity—and soon after with the founding of the first family planning clinic in the United States in 1916. Located in Brooklyn, New York, the clinic offered information and guidance, not actual birth control devices or products, yet authorities wasted no time in closing it and arresting Sanger. The ensuing controversy lasted for years and was marked by civil disobedience and arrests. The opposition was spearheaded by the Catholic Church, whose influence was strong in New York and other regions of the country and which was able to use the power of the police against the birth control advocates, whose crusade was considered beyond the pale of freedom of expression.

Despite the efforts of these powerful adversaries, in 1922 birth control was legalized in the United States via a Supreme Court ruling, and the American Birth Control League was founded, with Sanger as president, Anne Kennedy as executive secretary, and Juliet Barrett Rublee as vice president along with Mrs. Lewis L. Delafield. Kennedy and Rublee would soon have the chance to promote reproductive rights in Mexico as representatives of the League on an important trip to Mérida and Mexico City in August 1923.[30] Yet even before their visit, some Mexican feminists had followed in Galindo's footsteps and were promoting birth control and speaking openly about women's sexual freedom from diverse feminist, leftist, and anticlerical and anti-Catholic perspectives.

In 1922–1924, Yucatán was undoubtedly the center of radical feminist activity in Mexico. Under Elvia Carrillo Puerto's leadership, women's rights advanced, supported by the Socialist government of her brother Felipe.[31] Doctors at the state university's medical college were avid to establish birth control clinics for urban and rural women alike: hence the invitation to Sanger, who was not available but who sent Kennedy and Rublee in her place. Doctor Eduardo Urzaiz not only advocated family planning from his position at the hospital but also fantasized about it in his 1919 novel *Eugenia: esbozo novelesco de costumbres futuras*, alluded to in the introduction.[32]

Although the liberation of women from obligatory childbearing can be seen as part of a larger scheme of social engineering associated with socialist thought, it is important to emphasize the anticlerical elements of this project. Simply put, the Catholic Church functioned as the leading regulator of sexuality and reproduction and continued to define gender roles despite its nominal detachment from political power. Although the Church certainly organized women for other ends, serving as a semi-feminized space in which female-led sociability and activism could occur under the watchful eye of ecclesiastical authority, the notion of women's right to corporal and sexual self-determination automatically implied a challenge to its bio-control and thus to its dominion as an institution.[33]

A letter sent to Sanger by Roberto Haberman from Mérida is interesting in this respect. A Romanian-born, naturalized US citizen, Haberman lived in Yucatán and was a close associate of Felipe Carrillo Puerto and a frequent liaison between US leftists and Mexico.[34] On March 12, 1922, he informed Sanger about the "storm of protest that has been kicked up by the Knights of Columbus, the few remaining capitalists, and the reactionary press" regarding the governing Socialist Party's distribution of birth control pamphlets. According to Haberman, the "novelty" of this otherwise routine scandal was the response from government officials, who not only refused to suppress the pamphlet but had to print 10,000 more copies after the first run of 5,000 was immediately exhausted. The pamphlet, titled in Spanish "La regulación de la natalidad o la brújula del hogar. Medios seguros y científicos para evitar la concepción," was being translated into "the language of the Mayan Indians" and was to reach the public through teachers and "marrying officials" throughout the state. Moreover, Haberman mentioned that 100,000 copies of the pamphlet had just been printed in Mexico City, indicating that, beyond the pioneering policies of the Carrillo Puerto administration, interest in contraception was growing outside of Yucatán as well.[35]

Unsurprisingly, conservative forces voiced their opposition to family planning via what Haberman called the "reactionary press": in Mérida, the *Diario de Yucatán* led the attack on "masculinized" women whom it claimed were under the sway of foreign interests, while in Mexico City, the widely distributed newspaper *Excélsior* successfully instituted the Mother's Day holiday to be celebrated on May 10 as a bulwark against the feminist subversion of traditional Mexican values.[36] The notion that Mexican women were falling prey to misguided ideas about gender introduced by outsiders mirrors the arguments of male anticlerical revolutionaries who, as we have seen, considered women to be especially vulnerable to religious indoctrination and thus a potential "enemy in the home." Though opposed in their views on religion, both sides sought to force women into a particular role vis-à-vis the nation, either by reproducing religious values or by rejecting these in favor of secular reform; neither position recognized women's agency.[37]

Science, "Race Improvement," and Working Women's Rights

As birth control advocates struggled to break the stranglehold that religious doctrine and moralism maintained over discussions of sex and reproduction, they increasingly adopted the language of science and, in particular, that of eugenics. The topic of eugenics is, to this day, challenging to address, given its association with racism, classism, ableism, and, eventually, with genocidal policies carried out not only by the Nazis in Germany but by many twentieth-century political regimes. Although the history of eugenic thought is beyond the scope of this chapter, it is important to note, first, the broad spectrum of political positions that, before World War II, utilized eugenic language to support diverse ideas and initiatives;[38] and second, for anticlerical feminists in particular, the strategic advantage of covering the scandalous nakedness of female sexuality with the seemingly more objective—and masculine—fig leaf of science.

Illuminating in this regard is Esperanza Velázquez Bringas's lecture *La limitación racional de la familia como mejoramiento del proletariado y de la raza* (The rational limitation of the family as improvement of the proletariat and the race).[39] The talk, sponsored by the Liga de Maestros Racionalistas Francisco Ferrer Guardia, was presented to the Liga Feminista Rita Cetina Gutiérrez on February 22, 1922—only three weeks after

Felipe Carrillo Puerto's inauguration as governor. As Monique Lemaître notes, the location of the feminist league's headquarters in Mérida facilitated collaboration between Elvia Carrillo Puerto and her brother's administration; yet, far from simply following a party line, the group developed projects with sex workers and rural women and struggled against the often conservative views of male comrades regarding questions of gender.[40] Velázquez Bringas's address to Yucatec women took place in the context of this activist effervescence.

Velázquez Bringas, born in 1899 in Orizaba, Veracruz, studied law in Mérida and, by 1922, had a promising career as a journalist and educator; a few years later, she would be in charge of the Secretariat of Public Education's library department and director of the National Library.[41] Like Hermila Galindo, she was adept at working within male-dominated political structures and used her talents and relationships with political figures to advocate for women's rights. The published version of her talk gives her the title of "señorita profesora," continuing the association between feminism and the teaching profession that had defined the two feminist congresses, in which Velázquez Bringas had also participated.[42] The text itself places her as an intellectual and purveyor of "advanced" ideas; and these, she explains in her introduction, are anticlerical almost by definition:

> As soon as a new theory of social organization, a new tendency, appears, an alarmed society hurls anathemas and—spurred on generally by the clerics who aid capitalism in oppressing it—reaches the point of persecutions. However, little by little, comes familiarity with that which before was a new idea, adepts emerge, and [the idea] comes to serve as the basis for many others.[43]

Velázquez Bringas goes on to position herself as the bearer of revolutionary thought: one who does not seek applause and, indeed, expects a certain degree of disgust and rejection. Her aim is to aid women in becoming "physically, politically and morally" independent (física, política y moralmente); key elements of this process include an understanding of love without stigmas, formulas, or cowardice, and of maternity as a choice rather than an obligation.[44] In this context, she places the "betterment of the race" as a progressive and scientifically sound principle, free of religious prejudice: "My arguments are based on the important problem of scientific procreation, of family limitation not only from the point of view of socioeconomic reform, but also from the point of view of Eugenics."[45]

This capital-E Eugenics, whose scientific foundation she emphasizes by way of citation in subsequent paragraphs, is aimed at the well-being of the proletariat and of women; its contribution to the latter is spelled out as "the means to avoid conception" (los medios para prevenir la concepción), a notion she recognizes as both "audacious" and necessary for women's progress: "What we seek is that woman is no longer an incubator," but rather that she has a child "when she wants one, when she is able to support and educate one."[46] Echoing Sanger's observations from the health care field, she laments the fate of women who must bear many children as a social and intimate obligation, fulfilling the desires of their mates with little regard for their own well-being or for the couple's ability to provide healthy conditions for their offspring.

While Velázquez Bringas's speech seems to echo the judgmental aspect of eugenics discourse insofar as it assumes external knowledge of what is desirable or undesirable for proletarian mothers as a whole, her concern is less for the "betterment of the race" than for the quality of human relations enjoyed or suffered by women and their children.[47] Birth control is a means of liberation; the examples she cites of Holland and New Zealand, however distant, are meant to point the way toward freedom for Yucatec women as well.

In this text, Velázquez Bringas invokes international thinkers, all of whom except Margaret Sanger are male, and in doing so establishes the legitimacy of her proposal, utilizing the discourse of science to combat the Church and its hold over women's bodies. Interestingly, her final words are themselves evangelical in tone: "Woman: free yourself and ascend the mountain, for if the path to your redemption is heavy, in exchange, there on the mountaintop, you will see the light of a new East!"[48] In this new dawn, women are free to choose their partners and decide whether to have sexual relations. What is more, they will use the science of contraception, regardless of whether such relations will lead to childbearing. Citing a British doctor on the subject, she states emphatically that "the Church no longer has anything to say about it."[49]

Using Velázquez Bringas's speech as an example, Sarah A. Buck notes that feminist birth control advocates often shared with other social reformers "the same contradictory mixture of sympathy for the proletariat alongside a middle-class mentality"—evidenced, perhaps, by an exaggerated sense of civic duty and an equally exaggerated appeal to science as an unproblematic answer to social ills.[50] Yet despite this slippage between advocacy and imposition, or what Buck calls the juxtaposition of "democratic" claims for women's freedoms with "authoritarian recipes" in which women are recipients of social intervention,[51] Velázquez Bringas's rhetoric in fact recognizes women as subjects and calls on them as participants in their own liberation.

Moreover, her fervent conclusion, like Galindo's 1916 speech that cited the egalitarian teachings of Christ while rejecting the Church and its moralist dogma, hints at the possibility of a feminist, anticlerical, and anti-Catholic spirituality. Although the texts in question seem to appeal mainly to science and social engineering while deploying religiosity as a discursive strategy, feminist anticlericalism, often found in the same neighborhood as Spiritualism, Theosophy, and other alternative philosophies of the time, suggests a plausible configuration of the "religious dimension" that Matthew Butler encourages us to examine in the revolutionary period.[52]

The Gendered Reception of Feminism and Anticlericalism

The Pan-American Women's Conference held in Mexico City in May 1923 put these radical ideas to the test. As Ana Lau Jaiven notes, the views espoused by the Yucatec women were poorly received by other delegations; as in 1916, topics like sex education, free love, divorce, and birth control proved to be taboo even among feminists who would have preferred to concentrate on other matters, such as educational and economic equality.[53] Nevertheless, the existence of female sexuality, as the unavoidable underpinning of these issues, had escaped the secrecy of the confessional and become a subject of public, political discussion. Fernanda Núñez Becerra suggests that the Catholic Church's virulent counter-campaigning among women constituted a "moral crusade" whose success contributed to the refusal on the part of successive revolutionary governments to grant voting rights to the female half of the population.[54]

Although radical feminists were censored by their peers for their daring treatment of taboo subjects such as the sexual instinct, they, or rather, all feminists, were portrayed in the media as mannish and asexual. Press coverage of the 1923 congress took the form of caricature: newspapers from *Excélsior* to *El Universal Ilustrado* "reported" on the event as a kind of three-ring circus featuring women clowns playing at politics. Predictably, these accounts cited personal unattractiveness as the likely motivation for women's interest in this otherwise masculine sphere. As the satirical poet "Sánchez Filmador" wrote in *El Universal Ilustrado*: "Feminism has been and is refuge / of ugly women and spinsters / and if it is true that among the delegates / there are now actually / pretty little women, / they must at least be in despair."⁵⁵ Since photos show Elvia Carrillo Puerto and Esperanza Velázquez Bringas, among others, as stunning young women obviously concerned with fashion and appearance, we can only assume that their "despair" resulted from frivolous press coverage, fellow feminists' rejection of their radical proposals, and the difficulty of moving the Revolution beyond the rules and assumptions of patriarchy.

As mentioned earlier, press criticism of feminism often accused women of following foreign fads said to be out of place in the Mexican context. It is thus interesting to review the reception of Spanish feminist Belén de Sárraga in the same press. De Sárraga, as a Spiritualist, Freemason, anarchist, and freethinker, had first visited Mexico at the invitation of Francisco I. Madero. De Sárraga published in 1914 *El clericalismo en América a través de un continente*, a work that advocated women's education and independence but, as María Teresa Fernández Aceves points out, showed little understanding of Mexican popular religiosity and its role—for example, in the Zapatista movement, which de Sárraga considered to be "fanatically Catholic" and thus incompatible with modernity.⁵⁶

De Sárraga's speaking tours during the early 1910s and again in the 1920s—in alliance with candidate and then president Plutarco Elías Calles—were often addressed to audiences of organized workers, and anticlericalism and anti-Catholicism were prominent themes. According to Fernández Aceves, little is known about her links, if any, to Mexican feminists, the impact of her ideas, or the readership of her magazine *Rumbos Nuevos*, published in Mexico during 1925–1927.⁵⁷ What seems clear is that, while de Sárraga's feminism horrified Catholic organizations and their media, the mainstream press viewed her as a kind of honorary man, due to her "masculine" rhetorical talent: "Her public anticlerical actions and performances presented her as very close to the practices of men, except that she was a woman."⁵⁸ While her intention was probably not to set herself apart from Mexican women, press coverage worked to do just that.

In 1922, Stridentist (*estridentista*) writer and journalist Arqueles Vela interviewed de Sárraga for *El Universal Ilustrado*. The interview was titled "El feminismo antifeminista de Belém [sic] de Sárraga"; its opening paragraphs were devoted to distinguishing its subject from other women and, in particular, from other feminists. Vela, prefiguring the views of his narrator in *La Señorita Etcétera*, writes that "feminism in women was a pose. A rebellious pose! Yes. But nothing more than a pose."⁵⁹ De Sárraga, in contrast, rouses in him "an unusual feeling. Her words, her ideas, don't have the Soviet smoke nor the telephonic sound of feminism . . . She doesn't get stirred up. She doesn't get excited. She is serene. [. . .] She is very much a woman."[60] While superficially reviewing de Sárraga's ideas and trajectory, Vela's main interest is his own positive reaction, which he can only justify by differentiating her from others of her ilk.

This interview, like much of the reception of de Sárraga by the Mexican press, contrasts with the latter's usual treatment of feminism. A year later, during the Pan-American Congress, the aforementioned poem by "Sánchez Filmador" would be accompanied by an emblematic cartoon of a woman chasing a man and wielding an axe labeled "feminismo." Feminists as man-hating, resentful spinsters surely had little to say about the "sexual instinct," yet their discussion of birth control, which Megan Threlkeld calls "by far the most contentious issue at the conference," received a disproportionate amount of media attention: "Most of the delegates, in fact, did not support birth control, but that did not stop newspapers in Mexico City from labeling the congress as radical."[61] To make matters worse, the "Pan-American" aspect of the event was difficult to sustain, given the broad differences between US, Mexican, and other Latin American contexts.

Mexican women's road to citizenship was impeded by both clerical and male-defined anticlerical ideology. Conservatives lambasted feminists for betraying the "natural" virtues of Mexican womanhood, preaching free love and, as educators, seeking to impose their scandalous ideas on the nation's children. Cultural radicals like Vela, on the other hand, dismissed their movement as a pose, while working to keep discussion on a superficial and personal level, thus denying feminism's political potency. For male anticlerical ideologues, meanwhile, women—understood as nonfeminist—remained under the thumb of the priests, their gullible minds plagued by superstition, despite the occasional erudite exception such as de Sárraga. How could this group be trusted with the vote?

Final Thoughts

Although not all feminists of the Mexican Revolution challenged the Church nor raised issues pertaining to female sexuality, this brief survey of some who did both indicates that feminist anti-Catholicism, seemingly aligned with the anticlerical ideas of male-led movements and political forces, also included a gendered dimension that the latter forces lacked. While both feminist and nonfeminist anticlericalism portrayed women as particularly vulnerable targets of reactionary doctrine, thinkers such as Galindo and Velázquez Bringas addressed women as subjects and attributed their vulnerability to the lack of education and equal opportunity, rather than to any particularly feminine condition.[62] They encouraged women to overthrow religious domination not only to improve society as scientifically informed caregivers, workers, and citizens but also for their own physical, mental, and spiritual liberation. This liberation included the notion of motherhood as a choice, as well as the enjoyment of a healthy, equally voluntary sexuality.

The language of these early twentieth-century feminists may seem timid by today's standards to the extent that the boundaries of the scandalous have stretched considerably. Yet their proposals are in many ways contemporary: many of the battles of that time have yet to be won, including that of reproductive freedom. While birth control is widely if tacitly accepted even among practicing Catholics, the interruption of pregnancy is a volatile issue, and the language used to oppose it often reveals misogynist assumptions little different and perhaps more violent than those of the past. The decriminalization of abortion in Mexico City in 2007, as the culmination of prolonged feminist struggle, led many states to strengthen their anti-abortion laws, which pro-choice movements have only begun to dismantle.[63] Along with abortion, feminicide, homophobia, transphobia, sexual harassment, discrimination, and violence are problems around which the voices of the feminists of yesteryear find echoes, despite the achievement of women's political rights in the mid-twentieth century.

In 2019, for example, the archbishop of Xalapa, Veracruz, Hipólito Reyes Larios, responded to March 8 feminist mobilizations by complaining that "today most women dress like men; one sees them, there is no more glamour, instead they look like any little man with their jeans, with their cell phone walking down the street and with whatever they put on."[64] With this speech, which became national news and a topic of ridicule in social media, the archbishop not only criticized a style of dress but also questioned the right of women to be in the street and to disregard the male gaze in their choices of self-expression, a point of view closely related to his conservative positions on other issues, such as abortion, gay rights, and sexuality in general.

However "anachronistic," the views of the archbishop and the institution he represented have managed to dominate public debate on reproductive freedom in Mexico and much of Latin America. In the face of this ecclesiastical moralism, it is clear that the anticlerical emphasis of feminist struggle has not lost its relevance in the twenty-first century. On the contrary, just as it was a hundred years ago, deconstructing the religious and secular discourses that promote and justify the conversion of girls and women into objects, merchandise, and victims remains a pressing task for present-day feminist praxis.

Notes

1. Although Protestantism and other religions certainly existed in Mexico, the preponderance of Catholicism, even after the Liberal reforms of the nineteenth century (and, to a certain extent, to this day), made the Catholic Church and its ideologues the chief targets of feminist and other anticlericalisms.
2. Historical research on women in twentieth-century Mexican history, once limited to a handful of documents, is now a burgeoning subfield. Important works include: Olcott, *Revolutionary Women*; Olcott et al., *Sex in Revolution*; Lamas, *Miradas feministas sobre las mexicanas del siglo XX*; Smith, *Gender and the Mexican Revolution*; Espinosa Damián and Lau Jaiven, *Un fantasma recorre el siglo*; Tuñón, *Voces a las mujeres*, an annotated compilation of primary sources; Fernández Aceves, *Mujeres en el cambio social en el siglo XX mexicano*; Porter and Fernández Aceves, *Género en la encrucijada de la historia social y cultural de México*; Lau Jaiven and Mc Phail Fanger, *Rupturas y continuidades*; and Núñez Becerra and Ortiz, *La osadía se viste de mujer*, among others. Further contributions include monographs on specific women, groups, and sectors, such as Fowler-Salamini's *Working Women* or Castañeda López and Rodríguez de Romo's *Pioneras de la medicina Mexicana en la UNAM*, as well as others cited elsewhere in this chapter. The impossibility of exhausting the literature in a note itself indicates the dynamism of the topic.
3. Macías, *Contra viento y marea*, 52. This book originally appeared in English as *Against All Odds: The Feminist Movement in Mexico to 1940* (Westport, CT: Greenwood, 1982).
4. Galindo's training and subsequent employment as an office worker, one of few professionalized fields open to women, anticipates the phenomenon studied by Susie S. Porter of early twentieth-century office work as a route to economic and intellectual emancipation for many women. See Porter, *From Angel to Office Worker*.
5. "XI. LLEVAR A LA CONCIENCIA DE LA MUJER MEXICANA, LA CONVICCIÓN DE SU DEBER EN ESTE MOMENTO HISTÓRICO—nosotros podemos obtener todas las conquistas imaginables, pero si no conquistamos la inteligencia de la mujer, tendremos siempre un enemigo dentro de nuestra propia casa." "Programa," 2.
6. Cited in Valles Ruiz, *El discurso*, 74.
7. Valles Ruiz, *El discurso*, 85–88.
8. "Emanciparse de la férrea tutela clerical que es la más oprobiosa y más cruel, puesto que el sacerdote la domina moral y físicamente, es decir, embota a la mujer y adormece sus facultades, todas con la ventajosa arma de la fe, de la leyenda mentirosa de 'cree y te salvarás' o la tremenda de 'cree o te mato.'" Cited in Valles Ruiz, 77.

9. "¿Cuáles son los medios sociales que deben emplearse para manumitir a la mujer del yugo de las tradiciones?" Alvarado, "Convocatoria," 180.
10. Galindo, "La mujer en el porvenir," 182–91.
11. Galindo, 184.
12. The notion of religion in this and other feminist texts is inseparable from the Catholic Church because of its evident social and political power, even when Catholicism is not explicitly singled out for critique. While atheism prevailed among anarchists and Communists, many thinkers of the period viewed Protestantism as a possible alternative for Mexico; see the chapters by Dalton and Jantzen in this book.
13. "¡Aunque sea triste decirlo, el hombre nace animal y la mujer hembra!" Galindo, "La mujer en el porvenir," 186.
14. "Es que el instinto sexual impera de tal suerte en la mujer y con tan irresistibles resortes, que ningún artificio hipócrita es capaz de destruir, modificar o refrenar." Galindo, 187.
15. "Relegada al desprecio social, truncado su porvenir y arrojada al abismo de la desesperación, de la miseria, de la locura o del suicidio." Galindo, 190.
16. "Generalmente se procura en la mujer el desarrollo de lo que se llama vida del corazón y del alma, mientras se descuide y omite el desarrollo de su razón. Resulta de esto que padece una hipertrofia de vida intelectual espiritual y es más accesible a todas las creencias religiosas." Galindo, 188.
17. Galindo, 191.
18. The Constitutional Convention of 1916–1917 provides another example of divergence between masculine anticlericalism and that of feminists such as Galindo. As described by Adrian A. Bantjes, the debate over article 24, on religious freedom, "was conducted in an atmosphere of risqué, boisterous mockery"; male delegates invoked stereotypes of lusty priests and revealed an obsession with female virginity and the fidelity of married women, both of which—given women's lack of agency—inevitably fell to ruin in the confessional (Bantjes, "Saints," 142.
19. However, it is wise to remember that legend does not always correspond fully to fact. As historian Michael Ducey pointed out when I presented a version of this chapter at the SECOLAS conference in Oaxaca in 2019, at any public event, the reactions that go on record are those that are expressed openly, not those that people choose to keep to themselves, as may have been the case for at least a few women at the Yucatán congress.
20. Smith, 30, citing Francesca Miller's 1991 *Latin American Women and the Search for Social Justice* and Shirlene Soto's 1990 *Emergence of the Modern Mexican Woman*. One of the earliest accounts and a likely secondary source for the others is Macías in *Against All Odds* (*Contra viento y marea*, 99–100).

21. "Un requisito esencial o indispensable para que la mujer pueda acabar con las tradiciones que gravitan sobre ella es que sea libre." "Dictamen de la Comisión que estudió el Primer Tema," 195.
22. It is interesting to note that Matilde Montoya, the first woman to win the right to practice professional medicine in Mexico (in 1887) and whose years of experience in women's ob-gyn health care no doubt influenced her thinking on reproductive and sexual matters, defended Galindo's position at the congress. Her opinions were published in *Mujer Moderna* in its June issue (Valles Ruíz, *El discurso*, 80–81. On Montoya, see Castañeda López and Rodríguez de Romo, *Pioneras de la medicina mexicana*, 35–38 and 161–64.)
23. "Levantó en contra mía una tempestad difícil de ponderar, hacienda llover sobre mi humilde personalidad una tempestad de dicterios y saetas envenenadas en los manantiales de una virtud gazmoña y de una refinada hipocresía jesuítica." Galindo, "Ponencia de Hermila [Galindo] para el Segundo Congreso Feminista de Yucatán," 187.
24. "¿Quién será más de culpar / Aunque cualquiera mal haga: / La que peca por la paga / O el que paga por pecar?" in Galindo, "Ponencia," 189.
25. Read at the congress by Elena Torres, Galindo's essay was also published in *Mujer Moderna* in November 1916.
26. The 11 Mar. 1917 issue of *Mujer Moderna* featured a photo of González on its cover. The oxymoronic juxtaposition of strongmen like González and Carranza with the weekly's feminine name and logo seems not to have troubled Galindo, whose loyalty to Constitutionalism and its leaders was as much a part of her ideology as feminism. See Valles Ruiz, *El discurso*, 95–134, and *Sol de libertad*, 123–39.
27. Valles Ruiz notes that, in October 1920, the newly installed government demanded return, within six days, of 500 pesos that she had received in April as an advance for this mission, apparently a vindictive gesture against one of Carranza's faithful (*Sol de libertad*, 144–45).
28. Valles Ruiz relates that after Carranza's death, Galindo left politics and took up painting; in 1923, she married businessman and amateur opera singer Miguel Enríquez Topete and later painted portraits of her husband and Carranza that hung in her home at the time of her death in 1954 (*Sol de libertad*, 146).
29. Salomé Carranza, a Veracruz activist unrelated to the Constitutionalist leader, was one of Galindo's closest collaborators and equally radical in her critique of the church as the "biggest enemy of woman and her emancipation" (Valles Ruíz, *El discurso*, 75).
30. See Rashkin, "Conexiones feministas transnacionales," 86–91.
31. On Carrillo Puerto, see Lemaître's wonderful short biography, *Elvia Carrillo Puerto*.
32. A second version of this novel was edited by the Universidad de Yucatán in 1947 and reprinted by the same (now Universidad Autónoma de Yucatán) in 2002.

33. That Catholic women organized both in defense of the church and in defense of women's rights from an explicitly Catholic subject position is beyond dispute. "To maintain that women were tools of the clergy is to deny them agency," writes Bantjes ("Saints," 151), and historians have found much evidence to the contrary. Jean Meyer considers that women played a decisive role in the Cristero conflict of the 1920s and mentions the 1928 Cristero Plan de los Altos de Jalisco that advocates women's right to vote ("An Idea of Mexico," 288). María Teresa Fernández Aceves's work (such as "Guadalajaran Women and the Construction of National Identity" in the same volume, and *Mujeres en el cambio social*) shows how Jalisco women were protagonists in both Catholic and secular organizing, while Jocelyn Olcott documents similar participation in Michoacán, noting that female-led protests confounded authorities who could not conceive of women as self-directed agents (*Revolutionary Women*, 72). Militant Catholic women engaged in violence against teachers promoting secular education in the countryside during the Cárdenas administration, leading some feminists to acknowledge that the church had, in fact, long served as a supportive space for women that would need to be substituted if defanaticization was to succeed (Olcott, *Revolutionary Women*, 101–2). While such discussions emerged slightly after the period in question here, the recognition of women's agency is precisely what distinguishes feminist thinkers like Galindo and Salomé Carranza from their male revolutionary counterparts.
34. Delpar, *Enormous Vogue of Things Mexican*, 21–23.
35. Robert Haberman to Margaret Sanger, 12 Mar. 1922. Margaret Sanger Papers, Library of Congress.
36. Smith, *Gender and the Mexican Revolution*, 109; Buck, "El control de la natalidad y el día de la madre," 34.
37. Again, it is important to emphasize that Catholic women were in fact active subjects who often organized for social change on their own terms during this period. While the activities of the Unión de Damas Católicas Mexicanas and other organizations are beyond the scope of this chapter, they have been explored by scholars such as Patience A. Schell in books and articles including "Of the Sublime Mission," 99–123.
38. Alisa Klaus addresses the complex relationship between eugenic thinking and maternal and child welfare campaigns in "Depopulation and Race Suicide." On eugenics in Mexico and Latin America, see Stepan's *"Hour of Eugenics"*; Luz Suárez and López Guazo's *Eugenesia y racismo en México*; and Antebi's *Embodied Archive*.
39. Buck discusses this text at the beginning of "El control de la natalidad" (9–11), as does Ortiz Rangel in "Feminismo y Eugenesia in México," 47–49.
40. Lemaître, *Elvia Carrillo Puerto*, 80.
41. Hernández Carballido, "Esperanza Velázquez Bringas."

42. Ortega Castillo, "Esperanza Velázquez Bringas." This article incorrectly credits Velázquez Bringas with having been the first woman to serve on the Supreme Court, a breakthrough achieved by María Cristina Salmorán de Tamayo in 1961. In recent years, enthusiastic but erroneous reporting about women's history is common; Cecilia Alfaro Gómez points out that, while much material exists regarding aspects of Velázquez Bringas´s life, no serious study has been published of her participation in the public sphere and abundant contribution to various fields ("Puericultura, higiene y control natal, 109).
43. "Tan pronto como presenta una nueva teoría de organización social, una nueva tendencia, la sociedad alarmada lanza anatemas y azuzada generalmente por los clérigos que ayuda al capitalismo a oprimirla, llegan hasta las persecuciones. Mas luego, poco a poco llegar la familiaridad con la que antes era nueva idea, principian los adeptos y está viene a servir de base para otras muchas." Velázquez Bringas, *La limitación racional*, 4.
44. Velázquez Bringas, 4.
45. "Mis argumentos se basan en el importante problema de la procreación científica, de la limitación de la familia no solamente desde el punto de vista de la reforma económico-social, sino desde el punto de vista de la Eugenia." Velázquez Bringas, 5.
46. "Lo que queremos es que la mujer deje de ser una incubadora, y sea una mujer que tenga un hijo cuando lo desee, cuando esté en condiciones de sostenerlo y educarlo." Velázquez Bringas, 6.
47. Ortiz Rangel offers a similar reading of Velázquez Bringas in "Feminismo y Eugenesia," 49.
48. "Mujer: libértate y asciende a la montaña, que si el camino de tu redención es pesado, en cambio allá en la cima, verás la luz de un nuevo Oriente!" Velázquez Bringas, *La limitación racional*, 9.
49. Velázquez Bringas, 9.
50. "La misma mezcla contradictoria de simpatías hacia el proletariado, junto con una mentalidad de clase media." Buck, "El control de la natalidad," 13.
51. Buck, 13.
52. Butler, "Revolution in Spirit," 4.
53. Lau Jaiven, "Mujeres, feminismo y sufragio en los años veinte," 80–83. Lau Jaiven, citing fellow historians Gabriela Cano and Julia Tuñón, points out that delegates may have strategically assumed the role of model housewives and mothers as a means of countering a hostile press and defusing the threat implied by female suffrage (83).

54. Núñez Becerra, "Márgenes del pudor," 38–39.
55. "El feminismo es y ha sido refugio / de feas y quedadas y si es verdad que entre las delegadas / ahora hay mujercitas /en realidad bonitas, / han de ser cuando menos despechadas." "Sánchez Filmador," "Feminismo," *El Universal Ilustrado*, 31 May 1923, 19.
56. Fernández Aceves, *Mujeres*, 98.
57. Fernández Aceves, 130.
58. "Sus acciones públicas anticlericales y performances la presentaban muy cercana a las practices de los hombres, pero era una mujer." Fernández Aceves, 108.
59. "El feminismo en las mujeres era una 'pose.' ¡Una 'pose rebelde! Sí. Pero no pasaba de ser una 'pose.'" Vela, "El feminismo antifeminista," 27. *La Señorita Etcétera*, published that same year in the newspaper's Novela Semanal series, is a short, vigorous work of avant-garde fiction that interrogates various dilemmas related to urban modernity, using the female title figure as object and mirror, more than subject, of these dilemmas. This elusive character at one point adopts feminism and syndicalism as a pose, related conceptually to the chatter of elegant beauty salons (24).
60. "Una emoción inédita. Sus palabras, sus ideas, no tienen ni el humo soviético, ni el sonido telefónico del feminismo . . . No se exalta. No se emociona. Es serena. (. . .) Es muy mujer." "Vela, "El feminismo antifeminista," 27. I thank Rose Corral for bringing this interview to my attention.
61. Threlkeld, *Pan-American Women*, 85.
62. A broader study would include Elvia Carrillo Puerto, Elena Torres, and perhaps Communist Party members such as Cuca García, among others; the impact of Alexandra Kollontai's stint as Soviet ambassador in Mexico would also be of interest, given her important writings on women and sexuality.
63. The Mexican Supreme Court decriminalized abortion in September 2021 in a landmark ruling for the state of Coahuila that set a precedent for the rest of the country. Yet countrywide implementation has followed only slowly; in March 2022, Sinaloa became the seventh state to legalize abortion, after Mexico City, Oaxaca, Hidalgo, Veracruz, Baja California, and Coahuila, meaning that twenty-five states have yet to respond to the national ruling.
64. "Hoy la mayoría de las mujeres se visten como varones, las ve uno, ya no hay glamour, sino que ahora parecen como cualquier varoncito con sus pantalones de mezclilla, con su teléfono celular caminando por la calle y con lo que se pueden poner." López, "Arzobispo de Xalapa critica a mujeres que visten 'como varoncitos.'"

Works Cited

Alfaro Gómez, Cecilia. "Puericultura, higiene y control natal. La visión de Esperanza Velázquez Bringas sobre el cuidado materno-infantil en México, 1919–1922." *Historia Autónoma*, no. 1 (September 2012): 107–19.

Alvarado, Salvador. "Convocatoria." 1916. In *Voces a las mujeres. Antología del pensamiento feminista mexicano, 1873–1953*, edited by Julia Tuñon, 178–82. Mexico City: Universidad Autónoma de la Ciudad de México, 2011.

Antebi, Susan. *Embodied Archive: Disability in Post-Revolutionary Mexican Cultural Production*. Ann Arbor: University of Michigan, 2021.

Bantjes, Adrian A. "Saints, Sinners, and State Formation." In *The Eagle and the Virgin: Nation and Cultural Revolution in Mexico, 1920–1940*, edited by Mary Kay Vaughn and Stephen E. Lewis, 137–56. Durham, NC: Duke University Press, 2006.

Buck, Sarah A. "El control de la natalidad y el día de la madre: política feminista y reaccionaria en México, 1922–1923." *Signos Históricos* no. 5 (January-June 2001): 9–53.

Butler, Matthew. "A Revolution in Spirit? Mexico, 1910–1940." In *Faith and Impiety in Revolutionary Mexico*, edited by Matthew Butler, 1–20. New York: Palgrave Macmillan, 2007.

Castañeda López, Gabriela, and Ana Cecilia Rodríguez de Romo. *Pioneras de la medicina Mexicana en la UNAM: del Porfiriato al Nuevo regimen, 1887–1936*. Mexico City: UNAM/Díaz de Santos, 2010.

Delpar, Helen. *The Enormous Vogue of Things Mexican. Cultural Relations between the United States and Mexico, 1920–1935*. Tuscaloosa: University of Alabama Press, 1992.

"Dictamen de la Comisión que estudió el Primer Tema." 1916. In *Voces a las mujeres. Antología del pensamiento feminista mexicano, 1873–1953*, edited by Julia Tuñon, 191–96. Mexico City: Universidad Autónoma de la Ciudad de México, 2011.

Espinosa Damián, Gisela, and Ana Lau Jaiven, eds. *Un fantasma recorre el siglo. Luchas feministas en México, 1910–2010*. Mexico City: UAM/Itaca/Conacyt/Ecosur, 2011.

Fernández Aceves, Maria Teresa. *Mujeres en el cambio social en el siglo XX mexicano*. Mexico City: Siglo XXI/CIESAS, 2014.

———. "Guadalajaran Women and the Construction of National Identity." In *The Eagle and the Virgin: Nation and Cultural Revolution in Mexico, 1920–1940*, edited by Mary Kay Vaughn and Stephen E. Lewis, 297–313. Durham, NC: Duke University Press, 2006.

Fowler-Salamini, Heather. *Working Women, Entrepreneurs, and the Mexican Revolution: The Coffee Culture of Córdoba, Veracruz.* Lincoln: University of Nebraska Press, 2013.
Galindo, Hermila. "La mujer en el porvenir." 1916. In *Voces a las mujeres. Antología del pensamiento feminista mexicano, 1873–1953,* edited by Julia Tuñon, 182–91.
———. "Ponencia de Hermila [Galindo] para el Segundo Congreso Feminista de Yucatán." 1916. In *Sol de libertad. Hermila Galindo: Feminista, constitucionalista y primera censora legislativa en México,* by Rosa María Valles Ruiz, 187–225. Durango: Instituto Cultural del Estado de Durango, 2010. Originally published in *Mujer Moderna,* November 1916.
Hernández Carballido, Elina. "Esperanza Velázquez Bringas." *Enciclopedia de la Literatura en México.* May 15, 2018. http://www.elem.mx/autor/datos/117920. Accessed May 22, 2024.
Klaus, Alisa. "Depopulation and Race Suicide: Maternalism and Pronatalist Ideologies in France and the United States." In *Mothers of a New World: Maternalist Politics and the Origins of Welfare States,* edited by Seth Koven and Sonya Michel, 188–212. New York: Routledge, 1993.
Lamas, Marta, ed. *Miradas feministas sobre las mexicanas del siglo XX.* Mexico City: Fondo de Cultura Económica, 2007.
Lau Jaiven, Ana. "Mujeres, feminismo y sufragio en los años veinte." In *Un fantasma recorre el siglo. Luchas feministas en México, 1910–2010,* edited by Gisela Espinosa Damián and Ana Lau Jaiven, 80–83. Mexico City: UAM/Itaca/Conacyt/Ecosur, 2011.
Lau Jaiven, Ana, and Elsie Mc Phail Fanger, eds. *Rupturas y continuidades. Historias y biografías de mujeres.* Mexico City: UAM Xochimilco, 2018.
Lemaître, Monique J. *Elvia Carrillo Puerto. La Monja Roja del Mayab.* Monterrey: Castillo, 1998.
López, Lourdes. "Arzobispo de Xalapa critica a mujeres que visten 'como varoncitos.'" *Excélsior,* March 10, 2019. https://www.excelsior.com.mx/nacional/arzobispo-de-xalapa-critica-a-mujeres-que-visten-como-varoncitos/1301057.
Macías, Anna. *Contra viento y marea. El movimiento feminista en México hasta 1940.* Translated by María Irene Artigas. Mexico City: Programa Universitario de Estudios de Género, Universidad Nacional Autónoma de México, 2002. Originally published as *Against All Odds: The Feminist Movement in Mexico to 1940.* Westport, CT: Greenwood, 1982.
Margaret Sanger Papers. Library of Congress, Washington, DC.
Meyer, Jean. "An Idea of Mexico: Catholics in the Revolution." In *The Eagle and the Virgin: Nation and Cultural Revolution in Mexico, 1920–1940,* edited by Mary Kay Vaughn and Stephen E. Lewis, 281–96. Durham, NC: Duke University Press, 2006.

Núñez Becerra, Fernanda, and Rina Ortiz, eds. *La osadía se viste de mujer. En el centenario de un año crucial, 1917.* Mexico City: Secretaría de Cultura/INAH, 2019.

Núñez Becerra, Fernanda. "Márgenes del pudor: moral sexual en tiempos de la mujer moderna." In *La osadía se viste de mujer. En el centenario de un año crucial, 1917,* edited by Fernanda Núñez Becerra and Rina Ortiz, 21–50. Mexico City: Secretaría de Cultura/INAH, 2019.

Olcott, Jocelyn. *Revolutionary Women in Postrevolutionary Mexico.* Durham, NC: Duke University Press, 2005.

Olcott, Jocelyn, Mary Kay Vaughn, and Gabriela Cano, eds. *Sex in Revolution: Gender, Politics, and Power in Modern Mexico.* Durham, NC: Duke University Press, 2006.

Ortega Castillo, Héctor E. "Esperanza Velázquez Bringas: Feminista y letrada." *El Mundo,* December 19, 2020. https://www.diarioelmundo.com.mx/index.php/2020/12/19/esperanza-velazquez-bringas-feminista-y-letrada/

Ortiz Rangel, Andrea. "Feminismo y Eugenesia in México. Articulaciones posrevolucionarias en Yucatán, Veracruz y Tabasco, 1915–1935." Master's thesis, El Colegio de México, 2016.

Porter, Susie S. *From Angel to Office Worker: Middle-Class Identity and Female Consciousness in Mexico, 1890–1950.* Lincoln: University of Nebraska Press, 2018.

Porter, Susie S., and Maria Teresa Fernández Aceves, eds. *Género en la encrucijada de la historia social y cultural de México.* Zamora: El Colegio de Michoacán/CIESAS, 2015.

"Programa." *La Vanguardia,* April 15, 1915.

Rashkin, Elissa. "Conexiones feministas transnacionales. Juliet Barrett Rublee en México." In *La osadía se viste de mujer. En el centenario de un año crucial, 1917,* edited by Fernanda Nuñez Becerra and Rina Ortiz, 73–105. Mexico City: Secretaría de Cultura/INAH, 1919.

Schell, Patience A. "Of the Sublime Mission of Mothers and Families: The Union of Mexican Catholic Ladies in Revolutionary Mexico." In *The Women's Revolution in Mexico, 1900–1953,* edited by Stephanie E. Mitchell and Patience A. Schell, 99–123. Lanham, MD: Rowman and Littlefield, 2007.

Smith, Stephanie J. *Gender and the Mexican Revolution: Yucatán Women and the Realities of Patriarchy.* Chapel Hill: University of North Carolina Press, 2009.

Stepan, Nancy Leys. *"The Hour of Eugenics": Race, Gender, and Nation in Latin America.* Ithaca, NY: Cornell, 1992.

Suárez y López Guazo, Laura. *Eugenesia y racismo en México.* Mexico City: Universidad Autónoma de la Ciudad de México, 2005.

Threlkeld, Megan. *Pan-American Women: U. S. Internationalists and Revolutionary Mexico.* Philadelphia: University of Pennsylvania Press, 2014.

Tuñon, Julia, ed. *Voces a las mujeres. Antología del pensamiento feminista mexicano, 1873–1953*. Mexico City: Universidad Autónoma de la Ciudad de México, 2011.

Urzaiz, Eduardo. *Eugenia: esbozo novelesco de costumbres futuras* [1919]. Mérida: Universidad Autónoma de Yucatán, 2002.

Valles Ruiz, Rosa María. *El discurso en* Mujer Moderna: *primera revista feminista del siglo XX en México, 1915–1919*. Mexico City: Universidad Autónoma del Estado de Hidalgo y Miguel Ángel Porrúa, 2017.

———. *Sol de libertad. Hermila Galindo: Feminista, constitucionalista y primera censora legislativa en México*. Durango: Instituto Cultural del Estado de Durango, 2010.

Vela, Arqueles. "El feminismo antifeminista de Belém de Sárraga." *El Universal Ilustrado*, July 6, 1922.

———. *La Señorita Etcétera*. La Novela Semanal de *El Universal Ilustrado*, December 14, 1922. Facsimile ed.: Rose Corral, ed. Mexico City: El Colegio de México, 2020.

Velázquez Bringas, Esperanza. *La limitación Racional de la Familia como Mejoramiento del Proletariado y de la Raza*. Mérida: Biblioteca de la Liga de Maestros Racionalistas Francisco Ferrer Guardia, Imp. Mayab, 1922.

CHAPTER FIVE

"Desfanatizar y Desalcoholizar la Población"

The Interrelated Anti-Catholic and Anti-Alcohol Campaigns

GRETCHEN PIERCE[1]

In 1929, Colonel Francisco Lazcano wrote *Unificando la campaña antialcohólica*, a booklet justifying the creation of the Comité Nacional de Lucha contra el Alcoholismo (CNLCA), an organization leading the national anti-alcohol campaign. A member of this body as well as a Masonic lodge, he explained that the campaign would supplement the Revolution's larger goal of defeating priests who were "intoxicating the souls and the minds of Mexicans."[2] Five years later, an article in a magazine published by the Secretaría de Educación Pública (Department of Public Education; SEP) claimed that people should fight alcoholism because it destroyed business and industry, caused accidents in the workplace, and swallowed up a family's savings as the inebriate "drank their children's bread."[3] Meanwhile, two thousand kilometers away to the northwest, the president of the Sonoran chapter of the new Partido Nacional Revolucionario (National Revolutionary Party; PNR), Guadalupe Bustamante, discussed Cultural Sundays, events held by teachers consisting of things like sports, temperance-themed plays, and irreligious lectures. He claimed they were designed to "desfanatizar y desalcoholizar la población" (defanaticize and dealcoholize the population).[4] Finally, in 1937, members of the Sindicato Femenil of Tiripetío, Michoacán, a women's union located in the center-west of the country, angrily observed that during a Carnival celebration, the open sale of intoxicating beverages led to "deaths and wounds." Writing to their mayor, they demanded that alcohol be prohibited from such festivities and that exploitative priests be expelled from the town altogether.[5]

These examples demonstrate that the anti-alcohol and anticlerical campaigns intersected in a variety of ways.[6] First, irreligious (or more frequently, anti-Catholic) thought inspired some temperance reformers. Sources like Lazcano's booklet pinpoint Catholic clergy as one cause of the country's so-called alcohol problem. Many Masons, who were often irreligious, and Protestants, who were pious but tended to be strongly anti-Catholic, were leading members of the anti-alcohol campaign and some also blamed drunkenness on priests and religious festivals more generally.[7] As such, this chapter fits in with the book's overarching theme of anti-Catholicism in its connections to both unbelief and anticlericalism.[8]

Second, unlike Lazcano, most temperance advocates focused less on the causes of alcoholism (religious or otherwise) and more frequently on its effects. The SEP article and hundreds of statements made by bureaucrats from governmental offices such as the Secretaría de Salubridad Pública (Department of Public Health; SSP) mention poverty, disease, and, to a lesser extent, the lack of social justice as side-effects of chronic intoxication. As Sarah Osten and Ben Fallaw point out in chapters 2 and 6, Catholicism was also blamed at times for encouraging a premodern and unscientific mentality that oppressed the lower classes, thwarted efforts at forging a healthy populace, and weakened the economy.

Third, because of the supposed effects of alcohol and Catholicism, the campaigns against both were tied into the revolutionary government's projects of state-building (the act of imbuing the new regime with legitimacy) and identity formation (the process of forming modern citizens who would help the country to progress). In other words, if drinking and worshipping contributed to the public health and socioeconomic problems that plagued the nation, then both practices needed to be eliminated. Bustamante's claim shows that the anti-alcohol and the anticlerical campaigns were thus designed to mold Mexicans into sober and secular citizens. The resulting modern New Men and Women (and their children) would, he hoped, strengthen the economy and solidify the revolutionaries' power vis-à-vis the Church.

Fourth, some ordinary people also linked the anti-alcohol and the anti-Catholic movements. Some middle- or working-class individuals, like the women of Tiripetio, blamed alcohol consumption, crime, and violence on religious activities or the priests who led them. In other cases, ordinary citizens wrote of their work to eliminate both issues from their communities. The sources also demonstrate that these two revolutionary projects were not simply imposed from the top down.[9]

The primary sources used in this chapter are mostly from Mexico City and across the state of Sonora, representing the Central Valley and Northwest regions, respectively. Secondary sources provide evidence from eight other states, covering Mexico's Center-West, South, and Southeast regions. These examples help to demonstrate that the trends identified in the primary sources existed in other parts of the country as well. As such, the findings of this chapter mirror scholars' observations that while some of the strongest anticlerical movements were in the North and Southeast, pockets of anti-Catholicism could be found throughout the country.[10]

The Revolutionary Anti-Alcohol Campaign

Mexican revolutionary presidents blamed excessive alcohol consumption for problems that affected the drinkers themselves, their families, and the nation as a whole. One major concern was health related: temperance advocates linked chronic intoxication with diseases like cirrhosis of the liver, children born with mental and physical irregularities, and degeneration of the entire race. They further connected drunkenness to crimes such as domestic abuse, public fights, and rebellions. They also worried that drunkards caused economic problems when they spent their families' savings in the bar and when they either did not show up to work or did so in an alcoholic haze. In particular, political leaders and reformers associated these issues with urban and rural working-class (and to a lesser extent, Indigenous) men, who they argued were the nation's problem drinkers. These hypocritical associations ignored the fact that people of all ethnicities, classes, and genders drank, including the notorious alcoholic, President Plutarco Elías Calles, who ironically passed the country's strictest anti-alcohol decree while governor of Sonora.[11] Plenty of revolutionaries also financially benefited from the alcohol consumption that they decried: President Abelardo Rodríguez, for one, became rich as a casino owner in Tijuana, even though he had overseen anti-vice campaigns in the territory of Baja California del Norte while zone commander and governor in the 1920s and would strengthen the national anti-alcohol campaign in the early 1930s.[12]

The anti-alcohol campaign should be understood as part of the larger processes of state-building and identity formation. Political leaders worried that alcoholism challenged the success of the revolution itself, for the inebriated might be more inclined to rebel, something authorities wished to avoid once they began the process of rebuilding the nation in 1914. Indeed, stories abounded of the counterrevolutionary dictator, Victoriano Huerta's, penchant for drink during his brief rule from February 1913 to July 1914. Furthermore, sick and "lazy" drunks could not assist political officials in creating a stable government or rebuilding the economy.

Therefore, leaders realized that to achieve their political, economic, and social goals, Mexicans would need to be remade into modern citizens. These New Men, Women, and Children would be hard-working, healthy, peaceful, secular, and sober. Political officials worked with teachers, doctors, and other experts to help achieve these ends. As such, the anti-alcohol campaign overlapped with other, more commonly studied projects such as educational expansion, public health drives, economic development plans, and the anticlerical movement.[13]

The national anti-alcohol campaign was waged in a variety of ways. The Constitutional Convention of 1916–1917 featured a fierce debate of the topic. In the end, the new constitution eschewed a federal prohibition and left it up to the SSP to regulate the quality of beverages and the cleanliness of locations selling them; to the federal legislature, to use the power of taxation to reduce consumption of intoxicants; and to the states, to pass prohibitive measures if they chose. A few years later, the government empowered the SEP to teach people about the dangers of alcohol abuse. The CNLCA, from 1929 on, worked as an umbrella organization to help coordinate the activities of the various governmental bodies involved in fighting alcoholism. Presidents Rodríguez and Lázaro Cárdenas, from 1932 to 1940, were the most directly involved in the anti-alcohol campaign. They urged governors to honor requests from unofficial temperance leagues to close drinking establishments and passed decrees that limited when, where, and to whom alcohol could be sold. Although these measures were not total prohibitions, they were the most direct restrictions on consumption that Mexican presidents ever made.

The anti-alcohol campaign involved the state as well as the federal level. Several states restricted alcohol production, distribution, and consumption. These included Sonora, from 1915 to 1919; Yucatán, from 1915 to 1917; and Tabasco, from 1926 to 1934. In the latter two cases, the measures were almost absolute; only beer could be sold because of its low alcohol content. In Sonora, however, all intoxicating beverages were prohibited. The decrees were also apparently strictly enforced; in all three states, rumors abounded of violators being executed. Although the most ardent of anti-alcohol reformers admired the draconian nature of these radical state-level experiments (especially Sonora's), the majority of said reformers argued that they were ineffective, leading to increased clandestine production, as well as a violation of civil liberties.[14]

People of all races, classes, and genders participated in this movement.[15] In my research, I discovered 164 groups and 140 individual reformers, totaling more than 3500 participants, who were concerned

FIGURE 5. Unifying the Anti-Alcohol Campaign. Clemente Islas Allende, *Unificando la campaña antialcohólica*, 1929. Reproduced with permission from the Archivo General de la Nación.

about alcohol abuse. They were based in either Sonora or Mexico City (but with claims of being a national organization). These included temperance leagues that did work mirroring the CNLCA, educating young people and distributing propaganda about the negative effects of excessive drinking. They also consisted of organizations like labor unions or community associations. Their primary work was not geared toward temperance, but they wrote to their leaders to complain about an excessive number of cantinas in their neighborhoods or officials not enforcing dry laws. These popular activists were the eyes and ears that assisted national, state, and local governments, but they also kept them honest, demanding that their leaders live up to their stated revolutionary goal of helping the masses.[16]

Anti-Catholic Motivations in the Anti-Alcohol Campaign

Some promoters of temperance blamed alcohol abuse on Catholic priests and other unnamed exploiters. As we saw in this chapter's introduction, Francisco Lazcano's anti-alcohol pamphlet accused clergy of fomenting alcoholism. The text also claimed that priests were "strongly linked" to other exploiters who hoped to "drown the people (*el pueblo*) in the vice of drunkenness." Published in 1929, the year in which the religiously motivated Cristero Rebellion came to an end, Lazcano argued that priests had been defeated and now organizations like the newly created CNLCA needed to wipe out alcohol abuse as well. The image from the front of the pamphlet, by graphic artist Clemente Islas Allende, reinforced these assertions (see fig. 5). In it, a group of mounted as well as foot soldiers advance on an unseen enemy. In front of them stretches a banner with the words "Unifying the anti-alcohol campaign." Not only was this the title of the pamphlet, but the message also exhorted groups, like the military, to join in President Portes Gil's temperance movement. Thanks to the bayonet at the end of the largest soldier's rifle, the viewer's eyes are drawn to a quote attributed to the president, which reads, "Alcoholism is a powerful ally of all kinds of tyranny and unjust exploitation." Although the statement did not mention priests, the main text established the link between the two and the connection may have been implied in the image as well. The use of nationalistic symbols, like snow-capped volcanoes and a geometric Indigenous motif, further underscored the importance of defeating all kinds of tyrannies for the well-being of the nation, whether linked to the bottle or the Bible.[17]

Another image made an even clearer connection between priests, elites, and drunkenness. In a 1934 edition of *Izquierdas*, a Socialist and

FIGURE 6. Red Saturdays, Bourgeois Saturdays. Cayetano Caloca Valle, "Sábados Rojos, Sábados Burgueses," *Izquierdas*, December 17, 1934. Reproduced with permission from the Nettie Lee Benson Latin American Collection, University of Texas at Austin Library.

strongly anti-Catholic newspaper, an illustration by Cayetano Caloca Valle titled "Sábados Rojos, Sábados Burgueses (Red Saturdays, Bourgeois Saturdays)" appeared on the front and back covers (see fig. 6).[18] The front side, labeled "orgies of exploiters and priests," includes elites dressed in the style of the global Modern Man and Woman. One man wears a top hat; all three have on suits. The women have bobbed hairdos, makeup, jewelry, and tight, revealing dresses. One man's money bag further exemplifies the wealth of these individuals. However, this image did not just depict an upper-crust social event but, even more so, a night of debauchery and vice as the consequence of bourgeois excess. There are three glasses, one bottle of wine, a man who appears to be vomiting, and a pack of cards, suggesting binge drinking and gambling. The image also implies sexual depravity in the form of orgiastic prostitution, as two of the women are drinking, one with her skirt hiked up far enough to reveal her garter belt and another with an exposed breast. In addition to denoting moneyed status, the bag of coins could also signify payment for the women's sexual services. The caption also suggests a denunciation of Catholicism. One woman wears a rosary (admittedly in a less than pious way, as a choker), the man on the right has on a bishop's biretta, and the one on the bottom drinks sacramental wine.[19] The back side of the periodical contrasts with the decadence and degeneration of this scene. There, the proletariat wear simple, modest clothing, learn at a festival much like the Cultural Sundays discussed below, and there is no sign of alcohol or religious iconography anywhere.

Government officials linking clergy, elites, and alcohol abuse was not a new phenomenon in 1934. Federal legislators in 1917 had debated drastically increasing the tax on the fermented beverage *pulque* in the hopes of reducing consumption (and increasing revenue). One of the more radical representatives, José Siurob Ramírez, a man who would come to head the SSP in the mid-late 1930s and thus oversee the CNLCA, could not help noticing the connection between pulque producers and the Church. He claimed that these *hacendados* (hacienda owners) were "recalcitrant Conservatives," political Catholics, and *"ultramontanos"* or papists. He called them greedy (and many others in the room shouted their agreement), noting that if peons tried to demand better pay, *pulqueros* (pulque producers) turned to two time-honored traditions: sending in a "mission" of priests or loading up the peasants with alcohol. Once more, other legislators yelled, "Or both!" The notion of priests frequently interfering in labor relations was exaggerated, but Siurob and many of his colleagues believed there was a clear connection between alcohol, Catholicism, and exploitation.[20]

Educators across the country also decried the supposed link between Catholicism and chronic intoxication. Antonio Gutiérrez y Olivares, a teacher at the Casa del Estudiante Indígena (a boarding school for Indigenous youth), wrote a temperance booklet bemoaning the problems that alcoholism had created in Mexico. While he did not accuse priests of encouraging vice, he argued that they would not be willing to help either, because they were too busy with "politics, finance, and . . . intrigue in Rome."[21] An anonymous textbook from the state of Tabasco claimed that socialist education for the masses was essential because "the worker's ignorance is very dangerous . . . it allows him to be victimized by the exploiters, priests, and alcohol."[22] In Sonora, two SEP inspectors, one discussing the Mayo and the other, the Yaqui, blamed these people's poverty on fanaticism and alcoholism.[23] Although these examples merely suggested a link between Catholicism, alcoholism, and exploitation, some were much more direct. Teachers and school inspectors in Campeche and Michoacán argued that Catholic festivals encouraged the intemperate use of alcohol, while educators in Sonora had their students perform plays that satirized priests as "lascivious, corrupt, alcoholic charlatans."[24] The connection between anti-Catholicism and the anti-alcohol campaign was strongest in the context of the school.

Another example stands out from the rest. In 1933, after anticlerical teachers denounced Epigmenio Hernández, a priest from Camotlán, Oaxaca, he and municipal authorities came to an agreement that Hernández would be allowed to continue preaching as long as the "bad customs, superstitions, and other needless expenditures which are made on the pretext of both profane and religious festivals, and which encourage alcoholism, be suppressed."[25] It should be noted that, unlike the other, more confrontational examples, these municipal authorities were likely not particularly active in the anti-alcohol or anti-Catholic campaigns.[26] This makes their "acknowledgment," and the agreement by the priest himself, that Catholicism encouraged people to drink and robbed them of their hard-earned money (both through consumption and hosting lavish festivals) all the more powerful. It suggests that while the rhetoric of more radical reformers like Lazcano or Siurob was exaggerated and incendiary, it was nevertheless based in a degree of truth.

Other proponents of temperance noted the connection between religions and intoxicants more generally, especially for native peoples. At a 1935 meeting of the CNLCA, Siurob mentioned that the Maya of Yucatán had a religious ritual using alcohol, while the Otomí of Querétaro had one that involved marijuana. In his opinion, these examples demonstrated that religion was "always linked with vice."[27] A couple of newspaper editorials made similar observations. One suggested that people have always consumed inebriants as part of their social and religious customs, and the writer despaired that this would make it difficult to wipe out alcoholism.[28] These examples are some of the few on the irreligious end of the anti-Catholic spectrum.

Interrelations between the Anti-Alcohol and Anti-Catholic Campaigns

Not all reformers argued that Catholicism was responsible for alcohol abuse. Even still, most felt that so-called fanaticism and vice were interrelated: both challenged the revolutionary projects of economic development and modernization and therefore must be eliminated. The director of federal education in Sonora, Ramón G. Bonfil, argued in 1929 that the revolution was not merely about political change but also "economic and moral rehabilitation." He claimed that revolutionaries had already set their sights on defeating "large landowners, despots, capitalists, and priests" (individuals who challenged said rehabilitation), but that "the liberation of the oppressed will not be complete, materially or spiritually, while alcohol continues impoverishing homes and degenerating spirits."[29] José Manuel Puig Casauranc, secretary of education from 1924 to 1928 and 1930 to 1931, agreed that Mexicans would not reach their full potential because of the "tragic triangle of fanaticism, alcoholism, and premature sexual unions."[30] These men linked alcohol abuse and religiosity and posited that eliminating both "vices" was central to the success of the Revolution.

The fact that the individuals making these statements were educators is not a coincidence, for the SEP played a leading role in the identity formation process and both the anti-alcohol and anti-Catholic campaigns as Fallaw shows in chapter 6. Officials from this department did not want teachers simply delivering lessons on reading and writing. Rather, they should act as cultural missionaries, helping to transform young people and their parents into modern citizens.[31] They were expected to hold school assemblies and public festivals that taught about the problems of alcohol and priests. They were also to encourage youth organizations to host events of this nature. Teachers were to be held accountable for doing these things by the secretary of education, school inspectors, and, unrealistically, peasant and worker organizations themselves. In the charts that inspectors used to evaluate teachers, anti-alcohol and anticlerical events were listed in the same column, separate from those that had to do with public health, land reform, or economic development. This demonstrates how the anti-alcohol and anti-Catholic movements were interrelated in the minds of education officials.[32]

The connection between temperance and anti-Catholicism is also clear in government-sponsored public festivals, many of which took place on Sundays (or at times, Saturdays, as seen in fig. 6). The day of the week was important. Sunday, of course, was the day Christians went to church, but it was also the only day many workers had off for the weekend. As a magazine geared to teachers and peasants explained, "Sunday arrives and there is nothing to do . . . and the only recourse is for the woman to go to church, and the man to the cantina."[33] The so-called Cultural Sundays were thus filled with healthy and secular activities like sporting events, music, and anti-alcohol or anticlerical-themed talks. Indeed, as the Sonoran PNR president Guadalupe Bustamante remarked, these events were meant to "defanaticize and dealcoholize the population."[34]

The three states that had the most draconian laws against intoxicants were also some of those that repressed the Catholic Church most forcefully, although the two movements did not always reach their zeniths at the same time. In Tabasco in the late 1920s to early 1930s, a radio program called the "Anti-Fanatic Hour" featured, among other things, a song called "Anti-Alcoholic Protest." Governor Garrido Canabal's Red Shirts, the irreligious youth group mentioned in chapters 2 and 6, were also tasked with enforcement of the state's dry laws. They broke up parties where alcohol was being served, hosted sessions for the public to denounce violators, and led charges to get drunken employees fired. A supposed punishment for breaking the drinking laws was destroying churches as a form of "community service." As historian Massimo de Giuseppe claims, alcohol and religion were the governor's two "supreme enemies."[35]

The connection between the temperance and the anti-Catholic movements in Yucatán found inspiration from below rather than from above. In the early 1920s, the state government had lifted the previously mentioned ban on most intoxicants, but several less draconian laws remained on the books. Popular temperance leagues flourished, most of them peopled by women. When Governor Felipe Carrillo Puerto visited the village of Muxupip, female activists sought his support to close cantinas. Their male counterparts then took advantage of the governor's presence to press *their* issue and expel the local priest. Seven other towns also had both strong anti-alcohol and anti-Catholic campaigns, although it is unclear if they were also divided between genders. Regardless, Carrillo Puerto was proud to announce that these "little pueblos of Indian workers . . . do not permit the sale of rum in their towns, nor that priests come to exploit them as they did in the past."[36]

In Sonora, the two campaigns were also interrelated. While Plutarco Elías Calles decreed the nation's only true prohibition as governor of Sonora and was the most anti-Catholic of presidents (see chap. 1), his son, Rodolfo Elías Calles, did more for the latter campaign in the state than his father had. Governor from 1931 to 1934, he turned churches into schools, had statues of saints destroyed (one of which may have been burned in the brewery Cervecería de Sonora's oven), and expelled priests. Although he did not reinstate anything as drastic as his father's alcohol decree, he did attempt to revitalize the anti-alcohol campaign in Sonora by enforcing national measures that limited when and where alcohol could be sold and distributing temperance propaganda. These campaigns overlapped in the younger Calles's support for Cultural Sundays and the screening of both anti-alcohol and irreligious films. He helped to ensure the success of these events by asking mayors and state-level PNR officials to make sure they were held. Indeed, dozens of mayors, school inspectors, teachers, and police officers mentioned that they had had them, or were planning to, perhaps because of the governor's diligence. Rodolfo Calles also took the time to thank popular organizations that he knew had been fighting alcohol and religion. Acts like these may have inspired Guy W. Ray, US vice consul in Guaymas, to note that in Mexico (and particularly in Sonora), officials had been "connecting 'alcoholism' with 'fanaticism.'"[37] Although to a lesser extent than examples at the national or state level, some popular temperance advocates also expressed anti-Catholic sentiment. Out of the 304 groups and individuals that I studied, seven (2.3 percent) mentioned being concerned about both issues. For example, Manuel R. Lamas and Dr. N. Rodríguez of Mexico City wrote to President Cárdenas with advice on how to improve the anti-alcohol campaign. They suggested, among other ideas, teaching rural people how bad pulque is, as it would leave them "slaves to the Reactionaries that exploit and the clergy that atrophy and asphyxiate us." Similarly, the teacher Elvira Serrato G. Briseño, president of the National Women's Revolutionary Union (Unión Nacional Femenil Revolucionaria), asked Cárdenas if she could head a school of homemaking, where she would deliver lectures on "defanaticization, temperance, and hygiene" to workers.[38] These likely middle-class groups mirrored the rhetoric of national and state-level leaders, singling out rural and urban working-class individuals as problem drinkers, while linking alcohol consumption with exploitation in general and abuse by priests in particular.

A handful of other groups likely saw the anti-alcohol and anti-Catholic campaigns as connected. Four (1.3 percent) did not mention anything explicitly irreligious but did talk about hosting events on Sunday. Like SEP teachers, they may have addressed fanaticism as well as alcoholism in their activities. Others that did temperance work did not leave a record of fighting so-called fanaticism but may have done so based on their history (which will be discussed in the next section). These include five Masonic lodges (1.6 percent), including the Logia Simbólica Cruzada Ideológica Femenina, a women's Masonic lodge which G. Briseño was also a member of, five Protestant organizations, and three groups (1 percent) that contained a significant number of Protestant members but that were not specifically linked to that religion. Adding these numbers together, we can see that 2.3 percent of temperance-oriented organizations studied in Sonora and Mexico City also did anticlerical work, and another 5.6 percent may have done so.[39]

Furthermore, in Michoacán, there were also popular organizations that fought religion and alcoholism, including the previously mentioned Sindicato Femenil of Tiripetio. The Teremendo branch of the Federación Femenil Socialista Michoacana lodged complaints against municipal authorities they labeled "clericales" (clericals, an accusation that they were Catholic rebels called Cristeros) as well as at least two individuals who defied alcohol regulations. In this state, the issue of temperance seemed to be more important to women than anti-Catholic activism, but doing work in the latter category may have given groups legitimacy and provided them space to focus on the former, their true interest. On a limited scale, these examples reveal a number of popular organizations that worked on both the anti-alcohol and the anti-Catholic campaigns.[40]

Masons and Protestants: Further Links between the Anti-Alcohol and Anti-Catholic Campaigns

The final section turns to two groups who were well known for supporting both the anti-alcohol and anti-Catholic campaigns, although it is not clear if they saw these two movements as interrelated or distinct. Masons tended to emphasize principles like individual freedoms, rational thinking, and the desire to help or, better put, "improve" the less fortunate. With a great deal of influence from eugenics, their ideal country would no longer include alcoholics, drug addicts, the mentally ill, or individuals with "criminal tendencies."[41] These traditional Masonic tenets led many members to adopt an anti-Catholic stance. Additionally, a fair number of Masons were teachers who promoted irreligious values in children and led communal events like "bautizos socialistas" (socialist baptisms), a secular ritual meant to initiate a schoolchild into a life of free-thinking and class-consciousness.[42] The link between Freemasonry and anticlericalism was strong enough that it led protesting Catholic peasants in 1938 to cry "Death to the state governor, death to the president," and later, "death to the masons, long live religion!" One apostolic delegate went so far as to claim that Masons were responsible for "our persecution and almost all of our national misfortunes."[43] Many, but far from all Masons were irreligious.[44]

The Masons' significance to the anti-alcohol movement was disproportionate to their numbers. President Emilio Portes Gil, himself a Mason, realized the importance of his organization when he formed the CNLCA. He called for representatives from all like-minded groups to join, including Masonic lodges, mutual aid societies, and rotary clubs. This sentiment was reiterated in official documents about how to organize the CNLCA, as well as state and local-level temperance leagues, in 1929 and 1934.[45] Indeed, at least one Mason, and often more, served on the CNLCA governing board throughout its history. General Isaac M. Ibarra, a member of the Gran Logia Valle de México, was one of the three founders of the CNLCA, and he continued to act as a representative (albeit of the armed forces) through at least 1937.[46] Other Masonic representatives included Professor David F. España and Coronel Miguel Orrico de los Llanos. While Ignacio García Téllez, also of Gran Logia Valle de México, did not attend CNLCA meetings regularly, he was the secretary of education from 1934 to 1935 and secretary of the interior from 1938 to 1940, meaning he often oversaw the project.[47] Each of these individuals also played a secondary role in the movement. De los Llanos, editor of the military magazine *Adelante*, published a special issue dedicated to the anti-alcohol campaign. España and García Téllez encouraged "all true and revolutionary Masons" to do temperance work in their lodges, arguing they should "help out the people at the bottom of society."[48] Indeed, I found records of several other Masons who either joined popular leagues, participated in CNLCA events, or sent in their ideas to presidents about how best to fight alcoholism.[49] Although these individuals, other than the previously mentioned Lazcano and G. Briseño, may not have left records directly linking irreligious sentiment to their interest in promoting temperance, both of these governmental campaigns fit in with their values.

The relationship between Protestants, anti-Catholicism, and the anti-alcohol campaign is similar to Masonic connections with these two movements. Protestants of various denominations first began to arrive in Mexico in the mid-nineteenth century, with the support of Liberals who hoped to break the power of the Catholic Church. Similarly, individuals like the Methodist Samuel P. Craver claimed in 1877 that his goal for coming to Mexico was to defeat "Papism," since Catholicism was supposedly responsible for "the misery and incredibly sad ignorance that the Mexican people find themselves in."[50] Like Masons, Protestants were often intimately involved in the anticlerical campaign during the Revolution as high-level SEP officials and teachers, delivering lessons about priests exploiting the masses or leading their communities in the destruction of saints.[51]

The idea of temperance appealed to Protestant values and fit in with the movement called the Social Gospel, which rejected so-called vice and promoted civic engagement. As a result, during the presidency of Porfirio Díaz (the Porfiriato, 1876–1911), Protestants, including missionaries, American expatriates, and Mexican believers—many of them women—were forming anti-alcohol leagues as a way to "rescue" workers from their vices.[52] Once the revolutionary anti-alcohol campaign began, Protestants continued to spread their version of morality. Periodicals like *El Abogado Cristiano* and *Comino*—the former for adults, the latter, geared toward children—occasionally ran articles that supported the anti-alcohol campaign and sought to explain why alcohol abuse was detrimental to the nation.[53] Individuals such as Ivy V. Yeaworth and María Luisa Chagoyan, presidents of two different Protestant groups, praised leaders for their temperance work, offered suggestions for improvement, or attended events hosted by the CNLCA. They also formed or joined new popular temperance leagues that translated and distributed propaganda in support of their cause, delivered harangues promoting sobriety across the country, and lobbied for laws to restrict alcohol consumption.[54]

A number of Protestants participated in the official anti-alcohol campaign at various levels of involvement. Some, like Masons, represented their organizations on the CNLCA's governing board. For example, J. T. Ramírez, district superintendent of the Methodist Church of Mexico and also a teacher, was a member of two popular temperance leagues, the Asociación Nacional de Temperancia (ANT) and the Liga Antialcohólica Mexicana. He served as the latter group's liaison on the CNLCA in 1929, while teacher Gonzalo Báez Camacho represented the Asociación Cristiana de Jóvenes on the CNLCA in 1935.[55] Moisés Sáenz, a Presbyterian educator, played a slightly larger role. In the early 1920s, his name appears in the rosters of one of the most prolific popular organizations, the Asociación de Temperancia (AT), although it is unclear how active he was in this group. He may have been designated an honorary member, one who performed acts in support of the temperance movement but outside the specific purview of the Temperance Association. Sáenz served as the chief administrative officer of the SEP from 1924 to 1926 and its undersecretary from 1926 to 1931. This meant he oversaw teachers and school inspectors who were doing temperance work in their classrooms and communities. In the 1930s, while abroad as a diplomat, he occasionally wrote and lectured about how alcohol consumption negatively affected Indigenous peoples.[56]

The Protestant who perhaps made the biggest impact on the anti-alcohol campaign was Andrés Osuna, a Methodist minister, Mason, educator, and revolutionary. He was named the director of public education from 1916 to 1918 in Mexico City, where he surely was able to promote the value of sobriety. He continued to use his skills as an educator in the 1920s as an active member of two popular temperance leagues, the AT and the ANT, both of which had a number of other Protestant participants. He traveled around the country distributing propaganda and delivering scientific lessons at schools and workers' centers that showed why alcohol was bad for the body. He also wrote a well-researched book geared to elementary and middle-school students called *Alcoholismo*. It detailed the many problems caused by alcohol abuse. Despite Osuna's religious background, the manual was disseminated by the SEP beginning in 1929. Both the longtime director of the CNLCA, Luis G. Franco, as well as some Indigenous schoolboys in Sonora cited it in their own pro-temperance speeches and posters, and it was still being distributed as late as 1941.[57]

For Protestants, the anti-alcohol and the anticlerical campaigns overlapped in a variety of ways. Both movements were a way to spread their values of helping the masses by weakening the power of exploiters (in their minds, priests, owners of drinking establishments, and bartenders) and promoting self-help ideologies (like temperance).[58] In some cases, Protestants outright blamed priests for excessive alcohol consumption. For example, an article in the periodical *El Mundo Cristiano* in 1923 claimed that "the 'Romanists' promoted idolatry and the ingestion of alcohol in their celebrations."[59] It should be noted, however, that while Protestants were anti-Catholic, they were not irreligious. Students in the Legión Leal de Temperancia were required to take an oath that said they would abstain, with the help of God, while *El Abogado Cristiano* featured a testimonial from someone who read one of their anti-alcohol articles, decided to mend his ways, and converted to Protestantism as a result. Finally, Osuna, in

Alcoholismo, argued that "it is very important that churches of all types fight vices among their followers because the leaders have such influence." He went on to point out that it was precisely Protestants who led the temperance movement in the United States.[60]

When it comes to the anti-alcohol campaign, anti-Catholic sentiment was misguided. Political Catholics did not participate in the official anti-alcohol campaign to the same extent as some other groups, perhaps because of its connection to the revolutionary government's anticlericalism, agrarian reform, and rationalist education. Indeed, there are examples of priests asking their parishioners to resist anti-alcohol measures because of links to Protestant reformers.[61] This is not to say, however, that all Catholics were uninterested in fighting vice. Catholics during the colonial period and the nineteenth century bemoaned excessive alcohol consumption for a variety of reasons.[62]

During the Revolution, some Catholics maintained an interest in promoting sobriety. I found reference to three Catholic groups (1.8 percent) that disapproved of drinking: the Mexican Knights Templar, Legión Mexicana de Decencia, and Unión Femenina Católica Mexicana de Clases Trabajadoras. In the case of the second, members had to sign a pledge card in 1937, agreeing to combat alcoholism and other immoralities in the home, office, or sports team. Of course, any number of people who were members of groups that were not explicitly Catholic in nature may have been believers themselves.[63] Furthermore, some Catholic schools, like the Colegio Aquiles Serdán in Guadalajara, upheld temperance as one of the many virtues it taught female students, while Luis Ibarra, a leader of the Segunda (the second wave of Cristero violence) in Sonora outlawed drinking and other vices in the towns he and the rebels captured in the mid-1930s.[64] More research is needed, but plenty of Catholic sermons likely promoted sobriety as well.

At times, Catholics even approved of or worked with the revolutionary government's anti-alcohol campaign. Although they did so infrequently, the Catholic publications *El Mensajero del Sagrado Corazón* and *Christus* denounced alcohol consumption. Significantly, in an article published in August 1929, four months after the launching of the CNLCA, a Jesuit priest, Joaquín Cardoso, and a well-known Catholic doctor, José Meza Gutiérrez, openly praised President Portes Gil's anti-alcohol campaign. It seems Meza Gutiérrez was likewise well respected by revolutionary temperance advocates, perhaps because he was the former director of La Castañeda, a mental hospital that housed thousands of alcoholics. He wrote a sixteen-page booklet that was published by the CNLCA, *El alcoholismo como plaga social* (*Alcoholism as a Social Plague*), which chronicled the link between drinking, disease, and crime. While both of these authors disputed the idea that their religion contributed to the problem of alcoholism, in many other ways their ideas overlapped with the revolutionaries.'[65]

During the Revolution, thousands of Mexicans, including politicians, government bureaucrats, and ordinary people, worked to fight the so-called vice of alcoholism. Some of these reformers were inspired by anti-Catholic or irreligious motivations, arguing that religious festivals led to intemperate consumption or that priests allied with exploitative landowners who plied their peons with drink to keep them impoverished. It was much more common, however, for these individuals to focus on alcohol's effects rather than its causes, many of which overlapped with problems supposedly caused by "fanaticism." These effects included crime, poor health, economic decline, and a traditional worldview. As a result, creating citizens that were both sober and secular was seen as essential to the goal of forming Modern Men, Women, and Children and, indeed, the stability of the revolution. These interrelations can be seen at the national, state, and popular levels. The close connection between these two movements reveals that "desfanatizar y desalcoholizar la población" was an important part of the greater revolutionary project.

Notes

1. The author would like to thank Jürgen Buchenau, Jerry Pierce, Áurea Toxqui, and Robbie Weis for reading drafts of this paper, and Claudio Escandon Mendiola for help securing publication-quality images. I accept all responsibility for any mistakes in the text.
2. Francisco Lazcano and Emilio Portes Gil, *Unificando la campaña antialcohólica* (Mexico City: Centro Internacional de Prensa, 1929) in Archivo General de la Nación, Fondo Archivo Particular, Emilio Portes Gil, Fondo Emilio Portes Gil (AGN-FArP-EPG), Caja 5, Expediente (Exp.) 94; Autrique Escobar, *"Salvar a la Raza,"* 170n142. It should be noted that the CNLCA changed names several times between 1929 and 1940, but for simplicity's sake, I am referring to all iterations of this body as simply the CNLCA in the text. In the notes, I will use whatever name the body had at the time.
3. "El alcoholismo, azote social," *El Maestro Rural* (Mexico City) (*EMR*) 5, no. 5 (Sept. 1934): 18.

4. Guadalupe Bustamante to Rodolfo Elías Calles, 25 May 1934, Archivo Histórico del Estado de Sonora, Ramo Ejecutivo (AHES-RE) 1934, Caja 21, Tomo 23, 733"34"/24.
5. Olcott, *Revolutionary Women*, 86–87; Mitchell, "Por la liberación de la mujer," 173–74.
6. As this book argues, it makes more sense to call the latter movement the "anti-Catholic campaign," but at the time it was called the anticlerical campaign. Most previous scholarship uses this terminology as well. I use "anticlerical" when trying to reflect the sentiment of the time and "anti-Catholic" when inserting my own analysis.
7. I have not found records of Mormons or Mennonites participating in the anti-alcohol campaign in any primary or secondary sources. However, as Rebecca Janzen shows in chapter 8, both groups were opposed to alcohol consumption as well as strongly anti-Catholic.
8. Butler, "Revolution in Spirit," 7; Knight, "Mentality," 31.
9. Bantjes, "Regional Dynamics," 112; Butler, "Revolution in Spirit," 7.
10. Bantjes, 113–14, 116, 122; Knight, "Mentality," 31.
11. See chapter 1.
12. Pierce, "Sobering the Revolution"; Pierce, "Parades"; Pierce, "Fighting Bacteria; Sluis, *Deco Body*," 212–13; Pierce, "Altered States: Anti-Alcohol, State-Building, and Identity-Formation Projects during the Mexican Revolution, 1910–1940" (manuscript in progress).
13. Pierce, "Altered States."
14. Martínez Assad, *El laboratorio de la revolución*, 141–47; Fallaw, "Dry Law," 40–42; Giuseppe, "'El Indio Gabriel,'" 226; Pierce, "Sobering the Revolution," 188–223; Autrique Escobar, "*Salvar a la Raza*," 98–100, 149–65; Pierce, "Altered States." See also chapters 2 and 6 from this book.
15. In my research on popular temperance advocates, I tracked race, class, and gender using "real characteristics" (explicit naming of a race, class, or gender that a reformer identified as being part of) and "nominal characteristics" (more arbitrary traits used by researchers to categorize people like first or last names, titles, and occupations). Using these designations, I was able to surmise that about 11.8 percent of reformers identified as or were likely Indigenous, while 9.9 were not. Slightly more than one-fourth of temperance supporters were from the middle class, while 21.7 percent were definitely or likely from the lower class. At least one male was in 57.9 percent of groups, while females were in at least 20.7 of them. Even using these clues, the backgrounds of the vast majority of people was unknown. In 78 percent of reformers, race was unknown; in 53.6 percent, the class background was unknown; and in 37.5 percent, genders were unknown. Pierce, "Altered States."

16. Pierce, "Sobering the Revolution," 254–96; Pierce, "Altered States."
17. Lazcano and Portes Gil, *Unificando la campaña antialcohólica*, AGN-FArP-EPG, Caja 5, Exp. 94.
18. Cayetano Caloca Valle, "Sábados Rojos, Sábados Burgueses," *Izquierdas* (Mexico City) no. 23 (17 Dec. 1934), front and back covers, Benson Rare Books Collection (-F- GZ 056.8 lz61 no. 8–25), Benson Latin American Collection, LLILAS Benson Latin American Studies and Collections, University of Texas at Austin.
19. The article on the page following the cover claims that priests spent most of their days getting drunk, exploiting peons' hard work, and prostituting women. See Sojari Tereso, "Como viven los curas en los pueblos," *Izquierdas*, no. 23 (17 Dec. 1934), 2.
20. Secretaría de Hacienda y Crédito Público, *Memoria de la Secretaría Hacienda y Crédito Público 16 de abril de 1917 a 21 de mayo de 1920*.
21. Gutiérrez y Oliveras, *El sepulturero de la raza latinoamericana o el cantinero y la conquista pacífica*, 26.
22. "The Socialist ABCs," 410.
23. Leonides Ayala Escamilla to Ramón G. Bonfil, 24 Mar. 1931, Archivo Histórico de la Secretaría de Educación Pública, Departamento de Escuelas Rurales, Estado de Sonora (AHSEP-DERS), Caja 1673, Referencia (Ref.) 4632; Leonardo Magaña report, 28 Mar. 1936, Archivo Histórico de la Secretaría de Educación Pública, Dirección General de Educación Primaria en los Estados y Territorios, Dirección de Educación Federal, Sonora (AHSEP-DEFS), Caja 8447, Ref. 319, Exp. 11.
24. Bantjes, *Jesus Walked on Earth*, 17, 19. See also Knight, "Popular Culture," 405; Fallaw, *Religion and State Formation*, 40.
25. Meyer, "Religious Conflict," 197.
26. Meyer, 197.
27. Minutes, 24 June 1935, Archivo Histórico de la Secretaría de Salubridad y Asistencia, Fondo Salubridad Pública I, Sección Servicio Jurídico (AHSSA-FSPI-SSJ), Caja 42, Exp. 1.
28. "La estéril campaña contra el alcoholismo," *El Universal* (Mexico City), 15 Nov. 1935; "Opinión editorial," *El Nacional* (Mexico City) (*EN*), 24 June 1939.
29. Bonfil, "El aniversario de la revolución," 20 Nov. 1929, AGN-FArP-EPG, Caja 34, Exp. 8054.
30. Dawson, *Indian and Nation*, 21.
31. Vaughan, *Cultural Politics*, 5–6, 12, 27–35; Palacios, *La pluma y el arado*, 35–42, 52–58, 192–93.
32. Elpidio López to unknown, 30 Nov. 1933, AHSEP-DEFS, Caja 5507 (25), Exp. 20; Ordoñez Vila, "Alcoholismo y fanatismo," *EMR* 4, no. 3 (1 Feb. 1934): 16; AHSEP-DERS:

keys for bi-monthly graphs, Nov.–Dec. 1934, Caja 8447 (25), Exp. 4; circular #3, 25 Feb. 1935, Caja 8447 (25), Exp. 3; circular #6, 16 Apr. 1935, Caja 8447 (25), Exp. 3; "Programa de/para las escuelas primarias del estado de Sonora," n.d., Caja 8401, Exp. 5.

33. Palacios, *La pluma y el arado*, 180–81.
34. Bustamante to R. Calles, 25 May 1934, AHES-RE-1934, Caja 21, Tomo 23, 733"34"/24. See also circular #5, 30 Apr. 1932, AHSEP-DERS, Caja 8401, Exp. 16; state plan for the 1934–1935 school year, n.d., AHSEP-DERS, Caja 8447, Exp. 10; report, 15 Jan. 1937, AHSEP-DEFS, Caja 602, Exp. 22; Palacios, *La pluma y el arado*, 149–57, 192–93; Bantjes, *Jesus Walked on Earth*, 16–18; Lewis, *Ambivalent Revolution*, 107.
35. Giuseppe, "'El Indio Gabriel,'" 225–26, 228. See also Jorge Labra, "El refugio diabólico de la embriaguez," *Excélsior* (Mexico City) (*EX*), 19 Aug. 1935, 10; Parsons, *Mexican Martyrdom*, 243; Martínez Assad, *Laboratorio*, 143, 146–47.
36. Fallaw, "Dry Law," 46; Smith, "Salvador Alvarado of Yucatán," 48.
37. Guy W. Ray to US Secretary of State, 21 Jun. 1934, Records of the Department of State Relating to the Internal Affairs of Mexico, 1930–1939, 812.114 Liquors/101. See also Mario Aguilera D. report, 10 Nov. 1933, AHSEP-DERS, Caja 8443, Exp. 7; R. Calles to Wilfrido Oloño, 21 Feb. 1934, AHES-RE-1934, Caja 21, 1934, Tomo 23, 741"34"/1; Rodolfo Guajardo to R. Calles, 10 July 1934, AHES-RE-1934, Caja 21, 1934, Tomo 23, 733"34"/37; R. Calles to Salvador U. Bojórquez and Jorge Román, 8 Aug. 1934, Caja 21, 1934, Tomo 23, 738/3; several letters, AHES-RE-1934, Caja 21, Tomo 23, 733"34"/24; Carlos Puebla Valenzuela questionnaire, 15 May 1939, AHSEP-DERS, Caja 5719, Ref. 19297, Exp. 32; Bantjes, *Jesus Walked on Earth*, 10–20; Pierce, "Sobering the Revolution," 235–38; Pierce, "Altered States." The anti-alcohol and anti-religious films continued to be shown during the governorship of Emiliano Corella M.: Corella M. to mayors and police commissaries, 15 Jan. 1935, AHES-RE-1935, Caja 30, 1935, Tomo 57, 741"35"/3; dozens of others from Jan. to Sept. 1935.
38. R. Calles to Bojórquez and Román, 8 Aug. 1934, AHES-RE-1934, Caja 21, 1934, Tomo 23, 738/3; Elvira Serrato G. Briseño to Cárdenas, 6 Dec. 1934, AGN-FAP-LC, Exp. 702.2/316; flyer, 3–4 Feb. 1935, AHSEP-DERS, Caja 8447 (25), Exp. 2; Carlos Álvarez to Corella M., 6 Mar. 1935, AHES-RE-1935, Caja 23, Tomo 33, 231.5"35"/4; Corella M. to Luis Bálsamo Infante, 21 Mar. 1935, AHES-RE-1935, Caja 30, Tomo 56, 733"35"/4–20; Manuel R. Lamas and Dr. N. Rodríguez to Cárdenas, 9 Apr. 1935, AGN-FAP-LC, Exp. 553/18; Primer Congreso Nacional Antialcohólico to Cárdenas, 31 Oct. 1936, AGN-FAP-LC, Exp. 553/11.

39. X y Z (pseudonyms), "La campaña antialcohólica," *El Pueblo* (Hermosillo), 3 June 1929, 2; Ayala Escamilla report, 31 May 1932, AHSEP-DERS, Caja 8443, Exp. 15; "La cooperación infantil en la campaña antialcohólica," *EN*, 11 Apr. 1936. Jason Dormady found a Protestant church in Jalisco that wanted to use a former Catholic church for anti-alcohol talks and other secular events. See Dormady, "God, Cleanliness, and the City," 398–99.
40. Jocelyn Olcott and Stephanie Mitchell mention four different groups by name that did both anticlerical and anti-alcohol work but implied that were more such organizations. Olcott, *Revolutionary Women*, 63–64, 72–76, 82, 84–89; Mitchell, "Por la liberación de la mujer," 173–74.
41. Urías Horcasitas, "De moral y regeneración," 88, 96–98, 101, 104–5.
42. Urías Horcasitas, 93, 104, 110; Bautista García, "Maestros y Masones," 223, 226–27, 231–32, 236, 242, 254–57, 259–60, 265–66, 270–71; Smith, "Anticlericalism," 562, 569, 574, 577–83.
43. Smith, 559.
44. Bautista García, "Maestros y Masones," 221–22, 236, 258, 268; Smith, 570.
45. "Acuerdos a los secretarías de estado y departamentos dependientes del ejecutivo de la unión," *Boletín de la Secretaría de la Educación Pública* 13, no. 4 (1929): 141–42; Emilio Araujo to the representative of the SSP on the CNLCA, 11 June 1929, AHSSP-FSI-SSJ, Caja 18, Exp. 1; "Organización y funcionamiento de comités y sub-comités antialcohólicos en la república," 1 Dec. 1934, AHES-RE-1935, Caja 30, Tomo 56, 733"35"/21; Smith, "Anticlericalism," 574.
46. "El festival antialcohólico en la penitenciaria del D. Federal," *EN*, 1 May 1932, 1a. sec., p. 8; Cuerpo Consultivo of the Dirección de Educación Antialcohólica (DEA), 16 Nov. 1933, Archivo General de la Nación, Fondo Administración Pública, Abelardo Rodríguez (AGN-FAP-AR), Exp. 573/4; minutes, 24 June 1935, AHSSP-FSI-SSJ, Caja 42, Exp. 1; Dirección Antialcohólica (DAA) to Lázaro Cárdenas, 1 Aug. 1935, Archivo General de la Nación, Fondo Administración Pública, Lázaro Cárdenas (AGN-FAP-LC), Exp. 553/11.
47. Cuerpo Consultivo of the DEA, 16 Nov. 1933, AGN-FAP-AR, Exp. 573/4; DAA to Cárdenas, 1 Aug. 1935, AGN-FAP-LC, Exp. 553/11; "Recibe apoyo popular la campaña antialcohólica," *EN*, 27 Sept. 1937.
48. Ignacio García Téllez to Isaías L. Acosta, Apr. 1934, Archivo Histórico de la Secretaría de Educación Pública, Institución de Orientación Socialista, Caja 3954/3093/5, Exp 15. See also David F. España and Santiago Hernández to Plutarco Elías Calles, 26 July 1932, Fideicomiso Archivos Plutarco Elías Calles y Fernando Torreblanca-Archivo Fernando Torreblanca-Fondo Plutarco Elías Calles, Fondo 12, Serie 010805, Exp.

7, Inv. 563, Legajo (Leg.) 7/8; *Adelante: Revista Militar y de Cultura* (15 Aug. 1933); Bautista García, "Maestros y Masones," 241.

49. Isaac M. Ibarra to Portes Gil, 22 Apr. 1929, Archivo General de la Nación, Fondo Administración Pública, Emilio Portes Gil (AGN-FAP-EPG), Exp. 3/669, Leg. 2; Alfonso LaMadrid to Portes Gil, 26 Apr. 1929, AGN-FAP-EPG, Exp 3/669, Leg. 1; "El festival antialcohólico;" Ibarra to Luis I. Rodríguez, 5 Dec. 1934, AGN-FAP-LC, Exp. 553/1; José A. Granados to Cárdenas, 31 Dec. 1934, AGN-FAP-LC, Exp. 702.3/31; Augusto Fócil Díaz, "Combaten el alcoholismo las mujeres," *EN*, 30 Oct. 1935; Granados, "Boceto de cooperación anti-alcohólica," 1 May 1936, AGN-FAP-LC, Exp.553/11; "Campaña al alcoholismo en el país," *EN*, 30 Aug. 1936. AGN-FAP-LC, Exp. 553/11: Granados, "Boceto de cooperación anti-alcohólica," May 1, 1936; Primer Congreso to Cárdenas, 31 Oct. 1936; Gonzalo F. González to Cárdenas, 17 Apr. 1940; Méndez Reyes, "De crudas y moralidad," 259. Although not included in my official count, because it is not from Mexico City or Sonora, I also found a source from Jalisco mentioning Masons: Jesús Rodríguez Tostado and María Concepción Becerra to the mayor of Tequila, 15 Apr. 1931, Archivo Histórico Municipal de Tequila, Sección Presidencia, Serie Correspondencia, Caja 12, Exp. 7.

50. Bastian, *Los disidentes*, location 886–901.

51. Bastian, location 142, 705, 2487, 3375, 4048; Bastian, "Protestantismo y sociedad en México," 438, 444–45, 448–49; Fallaw, *Religion and State Formation*, 79, 81, 83, 86, 121.

52. Bastian, *Los disidentes*, location 117, 901, 1675, 2175, 2552, 2760, 2866, 3375, 4344, 5037; Bastian, "Protestantismo y sociedad," 444, 447; Méndez Reyes, "De crudas y moralidad," 245, 259; Pulido Esteva, *¡A su salud!* 122, 124–26; Autrique Escobar, "*Salvar a la Raza,*" 34–36, 217.

53. *El Abogado Cristiano* (Mexico City), 23 Apr. 1914, 270–71; 24 Sept. 1914, 591; 21 June 1917, 399–400; 25 Apr. 1929, 1–2, 7; and *Comino* (Mexico City), 2, no. 8 (Aug. 1936): 3, 7, 11–12; 6, no. 11 (Nov. 1940): 7–8. *El Mundo Cristiano* and *La Nueva Democracia* also discussed temperance. See Rojas Sosa, *La metrópoli viciosa*, 143, 161–62; Autrique Escobar, "*Salvar a la Raza,*" 133–39, 233–36.

54. Andrés Osuna to Fernando Torreblanca, 6 Aug. 1924, Archivo General de la Nación, Fondo Administración Pública, Álvaro Obregón-Plutarco Elías Calles (AGN-FAP-O-C), Exp. 814-A-119; Ivy V. Yeaworth and María Linsa Ortiz to Álvaro Obregón, 6 Sept. 1924, AGN-FAP-O-C, Exp. 104-E-23; Ramírez to Portes Gil, 17 Apr. 1929, AGN-FAP-EPG, Exp. 3/669, Leg. 2; "Notas del redactor," *El Vocero Antialcohólico: Organo official de la Liga Antialcohólica Mexicana* 1, no. 6 (May and June, 1929),

1–2, in Archivo Histórico de la Secretaría de Educación Pública, Departamento de Escuelas Rurales, Dirección General, Caja 8, Exp. 10; J. T. Ramírez to Cárdenas, 4 Sept. 1936, AGN-FAP-LC, Exp. 553/11; Primer Congreso Nacional Antialcohólico to Cárdenas, 31 Oct. 1936, AGN-FAP-LC, Exp. 553/11.

55. Osuna to Torreblanca, 6 Aug. 1924, AGN-FAP-O-C, Exp. 814-A-119; "Notas del redactor," 1–2; DAA to Cárdenas, 1 Aug. 1935, AGN-FAP-LC, Exp. 553/11.

56. "La campaña que se hará contra el alcoholismo," *EX*, 12 Apr. 1919, 1; Delgado to unknown, 20 Aug. 1921, AGN-FAP-O-C, Exp. 816-A-46; Moisés Sáenz to Cárdenas, 14 Sept. 1935, AGN-FAP-LC, Exp. 533/4/1, Leg. 1; memorandum, 21 Jan. 1939, AGN-FAP-LC, Exp. 533/4/1, Leg. 1; Bastian, *Los disidentes*, location 2736; Bastian, "Protestantismo y sociedad," 445; Autrique Escobar, "*Salvar a la Raza*," 128–29n32.

57. Ignacio Torres Delgado to unknown, 2 Dec. 1921, AGN-FAP-O-C, Exp. 816-A-46; Osuna to Torreblanca, 6 Aug. 1924, AGN-FAP-O-C, Exp. 814-A-119; Osuna, *El alcoholismo*; Franco, *Los hijos de la intemperancia alcohólica y el presidio*, 15, in AHSSA-SPI-SSJ, Caja 41, Exp. 6; flyer, 20 Nov. 1936, AGN-FAP-LC, Exp. 533.11/1; Aureliano Esquivel Casas to Director of Federal Education in Sonora, 9 July 1941, AHSEP-DEFS, Caja 602, Exp. 28; Bastian, *Los disidentes*, location 2614, 2736, 4566, 4653, 4910; Bastian, "Protestantismo y sociedad," 444, 446; Autrique Escobar, "*Salvar a la Raza*," 64n79, 183n14, 237.

58. Gutiérrez y Oliveras, *El sepulturero*, 17, 59; Pulido Esteva, *¡A su salud!*, 80.

59. Autrique Escobar, "*Salvar a la Raza*," 138, 162. See also Rojas Sosa, *La metrópoli viciosa*, 162.

60. Osuna, *El alcoholismo*, 249–50. See also Pulido Esteva, *¡A su salud!*, 123–24.

61. Autrique Escobar, "*Salvar a la Raza*," 155.

62. Corcuera de Mancera, *El fraile, el indio y el pulque*, 115; Earle, "Algunos pensamientos sobre 'El indio borracho' en el imaginario criollo," 20–21; Pulido Esteva, *¡A su salud!*, 118–20.

63. Joaquín Pardo Dufoo to Portes Gil, 22 Apr. 1929, AGN-FAP-EPG, Exp. 3/669, Leg. 1; pledge card, 1937, Biblioteca Francisco Xavier Clavigero, Archivo Acción Católica Mexicana, Exp. 1.5.8.3; "Comisión Central de la U. F. C. M. de Clases Trabajadoras," *Acción Femenina* (Mexico City), May 1938. See also Méndez Reyes, "De crudas y moralidad," 259; Schell, "Of the Sublime Mission," 111.

64. Knight, "Popular Culture," 415–16; Bantjes, *Jesus Walked on Earth*, 49; Fernández Aceves, "Guadalajaran Women," 307.

65. Meza Gutiérrez, *El alcoholismo como plaga social*; Rojas Sosa, *La metrópoli viciosa*, 137–38, 140, 145, 149–50, 160–61, 174n35, 235–36.

Works Cited

Archives

Archivo General de la Nación (Mexico City)
    Fondo Administración Pública
        Abelardo Rodríguez
        Álvaro Obregón-Plutarco Elías Calles
        Emilio Portes Gil
        Lázaro Cárdenas
    Fondo Archivo Particular
        Emilio Portes Gil
            Fondo Emilio Portes Gil
Archivo Histórico del Estado de Sonora (Hermosillo)
    Ramo Ejecutivo
Archivo Histórico Municipal de Tequila
    Sección Presidencia
        Serie Correspondencia
Archivo Histórico de la Secretaría de Educación Pública
    Departamento de Escuelas Rurales
        Dirección General
        Dirección General de Educación Primaria en los Estados y Territorios
            Dirección de Educación Federal, Sonora
    Institución de Orientación Socialista
Archivo Histórico de la Secretaría de Salubridad y Asistencia (Mexico City)
    Fondo Salubridad Pública I
        Sección Servicio Jurídico
Biblioteca Francisco Xavier Clavigero (Mexico City)
    Archivo Acción Católica Mexicana
Fideicomiso Archivos Plutarco Elías Calles y Fernando Torreblanca (Mexico City)
    Archivo Fernando Torreblanca
        Fondo Plutarco Elías Calles
Regenstein Library, University of Chicago
    Records of the Department of State Relating to the Internal Affairs of Mexico, 1930–1939 (812.00) (microfilm), RDS 1930-1939
University of Texas at Austin Library
    Nettie Lee Benson Latin American Collection

Periodicals

El Abogado Cristiano (Mexico City)
Acción Femenina (Mexico City)
Adelante: Revista Militar y de Cultura (Mexico City)
Alma Sonorense (Ures)
Boletín de la Secretaría de la Educación Pública (Mexico City)
Comino (Mexico City)
Excélsior (Mexico City)
Izquierdas (Mexico City)
El Maestro Rural (Mexico City)
El Nacional (Mexico City)
El Pueblo (Hermosillo)
El Universal (Mexico City)
El Vocero Antialcohólico (Mexico City)

Primary Sources

Franco, Luis G. *Los hijos de la intemperancia alcohólica y el presidio*. Monterrey, Mexico: Talleres Linotipográficos del Gobierno del Estado de Nuevo León, 1932.
Gutiérrez y Oliveras, Antonio. *El sepulturero de la raza latinoamericana o el cantinero y la conquista pacífica*. Mexico City: Casa Unida de Publicaciones, 1929.
Lazcano, Francisco, and Emilio Portes Gil. *Unificando la campaña antialcohólica*. Mexico City: Centro Internacional de Prensa, 1929.
Meza Gutiérrez, José. *El alcoholismo como plaga social*. Mexico City: Comité Nacional de Lucha Contra el Alcohólismo, 1930.
Osuna, Andrés. *El alcoholismo. Manual de enseñanza antialcohólica. Para uso de profesores de educación primaria y estudiantes de escuelas secundarias*. Mexico City: Sociedad de Edición y Librería Franco Americana, 1929.
Parsons, Rev. Wilfrid. *Mexican Martyrdom: Firsthand Accounts of the Religious Persecution in Mexico, 1926–1935*. New York: Macmillan Company, 1936.
Secretaría de Hacienda y Crédito Público. *Memoria de la Secretaría Hacienda y Crédito Público 16 de abril de 1917 a 21 de mayo de 1920*. Vol. 1. Mexico City: Talleres Gráficos de la Nación, 1957.
"The Socialist ABCs" (Tabasco: Redemption Press, 1929). In *The Mexico Reader: History, Culture, Politics*, edited by Gilbert M. Joseph and Timothy J. Henderson, 410–17. Durham, NC: Duke University Press, 2002.

Secondary Sources

Autrique Escobar, Cecilia. *"Salvar a la Raza": La prohibición del alcohol, los protestantes de Estados Unidos y los revolucionarios de México (1916–1933)*. Mexico City: Universidad Iberoamericana, 2020.

Bantjes, Adrian A. *As If Jesus Walked on Earth: Cardenismo, Sonora, and the Mexican Revolution*. Wilmington, DE: SR Books, 1998.

———. "The Regional Dynamics of Anticlericalism and Defanaticization in Revolutionary Mexico." In *Faith and Impiety in Revolutionary Mexico*, edited by Matthew Butler, 111–30. New York: Palgrave Macmillan, 2007.

Bastian, Jean-Pierre. *Los disidentes: sociedades, protestantes y revolución en México 1872–1911*. Mexico City: Fondo de Cultura Económica, 1989. Kindle.

———. "Protestantismo y sociedad en México, 1857–1940." In *Los intelectuales y el poder en México: memorias de la VI Conferencia de Historiadores Mexicanos y Estadounidenses*, edited by Roderic A. Camp, Charles A. Hale, and Josefina Zoraida Vázquez, 437–53. Mexico City: El Colegio de México, 1991.

Bautista García, Cecilia Adriana. "Maestros y Masones: La contienda por la reforma educativa en México, 1930–1940." *Relaciones: Estudios de historia y sociedad* 26, no. 104 (2005): 220–76.

Butler, Matthew. "A Revolution in Spirit? Mexico, 1910–1940." In *Faith and Impiety in Revolutionary Mexico*, edited by Matthew Butler, 1–20. New York: Palgrave Macmillan, 2007.

Corcuera de Mancera, Sonia. *El fraile, el indio y el pulque. Evangelización y embriaguez en la Nueva España (1523–1548)*. Mexico City: Fondo de Cultura Económica, 1991.

Dawson, Alexander S. *Indian and Nation in Revolutionary Mexico*. Tucson: University of Arizona Press, 2004.

Dormady, Jason. "God, Cleanliness, and the City: Local Uses of Hygiene and Anticlerical Language in Religious Conflict - Guadalajara, Mexico, 1939–1942." *The Latin Americanist* 64, no. 4 (December 2020): 393–422.

Earle, Rebecca. "Algunos pensamientos sobre 'El indio borracho' en el imaginario criollo." *Revista de Estudios Sociales* 29 (2008): 18–27.

Fallaw, Ben. "Dry Law, Wet Politics: Drinking and Prohibition in Post-Revolutionary Yucatán." *Latin American Research Review* 37, no. 2 (2001): 37–64.

———. *Religion and State Formation in Postrevolutionary Mexico*. Durham, NC: Duke University Press, 2013.

Fernández Aceves, María Teresa. "Guadalajaran Women and the Construction of National Identity." In *The Eagle and the Virgin: Nation and Cultural Revolution in Mexico, 1920–1940*, edited by Mary Kay Vaughan and Stephen E. Lewis, 297–313. Durham, NC: Duke University Press, 2006.

Giuseppe, Massimo de. "'El Indio Gabriel': New Religious Perspectives among the Indigenous in Garrido Canabal's Tabasco." In *Faith and Impiety in Revolutionary Mexico*, edited by Matthew Butler, 225–42. New York: Palgrave Macmillan, 2007.

Knight, Alan. "The Mentality and Modus Operandi of Revolutionary Anticlericalism." In *Faith and Impiety in Revolutionary Mexico*, edited by Matthew Butler, 21–56. New York: Palgrave Macmillan, 2007.

———. "Popular Culture and the Revolutionary State in Mexico, 1910–1940." *Hispanic American Historical Review* 74, no. 3 (August 1994): 393–444.

Lewis, Stephen E. *The Ambivalent Revolution: Forging State and Nation in Chiapas*. Albuquerque: University of New Mexico Press, 2005.

Martínez Assad, Carlos. *El laboratorio de la revolución: el tabasco garridista*. Mexico City: Siglo Ventiuno Editores, 1979.

Meyer, Jean. "Religious Conflict and Catholic Resistance in 1930s Oaxaca." In *Faith and Impiety in Revolutionary Mexico*, edited by Matthew Butler, 185–202. New York: Palgrave Macmillan, 2007.

Mitchell, Stephanie. "Por la liberación de la mujer: Women and the Anti-Alcohol Campaign." In *The Women's Revolution in Mexico, 1910–1953*, edited by Stephanie Mitchell and Patience A. Schell, 165–85. Lanham, MD: Rowman & Littlefield, 2007.

Olcott, Jocelyn. *Revolutionary Women in Postrevolutionary Mexico*. Durham, NC: Duke University Press, 2005.

Palacios, Guillermo. *La pluma y el arado: Los intelectuales pedagogos y la construcción sociocultural del "problema campesino" en México, 1932–1934*. Mexico City: El Colegio de México, 1999.

Pierce, Gretchen Kristine. "Sobering the Revolution: Mexico's Anti-Alcohol Campaigns and the Process of State-Building, 1910–1940." PhD diss., University of Arizona, 2008.

Pierce, Gretchen. "Fighting Bacteria, the Bible, and the Bottle: Projects to Create New Men, Women, and Children, 1910–1940." In *A Companion to Mexican History and Culture*, edited by William H. Beezley, 505–17. London: Wiley-Blackwell, 2011.

———. "Parades, Epistles, and Prohibitive Legislation: Mexico's National Anti-Alcohol Campaign and the Process of State-Building, 1934–1940." *Social History of Alcohol and Drugs* 23, no. 2 (2009): 151–80.

Pulido Esteva, Diego. *¡A su salud! Sociabilidades, libaciones y prácticas populares en la Ciudad de México a principios del siglo XX*. Mexico City: El Colegio de México, 2014.

Rojas Sosa, Odette María. *La metrópoli viciosa. Alcóhol, crimen y bajos fondos. Ciudad de México, 1929–1946*. Mexico City: Universidad Autónoma de México, 2019.

Schell, Patience A. "Of the Sublime Mission of Mothers of Families: The Union of Mexican Catholic Ladies in Revolutionary Mexico." In *The Women's Revolution in Mexico, 1910–1953*, edited by Stephanie Mitchell and Patience A. Schell, 99–123. Lanham, MD: Rowman & Littlefield, 2007.

Sluis, Ageeth. *Deco Body, Deco City: Female Spectacle and Modernity in Mexico City, 1900–1939*. Lincoln: University of Nebraska Press, 2016.

Smith, Benjamin. "Anticlericalism, Politics, and Freemasonry in Mexico, 1920–1940." *Americas* 65, no. 4 (April 2009): 559–88.

Smith, Stephanie J. "Salvador Alvarado of Yucatán: Revolutionary Reforms, Revolutionary Women." In *State Governors in the Mexican Revolution, 1910–1952: Portraits in Conflict, Courage, and Corruption*, edited by Jürgen Buchenau and William H. Beezley, 43–57. Lanham, MD: Rowman & Littlefield, 2009.

Urías Horcasitas, Beatriz. "De moral y regeneración: el programa de 'ingeniería social' posrevolucionario visto a través de las revistas masónicas mexicanas, 1930–1945." *Cuicuilco* 11, no. 32 (Sept–Dec 2004): 87–119.

Vaughan, Mary Kay. *Cultural Politics in Revolution: Teachers, Peasants, and Schools in Mexico, 1930–1940*. Tucson: University of Arizona Press, 1997.

SECTION III

ALTERNATIVES to CATHOLICISM

CHAPTER SIX

The Germ of Fanaticism

Anti-Catholicism, Scientism, and Tabasconization, ca. 1925–1935

BEN FALLAW

In 1930, General Cristóbal Rodríguez pontificated that "thanks to the horrible hygienic conditions in the churches, infant mortality and sickness in general have gone up."[1] Curing the "dangerous social cancer" of Catholicism demanded, in his words, "the radiation that destroys it—the radicalism of the liberals."[2] As a leading advocate of eugenics in Mexico, metaphorical associations of anticlericalism with biomedicine and religion with disease and filth came naturally to him.[3] Rodríguez's justification of anti-Catholicism on scientific grounds was no outlier. In 1929, strongman of Tabasco Tomás Garrido Canabal's administration asked the national health department to prevent the clergy from making the sign of cross with saliva "to prevent the spread of infectious diseases like tuberculosis, syphilis and cancer."[4] That same year, Dr. Enrique Beltrán Castillo, Mexico's first PhD in biology and remembered today as the father of Mexican conservationism, asked that the Department of Public Health close the Basilica of Guadalupe's well as a "focal point of infections" until its miraculous waters were made potable.[5] At the time, Beltrán self-identified as a "Jacobin Darwinist" and prescribed scientific education to "destroy prejudices and superstitions that darken the mind of the child."[6]

This chapter examines why and how a relatively small but very influential group of revolutionary politicos, soldiers, intellectuals, educators, and grassroots activists justified and understood the eradication of religious beliefs and practices as a scientific endeavor. For them, the scientific method was the ultimate and indeed the only source of all truth—a belief often termed *scientism*.[7] Like Porfirian positivists, scientistic revolutionaries embraced the idea of science as a powerful weapon against "fanaticism," meaning religious beliefs considered backward, irrational, or otherwise pernicious. Scientism enabled revolutionary anticlericals to override constitutional protections of freedom of religion, rewrite the educational curriculum, ignore widespread popular resistance, and advance the state's claims over the body—especially the female and Indigenous body.[8] For teachers, learning science not only enlightened the ignorant, but it also convinced the masses of the postrevolutionary state's ability to uplift; science was considered especially effective against fanatics and Indigenous Mexicans.[9] For anticlerical grassroots organizations and individuals, the idea of science provided a means of individual identity and sociability as well as overcoming popular apathy and resistance.

While the historiography of postrevolutionary anticlericalism has grown remarkably over the past twenty years, this represents the first study focused on scientism's place in anti-Catholicism.[10] This chapter also engages the abundant literature on everyday forms of state formation by problematizing the idea that the expansion of the postrevolutionary state into quotidian life in the name of science encouraged negotiation between state agents and society.[11] The application of scientific ideas like germ theory undoubtedly saved hundreds of thousands of lives and alleviated much suffering in postrevolutionary Mexico; such advancements were both meaningful and real.[12] At the same time, public health campaigns carried out by officials served as a vector for scientistic anti-Catholicism: fighting filth and disease could easily become a struggle against Catholic beliefs and practices deemed fanatical.[13] By foregrounding the role of the idea of science in revolutionary anticlericalism, we can see how the growth of the postrevolutionary state's presence in everyday life to eradicate not just germs but also fanaticism provoked resistance that sapped its legitimacy. This chapter also explores the contradictions and tensions in the idea of science as invoked by a number of different actors linked to the postrevolutionary state, ranging from state and federal schoolteachers to Tabasco's Garrido Canabal and his followers to a psychic herbalist and a theosophist magnetic doctor who represented their professions as scientific. While popular Catholic resistance to state formation has been widely studied, we know much less about the admittedly smaller cohort of anticlericals supporting it. This chapter seeks to remedy this.

To explore the meaning and practice of scientistic anti-Catholicism during the armed phase of the Mexican Revolution (1910–1920) and postrevolutionary state formation, I parse a range of primary sources, including tracts and correspondence from the personal archive of Tomás Garrido Canabal, Tabasco's revolutionary strongman and Mexico's principal advocate of anticlericalism; reports filed by inspectors and teachers with the federal Education Ministry (Secretaría de Educación Pública, or SEP); Interior Ministry (Secretaría de Gobernación) records of Catholic violations of anticlerical legislation; periodicals; and published secondary sources.[14] Methodologically, I heed Adrian Bantjes's call to closely examine key terms like "defanaticization," "fanatic," and "science" in primary sources.[15]

The chapter begins by examining Garrido Canabal's anticlerical regime in Tabasco—the epicenter of anti-Catholicism between 1925 and 1935—then turns to its proselytization efforts across Mexico and especially the campaign to "Tabasconize" state (as opposed to federal) educators across Mexico.[16] Attempts to encourage the SEP to adopt an explicitly antireligious scientist curriculum modeled on Tabasco's rationalist education across the country touched off a dispute among educators and national politicians— the subject of the next section. By drilling down into the debate over the adoption of a Tabasco-style, scientific, explicitly anticlerical curriculum in federal schools aimed primarily at eradicating Catholicism root and branch, we can better understand the reluctance of the national SEP bureaucrats and even Plutarco Elías Calles to support the model of rationalist schooling adopted in Tabasco. At the same time, scientism's role in solidifying organizations and informing texts that linked like-minded revolutionary anticlericals across Mexico becomes more apparent. I then consider how some federal educators in rural Mexico adopted scientistic Tabascan methods as well as relying on the idea of science to explain their successes and failures, overcome resistance deeply rooted in religion, and represent the expansion of the postrevolutionary state into rural areas as modernity. In the penultimate section, I examine how a variety of grassroots anticlerical organizations used vaccination rituals and putatively scientific spiritism to combat fanaticism, before concluding this chapter.

The Science of Revolution in Tabasco

For a decade, Tomás Garrido Canabal turned Tabasco into what Lázaro Cárdenas famously called a revolutionary laboratory. President and *jefe máximo* Calles, arch-leftist Francisco Múgica, and President Lázaro Cárdenas all hailed Tabasco as the proving ground for key elements of state formation: prohibition, cooperativism, mobilization of youth and women, sports, and the eradication of fanaticism. After Cárdenas broke with Calles and Garrido Canabal, the left pilloried Garrido Canabal for his authoritarianism and failure to carry out land reform. Ironically, the right

FIGURE 7. Tomás Garrido Canabal (1), 1923. FAPECFT. Fototeca. Archivo Fernando Torreblanca. (AFFT), Fondo Álvaro Obregón, Oficial (FFAOO), serie: *Presidencia de la República, 1920–1924.* Mfn: 389, imagen: 143, inventario: 430.

and supporters of the Catholic Church also vilified Garrido as a thuggish strongman and henchman of Calles, although Conservatives stressed above all his zealous atheism.[17]

Recent research has challenged the black legend of Tabasco. Sarah Osten has shown how Garrido's southeastern socialism was not a personalistic satrapy that disappeared after Garrido's exile. Garrido's regional party and his project had a long tail. It gave Calles and key national collaborators a prototype of a "functional" socialism bequeathed to Cárdenas and, later, the official revolutionary ruling party (the Partido Revolucionario Institucional, or Institutional Revolutionary Party) albeit shorn of its anticlericalism.[18] Stan Ridgeway showed Garrido's cooperatives were not patronage rackets or shields against agrarian reform but an effective response to monocrop dependency on bananas that taxed foreign enclaves to underwrite an ambitious social and education program.[19] Kristin Harper's research revealed that this Garridista social wage generated real support among substantial sectors of Tabasco's society despite the regime's "coercion and arbitrariness."[20]

Under Garrido, Tabasco was not just a place. It was also an idea, one that fascinated, inspired, and/or repelled Mexicans across the country from Yucatán to Sonora. As governor and regional strongman, Garrido sponsored a veritable army of intellectuals to staff his burgeoning bureaucracy and propagandize across Mexico during the late 1920s and early 1930s; as national secretary of agriculture and development in 1934–1935, his proselytization efforts expanded.[21] Among the Tabascan literati was José Malpica Hernández, a prolific proponent of science and scientistic anticlericalism. While his formal education ended with primary school, his early entry into journalism exposed him to a wide range of scientific and philosophical ideas. A dedicated popularizer of contemporary scientific theory, Malpica contributed prodigiously to *Redención*, Garrido's daily newspaper; guest lectured at the Tabasco's center of higher education, Instituto Juárez; and eventually wrote a column featured in the mainstream national daily newspaper *El Universal*. To fully elaborate his materialistic fundamentalism, he penned *El Universo sin Dios*, which Garrido gave away by the dozens to his admirers across Mexico, including many state and federal teachers.[22] Echoing Porfirian positivists, Malpica celebrated science as the only source of truth and viewed ideological systems in terms of their social function. Discoveries over the past fifty years in science meant that "[t]oday, religion is unnecessary, and rigorously unscientific."[23] Malpica proclaimed: "The dogma of the soul's immortality is antiscientific"; believers in religion were "deserters from Science."[24] Tabasco's radical ideology was ardently scientistic. In place of the Catholic Church's fear and false hopes, science offered rational knowledge and material progress. Garridista poet Domingo Borrego urged his readers to "[n]ot fear, death is a new life reproduced in perfumed flower and in the sap of the century-old tree."[25] Metaphysical questions had no place in the post-religious future imagined by Garrido and his followers.

Tabasco also served as a testing ground for perfecting the rationalist school (*escuela racionalista*) developed by Felipe Carrillo Puerto in neighboring Yucatán and was a seedbed for future educational leaders.[26] When the leading theorist of rationalist education, José de la Luz Mena, fled his native Yucatán after Felipe Carrillo Puerto's death and the dismantling of much of the rationalist school project, Garrido Canabal welcomed him.[27] Miguel Cantón (Carrillo Puerto's key lieutenant) and a small army of teachers trained in rationalist schooling in Yucatán between 1915 and 1923 decamped to Tabasco as well. This radical diaspora helped Garrido Canabal adopt the curriculum developed in Yucatán that emphasized science in so-called action pedagogy (learning-by-doing, egalitarian classrooms) to nurture a new revolutionary subjectivity in students who would graduate free of superstition and selfishness.[28] Instruction in science and hands-on learning would create a secular, reason-based, perfectible society without dogma or doubt.[29]

Through free subscriptions to papers and magazines, complementary tracts and books, and junkets to Tabasco, Garrido Canabal spread his message. Well-coordinated outreach efforts encouraged teachers and politicians across Mexico to imitate Tabasco's pedagogy. Garrido also effectively lobbied policymakers; his bribes (*iguales*) to congressmen and cabinet ministers also played a role in creating Tabasco's revolutionary cachet.[30] Acolytes of Tabasco-style education often advanced to the upper ranks of the state and federal education systems because rationalist education provided them a coherent, convincing, and radical pedagogy that promised to revive the flagging fortunes of the postrevolutionary state and realize its goal of fostering a more nationalist, egalitarian, and productive society free from fanaticism. This Tabasconization—to paraphrase one-time admirer Francisco Múgica—stimulated what I have called elsewhere a lateral as opposed to top-down radicalization. Rather than Mexico City ordering subordinates to root out fanaticism, middle- and lower-ranking officials imitated Garrido Canabal's tactics.[31] The key agent in Tabasconization would be teachers trained in rationalist education.

Tabasconizing State Teachers across Mexico

Among the many publications distributed by the Garridista regime, one work stands out for its ubiquity and combativeness when it came to the "religious question" in schools: Germán List Arzubide's 1933 *Practice of Irreligious Education*. In December 1933, Garrido Canabal doled out dozens of complementary copies of it to federal inspectors, teachers, and even generals across Mexico. List (1898–1998), remembered today as a leading light of the avant-garde Stridentist movement, earned notoriety after *Practice* appeared on the Vatican's *Index Librorum Prohibitorum*. List's action-centered pedagogy resembled rationalist education, encouraging children to observe and experiment to understand natural and social phenomena. In the process they would emancipate themselves from errors instilled by parents and priests.[32] List represented his methods as imminently reasonable and free of violence and crudeness. Practitioners of List's methods often ran afoul of SEP policies prohibiting offending religious sensibilities. Lesson plans encouraged children under ten to build a wooden saint's head and stuff it with salts to show how fake sweat could be produced in icons, to ask doctors if they can get diphtheria or typhoid from Communion wafers, and to write letters to proletarian papers criticizing local religious customs.[33]

When Garrido Canabal distributed List's book to educators and politicians, he explained that science would not replace religion or transfer its sacrality to the state would but in fact abolish all irrational belief systems:

> Our anti-dogmatic labor has been neither violent nor arbitrary, instead we have ensured that our school confronts religious absurdities, proclaiming the principles of science and wielding reason, not exactly as a religious system, but as a method to investigate the truths that are not yet under the dominion of contemporary science.[34]

In Yucatán, Miguel Cantón, state congressman and the former editor of an important Garridista newspaper in Tabasco, argued that the state's schools should adopt List's curriculum because

> the dogmas of the religions should be combated in the public schools because the citizens hope that the state's educational system imparts the clarification of obscurantism to make a generation of strong iconoclasts, with calm spirits nurtured

by the sources of science and truth. The modern philosophy, based in scientific materialism, has uprooted all the prejudices based in religion, and pulverized all the idols created by the exploitation of the workers.³⁵

Yucatán's state congress failed to adopt List's methods, likely because Bartolomé García Correa, head of Yucatán's Socialist party, pursued détente with the Church instead of incinerating idols.³⁶

Tabascan-style scientific anticlericalism was more warmly received in other states. In Sonora, Governor (and son of jefe máximo Plutarco Elías Calles) Rodolfo Elías Calles in his words "purified" his teaching cadre, firing many teachers (almost all female) who refused to teach "scientific truth... to eliminate from children all religious prejudice."³⁷ The superintendent of Jalisco implemented a Tabascan curriculum in state schools to defanaticize children via science, apparently by adopting List's methods.³⁸ The superintendent of Coahuila's state schools was inspired by List's *Práctica* to teach "the principles of science, based in reason, investigating methodically the truth of science and discarding religious dogma as anti-pedagogical and anti-social."³⁹ List's scientistic methods promised state educators the power to dispel fanaticism binding their students and prepare them to be productive, patriotic citizens with a social conscience and an empirical view of the world. In other words, classrooms from Chiapas to Chihuahua would be little Tabascos. Whether rationalist education actually trickled down to the classroom in states where superintendents and governors adopted List's methods is another question. Teachers and inspectors generally hesitated to implement the most controversial parts of the rationalist curriculum because of fears of resistance and personal reservations. Nevertheless, for both advocates and Catholic opponents, Tabasconization seemed to be spreading like a red ink blot during the early 1930s.

While Garrido Canabal boasted of successfully exporting rationalist education to several states outside of Tabasco in 1932–1934, truly transforming all Mexico's schools would have required its adoption at the federal level. This in turn necessitated the national congress to reform Article 3 of the Constitution of 1917 to adopt the scientific model of Tabasco's education. Given Garrido's boundless self-esteem, his ambitions to export his ideas and influence national politics, and the encouragement from many admirers he had among revolutionary apparatchiks and intellectuals, such a campaign was likely inevitable.⁴⁰ Moreover, as Sarah Osten explains in this volume, Garrido's almost paranoiac concern with preventing a possible coup attempt after the de la Huerta revolt claimed Felipe Carrillo Puerto's life in early 1924 profoundly shaped his political project and heightened his anticlericalism. In short, attacking fanaticism justified crackdowns on suspected opponents as well as reminding Obregón and Calles of Garrido's loyalty.[41]

In a Tabasconized Mexico, Garrido would be able to count on clients across the nation plus supporters in Mexico City should his enemies seek to launch an "invasion" of Tabasco to topple him. In other words, the best defense was a good offense.[42] Offending foes intentionally through parody, satire, and literal iconoclasm were favorite tactics; what today we would term trolling won few new adherents but seemed to be immensely satisfying to Garrido and his more ardent acolytes. Rather than proselyting, the performance of rituals like *quemasantos* (spectacular burnings of sacred items) served to create solidarity among participants, instilling an identity as the vanguard of a new Mexico—a modern, non-Indigenous, productive country ruled by reason and dedicated to work as "the only true religion" in Garridista discourse.[43]

Regardless of his motivation, Garrido had to wait for a propitious moment in national politics to launch a campaign to rewrite Article 3 of the 1917 Constitution to Tabasconize the nation's schools. It came when supporters of Calles in Mexico City attacked President Pascual Ortiz Rubio for tolerating the public celebration of the 400th anniversary of the apparition of the Virgin of Guadalupe on the hill of Tepeyac on December 12, 1931. Garrido considered the event nothing less than a "mockery of our laws and a challenge to Revolution."[44]

The Failure to Tabasconize Mexico's Federal Schools

Not satisfied with burning two thousand "fetishes" in Tabasco to retaliate against the December 1931 display of Guadalupanismo, Garrido was determined to see rationalist schooling adopted across Mexico through constitutional reform.[45] Garrido believed the Tabasconization of Mexico City would exploit the rift that the December 12, 1931, celebrations at Tepeyac had opened in the national political elite between supporters of Calles who condemned it and defenders of Ortiz Rubio who did not. In the end, however, the Tabascans failed to win over Calles and his inner circle or the leadership of the federal education ministry (SEP).[46] Not only did Garrido misread Mexico City politics; he also found that many elites proved reluctant to deploy science to aggressively defanaticize pupils. Instead of rationalist education with its scientistic pretensions, Calles, his key Mexico City allies, and the SEP's upper ranks opted for socialist education, a more moderate program that tempered anticlericalism. The differences between socialist education and rationalist education might seem small given their similarities, but in the contest between Tabasconizers backing the former and their foes within the revolutionary camp advocating the latter, there was a lot at stake. Whether to use the idea of science to fight fanaticism was one of the main points of contention. There were other, less ideological differences between the Tabasconizers and their opponents. From the point of view of Garrido's faction, socialist education lacked rationalist education's distinguished pedigree and tolerated too many individualist and conservative ideas.[47] For those who would Tabasconize Mexico, socialist education was too cautious when it came to religion and was thus part of the problem.

Early successes for Garrido's campaign to Tabasconize schools belied its eventual defeat by opponents within the SEP and state education systems and by national political elites who were much more moderate on the religious question and feared giving Garrido too much power nationally. In early 1932, Tabascan Senator Ausencio C. Cruz sprang into action, imploring governors to endorse the reform of Article 3; admirers of Garrido like Governor Lázaro Cárdenas of Michoacán approved. Like-minded educators at a teacher's convention in Guadalajara and delegates to an agrarian congress in San Luis Potosí seconded the proposal.[48] By early October 1934, Garridistas in the national congress led by former teacher and *diputado federal* Arnulfo H. Pérez—the self-proclaimed Personal Enemy of God—seemed close to victory.[49] Foes in congress acting apparently with Calles's tacit approval punned in Spanish calling it not *educación científica* but *educación científico*, since *científico* also referred to the positivist clique close to Porfirio Díaz.[50] It was more than an insult.

By now, Garrido's foes and supporters both understood scientific education not just as continuing rationalist education's emphasis on experiential learning and science but also as explicitly eradicating religion. The SEP's brand of socialist education, on the other hand, implicitly promised moderation on the religious question. Calles, acting indirectly through his congressional proxies and the ruling party's newspaper *El Nacional*, blocked the national adoption of the Tabascan model. In the end, an overwhelming majority of federal diputados (93 versus 26) rejected Garrido Canabal's call to directly attack religious fanaticism using the idea of science as among its most potent weapons.[51] Garrido Canabal's response to this setback was not recorded, but he reacted to a previous defeat in Mexico City by bulldozing a cathedral in Tabasco.[52]

Calles's reluctance to endorse rationalist education is at odds with standard depictions of him as the uncompromising clerophobe who issued the 1934 Grito de Guadalajara urging the state to wrest full responsibility for education from the Church and Catholic parents.[53] Historians should take into account his complicated political position and his own personal spiritual beliefs. Biographer Jürgen Buchenau notes not only Calles's "single-minded determination to weaken the Church" and a "desire to centralize education under the tutelage of the state" but also recognizes even as jefe máximo or hyper-executive Calles's power waxed and waned during the seven-year Maximato (1928–1935). In the introduction to this volume, Buchenau and Dalton show Calles was anti-Catholic but not against organized religion per se, and his personal beliefs were much more complex than usually portrayed. Like many other revolutionaries, Calles proved privately reluctant to completely reject the metaphysical as Garrido-style radicalism required.[54]

Shifting political circumstances (like the costs of another conflict with Catholics or the United States) forced Calles to make pragmatic choices and modify his public position on the religious question.[55] Pressure from the United States seems to have played a role, too, in encouraging Calles to sink Tabasconization of the SEP. Ambassador Josephus Daniels initially downplayed the firestorm the Grito de Guadalajara ignited on both sides of the Rio Grande, but President Franklin Delano Roosevelt's Democratic Party relied on the support of many US Catholics and feared political fallout from an investigation of Mexico's religious question threatened by Republican Senator William Borah.[56] Alberto J. Pani, consummate political insider who often criticized aspects of the Maximato despite serving President Calles, attributed Calles's intemperate attack on Mexican Catholics' faith delivered in the Grito de Guadalajara to pressure from individuals Pani derided as extremist lackeys in Calles's inner circle. Moreover, Pani noted, the jefe máximo's seemingly radical proclamation at Guadalajara "resulted in a lukewarm reform of article 3 of the Constitution of 1917."[57] Pani's account captures Calles's calibration when it came to anticlericalism ignoring actors far from Calles's inner circle, both Tabasconized politicians in the states and Garridista grassroots groups like the Red Shirts that sprang up across Mexico. Pani's focus on high politics also overlooks an important interest group with a huge stake in opposing the Tabasconization of Mexico's school: the SEP.

The SEP's upper ranks quietly fought Garrido's project tooth and nail.[58] Many inspectors and teachers likewise had real concerns over Tabasconizing their schools. The SEP's institutional memory recalled Garrido's closure of federal schools in Tabasco in 1925.[59] Moreover, excessive tampering with schools, SEP leaders feared, would incite dangerous resistance from Catholics and undermine the ministry's autonomy, upsetting all-important seniority by imposing ideological tests and provoking purges.[60] Many SEP officials recoiled from Tabasco-style iconoclasm, refusing to attend Mexico City's first *quemasantos* staged for their benefit.[61] The SEP waged a successful, very quiet campaign within the national government to defeat Garrido's initiative, but in public, federal educators often genuflected toward Tabasco. For example, SEP chief of staff Rafael Molina Betancourt praised Garrido Canabal's "scientific program and serious campaign against fanatics," and in 1935 he fired recalcitrant teachers and (rhetorically at least) included defanaticization in socialist education.[62] The SEP was not monolithic; it recruited many radical Tabascan teachers, along with Veracruzanos and Yucatecos who also harbored anticlerical beliefs.[63] There were deeper fractures, further complicating administration of a uniform policy. The SEP's reliance on Tabasconized teachers and its praise for some of their educational practices created space for federal teachers and even some inspectors to defy the SEP's moderate orthodoxy and employ the controversial methods developed in Garrido's revolutionary laboratory in SEP classrooms.

Science and Defanaticization in the Federal Classroom

Even though socialist education refrained from directly attacking religion and thus antagonized the Tabasconizers, it was far too radical for Catholics, Conservatives, and traditionalists within the SEP. They recoiled from it in part because it committed federal teachers to supporting agrarian reform, workers' rights, and secularizing society and culture.[64] In the end, the SEP got the revolutionary educational model that it wanted: the more moderate socialist education as opposed to rationalist education with its combative doctrines that wielded the idea of science against religion. Nevertheless, in many federal schoolhouses the idea of science came to play an important role in defining the SEP teachers' mission and curriculum. The scientific defanaticization that was a staple of Tabasco's rationalist education—along with a generic Marxist class-consciousness with a similar materialistic, antireligious bent—provided an ideological coherence and motivation absent from the SEP's institutional culture and the banal orthodoxy of socialist education. Moreover, a host of Garridista publications like List's book and a cadre of determined practitioners of Tabascan-style anti-Catholicism holding positions in the SEP influenced many federal educators.

Luis Ramírez was one of the Tabasconized SEP administrators. As federal superintendent of schools in Yucatán, he used List's book to teach defanaticization techniques at the August 1934 in-service training (*curso de mejoramiento*) attended by seventy federal teachers.[65] Some federal teachers openly engaged in Garridista iconoclasm. This was clearest in predominantly Indigenous areas of Campeche and Hidalgo states, where they mounted large *quemasantos*.[66] But such collective, public violations of SEP policy risked institutional sanctions. They could also provoke violent resistance. More common were semi-discrete attempts by Tabasconized federal educators to skirt strict SEP policy against direct attacks on religious sentiment.

One opportunity came in the SEP policy formally adopted in 1935 to give *pláticas* (motivational talks delivered to communities) to "scientifically explain phenomena attributed to divine forces."[67] The SEP believed such "indirect, but efficient means" would presumably avoid triggering Catholic anger yet still effectively defanaticize Mexico's youth.[68] An inspector based in Actopan, Hidalgo stated that scientific explanation of the universe would dispel "error, fetishism, witchcraft, and fanaticism."[69] Leopoldo Caro, federal inspector on Guerrero state's Costa Grande, reported his teachers' pláticas were "strengthening the view of the world and life when this is rational, or we work to change it when it is full of fantasies and superstitions."[70] In some of these pláticas the SEP's more moderate socialist education came to resemble its vanquished rival, rationalist education, with its radical, scientistic anticlericalism.

This Tabasconization of federal efforts to defanaticize were not necessarily the result of intentional infiltration by Tabasconized teachers. While the upper ranks of the SEP stymied Tabascan-style rationalist education for being too radical, the Communist Party, the CROM national labor federation, and Garrido-style socialists bitterly competed against each other for mass support. On the local level, federal teachers drew freely from rationalist education, socialist education, Garridista Socialism, communism, and the CROM's brand of anarcho-syndicalism.[71] In other words, anticlerical teachers like many anticlerical revolutionary politicians and intellectuals drew on these ideologies because they provided useful curriculum, symbols, and even tactics in combating fanaticism. Setting aside sectarianism, anticlericals drew on what Ray Craib has termed the "capacious left."[72] When it came to using the idea of science to fight backward ideas, disease, and superstition, the Tabascan emphasis on science and the model of rationalist education must have seemed especially compelling.

The mélange of generic leftism helps us understand the seepage of Tabascan practices into federal pedagogy despite the SEP's institutional policing. Tomás Cuervo, arguably the most anti-Catholic of all the SEP inspectors and a fervent admirer of Garrido, called for the defanaticization of Mexico's youth by teaching scientific explanations of natural phenomena. Cuervo regularly harangued Guanajuatan Catholics and dared to proclaim himself an atheist to their faces.[73] Fortíno López, while SEP inspector of south central Guanajuato, believed teaching a scientific explanation of the natural world would free workers from being "hypnotized" by priests. It would also liberate women from men's "depressing tutelage."[74] The Church's "plagues and sanctions" encouraged "ignorance" and "superstition" that held the people of Juchipila, Zacatecas, back from progress, explained federal inspector Manuel Cortina.[75]

For Tabasconized pedagogues, fanaticism (a term rarely if ever applied to non-Catholic Christians) was the enemy, but what did science mean to them and to the more moderate maestros of the SEP who eschewed directly injuring Catholic faith in favor of indirect, tactful methods? There emerged a spectrum of opinions. Moderates might shy away from adopting the hyper-materialistic scientism of Tabasco, but they too believed in teaching a scientific understanding of the world to address widespread superstitions, prejudices, and unhealthy practices. Radical Tabasconized educators and their more moderate peers believed in teaching their students to trust reason over faith, although they might differ over means to that end as well as science's ultimate authority. These radical teachers' discourse reveals some insights into how they thought about using science to "disenchant" the world. Inspector Fabio Belio C. gave talks to thirty-six communities in his district based in the city of Zacatecas during 1936 to "awaken in the citizens the spirit of investigation to replace erroneous beliefs about natural phenomena with scientific truth."[76] This trope of wakening people from the slumber of ignorance and fanaticism recurs in SEP reports and indeed in revolutionary narratives of all sorts.

To round out the curriculum, some inspectors encouraged their teachers to draw on the work of the world's great scientists to defanaticize Mexico. Inspector Manuel Cortina stressed Isaac Newton and

Pierre-Simon Laplace, the eighteenth-century polymath, to counter what he termed "ignorance" and "superstition."[77] There were limits to revealing the workings of nature. When it came to sexual education, SEP teachers proved reluctant to teach anything beyond rudimentary plant and animal reproduction and steered clear of any discussion of human sexuality. Even in officially atheist Tabasco, teachers feared the backlash the topic could provoke. Only a daring few discussed plant reproduction.[78]

To what extent did federal teachers' scientistic explanations of the natural world trickle down to the general population? It is debatable how much difference it made, at least in the 1930s. Most teachers were described politely by Eyler Simpson as "improvised." They were underpaid, overworked, and undertrained. Many had only a few years of primary school education supplemented by on-the-job training.[79] Had the campaigns against "fanatical" Catholicism continued for decades, more lasting results would certainly have been produced, although it seems likely that a reformed Catholicism like the Iglesia Católica Apostólica Mexicana (or the Mexican Catholic Apostolic Church), spiritism, and Protestantism—in particular newer denominations—would have flourished, a result that would have greatly offended Garrido Canabal but pleased more moderate anticlericals like Manuel Gamio (see Dalton in this volume). Whereas some of Garrido Canabal's most ardent acolytes of saw their efforts as irreligious, most of his admirers considered anticlericalism as anti-Catholicism. Indeed, some enterprising Pentecostals and other members of newer Protestant denominations joined Garridista literacy campaigns in Indigenous areas of Tabasco. For them, anti-Catholicism was a stepping stone to conversion to Protestantism, not atheism.[80]

For the SEP, the idea of science served other ends. For instance, it could serve to define success and explain failure, as demonstrated in the case of Roberto Oropeza Nájera, federal school inspector stationed in western Guanajuato in 1935. His bailiwick was in the hinterlands of León, a profoundly Catholic city that was a hotbed of pro-Cristero sentiment in both the first and second Cristiadas. This included sporadic attacks on *ejidos* and federal schoolteachers during the 1930s. To overcome suspicion and hostility toward his teachers, Inspector Oropeza convened pláticas that helped sustain sixteen new ejidos and several successful schools. SEP teachers around León faced—in his words—"fanatical resistance" from unlicensed priests who threatened to excommunicate Catholics who cooperated with the SEP. To counter this opposition, Oropeza spread "scientific knowledge" in pláticas given at twenty schools and at four community-wide Socialist Saturdays.[81]

In the end, science could only do so much or hang on for long. When teachers closed school for vacations or in-service training, "the priests gained ground," organizing truancy strikes that lowered school attendance to zero and closed about half of Oropeza's schools in 1934 and 1935. Faced with these failures, Oropeza encouraged his embattled teachers "to change their tactics in dealing with community members, in order to hide their true intentions regarding socialist education to attack religion."[82] Downplaying scientistic disenchantment of the world was necessary to reopen schools.

Like other SEP officials, Oropeza confronted complex, often intractable problems. Priests and lay leaders regularly organized attendance strikes and neo-Cristero armed bands menaced isolated teachers. Lack of resources and ineffective teachers, however, were probably even more daunting problems. The economic demand for child labor as well as cultural and religious resistance to schooling girls were also extremely difficult to overcome. The category of "fanaticism" simplified the problem, and the notion of science's eventual, inevitable triumph steeled these secular missionaries in the face of such setbacks. Blaming excessive religiosity, backwardness, and superstition also absolved the more radical educators of frequent failures.

Some took a different tack. Facing similar problems in the Celaya district of Guanajuato, Jenaro Hernández Aguilar used science in a different and more effective manner.[83] In assemblies with parents, he told them that their children would be ignorant and poor without schooling, linking fanaticism with poverty and social marginalization.[84] From March to June 1935, Hernández and his teachers abandoned direct attacks on fanaticism and instead undertook a sustained public health campaign, showing how science could improve everyday life through vaccination. Offering free breakfasts to those who came to school could not have hurt either.[85] In southern Guanajuato, two other SEP inspectors boasted of fighting fanaticism to open schools in hostile Catholic communities with "slow, always prudent tactics."[86] By planting new crops and exterminating insect pests, earnest SEP officials had faith that demonstrating science's potential to improve harvests would overcome popular adherence to rooted religious and cultural antipathy to the postrevolutionary state.

Seeing science as a font of useful knowledge applied to materially better life should not blind us to the symbolic place of the idea of science in postrevolutionary state formation, a legacy of Tabascan scientism absorbed by the SEP. The idea of teaching science stood in for a host of progressive transformations that the SEP promised to oversee via schooling and teachers' benevolent interventions into daily life. When SEP officials spoke of science's transformative impact, at times they even implied that it would promote cultural mestizaje among Indigenous Mexicans, a crucial part of the Garridista project.[87] Rubén Rodríguez Lozano, a future SEP standout and eventually intellectual adviser to President Gustavo Díaz Ordaz (1964–1970), hailed from a white, middle-class family in Zacatecas.[88] He saw the Maya villagers of the Chenes hills of Campeche as too backward for the standard SEP curriculum, claiming that "only through demonstration of what science has to offer will they be convinced" to take the path of "collective betterment." For Rodríguez Lozano, science would achieve "the defanaticization of the multitudes" by convincing them to abandon their "ancient rites, language, superstitions, and primitive customs."[89]

The SEP was institutionally robust enough to prevent the adoption of Tabasqueño rational education with its scientistic exclusion of any sort of religiosity. But even moderate SEP inspectors and teachers averse to Tabasco-style iconoclasm believed the idea of science could awaken Mexicans—especially Indigenous Mexicans—from a long slumber of superstition, sloth, and syncretic Catholicism. If Garrido's influence on the federal school system was marginal, it was much stronger over grassroots anticlerical groups and individuals who considered themselves islands of enlightenment surrounded by a sea of fanaticism. In this revolutionary archipelago, the idea of science served as a beacon of hope and a way of signaling to Garrido Canabal they needed his help.

The Spirit of Revolution: Grassroots Anti-Catholicism and Science

Between 1925 and 1935, Mexico's postrevolutionary state lacked a broad, mass base of support in the form of corporatist peasant, worker, and "middle sector" national organizations. Outside of a handful of strong regional parties like Garrido's Socialist party of Tabasco and the remnants of the CROM, the postrevolutionary state had to rely on weak regional and local political parties.[90] Anticlerical groups were important among the relatively feeble pro-revolutionary elements in civil society, yet aside from the schismatic Catholics recently analyzed by Matthew Butler, they remain largely understudied.[91] In this section, I examine local anticlerical groups and a few individuals inspired by scientism. For the anticlerical minority in overwhelmingly Catholic communities (most of Mexico outside the Gulf coast, the desert north, and the Pacific lowlands or Tierra Caliente), faith in the idea of science provided anticlerical teachers a sense of moral superiority that sustained them in a largely hostile social environment.

Anticlericals were always a minority in Mexico, an elect vanguard facing an indifferent or hostile majority.[92] The popularization of science and the technological revolutions that transformed daily life in the early twentieth century gave anticlericalism a much-needed boost. Faith in the idea of science bestowed a sense of purpose and even righteousness, as a letter to Garrido Canabal penned by an isolated anti-Catholic activist in Ocosingo, Chiapas, demonstrates: "I find myself in a truly filthy clericalist focal point struggling to destroy the horrible bandage blinding [them] for many years to the shining truth"—presumably science and Tabasco-style revolution.[93] Near Acapulco, Guerrero, in January 1935, local anticlericals led by a federal teacher formed the "Evolution" circle to combat priests and Christianity's "false doctrine" ("no one can affirm if the afterlife exists"; sin is "an erroneous idea"). For Acapulco's circle, only nature could guide man through life.[94] For this group, science would serve as the source of a new naturalistic and rational morality. The anticlericals of Salvatierra, Guanajuato, mocked Catholics who blamed drought on the opening of a local Masonic lodge.[95] These cases suggest an important part of science's appeal: it was limited to the elite. Only an enlightened few could apply pure reason; the rest would have to be freed from their own ignorance through education and energetic state action—an idea Porfirian positivists known as the *científicos* embraced. The dedicated populist President Lázaro Cárdenas advocated the teaching of "the scientific truth, pure and naked," a phrase he might well have heard from Garrido Canabal, a man he once admired.[96]

If Tabasconized anticlericals claimed science as a key ally and held up Garrido Canabal's Tabasco as a kind of scientific utopia, Garrido Canabal's rejection of anything with a hint of the supernatural prevented forging alliances with other groups with strong anticlerical beliefs. Garrido Canabal was so dogmatic that he opposed spiritism and had his suspicions about Freemasonry.[97] Yet spiritists numbered among the most vocal champions of revolutionary defanaticization in many communities.[98] They penned complaints about alleged Catholic crimes and violations to the federal government and were much more likely to end up joining the SEP. Beatriz Urías Horcasitas showed that spiritist lodges provided a crucial center of sociability for leading intellectuals, educators, and politicians who served in high government posts; the same was probably true in many localities as well.[99]

The Escuela Magnético Espiritual de la Comuna Universal (Magnetic Spiritual School of the Universal Commune, hereafter EMECU) was the most important and best-organized spiritist movement in all of Latin America during the decades treated in this chapter. It claimed Peruvian politician Raúl Haya de la Torre and Nicaraguan revolutionary Augusto César Sandino among its adherents. Founded in 1911 in Buenos Aires by a migrant Basque electrician, Joaquín Trincado, the EMECU claimed to be spiritist (*espiritista*) as opposed to spiritualist (*spiritualista*) because it was scientific and because it was not just distinct from Catholicism but actively antagonistic to it.[100] In Progreso, Yucatán, the EMECU chapter defined itself as a scientific center dedicated to study and investigation. The spiritists in Tixkokob, also in Yucatán, described themselves as "enthusiasts of this science."[101] The scientific teachings of EMECU, according to political scientist Marco Aurelio Navarro-Génie, helped some Mexicans rationalize their beliefs in extrasensory perception and reincarnation by drawing on a scientific understanding of electricity and magnetism.[102] "Trincado's thoughts," he posits, "were presented in a tightly packaged system based on scientistic assumptions—and shrouded in secrecy and exclusivity that made it seem even more authoritative."[103]

Scientistic spiritists of the EMECU and like-minded lodges provided often scarce local backing for the most radical elements of postrevolutionary state formation, above all defanaticization. In Huejutla, Hidalgo, the EMECU cathedral's delegate (leader) was also a federal teacher fighting "blind belief" in Catholic dogma; he helped the SEP and federal soldiers capture and expel a beloved local priest.[104] In several cases, spiritists used scientific EMECU doctrine to define revolutionary change. For instance, local members of the *Logia Psicológica Científica*, or Psychological-Scientific Lodge, campaigned to defanaticize the town of Progreso, Yucatán, in 1933. Members included Aurora C. de Cervantes, a leading feminist who sat on the Yucatecan state committee of the ruling party, the PNR.[105] In Tuxtla, Chiapas, María A. Brandi of the local EMECU penned an iconoclastic poem titled "Desfanatización" ("Why adore horrible idols, of wood, metal, clay and glue?") to turn people away from priests and toward the "only one true doctrine: spiritism."[106] At a time when the postrevolutionary state had only uneven support in much of Mexico, spiritism steeled a determined minority to fight what they regarded as Catholic fanaticism.

The cause of revolutionary defanaticization tapped other intellectual currents, again drawing on alternative science to debunk religion. Herbalist Rafael Saínz Arenas gave conferences and printed flyers "[t]o call

all groups of this port [Veracruz] to shake off the religious yoke, because it is anti-patriotic and irrational." Saínz explained to Garrido Canabal that "I practice scientific investigations through psychic occultism," which (among other things) predicted Obregón's assassination.[107] In Yucatán, the strongest local anti-Catholic movement outside the metropolis of Mérida was found in the town of Izamal. Here, Dr. Joaquín Burgos Medina, a theosophist, Freemason, and magnetic doctor trained at Paris's Sage Institute, led a campaign against "religious fanaticism" of "our humble classes."[108] Faith in the idea of science probably sustained these self-appointed apostles of revolutionary anticlericalism in dangerous times; when President Cárdenas visited Izamal, Dr. Burgos Medina required a police escort after being surrounded by a mob incensed over "professional, political, and religious" matters.[109]

The idea of science as an uncontested source of truth not only provided ideological justification for grassroots anticlericalism, but it also inspired revolutionary ritual. Such was the case with vaccination. Significantly, political elites pioneered ceremonial smallpox inoculations that were (at least once) imitated on the local level. The first ritual vaccination of the immediate postrevolutionary era probably took place in the early 1920s in Carrillo Puerto's Yucatán, where "Health Weeks" featured "The Day of the Vaccination."[110] Garrido Canabal found new meaning in the vaccination campaign by taking it to extremes—a defining feature of Garridista anti-Catholicism. At his second gubernatorial inauguration, the governor proclaimed his desire to eliminate sickness and death. To that end, he had his three children vaccinated in public to spurn "unhygienic" baptisms, then bared his own arm before an applauding crowd to receive the needle.[111] Tabasco's Medical Association launched a mass vaccination campaign including a "Healthy Child Pageant" (*Concurso del Niño Sano*).[112] As Gretchen Pierce's chapter in this volume demonstrates, Garrido Canabal's alcohol prohibition efforts were another characteristic feature of his project, one that promoted both health and a new revolutionary morality.

Revolutionary anticlerical intellectuals relished narratives spun by Garrido Canabal's propagandists that juxtaposed the vaccine's benevolent effect against pestilent fanaticism. A federal teacher in 1936 complained that her efforts to get peasants to start a cooperative to vaccinate cattle against an epizootic disease was thwarted by a wily priest who promised to cure the animals with a free blessing.[113] In at least one case, Catholics in Guanajuato rejected vaccines offered by federal teachers after lay leaders claimed they would sterilize them.[114] When retold by revolutionary intellectuals, the claim came to serve as a way to define themselves as rational and lifesaving while coupling Catholicism with contagion.[115] At the same time, vaccination could legitimize the authority of the revolutionary state over the human body.

The symbolic value of vaccination was heightened by incorporating children into revolutionary ceremonies, thus providing a much more attractive alternative to Catholic baptism than the rather drab socialist christening, which simply mimicked sacramental baptism.[116] Vaccination literally protected children from disease, and metaphorically suggested the power of the teacher to inoculate children against fanaticism. In late 1933, General (and future governor of Guerrero) Alfredo F. Berber wrote admiringly to Garrido Canabal that his recent gift of List's *Practice* would help teachers in their "labor of mental prophylaxes for the youth."[117] One self-appointed missionary of Tabasco, army captain Salvador V. y Sánchez Martínez, was so inspired by Garrido Canabal's vaccination of his children that he imitated it to spread "the new ideas of Tabasco." Like many letters to Garrido, Capitan V. y Sánchez Martínez's four missives combined genuine praise with clientelistic requests for favors (a spot on the Mexico City police or municipal bureaucracy, an invitation to join Garrido's bodyguard). The scientific vaccination ceremony for his son named Druso (after Garrido's son) would "register [him] before the Law and Science." The simple ceremony ("without ostentation of any nature") won over doubters among the curious neighbors by exposing them to "true Social Ideals of Tabasco." Even Catholics who had previously denounced the "atheist event" were swayed. As Sánchez pointed out, "The act of vaccination has significance . . . distinct in all meanings," perhaps comparing the power of science to save the child's body from disease to its power to save young minds from fanaticism. Instead of a homily, the captain spoke about Garrido's "personality and gifts." After learning of his transfer to "fanatical" Guadalajara, Captain Sánchez promised to hand out the Garridista weekly ironically titled *Cristo Rey* outside churches and Malpica's *el Universo sin Dios* in classrooms. He also planned to subject his company's enlisted men to Tabascan-themed barracks cultural assemblies[118] As President Lázaro Cárdenas's secretary of agriculture and development until his ouster for backing Calles against Cárdenas in mid-1935, Garrido was bombarded with petitions like the captain's, which combined sincere admiration with requests for propaganda, state sinecures, loans, or publication of anticlerical writings. Of course, Garrido learned as governor of Tabasco that there was no contradiction between cutting edge scientific radicalism and old-fashioned patronage.[119]

Conclusion

The idea of science gave revolutionary politicians, intellectuals, educators, and citizens a radical mandate to remake Mexico.[120] By taking its measure, we can better understand how the federal schools became a contentious place during the 1930s, when armed bands and rioting villagers killed an estimated three hundred teachers in the so-called Second Cristero War.[121] Scholars of Mexican anticlericalism have intensively studied socialist education and the widespread popular Catholic resistance it provoked.[122] More than a few have blamed Plutarco Elías Calles, Tomás Garrido Canabal, and Minister of Education Narciso Bassols (1931–1934) for sparking the conflict by injecting anti-Catholic ideas into the classroom.[123] Anticlericalism was far from a top-down affair, however. A relatively small but active and influential minority of revolutionary anticlericals, many of whom admired and often imitated Garrido Canabal, were key catalysts in the conflict. Even after Calles and the SEP rejected attempts by Tabasconized intellectuals, educators, and politicians to formally adopt the scientistic, combatively anti-Catholic rationalist education, many teachers and grassroots anticlerical groups and activists continued to fight fanaticism with the idea of science and iconoclasm.

While scientific education as conventionally defined (i.e., coursework in biology, astronomy, agronomy, and so on) had at best an uneven impact on Mexican society in the 1930s, its inclusion in the curriculum—along with SEP backing for agrarian reform and unionization—helped define the goals of the Mexican Revolution. It also helped define opponents of the SEP schools as superstitious, backward, and even unhealthy—in other words, as fanatics. Indeed, merely attempting to teach a scientific understanding of the natural world was seen as ushering in a new, revolutionary society. Perhaps even more importantly, devotion to science helped create a strong identity for agents of the postrevolutionary state, including beleaguered teachers who found themselves in hostile rural communities. Armed with science, they formed a progressive advance guard of the postrevolutionary state, sacrificing themselves for a higher cause.

Did the idea of science help win over Mexicans suspicious of federal schooling, at least during the 1925–1935 period? Whereas some SEP inspectors believed they persuaded communities to accept federal schools and ejidal or communal land grants by demonstrating how technology could improve harvests, they also advocated intrusive inspections of peasant households as necessary to "combat dirt and disease."[124] The seeds planted in the minds of Mexico's children took much longer to germinate; certainly, de-emphasizing direct attacks on religious sensibilities helped in the long run. That said, the SEP struggled to find cadres as dedicated as Tabasconized teachers.

This chapter also reveals how the idea of science was defined in profoundly different ways by officials and grassroots supporters of the postrevolutionary state. For Garrido Canabal and Tabasconized teachers, science was a source of certainty (as opposed to the skepticism encouraged by the scientific method). Despite the SEP refusal to adopt Tabasco's brand of scientistic anticlericalism, many federal educators—even moderates averse to Garrido Canabal's methods—deployed the idea of science to win over recalcitrant Catholics, explain their own shortcomings, and define their own identity in an indifferent or hostile social environment.

Even after President Lázaro Cárdenas purged Garrido Canabal from his cabinet and wound down Maximato-era anticlericalism, elements of Garrido's scientistic approach to state formation lived on. Even moderate revolutionaries who rejected Garridista extremism and the SEP, an institution that resisted Tabasconization, borrowed elements of the Tabascan-style rationalist education model. More so than any other antecedent of Mexico's long-ruling party known as the PRI after 1946, Garridista socialism showed how the postrevolutionary state could assert control over citizens' bodies and promise Mexicans a future free of fanaticism, disease, and poverty using the idea of science.

Notes

1. Rodríguez, *Sobre la Brecha*, 190.
2. Rodríguez, 181.
3. Stern, "From Mestizophilia to Biotypology," 207.
4. APTGC caja 141 exp. 14, Villa Hermosa correspondent of *Redención* to *El Universal*, 26 Oct. 1929.
5. *La Sotana* 1:3.
6. Cepeda, "Testimonios de la Génesis de la Facultad de Ciencia"; Ledesma-Mateos and Barahona Echeverría, "Alfonso Luis Herrera e Isaac Ochoterrena."
7. Marty, *Varieties*, 140–41. Timothy Ferris is a thoughtful, well-read defender of science who rejects attempts to define science as a source of power. See his *Science of Liberty*, especially 259.

8. On the postrevolutionary state's reliance on science to control women's bodies, see O'Brien, "Pelvimetry," and "Many Meanings of *Aborto*"; Smith, *Gender and the Mexican Revolution*. On the relationship between fanaticism and femininity, Indigeneity, and criminality, see Wright-Rios, *Searching for Madre Matiana*, 152 and 157. See also Vanderwood, *Power of God*, 135.
9. Following widespread but not universal scholarly conventions, I distinguish between the armed phase of the revolution (1910–1920) and the period of postrevolutionary state formation (1921–1940). Together they make up what Mary Kay Vaughan has called the Long Mexican Revolution (1910–1940). Vaughan "Pancho Villa," 22, 25, 28. I use the adjective "revolutionary" to refer to people, events, organizations, institutions, and processes during the entire Long Revolution.
10. Recent contributions to the study of anticlericalism in Mexico would be impossible to fully explore here. For an excellent overview, see Butler, *Faith and Impiety*. My approach owes much to Bantjes, "The War Against Idols." Jason Dormady explored an important topic related to scientism: the use of the discourse of hygiene after the end of the church-state conflict by both Catholic and Protestants citizens. See his "God, Cleanliness, and the City."
11. On the idea of state formation as an everyday process and the New Cultural History of Mexico, see Joseph and Nugent, *Everyday Forms of State Formation*; and Mallon, *Peasant and Nation*.
12. Mazzaferri, "Public Health and Social Revolution"; Birn, "Revolution in Rural Health."
13. The reasons why non-Catholic Christians were rarely accused of being fanatical is an important topic deserving closer inquiry. See Janzen in this volume; McIntyre, *Protestantism and State Formation*, 62; and Dormady "God, Cleanliness, and the City," 398.
14. Carlos Domingo Méndez Moreno used the Tomás Garrido Canabal archive in the Archivo General de México, but his focus is squarely on Tabasco itself. For a rare mention of Garridista sympathizers outside of Tabasco based on this archive, see his *El anticlericalismo en Tabasco*, 127.
15. Bantjes, "Idolatry and Iconoclasm," 117–18.
16. On Francisco Múgica's call to "Tabasconize" Mexico ("hay que Tabasqueñizar a México"), see Guzmán and Scherer Ibarra, "Furor tabasqueño," 14–15.
17. For an overview of the historiographical debate over Garrido's legacy, see Martínez Assad, *Laboratorio*, 61–76; and Tostado Gutiérrez, *El intento de liberar a un pueblo*, 187–218.
18. Osten astutely points out that Garrido's template for postrevolutionary partymaking centralized by absorbing caciquismo was inclusive and populist but not

democratic, and it sought to reform capitalism without radical nationalization. Osten, *Mexican Revolution's Wake*, especially 374–78.
19. Ridgeway, "Cooperative Republic of Tomás Garrido Canabal."
20. Harper, "Revolutionary Tabasco."
21. The medical doctors trained at the College of San Nicolás of Michoacán prominent in the presidential administration of Lázaro Cárdenas provide an interesting counterpoint to the anticlerical Tabascan teachers so influential during the Maximato. Both groups were provincial intellectuals with professional credentials based in part on science, but the *Nicolaitas* shied away from direct confrontation with the Catholic Church and instead sought to combine medical science with the social and economic aspirations of the revolution. See Kapellusz-Poppi, "Provincial Intellectuals," 239–57.
22. Malpica, *La Ciencia*; Universidad Autónoma de Tabasco, *Diccionario Institutional*.
23. Malpica, 27.
24. Malpica, 7, 11.
25. APTGC caja 133 exp. 2, Domingo Borrego, "No Receis." The translation is the author's.
26. Martínez Assad, *Laboratorio*.
27. Tostado Gutiérrez, *El intento*, 34–35.
28. Vaughan, *Cultural Politics in Revolution*, 27.
29. Martínez Assad, *Laboratorio*, 61–62.
30. Abascal, *Tomás Garrido Canabal*, 186–87.
31. Fallaw, "Varieties," 504, 508.
32. List Arzubide, *Práctica*.
33. List Arzubide, *Práctica*, 32, 37, 39, 43.
34. APTGC caja 133 exp. 13, Tomás Garrido Canabal to Manuel Avila Camacho, 19 Dec. 1933.
35. APTGC caja 133 exp. 14, Miguel Cantón to Tomás Garrido Canabal, 10 Jan. 1934.
36. Fallaw "Acrimony to Accommodation."
37. FAPECyFT APEC gav. 27 exp. 4 inv. 1733 leg. 19/24, Rodolfo Elías Calles to Plutarco Elías Calles, 13 May 1934.
38. APTGC caja 133 exp. 13, L. Villarreal to Garrido Canabal, 18 Dec. 1933; Martínez Moya and Moreno Castañeda, *Jalisco*, 273; Mena, *La Escuela Socialista*, 222–26.
39. APTGC caja 133 exp. 13, L. Villarreal to Garrido Canabal, 18 Dec. 1933.
40. The first attempt was made by the Liga Nacional de Maestros Racionalistas on 20 Oct. 1928. See Montes de Oca Navas, "La escuela racionalista."
41. Osten, *Revolution's Wake*, 132, 159–60.
42. I would like to acknowledge Sarah Osten for underscoring this point.
43. *A.B.C. Socialista para uso de los niños campesinos*, 38: "Piensa en que tu único Dios

es el Trabajo, porque te redime." The slogan was originally Masonic. On Garridista defanaticization aimed at eradicating Indigenous culture, see De Giuseppe, "El Tabasco racionalista frente a lo indígena."

44. Martínez Assad, *Laboratorio*, 45–46, 81–83. The translation is Stan Ridgeway's in his "Cooperative Republic," 206.
45. Martínez Assad, 45, 81.
46. On the conflict, see Tostado Gutiérrez, *El intento de liberar a un pueblo*, especially 50; Canudas, *Trópico Rojo*, 139; Britton, "Mexican Ministry of Education," 131; Abascal, *Tomás Garrido Canabal*, 126–29.
47. Martínez Assad, *Laboratorio*, 78–80.
48. Martínez Assad, 82–83.
49. APTGC caja 133 exp. 14, Arnulfo Pérez to Garrido Canabal, 8 Oct. 1934.
50. Pérez to Canabal.
51. Among the hardliners backing rationalist education were Lázaro Cárdenas's allies from Michoacán, as well as some from Puebla, Guerrero, Veracruz, Chiapas, and Tlaxcala. APTGC caja 133 exp. 14, Arnulfo Pérez to Garrido Canabal, 8, 10, and 24 Oct. 1934.
52. Abascal, *Tomás Garrido Canabal*, 121.
53. Krauze, *Mexico, Biography of Power*, 421–22. See also Abascal, *Tomás Garrido Canabal*, 90.
54. On the distinction between radicals and moderates on Mexico's religious question, see Fallaw, "Varieties."
55. Buchenau, *Plutarco Elías Calles*, 126.
56. Cronon, *Josephus Daniels in Mexico*, 88–99.
57. Pani, *Tres Monografías*, 194.
58. On the struggle within the SEP between supporters and opponents of Garrido Canabal and rationalist education from the perspective of the former, see de la Luz Mena, *La Escuela Socialista*, 280–92.
59. Ridgeway, "Cooperative Republic," 215.
60. APTGC caja 133 exp. 14, Rafael Molina Betancourt et al to Garrido, 22 Oct. 1934, and attached note from Prof. Jiménez de la Rosa. The translation is mine.
61. APTGC caja 133 exp. 14, Rafael Molina Betancourt et al to Garrido, 22 Oct. 1934, and attached note from Prof. Jiménez de la Rosa.
62. APTGC caja 133 exp. 14, Rafael Molina Betancourt et al to Garrido, 22 Oct. 1934, and attached note from Prof. Jiménez de la Rosa. See also Vaughan, *Cultural Politics*, 31–35.
63. On SEP recruitment of teachers from Tabasco, Veracruz, and Yucatán, see Fallaw, *Religion*, 78.

64. Vaughan, *Cultural Politics*, 29–36.
65. AHSEP caja 1096 exp. Missiones Educativos Culturales, Luis G. Ramírez, 11 Sept. 1934.
66. Fallaw, *Religion and State Formation*, 35–36, 86–87.
67. García Tellez's "Concepciones General del Socialismo" found in AHSEP ZAC caja 83 exp. 39, Javier Fernández report, 28 Oct. 1935. For an example of a typical (if uninspiring) report, see AHSEP GTO caja 1335 exp. 5, Ignacio B. Pamplona report, 19 Sept. 1935.
68. AHSEP GRO caja 1668 exp. 7, Salvador Gutiérrez report, 2 Dec. 1934.
69. AHSEP HGO caja 5328 exp.29, Bartolo Gómez report, 24 Dec. 1936.
70. AHSEP GRO caja 1336 exp. 13, Leopoldo G. Caro report, 30 Apr. 1935.
71. On the CROM's clash with Garrido over Tabasco workers, see Osten, *Revolution's Wake*, 136. For its part, the Communist Party, which was beginning to gain converts in the SEP's rank in the early 1930s, also despised Garrido-style socialism not just on ideological grounds but also because rationalist educators opposed recruitment of teachers from the Communist Party. Martínez Moya and Moreno Castañeda, *Jalisco*, 274; de la Luz Mena, *La Escuela Socialista*, 292.
72. Craib, *Cry of the Renegade*, 10, 60–62. Not all generic leftists' ideology was so elastic; members of the Communist Party or even fellow travelers who imbibed its ideology often criticized supporters of Garrido, CROMistas, as well as Freemasons. List Arzubide defined himself as an "integral leftist" who was sympathetic to all leftist causes and was indebted to Garrido Canabal for publishing and distributing over a thousand copies of his book. List Arzubide's own career—he began as an anarchist, later joined the Carrancistas, served moderate Veracruzano governor Heriberto Jara, joined the Communist Party, and worked for and was fired by Cárdenas when he was governor of Michoacán—seems like a case study of capacious leftist ideology in practice. Yet he called Tabasconized anticlericals' efforts well intentioned but counterproductive and repeated the Communist Party line on Garrido that he was a social fascist. List Arzubide might have chafed under party discipline, but communism gave him a coherent, doctrinaire worldview that would—he believed—help Mexican students see all organized religious as a racket based on irrational beliefs. List Arzubide's trip to Moscow gave him a kind of credibility and panache that most other revolutionary intellectuals lacked. List Arzubidé, *Frente a la Revolución Mexicana*.
73. AHSEP ZAC caja 83 exp. 1, Tomás Cuervo to President Lázaro Cárdenas, 26 Oct. 1935. Fallaw, *Religion and State Formation*, 165–66.
74. AHSEP GTO caja 1401 exp. 3, Fortino López R. report, Jan.–Feb. 1935.
75. AHSEP ZAC caja 85 exp.44, Manuel Cortina Vizcano report, Sept.–Oct. 1935.

76. AHSEP ZAC caja 80 exp.6, Fabio Belio C. report, 31 Dec. 1935.
77. AHSEP ZAC caja 85 exp.44, Manuel Cortina Vizcano report, Sept.–Oct. 1935.
78. Tostado Gutiérrez, *El intento*, 83.
79. Simpson, *Ejido*, 285; López Guzmán, "La Cuestión Educativa en Guanajuato," 238–39; Sánchez, *Mexico: A Revolution by Education*, 118.
80. Torres Vera, *Mujeres y Utopía*, 38.
81. AHSEP GTO caja 1401 exp. 5, Roberto Oropeza Nájera reports, 20 June and 21 Oct. 1935.
82. AHSEP GTO caja 1401 exp. 5, Roberto Oropeza Nájera report, 21 Oct. 1935.
83. AHSEP GTO caja 1335 exp. 4, Jenaro Hernández Aguilar report, 7 Mar. 1935 and 19 June 1935, and Jenaro Hernández Aguilar to Tomás Cuervo and report, 19 May 1935.
84. AHSEP GTO caja 1335 exp.4, Jenaro Hernández Aguilar to Tomás Cuervo, 7 Mar. 1935.
85. AHSEP GTO caja 1335 exp. 4, Jenaro Hernández report, 19 June 1935.
86. AHSEP GTO caja 1335 exp.13, Rafael Rosas Rosains report, 1935; AHSEP caja 3956 exp.18, AHSEP GTO Clemente J. Nápoles report, 16 Feb. 1940.
87. De Giuseppe, "El Tabasco racionalista."
88. On Rodríguez Lozano, see Fallaw, *Religion*, 73–78, 89–94.
89. AHSEP CAM caja 1802 exp. 8, Rubén Rodríguez Lozano report, 2 Aug. 1933.
90. See, for instance, Smith, *Pistoleros and Popular Movements*.
91. Butler, "*Sotanas Rojinegras*."
92. Vanderwood, *Power of God*, 64, 67.
93. APTGC caja 133 exp. 11, F. Quiñones León to Garrido Canabal, 28 Mar. 1932. See also APTGC caja 133 exp. 11, F. Quiñones León to Garrido, 22 Feb. 1932.
94. AGN DGG 2.340 caja 41 exp.42, act dated 25 Jan. 1935.
95. AGN DGG 2.347 caja 3 bis exp.18.
96. O'Rourke, *La persecución religiosa en Chihuahua*, 168,
97. Malpica Hernández, *La Ciencia*, 11.
98. AGN DGG 2.347(28) caja 18 exp. 7.
99. Urías Horcasitas, *Historias secretas del racismo en México*, 173–74. See also Devés-Valdés and Melgar Bao, "Redes Teosóficas y pensadores (políticos) latinoamericanos."
100. Navarro-Génie, *Augusto"César"Sandino*, 80n6.
101. AGN DGG 2.340 caja 98 exp.23.
102. Navarro-Génie, *Augusto"César"Sandino*, 82.
103. Navarro-Génie, *Augusto"César"Sandino*, 85.
104. AHSEP HGO caja 874 exp. 12, Francisco M. Moreno to SEP, 5 Feb. 1932. Fallaw, *Religion*, 79.

105. AGN DGG 2.340 caja 98 exp.17. On Aurora C. de Cervantes's political activities, see *Diario del Sureste*, 6 Dec. 1935 and 14 Dec. 1937.
106. Ríos Figueroa, *Siglo XX*, 254.
107. APTGC caja 96 exp. 165, Rafael Saínz Arenas to Garrido Canabal, 7 Jan. 1935.
108. AGEY PE 756 SG, Manuel J. Alcocer to Gov., 19 Feb. 1922; AGEY PE 969 SG 1, Estebán Kú to Gov., 9 Feb. 1933; AGEY PE 976 SG, Joaquín Burgos Medina to Gov., 17 Aug. 1933; AGN DGG 2.311 M, vol. 83 exp. 76, Joaquín Burgos Medina to Gov., 4 Jan. 1935; *Heraldo de Yucatán*, 8 Sept. 1934; *Diario del Sureste*, 19 Mar. 1934 and 13 Feb. 1938.
109. *Diario del Sureste*, 19 Mar. 1934.
110. Urías Horcasitas, "El poder de los símbolos," 195.
111. Abascal, *Tomás Garrido Canabal*, 143; Birn, "Rural Health," 43–76, 59.
112. Tostado Gutiérrez, *El intento*, 93.
113. AHSEP ZAC caja 83 exp., Inspector of Rio Grande to Director of Federal Education, 8 Dec. 1936.
114. López Guzmán, "La Cuestión Educativa," 211.
115. See also de la Peña, *Guerrero* I:323.
116. On the Masons' "abstemious and apparently rather solemn festivals at the summer and winter solstices" featuring orange juice, sandwiches, and crepe paper, see Smith "Anticlericalism," 567.
117. APTGC caja 133 exp.13, Alfredo F. Berber to Garrido Canabal, 19 Dec. 1933.
118. APTGC caja 96 exps. 164 and 167, various cor. Capitan Salvador V. y Sánchez Martínez to Garrido Canabal.
119. As governor of Tabasco, he was accustomed to doling out patronage. See Osten, *Revolution's Wake*, 140.
120. Hecht, *End of the Soul*, 310.
121. Raby, *Educación y revolución social en México*, 147, 190–91.
122. Other scholars have emphasized federal schools as a site of mediation between state and society. Vaughan shows that in at least some regions, federal teachers balanced the revolutionary curriculum against popular demands and expectations, making the classroom a key site of negotiations between agents of the state and society. Vaughan, *Cultural Politics*. Liberals, socialists, and even Catholics, as Patience Schell has shown, agreed on the need to forge a more productive, patriotic, and healthy nation through compulsory schooling. Schell, *Church and State Education*.
123. Vaughan, *Cultural Politics*, 31; Britton, *Educación y radicalismo en México*.
124. Vaughan, "Modernizing Patriarchy."

Works Cited

Archives

AGEY Archivo General del Estado de Yucatán
    PE Poder Ejecutivo
    SG Gobernación
AGN Archivo General de la Nación
    DGG Dirección General de Gobernación
AHSEP Archivo Histórico de Secretaría Educación Pública
    CAM Dirección de Educación Federal de Campeche
    HGO Dirección de Educación Federal de Hidalgo
    GTO Dirección de Educación Federal de Guanajuato
    ZAC Dirección de Educación Federal de Zacatecas
APTGC Archivo Personal de Tomás Garrido Canabal
FAPECyFT Fideicomiso Archivo Plutarco Elías Calles y Fernando Torreblanco
    APEC Archivo Plutarco Elías Calles

Periodicals

Diario del Sureste
Heraldo de Yucatán
La Sotana

Secondary Sources

A.B.C. Socialista para uso de los niños campesinos. Villahermosa, Mexico: Imprenta Redención, 1929.

Abascal, Salvador. *Tomás Garrido Canabal: sin Dios, sin curas, sin iglesias.* Mexico City: Tradición, 1987.

Bantjes, Adrian. "Negating the Image: Case Studies in Iconoclasm." In *Negating the Image: Case Studies in Iconoclasm*, edited by Anne McClanan and Jeff Johnson, 41–66. Burlington, VT: Ashgate, 2005.

———. "The War against Idols: The Meanings of Iconoclasm in Revolutionary Mexico, 1910–40." In *Negating the Image: Case Studies in Iconoclasm*, edited by Anne McClanan and Jeff Johnson. Burlington, VT: Ashgate, 2005.

Birn, Anne-Emanuelle. "A Revolution in Rural Health? The Struggle over Local Health Units in Mexico, 1928–1940." *Journal of the History of Medicine* 53 (Jan. 1998): 43–76.

Britton, John. *Educación y radicalismo en México. I. Los años de Bassols (1931–1934)*. Mexico City: SepSetentas, 1976.

———. "The Mexican Ministry of Education, 1931–1940: Radicalism and Institutional Development." PhD diss., Tulane University, 1971.

Buchenau, Jürgen. *Plutarco Elías Calles and the Mexican Revolution*. Lanham, MD: Rowman and Littlefield, 2007.

Butler, Matthew, ed. *Faith and Impiety in Revolutionary Mexico*. London: Institute for the Study of the America, 2007.

———. "*Sotanas Rojinegras*: Catholic Anticlericalism and Mexico's Revolutionary Schism." *The Americas* 65, no. 4 (Apr. 2009): 535–58.

Canudas, Enrique. *Trópico Rojo: Historia política y social de Tabasco. Los años Garridistas 1919/1934*. 3 vols. Villahermosa, Mexico: Gobierno del Estado de Tabasco and Instituto de Cultura de Tabasco, 1982.

Cepeda, Francisco. "Testimonios de la génesis de la Facultad de Ciencia." *Ciencias* 53 (Jan. 1999): 16–27.

Craib, Raymond. *The Cry of the Renegade: Politics and Poetry in Interwar Chile*. New York: Oxford University Press, 2016.

Cronon, E. David. *Josephus Daniels in Mexico*. Madison: University of Wisconsin Press, 1960.

De Giuseppe, Massimo. "El Tabasco racionalista frente a lo indígena: entre laboratorio social y experimentación cultural (1922–1934)." *Historia Mexicana* 61, no. 2 (Oct. 2011): 643–706.

Devés-Valdés, Eduardo, and Ricardo Melgar Bao. "Redes Teosóficas y pensadores (políticos) latinoamericanos, 1910–1930." In *Redes Intelectuales en América Latina. Hacia la constitución de una comunidad intelectual*, edited by Eduardo Devés-Valdés, 75–92. Santiago: Colección Idea, Instituto de Estudios Avanzados and Universidad Santiago de Chile, 2007.

Dormady, Jason. "God, Cleanliness, and the City: Local Uses of Hygiene and Anticlerical Language in Religious Conflict—Guadalajara, Mexico 1939–1942." *The Latin Americanist* 64, no. 4 (Dec. 2020): 393–422.

Fallaw, Ben. "From Acrimony to Accommodation: Church-State Relations in Revolutionary-Era Yucatán, 1915–1940." In *Peripheral Visions: Politics, Society, and the Challenges of Modernity in Yucatán*, edited by Edward Terry, Ben Fallaw, Gilbert Joseph, and Edward Moseley, 227–53. Tuscaloosa: University of Alabama Press, 2010.

———. *Religion and State Formation in Postrevolutionary Mexico*. Durham, NC: Duke University Press, 2013.

———. "Varieties of Mexican Revolutionary Anticlericalism: Radicalism, Iconoclasm, and Otherwise, 1914–1935." *The Americas* 65, no. 4 (April 2009): 481–509.

Ferris, Timothy. *The Science of Liberty: Democracy, Reason and the Laws of Nature.* New York: HarperCollins, 2010.
Guzmán, Armando, and María Scherer Ibarra. "Furor tabasqueño." *Proceso* 29, no. 1497 (10 July 2005): 13–17.
Harper, Kristin. "Revolutionary Tabasco in the Times of Tomás Garrido Canabal, 1922–1935: A Mexican House Divided." PhD diss., University of Massachusetts, 2004.
Hecht, Jennifer. *The End of the Soul: Scientific Modernity, Atheism, and Anthropology in France.* New York: Columbia University Press, 2003.
Joseph, Gilbert, and Daniel Nugent. *Everyday Forms of State Formation.* Durham, NC: Duke University Press, 1994.
Kapellusz-Poppi, Anne Marie, "Provincial Intellectuals from Michoacan and the Professionalization of the Post-Revolutionary Mexican State." PhD diss., University of Illinois-Chicago, 2002.
Krauze, Enrique. *Mexico, Biography of Power: A History of Modern Mexico, 1810–1976.* Translated by Hank Heifetz. New York: HarperCollins, 1997.
Ledesma-Mateos, Ismael, and Ana Barahona Echeverría. "Alfonso Luis Herrera e Isaac Ochoterrena: La Institucionalización de la Biología en México." *Historia Mexicana* XLVIII, no. 3 (Mar. 1999): 635–74.
List Arzubide, Germán. *Frente a la Revolución Mexicana: 17 protagonistas de la etapa constructiva. Entrevistas de Historia Oral,* edited by James Wilkie and Edna Monzón Wilkie, 247–54, 291–94. Mexico City: Universidad Autónoma Metropolitana, 1995.
———. *Práctica de educación irreligiosa: para uso de las escuelas primarias y nocturnas para obreros.* Mexico City: Ediciones Integrales, 1933.
López Guzmán, Jorge. "La Cuestión Educativa en Guanajuato. Proceso de Modernización y Cambio Político 1915–1939." MA thesis, Universidad Iberoamericana, 2004.
Mallon, Florencia. *Peasant and Nation: The Making of Postcolonial Mexico and Peru.* Berkeley: University of California Press, 1995.
Malpica Hernández, José. *La Ciencia y la Religión. Ensayo de divulgación científica y filosófica.* Villahermosa, Mexico: n.p., 1930.
Martínez Assad, Carlos. *El Laboratorio de la revolución: el tabasco garridista.* Mexico City: Siglo XXI, 1979.
Martínez Moya, Armando, and Manuel Moreno Castañeda. *Jalisco: Desde la Revolución. Tomo VII: Escuela de la Revolución.* Guadalajara: Gobierno del Estado de Jalisco and Universidad de Guadalajara, 1988.
Marty, Martin. *Varieties of Unbelief.* New York: Holt, Rinehart and Winston, 1964.
Mazzaferri, Anthony. "Public Health and Social Revolution in Mexico, 1877–1930." PhD diss., Kent State University, 1969.

McIntyre, Kathleen. *Protestantism and State Formation in Postrevolutionary Oaxaca.* Albuquerque: University of New Mexico Press, 2019.

Mena, José de la Luz. *La Escuela Socialista. Su desorientación y fracaso. El verdadero derrotero.* Mexico City: n.p., 1941.

Méndez Moreno, Carlos Domingo. *El anticlericalismo en Tabasco. Entre prácticas, símbolos y representaciones.* Morelia, Mexico: Universidad Michoacana de San Nicolás de Hidalgo, 2016.

Montes de Oca Navas, Elvia. "La escuela racionalista. Una propuesta teórica metodológica para la escuela mexicana de los años veinte del siglo pasado." *La colmena* 41 (Oct. 2017): 97–105.

Navarro-Génie, Marco Aurelio. *Augusto "César" Sandino: Messiah of Light and Truth.* Syracuse: Syracuse University Press, 2002.

O'Brien, Elizabeth. "The Many Meanings of *Aborto*: Pregnancy Termination and the Instability of a Medical Category Over Time." *Women's History Review* 30, 6 (2021): 952–70.

———. "Pelvimetry and the Persistence of Racial Science." *Endeavour* 37 (2013): 21–28.

O'Rourke, Gerarld. *La persecución religiosa en Chihuahua (1913–1938).* Chihuahua: Editorial Camino, 1991.

Osten, Sarah. *The Mexican Revolution's Wake: The Making of a Political System, 1920–29.* New York: Cambridge University Press, 2018.

Pani, Alberto. *Tres monografías.* Mexico City: Editorial Atlante, 1941.

Raby, David. *Educación y revolución social en México (1921-1940).* Translated by Roberto Gómez Ciriza. Mexico City: Sep-Setentas, 1974.

Ridgeway, Stan. "The Cooperative Republic of Tomás Garrido Canabal: Developmentalism and the Mexican Revolution." PhD diss., University of North Carolina-Chapel Hill, 1996.

Ríos Figueroa, Julio. *Siglo XX: Muerte y resurrección de la iglesia católica en Chiapas. Dos estudios históricos.* Mexico City: Programa de Investigaciones Multidisciplinarias sobre Mesoamérica y el sureste, 2002.

Rodríguez, Cristobál. *Sobre la brecha: Colección de artículos liberales y desfanatizantes.* Mexico: La Prensa, 1930.

Sánchez, George Isidore. *Mexico: A Revolution by Education.* New York: Viking Press, 1936.

Schell, Patience. *Church and State Education in Revolutionary Mexico.* Tucson: University of Arizona Press, 2003.

Simpson, Eyler. *The Ejido: Mexico's Way Out.* Chapel Hill: University of North Carolina, 1937.

Smith, Benjamin "Anticlericalism, Politics, and Freemasonry in Mexico." *The Americas* 65, no. 4 (April 2009): 559–88.

———. *Pistoleros and Popular Movements: The Politics of State Formation in Postrevolutionary Oaxaca*. Lincoln: University of Nebraska, 2009.

Smith, Stephanie J. *Gender and the Mexican Revolution: Yucatán Women and the Realities of Patriarchy*. Chapel Hill: The University of North Carolina Press, 2009.

Stern, Alex. "From Mestizophilia to Biotypology: Racialization and Science in Mexico, 1920–1960." In *Race and Nation in Modern Latin America*, edited by Nancy Appelbaum, Anne Macpherson, and Karin Rosemblatt, 187–210. Chapel Hill: University of North Carolina Press, 2003.

Torres Vera, María Trinidad. *Mujeres y utopía: Tabasco garridista*. Tabasco: Universidad Juárez Autónoma de Tabasco, 2001.

Tostado Gutiérrez, Marcela. *El intento de liberar a un pueblo. Educación y magisterio tabasqueño con Garrido Canabal: 1924–1935*. Mexico City: INAH, 1991.

Universidad Autónoma de Tabasco, *Diccionario Institutional*. Villahermosa, Mexico: Universidad Autónoma de Tabasco and Centro de Estudios e Investigaciones de la Frontera Sur, 2007.

Urías Horcasitas, Beatriz. *Historias secretas del racismo en México (1920–1950)*. Mexico City: Tusquets Editores, 2007.

———. "El poder de los símbolos/los símbolos en el poder: Teosofía y mayanismo en Yucatán (1922-1923)." *Relaciones. Estudios de Historia y Sociedad* XXIX: 115 (verano 2008): 179–212.

Vanderwood, Paul. *The Power of God against the Guns of Government: Religious Upheaval in Mexico at the Turn of the Nineteenth Century*. Stanford: Stanford University Press, 1998.

Vaughan, Mary Kay. *Cultural Politics in Revolution: Teachers, Peasants, and Schools in Mexico, 1930–1940*. Tucson: University of Arizona Press, 1997.

———. "Introduction: Pancho Villa, the Daughters of Mary, and the Modern Woman: Gender in the Long Mexican Revolution." In *Sex in Revolution: Gender, Politics and Power in Modern Mexico*, edited by Jocelyn Olcott, Mary Kay Vaughan, and Gabriela Cano, 21–32. Durham, NC: Duke University Press, 2006.

———. "Modernizing Patriarchy: State Policies, Rural Households, and Women in Mexico, 1930–1940." In *Hidden Histories of Gender and the State in Latin America*, edited by Elizabeth Dore and Maxine Molyneux. Durham, NC: Duke University Press, 2000.

Wright-Rios, Edward. *Searching for Madre Matiana: Prophecy and Popular Culture in Modern Mexico*. Albuquerque: University of New Mexico Press, 2014.

CHAPTER SEVEN

From Heaven to Earth

Rivera, Siqueiros, and the Mexican Muralist Project

HÉCTOR JAIMES

The Mexican Revolution, which sought to bring about land reform, social justice, and a more inclusive society, also left the country yearning for peace and unity. The country would not achieve relative peace and unity until the social, legal, and political reforms advanced during Álvaro Obregón's presidency (1920–1924). Key among the Obregón-era projects were the education reforms led by the prominent Mexican philosopher José Vasconcelos, who served as secretary of public education during those years. Although the education reforms under his leadership benefited the Mexican population at large, an inconspicuous sector of the population was also to benefit in unprecedented ways: the artists. Vasconcelos commissioned them to paint the walls of public buildings with instructive images, giving rise to the Mexican muralist movement. Soon, following the guidance as well as the artistic and creative spirit that Vasconcelos demanded, the first major revolutionary-era murals appeared: *Creation* (1922–1924) by Diego Rivera; *Feast of the Holy Cross* (1923–1924) by Roberto Montenegro; *Allegory of the Virgin of Guadalupe* (1922–1923) by Fermín Revueltas; *The Feast of Our Lord of Chalma* (1923–1924) by Fernando Leal; *Maternity* (1923–1924) by José Clemente Orozco; and *The Elements* (1922–1923) by David Alfaro Siqueiros. Given the themes and images that appear in these murals, one might think that religion lay at the heart of Mexican muralism. Nevertheless, the great wave of mural production that followed demonstrated precisely the contrary. Religion, as exemplified in the early murals, served only as a feeble and fuzzy theme, an inchoate launching point for an art movement that later acquired a more clear, solid, and historical grounding. Moreover, when the muralist David Alfaro Siqueiros writes about these first attempts, he says: "The true meaning of monumental painting, its organic quality of complementation in architecture, in accordance with 'classical laws,' had not been understood in the least."[1] In other words, the muralists were learning their craft along the way, drawing from known religious themes. At the same time, the painters' earliest work was closely guided and influenced by José Vasconcelos, a generally pro-Catholic *letrado* or prominent intellectual whose vision and philosophy greatly impacted the thematic content of the murals, their locations, and their intended audience.

The history and evolution of the Mexican muralist movement demonstrate not only its challenging artistic complexities but, most importantly, its divergent aesthetics, as expressed by the views of its many artists and their works. Indeed, contrary to the general perception, Mexican muralism as a whole was not a unified, homogeneous, and programmatic art movement projecting one vision and one idea but rather one in which different—and at times conflicting—artistic views converged. These competing views can be found among those who saw mural painting solely as an independent and free creative expression and among those who also aspired to carry out a political agenda within the arts. In the same vein, Robin Adèle Greeley asserts that "early muralism was certainly a heterogeneous affair, caught up in tensions between artistic imaginings and the often improvisational nature of Mexico's pre-World War II state formation" as it was never conceived "as a stand-alone project."[2] Also, according to John Lear, artists "shared reformist and nationalist ideologies but often diverged over the pace and degree of reforms, issues of organizational autonomy and artistic freedom."[3] Some painters demanded more radical political activism, some agreed on the political action but undertook painting as their preferred means of expression, and some initially embraced the social and political commitment but later on grew distant and skeptical of this approach.

Three determining factors seem to have intervened directly or indirectly in the aesthetic production of the early murals: 1) Vasconcelos's philosophy (Weltanschauung); 2) governmental politics, that is, the politics of representation (form) and the representation of politics (content); and 3) the limiting structure (layout and fixity) of the buildings. Insofar as the early murals depicted core aspects of Mexican culture alongside Vasconcelos's spiritual and philosophical commitments (principles of humanism and idealism), they also displayed contesting conceptions of aesthetics. It could be said that they generated their own disparate energies. Indeed, it did not take long for the Mexican muralist project to evolve politically and philosophically beyond the vision of Vasconcelos and the surrounding politics of the administration under which he served.

Contrary to popular belief, then, Mexican muralism did not start as a particularly political project, although the political and philosophical aspirations of the Mexican Revolution were always embedded within it. If art for art's sake may have been at the heart of Mexican muralism, its proximity to the Revolution inevitably engaged it politically. As such, this political engagement was exacerbated after Diego Rivera and David Alfaro Siqueiros, two of its leading painters, joined the Mexican Communist Party in the early 1920s. According to the historian John Lear, "the PCM (Partido Comunista Mexicano) inevitably influenced visual representations and labor discourses about the worker."[4] Indeed, while the first murals tended to represent religious themes in a positive light, those that came after took a more socially committed undertone with a Marxist perspective. As such, their approach to religion and religious symbols took on greater nuance. As the muralists explored more with Marxism—an ideology that provided an alternative to Catholicism—they began to produce an implicitly, and at times explicitly, anti-Catholic aesthetics.

Anti-Catholic discourses began to emerge ever-more explicitly among the muralists during the mid-1920s and beyond. We see this clearly in José Clemente Orozco's *The Carnival of Ideologies* (1937), where symbols of ideology (Marxism, Nazism, and even Catholicism) appear in complete disarray. Viewed as such, Orozco became a staunch critic of all ideologies, but his humanist convictions and struggle for justice remained intact throughout his career. By contrast, for Rivera and Siqueiros, history and society, politics and corruption, oppression and freedom, workers and peasants, and ideology—sometimes in a broad sense and sometimes in a very specific sense—became their main subjects of representation. And although the theme of religion appeared at the beginning of the Mexican muralist project, this project was to take a dialectical turn—from heaven to earth—toward a more socially and politically committed art form. This turn did not mean that these artists ignored the Church altogether; indeed, the conflicts of the day would not allow for this. Rather, they challenged the Church's hegemony either indirectly by pressing competing ideologies— particularly Marxism—or explicitly by decrying it for its role in hampering causes of social justice.

Rivera adapted and reconfigured religious themes toward social and historical realities and at times criticized the Church head-on, while politics and dialectics completely overtook the muralist project of Siqueiros. In the work of both painters, we can see that social realities overshadowed and superseded questions of religious thought. In this way, their independent vision and philosophy prevailed over the more traditional, pro-Catholic sentiments of Vasconcelos. This became evident through the themes the nation's two most famous muralists chose and also because of their opposing and critical views about religion. In many cases they only selected religious topics and iconographies to denounce the oppressive legacy of the Church. This is true in Rivera's mural series in Cuernavaca (*History of Morelos, Conquest and Revolution* [1929–1930]), which depicts priests as indifferent to Indigenous suffering as they greedily torture the native inhabitants of the land and take resources for themselves. The Church would continue to draw his ire well after the 1940 reconciliation between church and state when he blamed the former for continued Indigenous suffering in his painting *History of Religion* (1950).

In Siqueiros's overall body of work, we find the forces that govern human life are dictated by a materialist conception of history (class struggle) and not by God. A simple and clear example of Siqueiros's take on religion is in his painting *The Devil in Church* (1947), where rather than fear the evil presence of the devil, the oppressed masses express empowerment and a sense of liberation; indeed, they welcome the revolutionary change that the evil presence evokes. This is also true in the mural *The Elements*, where a celestial theme (an angel) is overshadowed by a mural Siqueiros painted, *Burial of the Worker*, in the same location. As the art historian Leonard Folgarait asserts, "the shift from the Christian allegory of *The Elements* to these militant subjects is dramatic. It is explained by an event that occurred in September 1923, concurrent with the work on *Burial of the Worker*: the sudden formation of the Syndicate of Technical Workers, Painters, and Sculptors (Sindicato de Obreros Técnicos, Pintores y Escultores), an event that seemed to come from no organizational or intellectual period of development or preparation on the part of its members. Its "Manifesto," produced on December 9, stated a commitment to populist revolutionary struggle.[5] But if we were to reconsider Siqueiros's unfinished (early) mural *Los mitos* (*The Myths* [1922–1923]), which is near *The Elements* and *The Burial of the Worker*, or even *América Tropical* (*Tropical America*), painted in Los Angeles in 1932, we can see how religious themes are transformed and, in a way, subverted altogether in his works. As Alejandro Anreus observes, regarding *Los mitos*: "Siqueiros painted an Indian Christ floating above a hammer and sickle, and next to the burial of a worker. From the beginning we see that Siqueiros identifies the figure of Christ not with the traditional bourgeois religion in which he was raised; but rather with the marginal and exploited elements in Mexican society:

the Indians, the workers."[6] In this way, the painter tapped into the symbols of the Church even as he repurposed their cosmological significance by subordinating them to a Marxist ideal.

But this is also a Mexican and Latin American story. The hammer and sickle are two very distinctive symbols of international Communism that signal Siqueiros's political commitment and future artistic direction. Yet by painting an Indian Christ, Siqueiros is providing an ethnic quality to Indian suffering in Latin America.

This notion of ethnic suffering is brought about again in a more visually dramatic and emotional way in *América Tropical*, where he painted a crucified Indian. When this mural was unveiled, it created so much controversy that it was partially destroyed and abandoned for many years until the mural was restored by the Getty Foundation.[7] These two examples, *Los mitos* and *América Tropical*, demonstrate how Siqueiros used the symbology of religion to advance, in a subtle way, a materialist vision that became pervasive throughout this mural production. And as Anreus observes, "the images of Christ that Siqueiros produced in 1963, 1965, and 1970 are earthly images of a suffering God. Through these works the artist mediated on the Christian-Marxist dialogue that was a result of the Second Vatican Council. He was paying homage to a 'God among us.'"[8] For Siqueiros, Marxism demanded political change and a social revolution. He subordinated religious symbols to his materialist cause for this reason. Siqueiros clearly felt that the only worthy spiritual cause was that of the true Mexican revolution.

The 1923 creation of the artists' union, its 1924 manifesto, and the active participation of many of the mural painters (Rivera, Siqueiros, Xavier Guerrero, among others) in the Mexican Communist Party helped to radically transform the aim of the Mexican mural project. This marked a true dialectical turn within the project, as abstract themes became more concrete, general human faces acquired recognizable features of the Mexican people, and abstract backgrounds and landscapes were imbued by historical ideas. Given that Marxism—a materialist (atheist) philosophy that opposes and distances itself from idealism and religion—formed part of the theoretical basis for the muralist production of Siqueiros and Rivera, it should come as no surprise that they would not promote religious thought in their works. After its quasi-religious and abstract beginning, then, Mexican muralism moved in an irreligious direction that focused primarily on grand narratives outside of religion while still voicing a continued skepticism of the Church through anticlerical and anti-Catholic discourses.

FIGURE 8. Symbols of the New Regime. Diego Rivera, *Symbols of the New Regime or the Allegory of Hardship of the Laborer and the Peasant or Symbols of the New Order*. 1926–1927. Mural, 5.53 × 6.08 m. Universidad Autónoma de Chapingo, Mexico City. Reproduced with permission of Art Resource.

Old Mexico as New Earth: The 1924 Muralist Manifesto

Supported by Diego Rivera, Xavier Guerrero, Fermín Revueltas, José Clemente Orozco, Ramón Alva Guadarrama, Germán Cueto, and Carlos Mérida, the "Manifesto of the Union of Mexican Workers, Technicians, Painters, and Sculptors," written by David Alfaro Siqueiros in 1924, became the political piece of the project, signaling the new direction it would take. Through its undeniable Marxist language, the "Manifesto" relaunched the Mexican muralist project. As we read, "The art of the Mexican people is the greatest and most vital spiritual manifestation in the world, and its Indian tradition is the best of these. It is great precisely because it is of the people and it is collective. That is why our primary aesthetic objective is to socialize artistic creation, in an effort to destroy all traces of bourgeois individualism. We reject so-called easel painting, and all the ultra-intellectual salon art of the aristocracy."[9] As this quote makes exceptionally clear, these painters viewed their work as one of inculcating a truth that the Church had long impeded. In this way, their Marxist project became an alternative to Catholicism that could serve as a more appropriate base for an egalitarian society.

Although deep ideological and political commitment is overtly expressed in the "Manifesto," let us not forget that the murals also adopted mythic, experimental, and philosophical qualities that would further support the notion that the Mexican muralist project must also be studied beyond its ideological and religious components. This is especially clear when it comes to interpreting Rivera's and Siqueiros's murals in terms of their Communist aspects: symbols as well as content. However, my statement merits much clarification: I agree that the ideological and political language is there, both in the writings and in the murals; I agree that the political commitment is there, because the muralists wished to carry out an aesthetic revolution and a revolution within aesthetics. They felt that the Mexican Revolution fell short of its principles and wanted to elevate the political struggle to the arts; I agree that Siqueiros's (and at one point Rivera's) alignment with the Stalinists and his participation in the attempt against Leon Trotsky's life made it almost impossible not to criticize his actions and his murals; I agree that Rivera was a controversial figure due to his political stance, switching from Stalinism to Trotskyism and back again to Stalinism, but I also disagree, as apparent as it may be, that ideology was the only, or the most important driving force of these two artists' mural production.

Put another way, painting ideology (symbols, emblems, and even revolutionary content) does not imply an ideological painting per se; and painting ideology does not imply that other qualities of the painting cannot prevent them from becoming even more important than ideology itself. This is precisely, I believe, what happened in both Rivera's and Siqueiros's murals. In the case of Rivera, it was almost impossible to overlook his fourteen years in Europe and how they shaped the painter that he was. When he returned to Mexico, for example, he had learned more from European painters—at least in terms of aesthetics—than he had from Mexican ones. In addition, despite his political leanings and political proposals in Rivera's murals, I believe that allegory prevailed over politics. Moreover, taking a closer look at Rivera's murals, one notices that his Marxism is somewhat fuzzy and guided by indeterminism. His revolutionary symbols at times seem to be taken from a cartoon, for they appear merely as allegorical figures. They frequently appear innocuous and dream-like, as depicted, for example, in *Dream of a Sunday Afternoon in Alameda Central* (1946–1947). As the Marxist philosopher Sánchez Vázquez asserts, regarding Rivera's aesthetic ideology, "in the absence of an inventory of Diego Rivera's readings, it must be assumed that his Marxist formation, more ideological than theoretical, was imbued by the philosophical, economic, and political ideas that circulated at the time, as articles of faith, among the Communist militants and sympathizers. Regarding aesthetics, his references to Marx and Marxism are even scarcer."[10]

At first sight, Rivera's mural *Creation* depicts a religious theme, especially if compared with Raphael's *The Trinity and the Saints*, but several elements have been added or changed to prevent it from being a purely religious mural. We can see upon further inspection that, even here, Rivera only used the symbols of the Church to promote a secular, nationalist ideal. According to the painter himself, "Adapting to Architecture in the most intimate and organic way possible, the artist took advantage of the little vault and walls of the niche that houses the organ to paint the original Cell, containing vegetables and animals around the Tree of Life, where, among the foliage are THE BULL, THE CHERUB, THE LION, AND THE EAGLE—signs of the Verb, beginning of everything—and on whose pinnacle emerges MAN, anterior entity to the masculine and the feminine."[11] As we can see, Rivera was thinking of "creation" in an encompassing manner, all the more so if we consider that the human figures have darker skin and Indian features, which by itself constitutes a revolutionary approach as to how the Mexican people were to be depicted and represented in the new

Mexican art. In other words, they were not shown as subdued subjects but as actual human beings with creative attributes. Furthermore, the robust man that emerges from nature with his arms outstretched becomes an emblematic image, as we find a similar image, generally speaking, in one of the panels (*Science/The Proclaimer*) of the mural series at the Secretariat of Public Education. And unlike in *Creation*, the human figures in *Science* appear much more terrestrial and historically grounded, thus alluding to the fact that Rivera's murals had overcome any religious leanings even as he continued to invoke alternative symbols to Catholicism. In addition, as Dina Comisarenco Mirkin explains, "inkling polyvalent symbols that integrate Judeo-Christian traditions, Pythagorism, and esoteric thought in Rivera's work refer to the essential unity of the divine and the human, characteristic of Vanconcelos' cosmological view."[12]

Turning to Siqueiros, if we set aside his early murals—even the ones he painted in Los Angeles (*Tropical America, Street Meeting*, and *Portrait of México Today*)—we can identify a constant thirst for experimentation and a desire to bring into play Marxist dialectics, which he viewed as the key element to his work. Marxist dialectics is a philosophical framework that explains the course of history through the interplay of contradictory and class-based forces. Critics have focused primarily on Siqueiros's ideology and not on his contributions to formal experimentation and the attempt to create a truly dialectical mural. For Siqueiros, dialectics meant everything: to incorporate motion into the murals; to integrate the arts (architecture, sculpture, and painting); to create his own paint and painting instruments, as well as to include tools not typically used for mural painting (spray guns); to work with abstract and conceptual figures (*From Porfirianism to the Revolution* [1957–1966] and *The March of Humanity* (1971) are two great examples); to actively involve viewers as they were expected to move along the mural due to its poliangularity.

Siqueiros laid this out in a 1935 conference as follows:

> We discovered then that we had to compose for a new viewer, the "mass-spectator." At the same time, we found that our composition should not be academic, symmetrical and peaceful, but had to be a superposition of angles that corresponded to the different spectacular points. Without realizing it, we began to use the dialectical method, and we said then: "Marxism gives us formidable elements, even for the plastic composition," and then we discovered that all the attempts of formal analysis of

the works and of the active forms that worried the cubists so much, were not but an attempt to analyze the dialectics in the arts, but they didn't know it; they didn't know they were using Marxist elements of dialectical materialism for the artistic composition.[13]

This passage, along with several aspects of Siqueiros's mural production, cast him as a dialectical rather than dogmatic painter. That said, his dogmatism or his voluntarism is incontestably found in his Communist politics and his radical life. In addition, in "El Sindicato" ("The Syndicate"), another essay from the 1930s, Siqueiros offers an assessment of the early mural productions that vehemently opposes their lack of political commitment while calling for a renewed muralist project: "The Revolutionary Union of Painters and Sculptors of Mexico will reappear once again, correcting the ideological deviations and technical mistakes that it suffered (. . .). It will be a joint movement of all the intellectuals of revolutionary ideology. This new organization will revise the ideological concepts and the items of the program that the other one did not carry out. From the failures of the previous one it will draw invaluable experiences for its activities."[14]

The one criticism that Siqueiros's view deserves and which, by the way, has been often overlooked is that no matter how socially and politically committed murals and muralists became, for him it was never enough; in this sense, he was a true radical activist and painter. I believe, however, that he underestimated the aesthetic revolution that was taking place before his eyes. The mere fact that we are still studying Mexican muralism today would seem to confirm this. Over a century after the muralist movement began, we continue to view these murals not only as paintings but as artifacts and pieces of history. Also, the mural series that Rivera painted at the Secretariat of Public Education (Secretaría de Educación Pública) and at the Autonomous University of Chapingo are undoubtedly beautiful and formidable murals, but Siqueiros considered their social aspect to be "contaminated" by "peasantry deviations."[15] That is, he rejected Rivera's belief that the peasantry, instead of the proletariat, would lead the revolution. While socialist and revolutionary themes appeared in the works of many lesser-known muralists, Siqueiros's radical criticism was primarily directed to Rivera; one may even consider it unjustified.[16] However, Rivera's murals give ample support to the idea that he was painting from the left, that he was a committed Marxist, but that he was not as blindly radical as Siqueiros. The two painters also differed not so much on the notion of painting dialectically but on how such dialectics should be depicted.

In the case of Rivera, a vague notion of Marxist dialectics, understood as an internal set of processes of contradictions and resolutions, with the result of the Revolution, can be found in the mural series of Chapingo, the Secretariat of Public Education, the National Palace (*Epic of the Mexican People*), and *Portrait of America*, at the former New Worker's School in New York. By calling it *vague*, I do not wish in any way to undermine or discredit the quality of his aesthetic project or insinuate that he had a distorted view of what dialectics meant. As a matter of fact, if by a dialectical process, particularly in regard to society, he meant—and indeed, he means this—that society at large is evolving and that this evolution involved a social struggle, he most certainly honors his dialectical vision.

What is interesting to me, especially with the mural series of Chapingo, is that Rivera not only included societal evolution but also the evolution of nature, and this is as a matter of fact, the true Marxist understanding of dialectics (from nature to society). That said, I also believe that, in comparison to Siqueiros, Rivera's depiction of dialectics was not as accomplished, perhaps because he emphasized artistic accomplishments over purely political achievements. There may be two reasons or possible explanations for this: 1) Rivera wanted to keep his own style, and indeed he kept it throughout his life; it was a style that gave prevalence to the arts, not to ideology or political change, as his critics tend to emphasize, although it was always implied. 2) Rivera, although always fascinated by modernity, industrial development, and new machineries, never truly incorporated the key element of dialectics: constant and flowing motion. For this reason, his historical murals seem to follow a historical narrative both visually and chronologically, but they appear somewhat undialectical because they do not successfully depict societal or natural contradictions (or even motion), which are so essential to Marxist dialectics.

Siqueiros viewed the historical narrative as conceptual and dialectical in nature. By this I mean that Siqueiros supports his notion of dialectics by abstract concepts, concepts that he attempted to paint. Rivera, on the contrary, never painted conceptually but rather figuratively or allegorically, perhaps because his theoretical foundation was not as strong as that of Siqueiros. I understand that the way he comprehended and depicted dialectics can generate much debate, but from my point of view he was aware of Marxist dialectics but chose not to reproduce this concept literally or take it at face value. These distinctions are crucial and absolutely relevant to

FIGURE 9. The Devil in the Church. David Alfaro Siqueiros, *The Devil in the Church*. Oil on canvas. Reproduced by permission of Art Resource.

understanding these two painters and their differences. Without these distinctions one may be tempted to believe that they occupy a similar pictorial space, both internally (as philosophy) and externally (murals), while in fact it is the contrary. For example, when Mary K. Coffey acknowledges their differences, she observes, "Both artists believed that they were leading the masses toward a Marxist, and therefore an emancipatory, understanding of history. Both artists viewed history as an objective reality unfolding according to a dialectical logic that was rooted in class conflict but that was ultimately progressive."[17] Although this is somewhat plausible as a general observation, I question Coffey's view. First, I do not believe Rivera and Siqueiros believed themselves to be leading the masses; their murals are and were too complex to effect any kind of social change, and in fact it never happened. Also, the mere fact that they both painted and that every painting is a subjective representation of reality would, in and of itself, imply that history was generally understood as dialectical, yes, but not as an "objective reality." Indeed, my disagreement goes much further. I would not treat Rivera and Siqueiros as if they were somehow equivalent at a philosophical level because Siqueiros precisely demonstrates a philosophical approach to painting, whereas Rivera's approach is not philosophical but artistic and allegorical. In short, the comparison and the nuances are, in my opinion, much more complex, and many critics tend to overlook these complexities and nuances. However, the differences of interpretations may also stem from the fact that from a philosophical point of view the terms "objective," "reality," "history," and "dialectical" must not be taken too lightly, as each of them constitutes a "red zone," no pun intended.

One very evident way in which Rivera supersedes religion, or at least the Catholic Church's version of it, is in the mural series at Chapingo. Let us not forget that Rivera was painting this series—as well as the ones at the Secretaría de Educación Pública—while Mexican society was experiencing the Cristero War, which started in 1926 after the state tried to enact some openly anticlerical articles of the 1917 Constitution. Indeed, we see explicitly anti-Catholic murals in this case that tied peasant collectivism, technological modernization, and the eradication of the clergy to a utopian future. All of this demonstrates that Rivera was very aware of what he was doing and what he aimed to accomplish. Some claimed that Rivera adhered to Rosicrucianism during this period, but he later discredited the rumor, confessing that he was acting under the direction of the Communist Party.

Rivera sought to "override" Catholicism in other ways. The name of the place where the main Chapingo murals were painted, "Capilla riveriana" ("Riverian Chapel"), echoes the Sistine Chapel, painted by Michelangelo at the Vatican. However, the religious aspects of the Sistine Chapel are here replaced by historical and revolutionary allegory. In this way, Rivera uses the idea of a chapel to communicate an alternative to Catholicism. *The Liberated Earth* (*La tierra fecunda*), the last mural at the end of the hall of the "Capilla riveriana," is flanked by two walls; on the right-hand side, nature (earth, agriculture, biology) bears fruit and prosperity; on the left-hand side, such prosperity and evolution are symbolized socially through the triumph of the social revolution. That is, on this side we find history, although foreshortened, crystalized in social change. Also, in the mural series at the Secretariat of Education, the one key Marxist concept that is repeatedly used by Rivera is that of exploited labor, both industrial and agricultural labor, and although we cannot detect a particular dialectical narration leading to social revolution, the viewer can identify its elements. As Mary K. Coffey asserts,

> The great accomplishment of Rivera's SEP [Secretaría de Educación Pública] cycle was his successful visualization of the ideals put forth by the Syndicate of Technical Workers, Painters and Sculptors in its 1923 *Manifesto*: to create an ideologically focused art, rooted in "indigenous traditions," that reflected the struggles of peasant, worker, and soldier in Mexico's "transition from an old order to a new one." In so doing, Rivera also offered the political regime the appearance of being a "revolutionary" state responsive to the demands of a mobilized peasantry as well as the growing power of a small but vocal confederation of communist and socialist labor organizations.[18]

However, what critics from the left tend to criticize, and Siqueiros was no exception, was the lack of ideology and dialectics in such "ideologically focused art." Evidently, this criticism was extremely radical and unfounded, and it speaks more about the kind of radical activist that Siqueiros was, and more about the times he lived in, than about the true accomplishments of Rivera as a painter. Rivera was, in my opinion, more concerned about showing off his grandiose aesthetics than about pleasing his critics. And this would explain why he took commissions from the Mexican government, the US ambassador to Mexico, and even the Rockefeller family.

American History 101: The Revolutionary Muralist's Dialectical View

A key set of Rivera murals, which were for the most part destroyed (although a few panels have survived), is *Portrait of America*. This mural was created in 1933 as a protest against the destruction of *Man at Crossroads*, a project commissioned by John D. Rockefeller for Rockefeller Center in New York City. To make a long story short, when Lenin's image appeared on the mural, Rockefeller canceled the project. In response, Rivera painted *Portrait of America* at New York City's New Workers School. The titles of some of the panels are politically charged and speak for themselves: *Colonial America, The American Revolution, Revolution and Reaction: Shay's Rebellion, The Civil War, The Labor Movement, Mussolini, Proletarian Unity*, etc. Like what we have seen in the Rivera murals discussed above, *Portrait of America* follows a historical process, with some sense of chronology that the artist perceived as dialectical. From a philosophical (and particularly Marxist) point of view, it becomes evident that the depiction of this dialectical process was overly simplistic. Yet again, Rivera maintained his artistic vision, keeping in mind that he was painting a mural with political content, and not just painting politics. Rivera himself claimed, however, that dialectics was at the core of this series. According to James Wechsler,

> As a Marxist painter Rivera relied on the theory and technique of dialectical materialism, which involved depicting an idea or thesis and a counter-idea or antithesis. As viewers resolved or synthesized these oppositions, they came to understand the artist's message. In *Man at the crossroads*, for instance, Rivera contrasted the social conditions in Depression-era USA with those in the Soviet Union. Even without the infamous portrait of Lenin, the viewer would have concluded that capitalist civilization was in decay and that Communism represented "a new and better future." In 1934 Rivera insisted that, of all his murals to date, *Portrait of America* was "the most correct in historical dialectics" and "the richest in materialistic synthesis."[19]

As we can see, according to Wechsler, Rivera needed only a basic notion of what dialectics was, as if following a manual, to then accurately portray the phenomenon. More surprisingly, Rivera himself claimed that this mural series was "the most correct in historical dialectics." Although

I give Rivera full credit for what he accomplished aesthetically in all his murals and in this one in particular, I would disagree as to how successful he was at depicting historical dialectics because, yet again, I find it too caricaturesque to be taken seriously, philosophically speaking. Furthermore, while Siqueiros placed too much attention on how closely (or not) Rivera followed his artistic agenda in relation to his politics, it is evident that Rivera was able to carry out an unprecedented artistic vision that included political and social elements without undermining the quality and artistic value of his murals.

Also, there is an obvious conclusion regarding the political mural production of Rivera and Siqueiros: their murals did not achieve the social revolution as they expected, and their representation of the Mexican people and the social struggle was exactly that: *their* representation. If Rivera's murals can be criticized because they are too caricaturesque or idealistic, in the case of Siqueiros, despite their philosophical originality, his murals also distance themselves from reality, making them at times too elevated and abstract for mass consumption, although I would not call him an elitist.

Nonetheless, Siqueiros's murals bring to the fore the other piece of the dialectical turn that was at the core of the Mexican muralist project: philosophical and theoretical dialectics. Depicting dialectics is not only a challenging task but also a daunting one, if not impossible altogether. The reason for this impossibility is because, in essence, dialectics is the inner dynamics of evolutionary processes, and, as such, it is a concept or an idea rather than a concrete thing, much less something that one can see. For example, would it be possible to paint how nature has transformed itself through millions of years? Or would it be possible to paint how a human cell has evolved, that is, the process itself? Maybe. But what kind of project would this be if not to emphasize the importance of evolution? As dialectical materialism aimed to take from nature its inner dialectics and apply it to the evolution of society, Siqueiros's goal throughout his life was precisely that: to depict the dialectical process by which society would transform itself to a higher—and better—social form.

Siqueiros is a dialectical painter in at least two ways: 1) he brings the content of (philosophical) dialectics to his murals; and 2) the murals, in a general way, conceptually encompass one another, thus giving the impression that his mural project is in a constant stage of progression, ascension, or even *becoming*: pursuing an unattainable concept, which at the end is essentially unrepresentable. All this, of course, if we take a radical criticism against his works; otherwise, his last mural, *The March of Humanity*, is, for all intents and purposes, the incontestable proof of my assertion and the success of the conceptual struggle that he underwent throughout his life, but that is accomplished in a wholesome way here. Yet, the one aspect that prevails in his mural production is the need to apply dialectics; that is why nature and society are the two concepts that constantly appear in motion, as if they were a force that aims to resolve its own contradictions. By this I mean that dialectics is so fundamental to his technique that he sought not only to represent it but to represent it integrating the arts, the artistic tools, the collaborative work through team work, and the viewer, because dialectics also implies recognizing the sets of relationships that are ever-present in objects, ideas, or processes, even intellectual ones.

In *Dialectics of Nature*, Frederick Engels defines three essential laws of dialectics: "[1] the law of the transformation of quantity into quality and viceversa; [2] the law of the interpenetration of opposites; [3] the law of the negation of the negation" and concludes: "It is, therefore, from the history of nature and human society that the laws of dialectics are abstracted."[20] Regarding the first law, as I have mentioned before, trying to paint such "transformation" is quite a daunting task to say the least, but Siqueiros sticks closely to this idea with dazzling results. That is why we find busy sets of images in his murals, aiming to represent the dialectical process in its essence: sets of accumulations that seek a dialectical resolution and reconfiguration. For example, the mural *Portrait of the Bourgeoisie* (1939) can be viewed as a dialectical process giving rise to the participation of the revolutionary forces to overcome the accumulation (quantity) of oppressive forces that give rise to a new society (quality). The premise of this mural is similar to that of *Portrait of Mexico Today* (1932), with the great difference that, in *Portrait of the Bourgeoisie*, Siqueiros incorporates more complex and challenging images. That said, the mural is painted under the same principles; in the latter, we can argue, Siqueiros is more successful. The transformation from quantity to quality, which is a simple and complex idea at the same time, is essentially that which is at play in *From Porfirianism to the Revolution* (1957–1966) and in *The March of Humanity* (1971): busy images that accumulate contradictions, these contradictions produce qualitatively new images that, by their inner dialectical forces, produce new images and so forth. In this vein, the images belong to an inner (invisible) and outer motion (visible), where the viewer is obliged to participate by moving along the mural, thus producing meaning dialectically; the mural has an inner dynamic, and it demands an outer dynamic as well. The second law, the idea of the interpenetration of opposites, basically implies their inseparable relationship: life is related to death and death to life; light is related to darkness and darkness to light; etc., and these sets of relationships establish new sets of relationships; matter is in motion, like the material forces of nature. If there is one aspect that Siqueiros emphasizes in *The March of Humanity*, it is the way nature evolved and how people built on their relationship with nature. Humans themselves are also nature, and that is why in this mural we find in two opposite sides, the (conceptual) figure of a man and a woman in a biological dialogue, which, by the way they are displayed, also seems a spatial relationship. Last, the law of "the negation of the negation" encompasses the principle by which, beyond and besides the relationships between opposites, every affirmation can be negated, and every negation also becomes an affirmation (which is the negation of the negation) that can be negated as well, ad infinitum. Historical time is an affirmation that is negated and affirmed throughout history; that is, the present negates the past, and the future negates the present. Historical materialism, which brings to the fore the question of new historical stages due to this dialectical process, in Marx's readings, is the history of the class struggle. This is, primarily, another key concept that can be easily identified in *Portrait of the Bourgeoisie, From Porfirianism to the Revolution*, and *The March of Humanity*.

The March of Humanity represents human life in its entirety: as nature (biology), as society (history), and as a constant process of *becoming*. The mural envelops the viewers, obliging them to see it from within, as if they had entered a cave or, conceptually speaking, a human cell. From all of Siqueiros' murals, this one is without a doubt the one that effectuates historical materialism at its core: the forces of nature in their fullest; the forces of humanity in relation to nature and to humans themselves; the process of nature as the continuation of life; the struggle of humanity to overcome its societal contradictions, etc. All of this provides the viewers with the actual feeling of motion, as they must stand at the center of the mural where a circular platform moves slowly and circularly while the viewer sees the mural. Although this motion is circular and one would expect that the linearity of the mural is circular as well, the viewer is impacted with the realization that the images follow all sets of shapes, thus giving the impression that the images jump out of the mural and yet continue the "march" in an ascending and spiral sequence and in a constant search for perfection and resolution. This progression is also conceptual, from the concrete to the abstract, and then back to the concrete; in short, it is the best depiction of an actual Hegelian's sublation (*Aufhebung*). But from a Marxist perspective, which Siqueiros follows tout court, this is also the best representation of the materialist conception of history. As we read in the *German Ideology*, "Men must be in a position to live in order to be able to 'make history' (...) The first historical fact is thus the production of the means to satisfy these needs, the production of material life itself."[21] *The March of Humanity*, then, must be viewed as matter, nature, and society interacting with one another, following their natural process of appearance and disappearance, life and death, and life back again, overcoming contradictions and even ideology. Last, my reading of Siqueiros's mural is done through Marxist texts but also and primarily through Siqueiros's texts, and this, I believe, sheds new light and possibilities for the reinterpretation of Siqueiros's works.

Conclusions

In the end, both Diego Rivera and David Alfaro Siqueiros imagined a Mexican future in which Marxism provided an alternative to Catholicism specifically and religion more generally. They largely avoided religious themes, although anti-Catholic discourses and images emerged in numerous ways. Sometimes the muralists cited religion to denounce it; other times they depicted religion to displace it. On still other occasions they forwent explicit references to Catholicism while casting Marxism as its successor. In each of these cases, the muralists produced anti-Catholic discourses that aimed to challenge the traditionally privileged role of the Church in national politics. As I have demonstrated, philosophical dialectics played a bigger role in the Mexican muralist project as Rivera and Siqueiros viewed dialectics as the key driving force of their works, but as we have observed, there are major differences as to how they viewed it and how they represented it. Regardless of how accurate, ideological, or comparable critics believe this representation to be, the fact is that this dialectical turn from heaven to earth led these painters to represent an irreligious and anti-Catholic reality at a time when religion and the Church experienced a crisis due to the Cristero war. That said, Rivera and Siqueiros aspired to more than a "representation"; rather, they wished to catalyze radical changes within Mexican society. As we know, these changes never occurred in the Marxist direction. In general, societal changes occur slowly, and they often do so in unpredictable ways and directions. The rich and diverse legacy of the Mexican muralist project reminds us that these murals are still alive, and they are still telling us something about our past, our present, and our future. Through these murals, the past becomes historical knowledge, the present becomes a permanent search for meaning, and the future becomes—artistically speaking—a connection back to the present, because the Mexican muralism still inspires viewers and artists alike. In sum, with regards to the interpretation of the murals, having Rivera and Siqueiros in mind, I believe that we all have to make a leap forward and reassess their murals beyond the ideological components that we find in them; that way, we do not oversimplify their meanings by placing before them a biased filter through which only a very narrow interpretation is possible. We have to chase the invisible (ideas and feelings) through the visible (mural); we have to let the murals speak for themselves and, in a way, set them free. If such freedom is achieved, we as viewers would have also effectuated a dialectical turn.

Notes

1. Siqueiros, "El Sindicato," 73.
2. Greeley, "Muralism," 17.
3. Lear, *Picturing*, 6.
4. Lear, 5.
5. Folgarait, *Mural Painting*, 50.
6. Anreus, "God among Us," 57.
7. Getty, "Conservation of *América Tropical*."
8. Anreus, "God among Us," 60.
9. Siqueiros, "Manifesto," 38.
10. Sánchez Vázquez, "Claves de la ideología estética de Diego Rivera," 207.
11. Quoted in Comisarenco Mirkin, "*La Creación*," 38.
12. Comisarenco Mirkin, "*La Creación*," 44.
13. Siqueiros, "Conferencia sobre arte pictórico mexicano sustentada el 12 de febrero de 1935, en el salón de actos de la Escuela Nacional de Medicina," 41.
14. Siqueiros, "El Sindicato," 62.
15. Siqueiros, 58.
16. For a list of lesser-known muralists who engaged in socialist and revolutionary themes, see Antonio Pujol, *Los alimentos y los problemas del obrero* [1935]); Fermín Revuelta, *Todo por la colectividad proletaria de México* [1934]; Raúl Gamboa Cantón, *Trabajo e injusticia social* [1936]. See also the collective works (by Máximo Pacheco, Roberto Reyes Pérez, Jesús Guerrero Galván, and Juan Manuel Anaya),

La *educación socialista* [1934] and *La lucha antiimperialista en Veracruz* [1936, by José Chávez Morado, Francisco Gutiérrez, and Feliciano Peña].
17. Coffey, *Orozco's American Epic*, 59.
18. Coffey, "'All Mexico on a Wall,'" 57.
19. Wechsler, "Portrait of America," 372.
20. Engels, *Dialectics of Nature*, 26.
21. Marx, *The German Ideology*, 47.

Works Cited

Anreus, Alejandro. "God among Us: Siqueiros' Christs." *Art Nexus* 44 (2002): 56–70.
Anreus, Alejandro, Leonard Folgarait, and Robin Adèle Greeley, eds. *Mexican Muralism: A Critical History*. Berkeley: University of California Press, 2012.
Coffey, Mary K. "'All Mexico on a Wall': Diego Rivera's Murals at the Ministry of Public Education." In *Mexican Muralism: A Critical History*, edited by Alejandro Anreus Alejandro, Leonard Folgarait, and Robin Adèle Greeley, 56–74. Berkeley: University of California Press, 2012.
———. *Orozco's American Epic: Myth, History and the Melancholy of Race*. Durham, NC: Duke University Press, 2020.
Comisarenco Mirkin, Dina. "*La Creación* by Diego Rivera." *Aurora, The Journal of the History of Art* 7 (2006): 35–61.
Engels, Frederick. *Dialectics of Nature*. Translated and edited by Clemens Dutt. New York: International Publishers, 1940.
Folgarait, Leonard. *Mural Painting and Social Revolution in Mexico, 1920–1940*. Cambridge: Cambridge University Press, 1998.
Getty. "Conservation of *América Tropical*." Accessed May 25, 2024. https://www.getty.edu/projects/conservation-america-tropical/.
Greeley, Robin Adèle. "Muralism and the State in Post-Revolution Mexico, 1920–1970." In *Mexican Muralism: A Critical History*, edited by Alejandro Anreus Alejandro, Leonard Folgarait, and Robin Adèle Greeley, 13–36. Berkeley: University of California Press, 2012.
Lear, John. *Picturing the Proletariat: Artists and Labor in Revolutionary Mexico, 1908–1940*. Austin: University of Texas Press, 2017.
Marx, Karl. *The German Ideology, including Theses on Feuerbach*. New York: Prometheus Books, Kindle edition.
Prampolini Rodríguez, Ida. *Muralismo mexicano: 1920–1940. Catálogo razonado I*. México: Universidad Veracruzana, 2012.

———. *Muralismo mexicano: 1920–1940. Catálogo razonado II*. México: Universidad veracruzana, 2012.

Sánchez Vázquez, Adolfo. "Claves de la ideología estética de Diego Rivera." In *A tiempo y destiempo: Antología de ensayos*, edited by Adolfo Sánchez Vázquez, 206–35. México: Fondo de Cultura Económica, 2003.

Siqueiros, David Alfaro. "Conferencia sobre arte pictórico mexicano sustentada el 12 de febrero de 1935, en el salón de actos de la Escuela Nacional de Medicina." In *Fundación del muralismo mexicano: Escritos inéditos de David Alfaro Siqueiros*, edited by Héctor Jaimes, 36–53. México: Siglo XXI Editores, 2012.

———. "El Sindicato." In *Fundación del muralismo mexicano: Escritos inéditos de David Alfaro Siqueiros*, edited by Héctor Jaimes, 54–108. México: Siglo XXI Editores, 2012.

———. "Manifesto of the Union of Mexican Workers, Technicians, Painters, and Sculptors." In *Manifestos and Polemics in Latin American Modern Art*, edited by Patrick Frank, 37–38. Albuquerque: University of New Mexico Press, 2017.

Wechsler, James. "Portrait of America: New Workers' School, New York." In *Diego Rivera: The Complete Murals*, edited by Luis-Martín Lozano and Juan Rafael Coronel Rivera, 371–86. Hong Kong: Taschen, 2007.

CHAPTER EIGHT

Immigrant Religious Communities in an Anti-Catholic Context

Mormons and Mennonites Petition the Mexican State, 1928–1936

REBECCA JANZEN

Significant conflict emerged in Mexico over the role of religion in public life in the 1920s and 1930s, culminating in the 1926–1929 Cristero War, and over the implementation of free public education for all that continued well into the 1930s. The national government mandated secularism, and yet it faced a population that was overwhelmingly Catholic. At the same time, there were groups of people in the country who were religious—but not Catholic—and who experienced officially imposed anti-Catholic policies in different ways than other Mexicans.[1] This chapter will consider the experiences of two such groups, Mormons and Mennonites, who came to Mexico from the United States and Canada seeking religious freedom in the late nineteenth and early twentieth centuries.[2] Examining how Mexico's federal government related to members of these religious minorities expands the scope of anti-Catholicism as a general phenomenon, moving toward what Butler describes in his afterward to this volume as a *catholic* (all-encompassing) definition of anti-Catholicism.

This chapter is in dialogue with other chapters in this volume, as well as *Liminal Sovereignty*, where I elaborated on how state policy relating to immigration and land redistribution programs occasionally favored Mormons and Mennonites and viewed them as a way to modernize or improve the country.[3] The Mexican government may have viewed the members of these foreign, religious communities as allies to building an anti-Catholic order. On other occasions, as I show in this chapter, Mexican state leaders and bureaucrats viewed these religious minorities unfavorably, perhaps because their members belonged to non-Mexican, religious organizations, and these organizations often tried to carry out functions that the state had reserved for itself. I then analyze interactions between Mormon men and the government about issues around education, water, and taxation because it compliments research that I have done about land conflict between Mennonites, Mormons, and the Mexican government during this period and how each group imagined national belonging and citizenship depending on the situation. I expand on that work by focusing on documents that highlight the contested issues of water and taxation. The two issues may seem unrelated, but in northern Mexico, where water was scarce and government presence was thin, few things could pair so readily to generate conflict. As will be seen, "foreign religion" entered the picture as a kind of third rail, complicated by the aims of Mexico's revolutionary state.

I situate this fraught relationship within the context of non-Catholic Christians in Mexico, the role of immigration in early twentieth-century Mexico, and the ways that anti-Catholicism is expressed in one of the many areas Butler's afterward mentions in his discussion of the encompassing nature of anti-Catholicism in revolutionary-era culture. I engage with Mormon and Mennonite anti-Catholic rhetoric and a brief case study of disputes between Mennonites and state and federal governments over private religious education and land use.[4] In a longer case study, I examine interactions between Mormons and the federal government that show how each group understood the Mormons' rights to Mexican citizenship. In dialogue with the work of historians George Ryskamp and Barbara Jones Brown on the lives of Mormons in the Mexico-US borderlands in this time period, I analyze the rhetorical use of Mexican citizenship and nationality in the petitions of Harvey Taylor and Daniel Skousen. These two Mormon men petitioned the government to be able to use bodies of water for agricultural purposes (for irrigation and hydroelectric power for agribusinesses). As will be seen, Harvey Taylor was deemed not Mexican enough to avoid paying special taxes levied on foreigners, whereas Daniel Skousen was thought to be just Mexican enough to be exempted. Skousen was a polygamist and a naturalized citizen; Taylor was born in Mexico to a family of polygamists. For fear of persecution, Taylor's parents chose to delay registration of his birth, which complicated his legal situation. In both cases, it was the intersection of belonging to a predominantly white racial and ethnic minority, as well as practicing Mormonism, that led to a struggle to claim Mexican citizenship.

Harvey Taylor was born in Colonia Juárez in 1890, the child of devout Mormon polygamists Ernest L. Taylor and Hannah Skousen. Harvey's father was so committed to the idea of polygamy that he contracted marriage even after the Church of Jesus Christ of Latter-day Saints' second official declaration against polygamy in 1904. Mexico recognized only one spouse. Harvey Taylor would have therefore been an illegitimate child per Mexican law. Ernest Taylor registered Harvey's birth in 1909, when his son was already an adult.[5] This gave Harvey the documentation necessary for marriage, but it did not automatically validate his claims to Mexican citizenship.[6] For that, he would have had to register his birth the year after he turned twenty-one in 1911.[7] Taylor's claims to citizenship were ultimately muddled by a legal framework that made it difficult for polygamists to register their children.

Daniel Skousen was Harvey Taylor's uncle.[8] He emigrated to Mexico from the United States in 1885 along with his first wife, his brother, and his mother. Skousen was a devout Mormon, and because of his beliefs he had two wives and fourteen children who lived to adulthood. According to his second wife, Sarah S. Skousen, he "worked on committees to visit the governor and often went to Mexico City on legal matters."[9] Skousen would have been familiar with the formal and informal processes that could lead to decisions being taken in his favor.

The Mexican Government's Relationship with and Mennonites

The Mexican state's relationship with Mormon and Mennonite communities was neither uniformly positive nor uniformly negative. The Mexican federal government may have been inclined to act positively toward Mennonites and Mormons because they were not Catholic, and so, for this reason, some government officials thought that these religious groups would have aligned with their understanding of the Mexican nation because of the tendency to equate all non-Catholic Christians with ideals of progress and the growing middle classes.[10] Indeed, in the 1920s and 1930s, the Mexican federal government largely favored what it considered to be Liberal secular values. These ideas were associated with Protestantism in Latin America and elsewhere and thus would have been opposed to Catholicism.[11] Although the Mennonites and Mormons would not have used the term Protestant to describe themselves, the Mexican government perceived them as potential allies in its struggle for progress and to supersede what it considered to be regressive Catholic views.

In Mexico and elsewhere in Latin America, elites had affiliated themselves with Protestant ideals since the struggle for independence in the nineteenth century. According to historian Jean-Pierre Bastian, Liberal elites in Mexico at that time found that Protestants were helpful allies first against the Conservative monarchy allied with the Catholic Church in Mexico's bid for independence (1810–1820) and then later on in the same century, aligned with elite ideas of Liberal reforms (1857) and the fight against the Porfiriato (1876–1911).[12] The Mexican government's belief that Protestants would be useful to what they considered to be progress follows what scholars of secularism have argued about other places and time periods. Talal Asad's study of Islam in the twentieth century, for instance, shows that Liberal governments supported religion when it adhered to Liberal conventions such as private religious devotion and Liberal social and philosophical ideals.[13] In supporting the Liberal components of Mexico's Constitution, non-Catholic, Christian faiths aligned themselves explicitly with anti-Catholic projects and policies. Indeed, nineteenth-century Mexican governments, much like those Asad studies, appreciated that people from these faiths would not seek public religious devotion because that would supersede nationalist displays. Furthermore, the religious messaging Protestants received in their services would reinforce the government's ideals about how to bring the country into the future through science, technology, and social programs that the government would administer.

The postrevolutionary Mexican government continued in the same vein, although its attempts at secularization were more extreme than those tried in the nineteenth century. Religious minority groups unaffiliated with Catholicism were still favorably understood by some Mexican intellectuals and politicians, but the limits would be tested by an array of new programs in education, health, and culture that attempted to replace the role of the Catholic Church in society. As Osten states in her chapter, while it was understood that socialists were not to practice religion, Catholicism was criticized more than other religions. In 1921, for instance, the Mexican federal government created the Public Education Secretariat (Secretaría de Educación Pública), with the stated goal of establishing public schools throughout the country. It also began to implement cultural missions and revolutionary festivals to supplant traditional Catholic festivals in honor of saints and the Virgin Mary, particularly her apparition in Mexico, the Virgin of Guadalupe. The government also implemented public hygiene, public health, anti-alcohol, and agrarian reform programs.[14] Mennonites and Mormons lived a lifestyle that already adhered to many of these goals. This, plus the fact that they were loosely Protestant (or at least vociferously *not* Catholic), would have meant that the government and those in power could have considered them to be groups aligned with revolutionary progress rather than with Catholicism.

Alignments with Postrevolutionary Governments through Anti-Catholicism and "Healthy Living"

Mennonites and Mormons held anti-Catholic beliefs, rooted in sacred texts, sermons from Church leaders, or in a belief in their superiority toward their neighbors, which differs from what Osten describes in her chapter as strategic and pragmatic anti-Catholicism.

Mormon anti-Catholic beliefs appeared in texts from Church leaders both before and after the period I study. James Talmage, Anthony W. Ivins, Rey L. Pratt, and Bruce R. McConkie's ideas are based on an interpretation of Church history in the *Book of Mormon* that suggests that the Catholic Church had ignored the true message of the Christian Savior.[15] Talmage, an LDS Church leader, criticized the Catholic Church in the *Great Apostasy*, a book that he published in 1909. He stated that the roughly eighteen centuries between Jesus Christ and Joseph Smith were a period of "the virtual overthrow and destruction of the Church established by Jesus Christ," whose conditions were "thoroughly apostate and utterly corrupt."[16] Three years later, Ivins, another church leader, characterized these eighteen centuries in the following way: "There evolved another system of religion, taking upon it the name of Christ, but in reality being anti-Christ, for it failed in all those things which he essayed to do."[17] Both Talmage and Ivins were undoubtedly referring to the Catholic Church. Rey L. Pratt, the leader of the LDS church's missionary efforts in Mexico, was more direct, stating in 1913 that "the power of the Catholic Church is almost supreme in the hearts of the people that received it under the iron pressure of the Spanish conquerors," whose "souls and consciences are in the hands and at the mercy of that great and abominable church, the whore of the whole earth, seen and spoken of by Nephi."[18] These negative ideas about Catholicism remain at least until 1958, when McConkie stated that the Catholic Church was the domain of the anti-Christ, whose foundation was the devil.[19] Talmage, Ivins, Pratt, and McConkie's ideas undoubtedly influenced Mormon people in Mexico, particularly those who would have met regularly with Pratt.

Mennonite ideas about Catholic people in Mexico are harder to trace—in part because for the Mennonites who immigrated to Mexico, anyone outside of their community was not living the way real Christians ought to live and so was simply irrelevant. They emigrated from Canada explicitly seeking separation from its society and in Mexico sought separation from the "Catholic, Spanish-speaking, post-revolutionary society in Mexico."[20] Andrea Dyck's study of Mennonites' letters from Mexico to their families and friends in Canada in the 1920s and 1930s shows that Mennonites understood themselves to be German-speaking, Anabaptist Canadians living as foreigners in the Spanish-speaking, Catholic culture of Mexico, and their letters sharply criticized their neighbors' morality, work ethic, and use of money.[21] These perceptions continue in the twenty-first century. In 2018, Mexican Mennonite teacher Peter Rempel explained that Mennonites see all outsiders as essentially the same and described stereotypical beliefs about Mexicans' morality and work ethic.[22] Veronica Enns elaborated on these perceptions in an interview from the same year where she described her Mennonite family's initial reactions to her non-Mennonite partner, including the stereotype that he would have a second family.[23] These statements from the 1930s to the present suggest that Mennonites understood Catholicism as integral to Mexican identity, and it follows that Catholicism would also be part of their negative stereotypes of their neighbors.

Both groups were undoubtedly anti-Catholic; perhaps because of this and their particular lifestyle guidelines, they were treated differently than Catholics in the post-revolutionary period.[24] Their community behavioral norms inadvertently aligned with revolutionary goals for progress in the areas of health, culture, and family structure. One significant way is their beliefs about alcohol use, which aligns with the revolutionary goals for health, described in Buchenau's chapter, and contrasts with the way Pierce's chapter illustrates the perceived connection between Catholicism and alcohol use. Mormons followed what they call the Word of Wisdom, and Mennonites followed a general policy of prohibition.[25] The Mexican government and the Mexican people thus largely perceived these nondrinking immigrants as "healthy" and "hard workers." In terms of culture, neither group had sufficiently public rituals or ornate spaces of worship that would compete with revolutionary programs and would align with revolutionary hygiene goals, which Fallaw elaborates on in his chapter. The Mennonites who opted to migrate to Mexico took the biblical prohibition on images in the ten commandments very seriously, and their austere church buildings were painted white on the outside and inside. There was no stained glass, and the benches (where people sat during religious services) did not have cushions or backs. Mormon buildings could be slightly more ostentatious than the Mennonite ones, but even those that did have stained glass or were architecturally interesting appear plain when compared to a Catholic Church.

Neither group's most significant services, marking membership in the religious community via baptism, marriage, or funerals, took place in a public way. Indeed, Mormons were married in their temples in front of fellow church members in good standing, and at that time the closest temples were at quite a distance from northern Mexico, and Mennonites were married at the end of a church service. Neither approach would have interfered with the Mexican government's desire to be the sole entity that could legalize a marital union. Moreover, the two groups' marriages produced what the Mexican government considered to be the ideal revolutionary family. The Mennonites had large monogamous families, and by the 1920s most Mormons were contracting monogamous marriages only and placing a similarly high value on large families.[26] Of course, as we see with Harvey Taylor's claim to citizenship, Mormons continued to grapple with the repercussions of their polygamous past well into the twentieth century. Thus, in these significant ways, the Mennonites and Mormons aligned with revolutionary ideals of health, culture, and family. Their private religious beliefs were celebrated only with members of their community and not in ways that attempted to compete with revolutionary festivals.

Well before the Revolution, the Mexican government treated Mennonites and Mormons differently than it treated Catholics because of this positive perception. In the late nineteenth century, Mormons were invited to colonize parts of northwestern Mexico because the government of Porfirio Díaz believed that immigrants from "civilized" countries would help modernize the nation. Moreover, both under Díaz and after the Mexican Revolution, the state of Chihuahua was vulnerable to American interests and incursions. A large part of the region was ceded to the United States in the treaty of Guadalupe-Hidalgo (1848), and nearly seventy years later, revolutionary fighting decimated the borderland region's population and agricultural production.[27] The Mexican government needed to reduce the chance of future incursions from the United States, and one way to do this was by accepting immigrants with agricultural skills who could thus bolster Chihuahua's economy.[28] Known for their high rates of procreation and productivity, Mormons and Mennonites might build a buffer.

The government's relationship with the Mormons began in the 1880s, when groups who wanted to remain in their polygamous family formations needed a place to live where this would not be criminalized.

The US government prosecuted polygamy, whereas the Mexican government chose not to intervene (although polygamy was technically illegal). As incentives, Mexico granted Mormon immigrants a series of legal exemptions from certain kinds of taxes and military service, and it allowed them to issue their own passports. Mormon settlers established approximately twelve distinct colonies in the states of Chihuahua and Sonora, building each town on the model of the Platt of Zion, not unlike the typical Mexican village grid that centers on a public square surrounded by a church and a municipal building.

Mormon settlers lived in these colonies until 1912, when revolutionary violence drove them to return to the United States. These Mormon refugees began returning to their homes in Mexico during the late 1910s, continuing to live in largely separate communities. They built and operated their own religious schools, and they held their own religious services.[29] This was despite the fact that such setups seemed to violate the anti-Catholic elements of the Constitution of 1917. Mormons did not face issues with their schools: their high school in Mexico City, the Benemérito de las Américas, was widely celebrated during its period of operation (1963–2013), and the Academia Juárez remains well known as a high school in Chihuahua, Mexico.[30] Perhaps because they were not Catholic, Mormons were able to get away with this parallel form of governance and education.

Mennonites, for their part, migrated to Mexico from Canada seeking religious freedom. Some Mennonites found that performing alternative service during World War I was onerous and against their faith. Others felt that the Canadian government's requirement to send their children to public nonreligious schools in English was too much of an imposition. They sought a country that would let them create the type of community that they wanted. In Mexico the Mennonites were allowed to set up religious education in German and attend church services that were also conducted in German. They also constructed their own communities, setting up colonies or groups of villages. Each village aligned along a street, with its own school and likely its own church. Each colony had a secular and religious leader to look after government matters and those pertaining to the community's religious health.

The Mexican federal government encouraged Mennonite and Mormon communities to live in accordance with their religious beliefs even though it was also engaging in a revolutionary push for public education and advocating for the understanding that land belonged to the nation via a massive land reform program. The revolutionary government expressed a generally positive view of these quasi-foreign cultural enclaves, and it clearly viewed them as allies on multiple fronts as it strove to effect anti-Catholic policies throughout the nation.

Negative Aspects of the Government's Relationship with Mennonites and Mormons

Not all was harmony despite many points of convergence, and indeed there are some significant examples of a negative relationship between Mennonites, Mormons, and the Mexican government. While the government had initially encouraged Mormon settlement, for some Mexicans, Mormon presence was a source of significant suspicion.[31] In the 1920s and 1930s, immigrants from the United States were subjected to removal orders for irregularities in their paperwork. Removals peaked between 1928 to 1934, and at least half of those deported were either from the upper classes or were landowners engaged in agriculture.[32] The Mormons in Chihuahua fit this profile nearly exactly, as they were landowners heavily invested in agriculture and US citizens. The official climate, then, was not exactly in their favor. Popular sentiment is harder to gauge, but there were reasons for resentment.

Mormons were also allowed to celebrate their religious services, performed by foreign clergy, and send their children to private religious schools at a time when Catholic people in Mexico did not have that option.[33] Some Mexicans may have been bothered by the fact that Mormons could hold religious marriage ceremonies during a period in which Catholic priests were not allowed to perform them. Mormons seemed generally unbothered by the Mexican state's civil marriage requirement, which they simply added to their own. The fact that a foreign religious minority had access to important religious rituals and was able to create a community almost entirely religious in nature likely increased resentment from people in surrounding communities who did not have the same access to rituals or community as the foreign minorities—or the same access that they had had before the Mexican Revolution.

Mormon lore focuses on anecdotes regarding events that took place during the revolution. It generally sustains that Mormons in Mexico were persecuted specifically because of their religious beliefs.[34] Mormons faced a new problem after the revolution: ongoing conflict over landholdings in the states of Chihuahua and Sonora. Thanks to the expansion of ejidos or communal lands under the new land reform system, the immigrants experienced an overall reduction in private landholdings.[35]

Mennonites also experienced conflict associated with landholding and land use. For instance, between 1922 and 1924, Mennonites in Chihuahua found that people were already living on the land they had purchased. The Mennonites typically sought out armed protection from police or other armed forces to resolve land issues in their favor.[36] Then in 1935 and 1936, the governor of the state of Durango closed all Mennonite schools in that state.[37] Mennonite leaders made successful appeals to federal authorities in this case.[38]

Mormon and Mennonite people in Mexico thus experienced events that detrimentally affected the lives of people in their communities. These experiences revealed the limits of their alignment with revolutionary ideals and thus exposed them to popular resentment. In some cases, the immigrants were able to resolve these issues through official channels and, in other cases, by using force (by state or hired proxy).

Seeking Favor and (not) Finding It: Taylor and Skousen's Petitions for Tax Exemption

We turn now to interactions between Mormons and the Mexican government in the late 1920s and early 1930s. Both positive and negative perception of Mormons came into play, as did the ongoing implications of how Mormons negotiated their religious belief in polygamy with living in a country where it was illegal. I have opted to analyze two very similar cases in which Mormon men Harvey Taylor and Daniel Skousen sought a tax exemption (which amounted to free water use) because they come to different resolutions: negatively for Taylor and positively for Skousen.

In January and February 1928, Harvey Taylor sent two separate letters to the Secretariat of Agriculture and Development in Mexico City, the federal water authority, and in both cases, he claimed that he was Mexican and thus should not pay additional taxes to access this water. In January, he asked to use water to power small machinery, and in February he wanted to confirm his right to access a well, create a dam, and use well water for irrigation. Daniel Skousen made a similarly straightforward claim to the water authority in 1930. He sought permission to use water from the Piedras Verdes River to irrigate his orchards in Colonia Juárez, Chihuahua state, approximately three hundred kilometers southwest of Ciudad Juárez.

Taylor made his claim to Mexican citizenship in a straightforward way.[39] He stated in two letters and two sworn statements that he was a Mexican citizen.[40] Taylor—first by himself in January 1928 and then with a group of local farmers in February 1928—hired a local notary, Lic. Augstín Landeros Díaz, to draft a petition to the government. The first letter introduces Mr. Taylor by his citizenship, age, marital status, profession, and residence. He is, the document states, a "Mexican citizen, 37 years of age, married, farmer, born in Colonia Juárez . . . and resident of Colonia Dublan . . ." ("ciudadano mexicano, 37 años de edad, casado, agricultor, originario de Colonia Juárez . . . y vecino de Colonia Dublán . . .").[41] Taylor's citizenship claim is simply one of several pieces of important information about him, as obvious as his age, profession, place of birth, and place of residence.

The second letter grouped Harvey Taylor with other local men. It introduces him as part of a list, stating that he is "Harvey Taylor, resident of Colonia Dublán, Municipality of Nueva Casas Grandes . . . all of them of Mexican nationality" ("Harvey Taylor, vecino de Colonia Dublán, Municipalidad de Nueva Casas Grandes . . . siendo todos de nacionalidad mexicana").[42] This is a similarly forthright declaration of identity, also tied to Taylor's place of residence. This letter differs slightly from the first one because Taylor's claim to Mexican nationality is indistinguishable from that of the other people who signed this letter.

In addition to these introductory letters, Taylor gives sworn statements attesting to his nationality for each petition for water concessions. The statement attached to his first petition introduces him as "HARVEY TAYLOR, Mexican exercising my rights" ("HARVEY TAYLOR, mexicano en pleno uso de mis derechos").[43] The statement attached to the second petition is similar, stating: "HARVEY TAYLOR, Mexican citizen exercising my rights" ("HARVEY TAYLOR, ciudadno [sic] mexicano en pleno uso de mis derechos").[44] The first statement simply states he is Mexican, and the second one adds a claim to citizenship. In both cases the statement is made in such a way as to brook no argument or foster further discussion.

Taylor and his notary justified this straightforward claim to citizenship and nationality in two ways. First, they offered further documentation. They added a notarized copy of his father's naturalization certificate, as his eligibility for birthright citizenship was contested given changes in Mexican law.[45] Ernest Taylor, Harvey Taylor's father, only registered Harvey's birth in 1909, when Harvey was already nineteen years old. No mother is named in this document. Delaying birth registration was common among polygamous parents, who often registered the child under the father's name only.⁴⁶ Taylor needed to prove his father was Mexican and to justify his claim to citizenship via his father's citizenship rather than by his own birth. This is why he included a notarized copy of his father's naturalization certificate with his petition.⁴⁷ Bureaucrat Manuel Aguilar Sáenz, the government general secretary for the state of Chihuahua, approved the notary's verification.⁴⁸

Second, Taylor's proposal promised benefits to the broader community. The first letter adds that should he be granted the requested water concessions, Taylor would "provide free electricity to the Official Schools of Llano Largo and Colonia Madera, and as many as 3000 watts to the Municipality of Casas Grandes for public services" ("proporcionaré luz gratuita a las Escuelas Oficiales de Llano Largo y Colonia Madera, y hasta 3000 wats al Municipio de Casas Grandes, para los servicios públicos").⁴⁹ Taylor and his attorneys or notaries offered what they considered to be legal proof. Moreover, they promise that once the government offered them water concessions with tax concessions, they would engage in actions that benefited the public good. Interestingly, however, they choose not to mention the petitioner's religious affiliation. Given that, in earlier periods, Mormons had tended to identify themselves as such in legal proceedings and were almost always identified this way by others, this may be evidence that Mexico's revolutionary anti-Catholic policy had made it so that proclaiming ties to any religion would not help one's case.

Taylor made his claim to citizenship and nationality in a straightforward fashion with what he and his notaries considered to be appropriate documentation. He believed that he was Mexican enough for water rights and related tax exemptions.

Daniel Skousen also matter-of-factly stated that he was a Mexican citizen. He and his notaries provided a letter, a list of all community members who would benefit from his irrigation project, a form that reiterated the content of his letter, and a certified copy of his naturalization certificate. Skousen's initial letter states that he is a "resident of Colonia Juárez, in transit in this place, Mexican citizen by naturalization as I show with the certified copy of my naturalization letter" ("vecino de Colonia Juárez de este Municipio, de tránsito en el lugar, ciudadano mexicano por naturalización como lo acredito con la copia certificada de mi carta de naturalización").⁵⁰ Citizenship was tied to his place of residence and to the bureaucratic process of naturalization. Skousen attached other documents to this letter. He (or his notaries) drew up a two-page list of local people who would benefit from this project. The form reiterated Skousen's claim to Mexican citizenship, simply stating that he is a "Mexican citizen through naturalization" ("C. Mexicano por naturalización").[51] The accompanying certificate of naturalization, however, is somewhat problematic. The notary's description begins by stating that the original is "a deteriorated document that is ripped on the edge opposite to the margin" ("un documento deteriorado que tiene rota una parte del lado contrario al márgen").[52] Much of the certified copy is ellipses, which indicates parts the notary was not able to read. So this document only offers a tentative claim to citizenship, and Skousen and his notary completely ignore the obvious blank spots in his naturalization certificate. These documents assert Skousen's citizenship even as they leave some room for other interpretations.

Skousen's petition also included another type of document presented matter-of-factly: sworn statements from fellow community members. The letters—like Harvey Taylor's—identify Skousen's supporters by age, citizenship, country of origin, marital status, and profession and claim citizenship without explanation or detail their authors' naturalization status. Martha H. Haus, for instance, attests that she is a "Mexican ... originally from Utah, United States of America,/ from neighboring Colonia Juárez" ("mexicana ... orginaria de Utah, Estados Unidos del Norte, / y vecina de Colonia Juarez [sic]").[53] Isaac Turley states that he is a "Mexican citizen ... originally from Showike, Arizona, United States of America and from neighboring Colonia Juárez" ("ciudadano mexicano ... originario de Showike, Arizona, Estados Unidos del Norte y vecino de Colonia Juarez").[54] These witnesses do not elaborate on how they became Mexican citizens. Another supporting letter establishes their ties to Mexico via naturalization and by birth. Anson B. Call and Smith H. Skousen state that they are "Mexican citizens through naturalization firstly and by birth secondly" ("ciudadanos mexicanos por naturalización el primero y por nacimiento el segundo").[55] These supporters' statements imply that Skousen's actions will benefit the community's Mexican members and, in this way, strengthen Skousen's claim to Mexican citizenship and tax exemption.

The government's responses to Daniel Skousen's and Harvey Taylor's petitions differ substantially. The government questioned Taylor's claim to citizenship; that is, officials did not think that he was a Mexican citizen. On April 14, 1928, Gumaro García de la Cadena, then the head of the Department of Water, Land and Colonization in the Secretariat of Agriculture and Development, wrote a letter in response to Taylor's first petition. The letter begins with the heading: "Submit proof of being a Mexican national" ("Que remita el comprobante de ser de nacionalidad mexicana").⁵⁶ The brief missive that follows this heading concludes that "it is necessary that you provide proof that you are a Mexican national" ("es necesario que se sirva comprobar que es de nacionalidad mexicana").⁵⁷ This communication thus confirms that the government did not perceive Taylor as a Mexican citizen.⁵⁸ Internal memos reiterated this. A bureaucrat named Marcelino B. Flores summarizes the case, stating that Taylor had been asked to "prove his Mexican citizenship" ("comprobara su nacionalidad como mexicano") and had submitted a document "that shows that his father became a naturalized Mexican" ("que consta que su padre se nacionalizó mexicano") as well as a "a certified copy with which he hopes to prove that he is Mexican" ("copia certificado con la que pretende probar que es mexicano").⁵⁹

Flores did not believe these documents proved Taylor's claim. The documentation submitted was considered insufficient proof of citizenship. The government told Taylor that he was not Mexican in July 1928. His imperfect documents "do not prove that Mr. Harvey Taylor is a Mexican citizen" ("no compruebe que el Sr. Harvey Taylor es de nacionalidad mexicana") and "the birth certificate and recognition as an illegitimate child . . . is amended or corrected" ("el acto de nacimiento [y] reconocimiento como hijo natural . . . está enmendado o corregido"). Moreover, since Taylor's father became a citizen in 1897, seven years after Harvey was born (and recognized as Ernesto L. Taylor's natural child, i.e., born out of wedlock) in 1890, the prevailing citizenship law states that despite being born in Mexico, Harvey Taylor cannot claim Mexican citizenship.⁶⁰ This ruling aligns with a certain tendency to deny Mormons from belonging to the Mexican nation. Taylor's citizenship claims were ultimately denied because of the legal framework that prohibited polygamy and thus made it difficult for parents to register their children. In the 1920s, the revolutionary state was occasionally willing to make exceptions to birthright citizenship requirements and speed up bureaucratic processes to favor otherwise desirable non-Catholic immigrants.

The government's response to Skousen was more favorable, aligning with the other tendency I mentioned earlier in this chapter. The initial internal communications from the government to Skousen confirm his citizenship claim as a secretary writes that Skousen is "Mexican citizen through naturalization" ("C. Mexicano por naturalización") in pencil over the typed letter.⁶¹ There may have been debate about the veracity of this claim, as the notarized copy of the naturalization certificate was deeply imperfect—however, unlike Taylor's case, it does not matter where or when he was born, when his father registered his birth, or whether his parents were married in a way recognized by the Mexican government.

Another factor is that Skousen did not give up. In addition to the many supporting documents he submitted with his initial claim, Skousen continually followed up.[62] As we recall from the somewhat hagiographic interpretation of Skousen, he was known to be good at negotiating with Mexican authorities. Eventually the case was decided in Skousen's favor: "There is no problem" ("no hay inconveniente"). Skousen's continual persistence effectively drowned the bureaucracy in documents until it agreed with him. As Skousen was a naturalized citizen himself, he did not face the same impediments to being registered at birth that Taylor did. There was not as much of a chance for structurally anti-Mormon, anti-religion, or anti-American bureaucratic practices to keep him out.

Harvey Taylor and Daniel Skousen experienced different responses to their claims to Mexican citizenship as they attempted to avoid certain taxes that were levied on foreigners. In light of the similarities in their claims, the fact that the same notary prepared their letters, and the similarity in the bureaucrats who responded to them, their experiences illustrate the vagaries of Mexican bureaucracy. The people handling the case may have had a negative view of Mormons who lived in the colonies, or they may simply have decided in one instance that it was not worth fighting with someone who would persist in submitting paperwork.

Taylor and Skousen's cases, moreover, illuminate the tensions of belonging to an ethnic and religious minority associated with the United States in Mexico in the tumultuous early twentieth century. There were positive aspects of this perception, in light of the associations between Mormons, Mennonites, and Protestants, which implied that their religious rituals and religious communities were restricted to the private sphere and thus would not conflict with the government's desire to monopolize the public one. Moreover, their lifestyle aligned with revolutionary goals for progress via education and health and, in particular, in the fight against alcoholic beverages, as did their largely anti-Catholic beliefs. This does not give us an overall view of Mennonites or Mormons in the 1920s and 1930s, but it does illustrate certain tendencies. As I have shown, Mormons' and Mennonites' anti-Catholic tendencies may have allowed them to curry favor with the state, and as much as they expand our understanding of what revolutionary anti-Catholicism could look like, their members still often faced certain challenges as predominately foreign, religious communities in a secularizing state.

Notes

1. I engage with both Mennonites and Mormons in this chapter, building on my monograph *Liminal Sovereignty*, which looked to earlier work that had compared both groups—from Janet Bennion (*Desert Patriarchy*), Jason Dormady, and Philip R. Stover (*Religion and Revolution in Mexico's North*).
2. In this essay I use the term Mormon to refer to people who were members of the Church of Jesus Christ of Latter-day Saints even though it is a term used by many religious groups who follow the teachings of Joseph Smith, a man whom they consider to be the prophet. Mormons from what is now Utah migrated to Mexico to preserve polygamy. As the largest group of Mormons distanced itself from this type of marriage, an array of splinter organizations emerged in Mexico as well as in the United States. Elisa Pulido's *The Spiritual Evolution of Margarito Bautista* chronicles the life of a significant Mormon leader in Mexico and, in so doing, explores the development of Mormonism and of polygamy in that country. Today, the vast majority of Mormons in Mexico do not have roots in migration from the United States. My more recent work on Mormon art and architecture in Mexico, "Mormon Art and Architecture in Mexico: Between Mexico and the United States," takes this broader history into account, seen in the forthcoming collection, *Mormon Art: A Critical Reader*.
3. Janzen, *Liminal Sovereignty*, chap. 1, on immigration (1–33); chap. 2, on Mormons and land redistribution (33–60); chap. 3, on Mennonites and land redistribution (61–82).
4. Pablo Yankelevich highlights the fact that foreigners could not be ministers of religion ("Extranjeros indeseables en México"), 718.
5. "México, Chihuahua, Registro Civil, 1861–1997," database with images, *FamilySearch* (https://familysearch.org/ark:/61903/3:1:33SQ-G5HD-9ZD4?cc=1922462&wc=MKCR-4WL%3A1021829501%2C1021856801 : 12 March 2018), Casas Grandes > Nacimientos 1905–1911 > image 413 of 689; Archivo General del Registro Civil (Chihuahua City Central Archives), Mexico.
6. Ryskamp, "Mormon Colonists," 45.
7. The 1886 "Ley sobre extranjería y naturalización" states that one is Mexican if one has a Mexican father; if one is born to a Mexican mother and unknown father or a father with an unknown nationality; or a person may become Mexican by registering the year after one turns twenty-one ("Son mexicanos I. Los nacidos en el territorio nacional, de padre mexicano por nacimiento ó por naturalización. II. Los nacidos en el mismo territorio nacional de madre mexicana y de padre que no sea legalmente conocido, según las leyes de la Republica. En igual caso se considerarán los que nacen de padres ignorados, ó de nacionalidad desconocida. II, Los nacidos fuera de la República, de padre mexicano que no haya perdido su nacionalidad. Si

esto hubiere sucedido, los hijos se reputarán extranjeros; pudiendo, sin embargo, optar por la calidad de mexicanos dentro del año siguiente al día en que hubieren cumplido veintiún años, siempre que hagan la declaración respectiva ante los agentes diplomáticos ó consulares de la República, si residiesen fuera de ella, ó ante la Secretaria de Relaciones si residiesen en el territorio nacional. Si los hijos de que trata la fracción presente residieren en el territorio nacional, y al llegar a la mayor edad hubieren aceptado algún empleo público ó servido en el ejército, marina ó guardia nacional, se les considerará por tales actos como mexicanos, sin necesidad de más formalidades") (1038–39).

8. "Daniel Skousen."
9. Hatch, *Stalwarts*, 610.
10. Gill, *Rendering unto Caesar*, 81. For more information, see also Gamio, *Mexican Immigration*, 114–15.
11. Mormons who belong to the Church of Jesus Christ of Latter-day saints as well as to other movements can be classified as "restorationist," that is, following the restored or additional teachings of Joseph Smith, which other Protestants would not follow. For a discussion of how these beliefs in a restored or corrected Christianity play out in Mexico, see Dormady, *Primitive Revolution*, 71–72. Carlos Loret de Mola's "Con los domadores del desierto" offers a Mexican understanding of Mormonism as restorationist Christianity (30). Mennonites are the spiritual descendants of Anabaptists or re-baptizers involved in the sixteenth-century Radical Reformation and see themselves as different from the European reformers who founded what would become Lutheran and Reformed churches. For more information, see Klaassen, *Anabaptism*.
12. For more information, see Bastian, "Les réponses de l'Église catholique à l'expansion du protestantisme en Amérique latine"; Jean-Pierre Bastian, "Metamorphoses."
13. Asad, *Formations of the Secular*, 181, 183.
14. Kloppe-Santamaría, *In the Vortex*, 19. See also Knight, "Popular Culture," 394–95. For general information about agrarian reform or land redistribution, see, for example, Hart, *Empire and Revolution*, particularly 343–70.
15. "I saw among the Gentiles the formation of a great church . . . And the angel said unto me: Behold the formation of a church which is most abominable above all other churches" (1 Nephi 13:4–5a).
16. Talmage, *Great Apostasy*, 21, 150.
17. Craig Livingston discusses the work of Anthony W. Ivins, a church leader in Salt Lake City, and Rey L. Pratt, who led the LDS Church's missionary efforts in Mexico and was also a church leader. His article provided helpful information for primary sources from Livingston ("Lions, Brothers, and the Idea of an Indian Nation" 124); Ivins, *Eighty-Second Annual Conference*, 63.
18. Pratt, "Gospel to the Lamanites, IX–XII," 686.
19. McConkie, *Mormon Doctrine*, 66, 130.

20. Dyck, "And in Mexico,'" 2.
21. Dyck, 36.
22. "Peter Rempel: Me di cuenta."
23. "Raúl Kigra and Veronica Enns."
24. Coviello, *Make Yourselves Gods*, 13, engages with the question of Mormons and secularism and notes that the development of Mormon behavior and belief in the nineteenth century oscillates between the two poles of acceptably private and inappropriately public.
25. The Mormon prohibition on alcohol is part of *The Doctrine and Covenants of the Church of Jesus Christ of Latter-Day Saints*, section 89. For more information about Mennonites and alcohol—from the tendency toward prohibition, alcohol-related businesses, and substance use disorders—see Friesen, "Mennonites and Alcohol."
26. George Ryskamp has studied Mormon marriage tendencies in northern Mexico from 1885 to 1912. The number of Mormon children registered as illegitimate (i.e., with parents in polygamous unions) was at least 37%, compared to an average in surrounding states of 10 to 20 percent ("Mormon Colonists," 44–45).
27. Dormady, "Mennonite Colonization in Mexico," 172.
28. Will, "Mennonite Colonization of Chihuahua," 366.
29. Kathleen McIntyre's *Protestantism and State Formation in Postrevolutionary Oaxaca* examines many of the same tensions related to education in Oaxaca, primarily around Presbyterian and Baptist missions.
30. The LDS Church had over two dozen schools by 1978, and they were well regarded; for further information, see Juarez Rubio, "Benemérito!" and Morgan, "Century of LDS Church Schools."
31. This was in part because their initial immigration came soon after the Tean movement for independence and the Mexican-American war. Janzen, *Liminal Sovereignty*, 39; 45–47.
32. Yankelevich "Extranjeros indeseables en México," 717, 721.
33. At that time, no religion could have clergy members who were not Mexican (Yankelevich, 718). Mennonites and Mormons only had lay unpaid leaders and so were able to skirt the letter of the law.
34. See, for example, Whitaker, *Aunque nos toque morir*. A more recent effort to rectify this sensationalist history comes from John Hatch, an Anglo Mormon in Mexico, and his documentary *Over the Years and Roads*. *Aunque nos toque morir* was released only seven years after Mexican Mormon Ambrosio de Aquino was murdered (Sanchez Xicali).
35. See Janzen, *Liminal Sovereignty*, chap. 2.
36. See, for example, Schmiedehaus, *Ein festes burg*, 213–15; Quiring, *Mennonite Old Colony*, 27.

37. For more information, see Janzen, *Liminal Sovereignty*, 62–63; Rempel and Rempel, *75 Jahre*, 299; Sawatzky, *They Sought a Country*, 70; Will, "Mennonite Colonization of Chihuahua," 368.
38. Stover, *Religion and Revolution in Mexico's North*, 309; Dyck, "'And in Mexico,'" 77.
39. Aprovechamientos Superficiales collection, 1208, exp 16779.
40. Aprovechamientos Superficiales collection, 1580, exp 18898.
41. Harvey Taylor to the Secretaría de Agricultura y Fomento, 17 Jan. 1928, Aprovechamientos Superficiales collection, Archivo Histórico, Comisión Nacional del Agua, Mexico City.
42. Harvey Taylor, Genaro Galaz, Santos Miranda, Jesús José Rico, Rafael Ponce, Eutimio Ponce and Jesús Rico Vda de Quevedo to C. Secretario de Agricultura y Fomento, 16 Feb. 1928, Aprovechamientos Superficiales collection.
43. Harvey Taylor sworn statement to C. Secretario de Agricultura y Fomento, 17 Jan. 1928, Aprovechamientos Superficiales collection.
44. Harvey Taylor sworn statement to C. Secretario de Agricultura y Fomento, 19 Nov. 1927, Aprovechamientos Superficiales collection.
45. Gleizer, "Nacionalidad, naturalización y extranjería," 267.
46. Ryskamp, "Mormon Colonists," 45.
47. Luis A. Ornelas, notarized copy of "Carta de Naturalización de Ernesto L. Taylor," 1 May 1928, Aprovechamientos Superficiales collection.
48. Manuel Aguilar Saenz, of signature, 9 May 1928, Aprovechamientos Superficiales collection.
49. Daniel Skousen to the Secretaría de Agricultura y Fomento, 17 Jan. 1928, Aprovechamientos Superficiales collection.
50. Daniel Skousen to C. Secretario de Agricultura y Fomento, 26 Mar. 1930, Aprovechamientos Superficiales collection.
51. Daniel Skousen to C. Secretario de Agricultural y Fomento, form regarding water concessions, 25 Apr. 1930, Aprovechamientos Superficiales collection.
52. Luis A. Ornelas, Copia certificada del certificado de naturalización, 29 Aug. 1928, Aprovechamientos Superficiales collection.
53. Martha H. Haus, sworn statement to C. Secretario de Agricultura y Fomento, 28 July 1930, Aprovechamientos Superficiales collection. This is likely Martha Haws, Ryskamp 45–47, in Dormady and Tamez. https://www.familysearch.org/tree/person/details/KWCG-PRG.
54. Isaac Turley, sworn statement to C. Secretario de Agricultura y Fomento, 29 July 1930, Aprovechamientos Superficiales collection. https://www.familysearch.org/tree/person/details/MZWB-7DB.
55. Anson B. Call and Smith H. Skousen to C. Secretario de Agricultura y Fomento, 6 Dec. 1930, Aprovechamientos Superficiales. Call was a bishop in Colonia Dublán

and a polygamist, Brown, *1910 Mexican Revolution*, 23. Smith Skousen was Daniel Skousen's great-nephew. See Smith Hollister Skousen on entry for Peter Niels Skousen, Daniel Skousen's brother: https://www.familysearch.org/tree/person/details/KW89-D8Q.

56. Gumaro García de la Cadena to Harvey Taylor, 14 Apr. 1928, Aprovechamientos Superficiales collection.
57. Gumaro García de la Cadena to Harvey Taylor.
58. Marcelino B. Flores to the head of the department, Secretaría de Agricultura y Fomento, 6 June 1928, Aprovechamientos Superficiales collection.
59. Flores to head of department.
60. Octavio Andrade to the head of the "Departamento Consultivo y de legislación," Departamento Jurídico, 4 July 1928, Aprovechamientos Superficiales collection.
61. Daniel Skousen, application to Secretario de Agricultura y Fomento, 25 Apr. 1930, Aprovechamientos Superficiales collection.
62. These include documents already cited as well as additional documents in the Aprovechamientos Superficiales collection (18810, 18900, 27760) and in the Aguas Nacionales collection (212).

Works Cited

Aguas nacionales collection, Archivo Histórico, Comisión Nacional del Agua, Mexico City.

Aprovechamientos Superficiales collection, Archivo Histórico, Comisión Nacional del Agua, Mexico City.

Asad, Talal. *Formations of the Secular: Christianity, Islam, Modernity*. Stanford: Stanford University Press, 2003.

Bastian, Jean-Pierre. "Les réponses de l'Église catholique à l'expansion du protestantisme en Amérique latine." *L'Ordinaire des Amériques* 210 (2008): 81–95.

———. "The Metamorphosis of Latin American Protestant Groups: A Sociohistorical Perspective." *Latin American Research Review* 28, no. 2 (1993): 33–61.

Bennion, Janet. *Desert Patriarchy: Mormon and Mennonite Communities in the Chihuahua Valley*. Tucson: University of Arizona Press, 2004.

Brown, Barbara Jones. "The 1910 Mexican Revolution and the Rise and Demise of Mormon Polygamy in Mexico." In *Just South of Zion: The Mormons in Mexico and its Borderlands*, edited by Jason H. Dormady and Jared Tamez, 23–38. Albuquerque: University of New Mexico Press, 2015.

Coviello, Peter. *Make Yourselves Gods: Mormons and the Unfinished Business of American Secularism*. Chicago: University of Chicago Press, 2019.

"Daniel Skousen." *FamilySearch*. July 5, 2021. Accessed March 14, 2022. https://www.familysearch.org/tree/person/details/KWCG-99W.

The Doctrine and Covenants of The Church of Jesus Christ of Latter-day Saints. Salt Lake City, UT: The Church of Jesus Christ of Latter-day Saints, 1981.

Dormady, Jason H. "Mennonite Colonization in Mexico and the Pendulum of Modernization, 1920–2013." *Mennonite Quarterly Review* 88, no. 2 (2014): 167–94.

———. *Primitive Revolution: Restorationist Religion and the Idea of the Mexican Revolution, 1940–1968*. Albuquerque: University of New Mexico Press, 2011.

Dyck, Andrea. "'And in Mexico We Found What We Had Lost in Canada': Mennonite Immigrant Perceptions of Mexican Neighbours in a Canadian Newspaper, 1922–1967." MA thesis, University of Winnipeg, 2007.

Esplin, Scott C., E. Vance Randall, Casey P. Griffiths, and Barbara E. Morgan. "Isolation, Exceptionalism, and Acculturation: The Internationalization of Mormon Education in Mexico." *Journal of Educational Administration and History* 46, no. 4 (2014): 387–404.

Friesen, Aileen. "Mennonites and Alcohol." *Preservings* 43 (2021): 1–2.

Gamio, Manuel. *Mexican Immigration to the United States: A Study of Human Migration and Adjustment*. Chicago: University of Chicago Press, 1930.

Gill, Anthony. *Rendering unto Caesar: The Catholic Church and the State in Latin America*. Chicago: University of Chicago Press, 1998.

Gleizer, Daniela. "Nacionalidad, naturalización y extranjería en el Constituyente de 1917." *Cuestiones Constitucionales* 38 (2018): 259–78.

Hart, John Mason. *Empire and Revolution: The Americans in Mexico since the Civil War*. Berkeley: University of California Press, 2002.

Hatch, John, dir. *Over the Years and Roads*. December 31, 2021. Phoenix, AZ. Byron's Technology Services, LLC. YouTube video. https://www.youtube.com/watch?v=n1r0YRK_puY&ab_channel=Byron%27sTechnologyServices%2CLLC.

Hatch, Nelle Spilsbury. "Daniel Skousen: 1865–1940." *Stalwarts South of the Border*, 610. Qtd. in *Las colonias—The Mormon Colonies in Mexico*. March 7, 2014. http://www.lascolonias.org/tag/daniel-skousen/.

Ivins, Anthony W. In *Eighty-Second Annual Conference of the Church of Jesus Christ of Latter-day Saints Held in the Tabernacle and Assembly Hall Salt Lake City, Utah, April 5, 6, 7, 1912*, 60–67. Salt Lake City, UT: Deseret News, 1912.

Janzen, Rebecca. *Liminal Sovereignty: Mennonites and Mormons in Mexican Culture*. Albany: SUNY Press, 2018.

———. "Mormon Art and Architecture in Mexico: Between Mexico and the United States." In *Mormon Art: A Critical Reader*, edited by Amanda K. Beardsley and Mason Allred. New York: Oxford University Press, forthcoming.

Juarez Rubio, Tarcisio R. "Benemerito! Church's Vanguard School in Mexico." *Church News* November 27, 1999. https://www.thechurchnews.com/1999/11/27/23247527/benemerito-churchs-vanguard-school-in-mexico.

Klaassen, Walter. *Anabaptism: Neither Catholic nor Protestant.* Waterloo, ON: Conrad Grebel Press, 1973.

Kloppe-Santamaría, Gema. *In the Vortex of Violence: Lynching, Extralegal Justice, and the State in Post-Revolutionary Mexico.* Berkeley: University of California Press, 2020.

Knight, Alan. "Popular Culture and the Revolutionary State in Mexico, 1910–1940." *The Hispanic American Historical Review* 74, no. 3 (1994): 393–444.

"Ley de extranjería y naturalización." In *Código de colonización y terrenos baldíos de la república mexicana, formado por Francisco de la Maza*, 1038–1050. México, DF: Oficina de la Secretaría de Fomento, 1893.

Livingston, Craig. "Lions, Brothers, and the Idea of an Indian Nation: The Mexican Revolution in the Minds of Anthony W. Ivins and Rey L. Pratt, 1910–1917." *Dialogue: A Journal of Mormon Thought* 35, no. 2 (2002): 115–38.

Loret de Mola, Carlos. "Con los domadores del desierto." *Siempre!* Nov. 16, 1960, 30–31, 70.

McConkie, Bruce R. *Mormon Doctrine.* Salt Lake City, UT: Bookcraft, 1958.

McIntyre, Kathleen. *Protestantism and State Formation in Postrevolutionary Oaxaca.* Albuquerque: University of New Mexico Press, 2019.

"México, Chihuahua, Registro Civil, 1861–1997." *FamilySearch.* Accessed March 2, 2021. https://www.familysearch.org/ark:/61903/1:1:QGCB-ZRLJ.

Morgan, Barbara E. "A Century of LDS Church Schools in Mexico Influenced by Lamanite Identity." In *The Worldwide Church: Mormonism as a Global Religion*, edited by Michael Goodman and Mauro Properzi, 354–78. Provo, UT: Brigham Young University; Deseret Book, 2015.

"Peter Rempel: 'Me di cuenta de lo racista que soy.'" *Darp Stories Project.* YouTube video, November 9, 2018. Video, 12:20. https://www.youtube.com/watch?app=desktop&v=yasffIjpqUk.

Pratt, Rey L. "The Gospel to the Lamanites III." *Improvement Era* 16, no. 5 (1913): 497–503.

——. "The Gospel to the Lamanites, IXXII." *Improvement Era* 16, no. 7 (1913): 686–90.

Pulido, Elisa Eastwood. *The Spiritual Evolution of Margarito Bautista: Mexican Mormon Evangelizer, Polygamist Dissident, and Utopian Founder, 1878–1961.* Oxford: Oxford University Press, 2020.

——. *The Spiritual Evolution of Margarito Bautista: Mexican Mormon Evangelizer, Polygamist Dissident, and Utopian Founder, 1878–1961.* Oxford: Oxford University Press, 2020.

Quiring, David M. *The Mennonite Old Colony Vision: Under Siege in Mexico and the Canadian Connection*. 2003. Winnipeg, MB: DF Plett Historical Research Foundation, 2009.

"Raúl Kigra and Veronica Enns: Full Interview – Cross Cultural Relationships, and Becoming Artists." *Darp Stories Project*. YouTube video, November 16, 2018. Video, 1:16:14. https://www.youtube.com/watch?v=nLUq-rnA9VY.

Rempel, Gerhard, and Franz Rempel. *75 Jahre: Mennoniten in Mexico* [*75 Years: Mennonites in Mexico*]. Ciudad Cuauhtémoc, Mexico: Comité Pro Archivo Histórico; Museo Menonita, 1998.

Ryskamp, George. "Mormon Colonists in the Mexican Civil Registration: A Case Study in Transnational Immigrant Identity." In *Just South of Zion: The Mormons in Mexico and its Borderlands*, edited by Jason H. Dormady and Jared Tamez, 39–54. Albuquerque: University of New Mexico Press, 2015.

Sanchez, Xicali, and Martha Selene. "Ambrosio de Aquino, pionero y mártir de la Iglesia de Jesucristo de los Santos de los Últimos Días en México." *FamilySearch*, March 27, 2019. Accessed April 10, 2023. https://www.familysearch.org/photos/artifacts/80457696/ambrosio-de-aquino-pionero-y-m%C3%A1rtir-de-la-iglesia-de-jesucristo-de-los-santos-de-los-%C3%BAltimos-d%C3%ADas-en-m%C3%A9xico.

Sawatzky, Harry Leonard. *They Sought a Country: Mennonite Colonization in Mexico*. Berkeley: University of California Press, 1971.

Schmiedehaus, Walter. *Ein feste Burg ist unser Gott: Der Wanderweg eines christlichen Siedlervolkes* (*A Mighty Fortress Is Our God: The Wanderings of a Group of Christian Settlers*). Ciudad Cuauhtémoc, Mexico: G. J. Rempel, 1948.

Stover, Philip R. *Religion and Revolution in Mexico's North: Even Unto Death . . . Tengamos Fe*. Deming, NM: Rio Vista Press, 2014.

Talmage, James E. *The Great Apostasy: Considered in the Light of Scriptural and Secular History*. Salt Lake City, UT: Deseret News, 1909.

The Book of Mormon. Translated by Joseph Smith, Jr. Salt Lake City, UT: The Church of Jesus Christ of Latter-day Saints, 1981.

Whitaker, Wentzel, dir. *Aunque nos toque morir*. Brigham Young University and the Church of Jesus Christ of Latter-day Saints. YouTube video. Salt Lake City, UT, 1966. https://www.youtube.com/watch?v=oC9nrnlfTO4&ab_channel=DiscursosSUD.

Will, Martina E. "The Mennonite Colonization of Chihuahua: Reflections of Competing Visions." *The Americas* 53, 3 (1997): 353–78.

Yankelevich, Pablo. "Extranjeros indeseables en México (1911–1940). Una aproximación cuantitativa a la aplicación del artículo 33 constitucional." *Historia Mexicana* 53, no. 3 (2004): 693–744.

Afterword

The Ever-Cooling Worlds of Mexican Anti-Catholicism

MATTHEW BUTLER

Many readers first encounter Mexican anti-Catholicism in *The Power and the Glory*, Graham Greene's 1940 novel about an ecclesiastical manhunt in postrevolutionary Tabasco. Who can forget the materialistic cosmology of Greene's lieutenant, staring as beetles drop to the floor, wings broken, after crashing into the barracks wall in the tropical night? As the irate lieutenant counts the pitiful, downed flying machines, Greene give us the image of a rosary without aim—one whose black, stricken beads proclaim only that there is no mystery:

> It was the hour of prayer. Black-beetles exploded against the walls like crackers. More than a dozen crawled over the tiles with injured wings. It infuriated him to think that there were still people in the state who believed in a loving and merciful God. There are mystics who are said to have experienced God directly. He was a mystic, too, and what he had experienced was vacancy—a complete certainty in the existence of a dying, cooling world, of human beings who had evolved from animals for no purpose at all. He knew.[1]

As a fictional depiction of anti-Catholic fervor, the scene is a tour de force: it ends with a modern John the Baptist announcing the kingdom of Nothing, the nullity of the Word, the biblical locusts and wild honey returning, just as unappetizing, as black-beetles and *gaseosa* (Garridista soda). As the novel progresses, the lieutenant directs his ire, and finally his pistol, at priests, drapers of the world who trick the unwary into thinking that there might be some ultimate point, not this bleak, cosmic deceleration. It is the lieutenant's ontological certainty, not his gun, that makes him frightening. Unlike other revolutionaries, he detests the Lie—the falsehood of God's planned Creation—as much as the Church's second-order hypocrisies, its Friar Tucks, silly miracle tales, and profligate fiestas. Even if he is right, however, the lieutenant is a fanatic, a true believer.

As historians, it is fair to say, we have been slow to treat revolutionary unbelief with Greene's sophistication; that is, with the same eye to calibration and to the phenomenon's situational range, emotional depth, philosophical bases, and contradictions. For starters, we have usually defined the problem in relation to church-state affairs and (more recently) revolutionary state formation, not culture. For the same reason, perhaps, we have been shy about taking a broader, more interdisciplinary approach that draws on and connects the insights of, say, art historians, historians of science, or women's studies scholars. Conceptually, too, we have sometimes confused basic categories (atheism, secularism, anticlericalism, *odium theologicum*) or conflated parts with the whole (e.g., socialist education, 1930s "defanaticization"). A book that I once edited, and which the coeditors of the present volume kindly cite in the introduction, threw a hopeful, generic lasso ("impiety") around the whole subject.[2] As far as interdisciplinary insights go, the usual method has been pop psychology—though this has led us to treat Mexican anti-Catholicism as a Freudian, even adolescent, projection rooted in individual trauma. Often the analysis describes a revolt against the Church rooted in childhood or pubescent angst. Thus, for Calles, the shock was the social stigma of bastardy; for Múgica, expulsion from the Zamora seminary; for Morones, vicarious childhood exposure to sacristy sex in Acatlán.[3] This Freudian thesis stresses the exceptionality of such ruptures: therein lies its utility, perhaps. After all, it is not just Catholic historians who are drawn to, perhaps even *need*, the myth of a Catholic Mexico. It is sometimes tempting, therefore, to write off revolutionary skeptics as Catholic duds—the ones that fell off the conveyor belt. Some of their wider societal importance is lost.

This said, there are also good historical reasons for historians' perplexity and church-state focus. One is that real-world political and cultural actors, for whom leveling or disproving charges of anti-Catholicism was absolutely no laughing matter, deliberately and perhaps permanently confused things for political advantage. Rome's strategy, under assault from Liberals and revolutionaries, was to treat attacks on the institutional Church and clergy, especially the papacy, as attacks on faith itself. The Vatican Council (1869–1870) raised papal primacy—jurisdiction over the universal Church—to the status of dogma, not just the well-known doctrine of papal infallibility in matters of faith and morals. Henceforth, to attack the Church's governing structure and discipline, even while accepting its basic spiritual premises, was heresy. How, then, to distinguish between existential and doctrinal assaults on Catholicism and shallower political critiques, as when, for instance, the Mexican state demanded that priests conform to a licensing system in June 1926? Sharing the blame around, Mexican revolutionaries' claims to be good Liberals, "sons of the immortal Juárez," were dishonest. The Liberals' 1857 Constitution led to church-state separation, arguably spiritualizing the Church by liberating it from wealth and power. The 1917 revolutionary magna carta denied the Church legal standing but gave it a Mexicanized civil constitution whereby priests could be appointed by ad hoc citizens' juntas, not bishops. This was an invasive ecclesiological experiment borrowed from Socialist France, yet revolutionaries glibly portrayed it as a simple exercise of national sovereignty. Nobody wanted to "decatholicize" Mexico, Calles promised a US audience, also in 1926.[4] If *nothing* was anti-Catholic, or *everything* was, what hope for historians?

■■■

The editors of this book devise a suitably catchy, momentous phrase—"the hour of unbelief"—to describe the rise of an anti-Catholic animus from the middle years of the Mexican Revolution through the conventional postrevolution (1913–1940). It sounds dramatic, as indeed it should for a period that saw anti-Catholicism expressed in attempts by CROM to dynamite the Virgin of Guadalupe (1921) or in 1930s peep shows where priests lustily flogged naked women (Greene, who saw one such spectacle in Mexico City, disapproved).[5] As this book defines the genre, however, revolutionary anti-Catholicism ranged far wider than pornographic shock therapy or bombings. Instead, we are told, anti-Catholicism should be understood to include "*all* beliefs and measures opposed to the worldview, beliefs, and practices of the Catholic Church, its clergy, and its faithful." That is about as foolproof as a definition gets. It is, dare I say it, a most *catholic* (all-encompassing) definition. It is clearly intended to subsume within the broad church of anti-Catholicism the more restrictive subgenres—such as anticlericalism (hatred of priestcraft), irreligion (lack of faith), and laicism (religion-free states)—that Mexicanist scholars, especially historians, sociologists, and political scientists, have long used. It is also designed, I suspect, to make room for phenomena that are not avowedly anti-Catholic or *necessarily* interpreted as being so: a Diego Rivera frieze, a temperance pledge, a contraception pamphlet, or a scientific campaign (such as the 1947 *rifle sanitario* policy that enraged the Sinarquistas) is just as at home in this irreligious field as a dogmatic old relic like "socialist education" or the Calles Law, previously mentioned.[6] It is the concept that an interdisciplinary history book needs.

The definition is a useful, clear, and above all holistic one. By being inclusive it emphasizes the idea of affinity and so encourages us to make connections between things and domains that might otherwise be regarded as being separate. That in itself constitutes a real advance. Equally, it recognizes that there will be many anti-Catholicisms, as there are many Catholicisms, and that they will be found in many different places. The book at hand, which enriches our knowledge of Mexican anti-Catholicism through studies of mural art, anthropology, feminism, scientism, temperance, and migration (in addition to church-state relations or state and federal politics), certainly delivers on its eclectic promise and provides an interconnected history of revolutionary anti-Catholicisms. No other book that I know of is so alert to the possibilities of seeing anti-Catholicism as *culture*, or finds anti-Catholic ideas expressed so vividly across the sweep of revolutionary-era culture, as this one does.

This said, it may still be worth making two or three brief conceptual asides and an empirical, more comparative one. The first is that the term "anti-Catholicism" describes overlapping categories—a multitude of sins, a theologian might say—some of which cannot always be folded into one another. It is the case, for example, that many anti-Catholics were, and are, and perhaps as a matter of course, anticlerical, secularist, and irreligious.[7] Unhelpfully, though, some anticlericals were *not* anti-Catholic. In this non-intersecting set, for instance, we find Patriarch Pérez, pope-hating leader of the pro-revolutionary "Mexican" Church, and also—impossible bedfellows though they are—the *ultras* of the National League of Religious Defense (LNDLR) who in 1930 plotted to assassinate Pascual Díaz y Barreto, the archbishop of Mexico, for signing the *arreglos*. It is also possible to be in some sense anti-Catholic but *not* anticlerical. Thus the spartan youth of Mexico City's 1920s Catholic underground despised the vapid "sugar Catholics" they saw around them but lionized the Jesuit martyr Father Pro.[8] Greene himself admitted to liking only two types of people in Mexico: pilots and priests. He generally had a low opinion of Mexican Catholics, except for the Indigenous devotees at Tepeyac whose agonized praying, arms stretched out cruciform, reminded him of the stigmata.[9] In a conceptual sense, as we have seen, such perfectly symmetrical alignment is impossible.

A second observation is that defining anti-Catholicism in an inclusive way should not, to my mind, make us think that it is a catch-all or, using a suitably evolutionary metaphor, the earliest common ancestor of our taxonomy of impieties. And it definitely should not make us lose sight of revolutionary anti-Catholicism's basic, radical quality, even when compared to subgenres such as anticlericalism, laicism, and irreligion. Anticlericalism, for instance, is a less than total form of attack: tacitly, it stresses Catholicism's perfectibility in its endless hectoring about priests' feet of clay or political meddling. It presupposes an ecclesiastical ideal.[10] Even Mexico's vaunted laicist tradition—assigning religion its proper, private, place outside the state—is compatible with a Catholic framework: Juárez, the great separator, tried to conjure a Reform-friendly Mexican Church; so, mutatis mutandis, did Calles. True anti-Catholicism cannot be reconciled with Catholicism in this way. I say that even though we might also identify revolutionary Mexico with a kind of vexatious, everyday anti-Catholicism. This type was diffuse, and sometimes despicable, because it took issue with everything Catholic, even trivial things. The list of secondary, para-religious targets that Mexican revolutionaries painted on Catholicism is a long one. Using it, many revolutionaries could be defined as "anti-Catholic," even corrupt policemen who harassed penniless old pilgrims for wearing scapulars or who broke up quiet masses in people's homes just in case a *mordida* was forthcoming.[11]

Some revolutionaries, however, held to a radically committed form of what we might call fundamentalist anti-Catholicism. In this deeper and existential, but undeniably sincere and meaningful form, anti-Catholicism denoted *systemic* contempt—root and branch opposition to a whole Catholic order, to its entire theology, epistemology, institutional life, pastoral action, and infinite sociocultural extensions. The aims—theological replacement, outright extirpation, or Nietzschean deicide over time, not reformist tinkering or consigning Catholicism to the laicist closet—were of a different magnitude. Such apocalyptic desire, which prophesied and strove frankly for a post-Catholicism, was less common than anticlerical angst or religious apathy, but it existed.[12] Garrido, Carrillo Puerto, Múgica, Belén de Sárraga, and army brass like Cristóbal Rodríguez (to say nothing of Greene's lieutenant) all possessed it. They were *científicos* on steroids. Manuel Gamio likewise had it: albeit favoring gentler, anthropological methods, he dreamed of and worked for a future without God. Purely on theological grounds, I would count the Protestant Sáenz brothers, Moisés and Aarón—the Old Testament names tell their own story—as anti-Catholics of this type. They and other militant Protestants wanted to throw Rome's golden calf into the flames. Still, it bears repeating that this proof-strength anti-Catholicism, if it took many forms as the chapters here vividly show, was still unusual. It was too strong for some revolutionaries to stomach. After reading the excellent essays here, it seems unlikely that even Calles—by a distance, Mexico's most notorious *comecuras*; an anticlerical strictly defined—possessed or ever wanted it.

Anti-Catholicism as I understand it thus trends maximalist and is defined not only by its multiple polarities and range but by the totalizing, structural importance of the things it disagrees with or else wants to achieve in a transformative sense. As a description of the world to come, it requires faith (not just criticism, which is the hallmark of anticlericalism). It therefore creates purpose and meaning and has its own mystique, as Greene intuited, which is not necessarily a form of mockery.

A third, lesser point is that even everyday anti-Catholicism should be intentional in order to count. Too many things otherwise *might* be said to hinder Catholicism, accidentally: beer and hair commercials, soccer matches, movie theaters, dancehalls, etc. . . . Materialism-lite—the flotsam of Mexican revolutionary capitalist development—does not count. Therein lies its seductive danger, no doubt; but for something to be *anti*-Catholic, there must be design.

■□■

As an empirical proposition, fourth and last, the editors suggest that "anti-Catholic voices" in Mexico have waned since 1940.[13] I have real doubt about this. True, the voices quietened for a long stretch (c. 1940–1990) after *cardenismo*. The staleness of official anti-Catholicism by the mid-1980s can be glimpsed, perhaps, in Miguel de la Madrid's (1982–1988) prehistoric, unaware response to the episcopate's calls for a constitutional shake-up after the 1979 papal visit; almost unbelievably, he told the bishops to phone the Confederación de Trabajadores Mexicanos (Confederation of Mexican Workers) and read Alfonso Toro, as if Mexico were still stuck in the 1930s (a few years later, as we know, Carlos Salinas would unilaterally reform the 1917 Constitution's anticlerical articles without any such regard for PRI *dinosaurios*).[14] Nonetheless, a new kind of anti-Catholicism was not long in coming; and it, too, emerged, I would suggest, not long after Salinas's 1992 constitutional reform, which liberated the Mexican Church in law but at the cost of emphasizing its submission to Rome and pushing it in a conservative and pietistic (statistically less popular) direction. Since 2000, and 2010 especially, anti-Catholic voices undeniably have been on the rise. It is not mere hyperbole, in my opinion, to suggest that in some ways we are *now* heading back to the 1930s. Whether the assessment is accurate or not, I do presume that anti-Catholicism is an evolving, periodic value, found wherever Catholicism is found. Historians therefore need to make more effort to understand its historical specificity and find through lines connecting Mexico's hours of unbelief. Such a daunting, long-term task, of course, makes this benchmark collection a prescient and even more valuable one.

By "hours of unbelief," I do not just mean rising disenchantment—though it is true that the number of Mexicans reporting no religious faith rises by the census, and faster than both Catholic *and* non-Catholic affiliations.[15] Nobody has written a book, yet, called *Is Latin America Turning Anti-Catholic?* in the way that 1990s sociologists of religion confidently predicted the region's Protestantization. Yet this secular trend does correlate in some unclear way with a revival of aggressive incredulity and the anti-Catholic vindictiveness we once associated with, say, Garridismo and analyzed comfortably in the preterite. Some Mexicans, clearly, are turning *on*, not away from, Catholicism. Today's anti-Catholicism exhibits the same intolerance as the old kind and arguably more shallowness and viciousness. Its practitioners, for example, are very willing to desecrate Catholic churches, hundreds of which have been profaned in recent years. These crimes are only sometimes economic. In attack after attack, there is profanation of Eucharistic specie: since 2020, this has been reported in dioceses in Mexico City, Cuernavaca, Querétaro, Michoacán, Jalisco, San Luis Potosí, Durango, Saltillo, Sonora, Chihuahua, Yucatán, and Tabasco. The profanations, once again, are sometimes sexual or scatological. In one Mexico City church in 2019, social justice artists took pornographic photos for posting online; in 2020, a Xalapa (Veracruz) church was smeared with human excrement, and relics (of Saint Rafael Guízar Valencia, the *cristero*-era bishop canonized in 2006) were trashed. Shit was also thrown over the Virgin's veil.[16] Anti-Catholicism is becoming common: just in the month of writing (mid-May to mid-June 2023), an arsonist gutted Irapuato's Santiaguito church (Guanajuato), the tabernacle in Jiutepec (Morelos) was smashed; a man shouting that Catholics were "fanatics" smashed images in Santa María Magdalena church (Sonora), resting place of Father Kino; a gang of twelve hooded and armed men in three SUVs pillaged the church of San Luis Gonzaga in Iztacalco (Mexico City), having held a gun to the sacristan's head; a gang poured 700 bullets into a church in Guachochi (Chihuahua), in the Tarahumara sierra, with a decapitated corpse left outside as a warning; and a demand to outlaw Nativity displays in public places, launched by a mysterious Yucatecan NGO calling itself "Kanan Derechos," reached Mexico's Supreme Court. Mainstream media rarely report such events and to that extent are complicit in them. Likewise religious assaults and homicides: in the same period in 2023, a man tried to stab the archbishop of Durango during Mass, and an Augustinian religious was riddled with bullets near Cuitzeo (Michoacán).[17] Murders of Catholic priests in fact reached shocking, *cristero*-era levels years ago, but this time there are no postcards of boy priests crying ¡*Viva Cristo Rey!* doing the rounds. More than seventy Catholic priests have been murdered, and other priests disappeared, since 1990, with a big spike (twenty-six) coming in the Enrique Peña Nieto *sexenio* (2012–2018). The killings show little sign of abating under AMLO (nine and counting). In numerous cases, it is parish priests and religious who are slain as punishment for resisting cartel activity or other illegality such as human trafficking. Whatever the reasons, "Catholic" Mexico is now the world's most "clericidal" country, along with Nigeria and Nicaragua. Kidnappings and extortions of priests are growing problems too.[18]

The difference between the 1930s and 2020s is not so much repertoire but dramatis personae and philosophy. The Mexican *state* pushes anti-Catholicism far less than it used to, though it perhaps gains from it and does little to deter it; revolutionary anti-Catholicism, as this book shows, was very state centered. Today's principals (amoral *sicarios*; lumpen iconoclasts; the progressive, postmodern Left; shadowy NGOs and activist judges; complacent media) are typically non-state actors, with officials involved only if judicial impunity is a factor. Their ideology is also different. The religious orders, absolved by Liberals and revolutionaries because of their sixteenth-century missionary work, are now denounced as settler colonists, as with Franciscan friar Junípero Serra. Despite the recent attack on Kino's shrine, the old anti-Jesuitism—once totemic to Mexican anti-Catholics—has seemingly withered: witness the unusual response to the murder of two Chihuahua Jesuits in 2022.[19] More significantly, anti-Catholicism is less sectarian and rationalist than it was. Then again, other religions are more secure in Mexico than they were and less defensive, while the progressive Left, progenitor of some of today's anti-Catholicism, is itself suspicious of science's objectivity claims. Nor, logically, is anti-Catholicism really Marxist: we do not see murals of fat priests clinking glasses with top-hatted bourgeois any more but SEP schoolbooks invoking gender theory instead. Prima facie, the new anti-Catholicism is not driven primarily by anger at clerical sexual abuse scandals, past or present.[20] Rather, it is a cocktail that combines entrepreneurial and narco-capitalist ruthlessness; dull, anomic vandalism; and the fervor of contemporary identity politics, as seen in the Manichean claim that the Church forever oppressed women or Indigenous people. For twenty-first-century anti-Catholics, Catholicism's missionary past and pastoral views—on sexuality, abortion, and the human body, or its opposition to drug or human trafficking—make it a deserving or collateral target. It is not easy to discern a grand, utopian vision: despite the cartoon historicism, there is no dialectical endpoint on offer, no book of revelation. This in itself is unsurprising, given that modern anti-Catholics—*narcos*, nihilists, social justice warriors—are disparate. Unlike our lieutenant, telling his beads with black-beetles, Garrido's great great grandchildren have no interest in dispelling Catholicism's supernatural claims, just debunking its missiology or sexual ethics for economic or identitarian purposes. Mexico's Church has sins to atone for, but let us call this disturbingly contradictory thing what it is: a reviving, illiberal, and sometimes murderous anti-Catholicism.[21]

■□■

Readers will find no better starting point than this book to explore the history of Mexican anti-Catholicism and its ever-cooling worlds. There are, of course, some thematic and (since the approach is multidisciplinary) methodological lacunae. We might wish for a discussion of anti-Catholicism and war. Did the death and pestilence of the armed revolution (1910–1920) make religious faith unsustainable to some? A religious sociologist could perhaps find the answer in church registers, though possibly it took an infernal trench war like WWI to create that kind of spiritual shellshock.[22] Another gap, for a historian of sport or animal historian, is revolutionary Sabbatarianism. Bans on traditional—to that extent "Catholic"—pursuits such as bullfighting and cockfighting were a key component of the Constitutionalist revolution. This is usually put down to developmentalism, yet arguably they were a Protestant-inspired injunction against despoliations of Sunday in Catholic countries and a soft imperial attack on "Mexican" cruelty, just as much as they were a ban on the ritualized shedding of animal blood. Legal and medical historians would also have germane things to add: the 1928 Civil Code gave as grounds for divorce adultery by man or woman, prostitution (or incitement thereof), the wife's birthing in wedlock of another man's child, the corrupting of minors, and a spouse's carrying of syphilis and TB. This suggests a legal dissection of pre-1910—default Catholic—mores and an elevation of the medical state to the role of moral arbiter, giver of ethical commandments. Reproductive medicine, a closely related and major topic, is soon to be analyzed by Elizabeth O'Brien.[23]

It would be invidious to single out chapters in a strong, well-executed collection, and impossible to do them all justice; so instead I will pick out four common themes that many of the authors address and that together perhaps represent the book's main advances in the study of Mexican anti-Catholicism. They are: one, pragmatism—especially political pragmatism; two, the roots of Mexican anti-Catholicism; three, anti-Catholicism and science; and four, the emotions of anti-Catholicism. I will say a few words about each in turn.

Pragmatism is not at all something we associate with anti-Catholicism. Exactly the opposite: we are used to seeing it as sheer, maddening ideology, a redshirted fanaticism. We also read that it was politically costly, if not borderline irrational, and driven home bloody-mindedly or tyrannically.[24] Yet readers will notice many references to political pragmatism here. Jürgen Buchenau suggests that Calles's anticlericalism was forced on him by radical ministers (Tejeda, Morones, Amaro) and absent from his early career. The "natural-born clerophobe" is a retrofit, the allergy to priests perhaps stemming from a story that Calles's niece was seduced by a *cura* in Sonora.[25] Sarah Osten's search for Garrido's motives turns up unexpected answers, too. Though Garrido boasted in 1935 of leaving Tabasco purged of priests, Osten does not credit the bravado. Instead, she finds the root cause of his anti-Catholicism in political insecurity, mainly resulting from *delahuertismo* (1923–1924). This mutiny killed off Garrido's Yucatecan mentor, Carrillo Puerto, and threatened the southern revolution. Garrido was besieged in Villahermosa (it might soon have reverted to San Juan Bautista) by the mutineers' "Virgin of Guadalupe" brigade. Saved from this Virgin in khaki, however, he unleashed his Camisas Rojas on Catholicism.[26] Last, Ben Fallaw observes how in the early 1930s Calles personally intervened to ensure that the SEP's constitutionally mandated attack on "fanaticism" would be prosecuted vaguely under the banner of "socialist" education, not through systematic "scientific" education, as Garrido (by this time a national figure) wanted. Calles even jested (the pun was an amusing one) that Garrido's plan would only promote *educación científico*—a positivistic, Porfirian throwback.[27]

Anti-Catholicism as insurance policy against death by siege; Calles (the anticlerical ex-schoolteacher) pulling his punches in education—this is not what we expect! Yet, as I read them, these chapters are not really suggesting that anti-Catholicism was significantly non-ideological, prudent, or feigned, only that it is important to contextualize it politically, seeing it in terms of the art of the possible, and not to reify it, as we sometimes have, like a revolutionary King Herod. We need to know how anti-Catholic ideas came down from revolutionaries' bookshelves; but we also need to explore how and why they acquired political traction or significance in local or institutional settings (*municipios*, states, bureaucracies, parties, elections). We also need to understand where, why, and how successfully, anti-Catholicism was deployed—as a concession to radicals whose support was needed elsewhere, as a political volume control to frighten the Church, to signal revolutionary virtue, or as the leading edge of some other state project. We need, in other words, an integral political history of Mexican anti-Catholicism, with these chapters (and others) being models of how it can be done. Incidentally, the task requires us to have a better understanding of political Catholicism beyond *cristerismo*, too, and to revisit its influence in such understudied things as *delahuertismo*, Jorge Prieto Laurens's National Cooperativist Party, electoral politics in general, and *vasconcelismo* (1928–1929).

A related, equally significant, contribution of the book is the way that it finesses the ideology of Mexican anti-Catholicism, showing an acclimated, rooted phenomenon, not a doctrinaire copy of grand European radicalisms (Protestantism, anarchism, Marxism). As the book shows very well, anti-Catholicism was a multi-domain, bonding, ideology. Its success, in fact, was often predicated on the power with which it could or could not bond with phenomena in the sociocultural realm. We see this, respectively, in Rashkin's chapter on feminism (plus women's sexual liberation) and Jaimes's on mural Art, around which anti-Catholicism became wrapped tight, like ivy on brickwork; conversely, in two contrasting chapters on US-style prohibitionism (Pierce) and the bureaucracy of migration (Janzen), where the bond, being weak or contradictory, failed. Elissa Rashkin's study of women anticlericals, for its part, complicates the association between anti-Catholicsm and masculinity (hence, between Catholicism and femininity). Rashkin does this by exploring the anti-Catholic feminist ideas of Hermila Galindo, who railed against "clerical tutelage" of women and sent a speech to Yucatán's feminist congress in praise, daringly for the time, of women's "sexual instinct." Yucatecan Elvia Carrillo Puerto and *jarocha* Esperanza Velázquez Bringas, meanwhile, argued publicly for birth control and pamphleted Mérida. These were radical ideas, contravening Catholic sexual mores, but they stayed the course and are less controversial (or controversial for partly different reasons) nowadays.[28] Héctor Jaimes's chapter, like Rashkin's, confirms the value of an interdisciplinary approach. Here we see, painting by painting, the gestation of an aesthetic anti-Catholicism rooted in Marxist dialectics. While early murals, such as

Rivera's *Creation*, worked in a still Catholic idiom, the muralists' works soon took a "dialectical turn" from heaven to earth, via the incorporation of historical-materialist motifs such as class struggle, as well as the ironic use of industrial-capitalist artifacts such as spray paint. The tone was set in the muralists' manifesto (1924), where the artists made an apparently solemn commitment to abandon in their work the "masturbation" of bourgeois individualism. That particular claim must have turned up in a few priests' sermons, and one suspects that it was probably supposed to.[29]

Anti-Catholicism and sex went well together, compared to other formulations which fell by the wayside. Gretchen Pierce's chapter, for instance, explores anti-Catholicism's role as a factor in Mexico's temperance movement. Mexican prohibitionists, she shows, were often Protestant, and of puritanical, bent. They wanted to dry out and unchurch Indigenous Catholic Mexicans, leaving "sober and secular citizens" in their place. There was some popular buy-in to these campaigns, among Mexican women, especially, some of whom again seemed receptive to a policy that criticized their faith; in general, however, campaigners' attempts to describe social problems (squalor, disease, crime) as effects of Catholicism and booze were "misguided," Pierce writes, because they created religious resistance to what was, at bottom, a Salubridad issue.[30]

Janzen's chapter shows how Mexican revolutionary anti-Catholics, desiring to spite Rome, could enter into preferential, ambivalent, relationships with other religions, in this case Anabaptism (Mennonites) and Mormonism (the LDS). Revolutionary anti-Catholicism thus proved itself, once again, to be a sectarian, not just a secularizing, phenomenon, especially in the north. As Janzen shows, in the 1920s and 1930s revolutionary officialdom tolerated the active (hence illegal) presence of foreign religious ministers in Chihuahua, so long as they were not Catholic but Mormon; and overturned state-level bans on religious primary schools in Durango, so long as the schools were not Catholic but Mennonite. In part, this enlightened hypocrisy reflected the fact that Mormons and Mennonites owned a theological hatred of Catholicism that reinforced official ideology: the LDS's missionary leader, Rey L. Pratt, for instance, described Roman Catholicism as "the abominable church, the whore of the whole earth"; Mennonites viewed Mexican Catholics as indolent and profligate, and so advocated religious separatism. Revolutionaries' belief that Mormons and Mennonites would spread religious liberty and turn northern deserts into gardens—thus meriting privileges that were denied to Catholics—was an act of faith all of its own, one that was not repaid if Janzen's case studies were typical. As her essay shows, indeed, religious migrants such as Harvey Taylor and Daniel Skousen tried to game the regime's non-Catholic preferences, one by appealing for tax breaks and water rights, the other successfully asserting Mexican citizenship while violating laws prohibiting polygyny. Here, at the intersection of migration and state religious bigotry, was an instrumental, and opportunistic, form of popular anti-Catholicism.[31] Following these social and ideological webs, nonetheless, we see that anti-Catholicism was a more humanistic tradition than we might think, not just barking ideology. Sometimes it spoke to human desires: for sexual intimacy (even polygamy), artistic expression, or migration to a new home.

What would seem, on the face of it, to have been an easy marriage—anti-Catholicism and science—turns out, after all, to have been complicated and contradictory. "Science is the record of dead religion," Wilde said. Yet in postrevolutionary Mexico the affinity of science and anti-Catholicism was not automatic or complete, because the science was subordinated to politics or used to endorse prejudice. David Dalton's chapter on Gamio, which revisits the oft-cited, rarely studied *Forjando Patria* (1916), stresses Gamio's positivistic roots and scientific mestizophilia, so different to Vasconcelos's cosmic race mysticism. Gamio's answer to the problem of what he viewed as a corrupt Church was to use social science to reeducate Indigenous ("pagan") Catholics and orthodox ("true") Catholics, thereby isolating what he called the "utilitarian" (we might now say *political*) Catholics who manipulated the others. Having created his typology, Gamio was shocked by Calles's strong-arm anticlericalism. To Gamio, it was "fundamentally unscientific," a bludgeon that turned "pagan" and "orthodox" Catholics into political ones by the thousand.[32]

Ben Fallaw's colorful study of revolutionary Scientism—dogmatic faith in omniscient science—shows how a small Tabascan cadre of white-coated anti-Catholics used scientific ideas about germs to justify all-out attacks on Catholicism, mischaracterized as a plague. "Scientistic" Garridistas obsessed over popular Catholicism's supposed infectiousness like teenagers repulsed by the thought of emerging from their parents' distant sexual trysts. They yucked at everything involving touch: pilgrims' kissing of images' feet or drinking of holy water from miasmic stoups; priests' allegedly lethal habits of crossing people's foreheads with saliva or handing out dysentery on Eucharistic wafers. Catholicism, to don Tomás's illuminati, was a pox, a game of ring-a-ring o' roses at the end of which everyone sneezed and fell down. One has to wonder where such hysterical, morbid squeamishness came from—yet it is surprising how far these scientistical stirrers were able to spread their views through SEP on the strength of their authoritative-sounding claims and Garrido's political kudos. Even here, though—even here!—the rationalism was compromised, impure. In a significant number of cases, Fallaw finds, the Tabascan doctors' authority was founded not just on germ theory but on those universally acknowledged hardest of hard sciences, magnetic Spiritism and "psychic occultism."[33] Catholics were being mocked for their irrationality and treated like lepers by people who believed in ectoplasm.

We are, however, closer to these hygienic disputes than we might imagine, so perhaps we should not mock. The Mexican Church made the "historic" decision to shutter the Basilica of Guadalupe in December 2020, in order to prevent Covid 19 infections. This came after the Comité Episcopal Mexicano tweeted a communiqué ("Covid-19 Emergencia Sanitaria," March 16, 2020) suspending Sunday Mass and calling for priests' private masses to be transmitted publicly wherever possible via digital platforms, a measure that was followed by a second suspension that December. But what would have happened, one wonders, if Cardinal Norberto Rivera had died of Covid 19 during the pandemic, or indeed during his long 2021 hospitalization with the disease? Government norms requiring cremation in cases of Covid 19 death might have clashed with Catholic calls to place his body, as a cardinal archbishop (hence a prospective saint) in the Metropolitan Cathedral crypt, so that a relic might be preserved.[34] The prospect of a twenty-first century, unpredictable, Tabascan-style clash might have presented itself.

The most humanizing aspect of this book, however—by way of conclusion—are the many, sometimes unprecedented insights that it gives into the emotional lives of Mexican revolutionary anti-Catholics. They were an unforgiving lot, yet the book's authors do the decent (the vengefully Christian?) thing in being merciful when confronting them with their own moral weaknesses. To me, the most fascinating thing about Buchenau's essay are the vivid, moving, flashes it gives of Calles's spiritual seeking in later years, right down to the minutes of the séances he attended in the 1940s, where he discussed with the spirit of a nineteenth-century doctor the forlorn possibility of prolonging his life. His time was almost up and it had come to that—tapping the spirit world for echoes that might, somehow, bring him hopeful news. Calles was an anticlerical, but no Garrido, we finally intuit, because he could not face the solitude that being fully "anti-Catholic"—in the fundamental sense of being defiantly, metaphysically inert, possessed of no soul and no future—implied.³⁵ If that sounds like too much of a capitulation, or a Mexican rerun of Pascal's wager, it is worth remembering that in a philosophical sense Mexico's Revolution was built on an *ateneista* rejection of straight-out Positivism, which opened the door to more enlightened spiritualities.³⁶ Whatever Garridistas might say to the contrary, therefore, revolutionaries such as Calles believed that a purely materialist conception of life did not belong in some utopian future—it *already* belonged in the past, and was dead and buried with Díaz and the *científicos*. After reading Osten's essay, we might even spare a thought for Garrido, the brashest of the godless. From 1924, it turns out, to him the Church was Brutus, ever ready to put a knife into Caesar: this fear hardened him against Catholics forever. It must have been a burden, not a liberation, to think like that. Gamio's conversion to *callismo*, following Calles's suppression of the Anthropology Department in 1924, was cynical, Dalton tells us, an attempt to win the *jefe máximo*'s favor and keep his research funding: he avenged the slight in a vindictive op ed as Calles lay dying in 1945. Fallaw's "scientistic" types found that anti-Catholicism gave them righteous purpose; Rashkin's feminists wanted sexual freedom; and Janzen's Mormons and Mennonites were looking for a place to stay. Revenge; fear of dying, of pain, and of betrayal; the sexual urge; rootlessness; and above all justification—anti-Catholicism's cardinal virtues and deadly sins were all mixed up. Perhaps the inner worlds of Mexico's anti-Catholics were not nearly so cold as we think, but then nor were they nearly so brightly lit as they themselves hoped.

Notes

1. Greene, *Power and Glory*, 24–25. Reproduced by permission of David Higham Associates.
2. Butler, *Faith and Impiety*. I mean no disrespect to the authors—Alan Knight, Adrian Bantjes, Ben Fallaw, Keith Brewster, Jean-Pierre Bastian—who wrote fine essays on aspects of anti-Catholicism (even though we did not call it that).
3. As Morones recalled in 1926: "When I speak of perverted individuals, I have my reasons; for five years I was an altarboy in the church of Santa Cruz Acatlán. The things I saw then! I saw in May, which is called the Month of Mary, amid the warmth of the canticles, by the light of the candles, and in the quiet of the church, which serves as well for prayers as for crimes, that Father Villegas, who still lives, which is why I mention him, converted not just the church but the sacristy into a

real brothel... The then priest of the Santa Veracruz was another don Juan, which is how I got to know him. When he made his invocations to the Immaculate Virgin, filled with pagan enthusiasm, he fixed with his satyr's eyes the black eyes of one of his faithful daughters from the confessional." Barbosa Cano, *La CROM de Luis N. Morones a Antonio J. Hernández*, 296–97. On Calles, see Monteón, "Child Is Father," 43–61. On Múgica, see Krauze, *Mexico, Biography of Power*, 361.

4. "La legislación sobre cultos no pretende la 'descatolización' de México," in Macías, *Plutarco Elías Calles*, 190–95.
5. Greene, *Lawless Roads*, 85.
6. Introduction, 2, 4, 12. My emphasis.
7. Andrea Mutolo and Franco Savarino distinguish between "anticlericalismo, laicismo, e irreligión." Savarino and Mutolo, *El anticlericalismo en México*, 11.
8. Butler, *Mexico's Spiritual Reconquest*. On the plot to kill Díaz, which Liga apologists tried to bury by destroying copies of the offending book (Carreño, *El arzobispo de México Excmo. Sr. Don Pascual Díaz y el conflicto religioso*), see the 1932 edition (or the 1940s reprint), 432–36. On *católicos de azúcar*, see Weis, *For Christ and Country*.
9. Greene, *Lawless Roads*, 116.
10. As René Rémond had it, when it comes to religion, the anticlerical thinks of *nothing but* ("il ne pense qu'à elle"). Rémond, *L'anticléricalisme en France*, 10.
11. The social manifestations of Catholicism that revolutionary anti-Catholics periodically attacked (and fined or jailed people for), many of which were not directly related to priests, included the following: the act of crossing oneself when passing a church; the ringing of bells; the parading or kissing of religious images; schoolroom crucifixes; sports, drinking, and dancing (especially when done after church on Sundays and feast days); wearing scapulars and insignia; pilgrimages and *romerías* (especially when tagged to school truancy and penitences); sprinkling with holy water; sacred toponyms; burying corn dollies; tithing; bodily mortification; feasting and drinking; folk medicine and faith healing; Catholic-flavored superstitions; Judas burnings...
12. An equally long list could be made for this and would include opposition to everything formally, doctrinally, Catholic. In no particular order: God and the Trinity; heaven, hell, and purgatory; the Catholic Mass (especially transubstantiation); the other Catholic sacraments (especially auricular confession and the Viaticum); religious vows (especially celibacy) and attire; liturgical Latin; church buildings and fabric (altars, stoups, stained glass, cemeteries, sacristies, niche saints); Catholic schools, convents, and seminaries; the Bible; intercessory saints; bishops and popes (especially ultramontanes); canon law; burning incense; indulgences; genuflection; infallibilism; the miraculous...
13. Introduction, 11.

14. Olimón Nolasco, *Servidor fiel*, 162.
15. According to Mexico's 2020 census, 90,224,559 people identified as Catholic (77.7%); 16,118,762 people identified as belonging to another religion (11.2%); and 9,156,555 (8.1%) identified as having no religion at all. A comparison with the 2010 figures (Catholics, 84,217,138 [82.7%]; non-Catholics, 10,076,056 [7.5%]; and nonreligious, 4,660,692 [4.7%]) suggests that Mexicans professing a non-Catholic religion are growing faster as a group than Catholics, at least in relative terms, but have themselves been rapidly outstripped by nonbelievers. That still means that there were 6 million more Catholics in Mexico in 2020 than in 2010. For the underlying INEGI data, see https://www.inegi.org.mx/contenidos/productos/prod_serv/contenidos/espanol/bvinegi/productos/nueva_estruc/702825197261.pdf. For a summary, https://datos.nexos.com.mx/que-nos-dice-el-censo-2020-sobre-religion-en-mexico/.
16. These protests are clearly meant only to befoul and defile what is, to many Mexicans, sacred—and not, I think, to be a more or less legitimate means of questioning official ideology, as in Pamela Voekel's study of scatalogical resistance to Bourbon work discipline, "Peeing on the Palace."
17. The source I have used for reports of attacks on Catholic churches is ACI Prensa (Agencia Católica de Informaciones):

    https://www.aciprensa.com/noticias/profanan-sagrario-en-iglesia-en-mexico-y-destruyen-objetos-sagrados-65041;

    https://www.aciprensa.com/noticias/obispo-pide-actos-de-desagravio-tras-robo-de-la-eucaristia-en-iglesia-en-mexico-64200;

    https://www.aciprensa.com/noticias/arzobispo-decreta-excomunion-tras-profanacion-de-la-eucaristia-en-iglesia-de-mexico-37713;

    https://www.aciprensa.com/noticias/profanan-iglesia-y-realizan-sacrilegio-con-la-eucaristia-en-el-norte-de-mexico-52547;

    https://www.aciprensa.com/noticias/imagenes-de-profanacion-del-santisimo-expuesto-conmueven-a-mexico-14613;

    https://www.aciprensa.com/noticias/roban-eucaristia-en-templo-de-cristo-rey-y-danan-imagen-de-san-joselito-en-mexico-36758;

    https://www.aciprensa.com/noticias/ingresan-a-iglesia-y-profanan-eucaristia-en-primer-dia-del-ano-en-mexico-27307;

    https://www.aciprensa.com/noticias/mexico-sufre-segunda-profanacion-y-robo-del-santisimo-en-menos-de-una-semana-63664;

    https://www.aciprensa.com/noticias/profanan-la-eucaristia-en-catedral-de-nuestra-senora-de-la-asuncion-en-mexico-24372;

    https://www.aciprensa.com/noticias/roban-y-profanan-iglesia-en-mexico-fotos-21017;

https://www.aciprensa.com/noticias/celebran-misa-de-desagravio-en-iglesia-profanada-en-mexico-25613;

https://www.aciprensa.com/noticias/profanacion-en-mexico-mujer-se-desnuda-en-iglesia-y-publica-fotos-en-redes-65911;

https://www.aciprensa.com/noticias/mexico-profanan-capilla-en-ciudad-fronteriza-con-estados-unidos-76155;

https://www.aciprensa.com/noticias/incendian-emblematica-iglesia-en-mexico-obispado-condena-el-sacrilegio-22673;

https://www.aciprensa.com/noticias/profanan-iglesia-y-destruyen-imagenes-de-santos-en-mexico-81170;

https://www.aciprensa.com/noticias/asesinan-a-sacerdote-a-balazos-a-bordo-de-su-automovil-en-mexico-69688;

https://www.aciprensa.com/noticias/mexico-radiografia-de-la-violencia-contra-la-iglesia-catolica-81036?utm_campaign=ACI%20Prensa%20Daily&utm_medium=email&_hsmi=260097158&_hsenc=p2ANqtz-83dxKHLlQTx1xIQcjISiYxht3-Ygd1zgKCWRByxfkwZbUHNHjifJGB7LbieJfnWGnguocIFxsr39kFd5qbFeGKGoxP1pq6iYCuoGjIpZRztZtEiSI&utm_content=260097158&utm_source=hs_email;

https://www.aciprensa.com/noticias/hombres-armados-atan-a-sacerdote-y-asaltan-parroquia-en-mexico-37752?utm_campaign=ACI%20Prensa%20Daily&utm_medium=email&_hsmi=260977876&_hsenc=p2ANqtz-8jLERm1_FHMmk_D0AU0JmdsFmUHxKzU1XDLDvSohtVYeFPEdJcq3uz06aeWZ6x7R3GIUkqUkY6hbzO6Oug6ostGsYyOJU16wfRyDBv1aZ7LAM4PTE&utm_content=260977876&utm_source=hs_email;

https://www.aciprensa.com/noticias/sacerdote-salva-3-ninos-tras-enfrentamiento-que-dejo-un-muerto-y-una-iglesia-baleada-en-mexico-36192?utm_campaign=ACI%20Prensa%20Daily&utm_medium=email&_hsmi=261486840&_hsenc=p2ANqtz-958W68OjfmiISUBhvZLJyYOfK3QeTxoqRRycpdhkkUzlMr5gcW2xuJIEj57-bpJkRx7wH8CDz8_h50ZHwpdz04QsWdRrSpKw60cf9HG_Q7eA8jElA&utm_content=261486840&utm_source=hs_email;

https://www.aciprensa.com/noticias/obispos-de-mexico-alertan-sobre-proyecto-que-censuraria-pesebres-en-lugares-publicos-12004?utm_campaign=ACI%20Prensa%20Daily&utm_medium=email&_hsmi=262085593&_hsenc=p2ANqtz-_8ICm1rxCOUA5cLyVOKPsEcIatk9EBbbUOJQyXH4Bupmhr6vhae_2_gaXYh6ONqKsRR1sHl-G69LN-DlPWl4G-yzeu49F_b9qkZKAMhn7d2tZWyBM&utm_content=262085593&utm_source=hs_email.

Accessed May 20 to June 12, 2023.

18. For the homicide statistics: http://ccm.org.mx/2022/07/elenco-de-sacerdotes-y-religiosos/. The term *clericidio* was coined by Paulist priest Omar Sotelo Aguilar,

https://www.proceso.com.mx/reportajes/2017/9/14/la-iglesia-enfrenta-un-clericidio-191128.html.

19. The assassination of the two Jesuits, Javier Campos Morales and Joaquín Mora, in Cerocahui in the Sierra Tarahumara on June 20, 2022, as they attempted to give sanctuary to a local tour guide pursued by a notorious *sicario*, "El Chueco," prompted popular outrage, a media frenzy, and some base political opportunism in Mexico. The *panista* state government put up a $5 million peso bounty and publicly promised both the Society of Jesus and *chihuahuenses* that such killings would not be tolerated. Meanwhile, federal troops and national guard units flooded the area to search for the bodies, which had been removed from the crime scene, and in pursuit of "El Chueco." The incident then prompted a political dispute between President López Obrador and panista governor Maru Campos, with the former alleging that local officials themselves had sequestered the bodies and offered to give them up in exchange for the withdrawal of federal forces. This putatively "indecent proposal," in AMLO's words, was interesting inasmuch as it showed that the killings had been politicized in relation to the question of federal security policy and state autonomy, not their religious aspect. "El Chueco" was later found murdered in Sinaloa with a bullet to the head, in March of 2023. https://www.jornada.com.mx/notas/2023/03/24/politica/gobierno-de-chihuahua-condiciono-al-federal-tras-asesinato-de-jesuitas-amlo/.
20. I do not deny the seriousness of that problem. On an atrocious case, see González, *Marcial Maciel. Los Legionarios de Cristo*.
21. Cf Jenkins, *New Anti-Catholicism*.
22. Ellis, *Eye-Deep in Hell*.
23. O'Brien, *Surgery and Salvation*.
24. Following Jean Meyer's *La cristiada*.
25. Buchenau, this volume.
26. Osten, this volume.
27. Fallaw, this volume.
28. Rashkin, this volume. A less convincing element in the analysis, perhaps (18), is Rashkin's exculpation of Carrillo Puerto et al. from the suggestion that their demands for birth control were not just about female sexual autonomy—they were also about eugenics. Rashkin wonders if feminist eugenicism was not pragmatic: an attempt to cloak Eve's sexuality in the fig leaf of Adam's patriarchal, scientific power, so to speak. Yet Velázquez Bringas's 1922 lecture on "rationally" limiting the family in the interests of improving the Mexican race and proletariat—subordinating individual female reproductive agency to the collective interest—seems pretty sincere and period to me, however anachronistic it might look now.
29. Jaimes, this volume.

30. Pierce, this volume.
31. Janzen, this volume.
32. Dalton, this volume.
33. Fallaw, this volume.
34. For these measures, which eerily recall the 1920s suspension of public worship (though the 2020 prohibition was of in-person, not public, worship, and came from the episcopate not the government), see:

    https://desdelafe.mx/editorial/ultima-llamada-quedate-en-casa/;

    https://twitter.com/IglesiaMexico/status/1239670897780428801?ref_src=twsrc%5Etfw%7Ctwcamp%5Etweetembed%7Ctwterm%5E1239670897780428801%7Ctwgr%5E1ce61f44cb97f2e0dcf1c7bddecacd4b6a7a17f6%7Ctwcon%5Es1_&ref_url=https%3A%2F%2Faristeguinoticias.com%2F1603%2Fmexico%2Fsuspenden-misas-por-coronavirus%2F;

    https://twitter.com/ArquidiocesisMx/status/1340338740896690176?ref_src=twsrc%5Etfw%7Ctwcamp%5Etweetembed%7Ctwterm%5E1340338740896690176%7Ctwgr%5E6f54665d8322a51bb5b51a5d549db549e472e56c%7Ctwcon%5Es1_&ref_url=https%3A%2F%2Fwww.aciprensa.com%2Fnoticias%2Fsuspenden-nuevamente-la-celebracion-de-misas-con-fieles-en-ciudad-de-mexico-por-pandemia-75324.

    This is a technical point: I make no assessment of Rivera's saintly credentials. For a range of responses, see Barranco, *Norberto Rivera*.
35. Ignacio Solares, in perhaps the best novel about Calles, *El jefe máximo*, has more sport with the ailing chief and his séances—the only spirits who are willing to talk to Calles are those of people he sent to the firing squad, such as generals Gómez and Serrano or Father Pro.
36. Ateneo de la Juventud Mexicana (1907–1913): anti-positivist salon whose leading lights were Alfonso Reyes, Pedro Henríquez Ureña, José Vasconcelos, and Antonio Caso.

Works Cited

Barbosa Cano, Fabio. *La CROM de Luis N. Morones a Antonio J. Hernández*. Puebla, Mexico: Universidad Autónoma de Puebla, 1980.
Barranco, Bernardo, ed. *Norberto Rivera: el pastor del poder*. Mexico City: Grijalbo, 2017.
Butler, Matthew, ed. *Faith and Impiety in Revolutionary Mexico*. New York: Palgrave Macmillan, 2007.
———. *Mexico's Spiritual Reconquest: Indigenous Catholics and Father Pérez's Revolutionary Church*. Albuquerque: University of New Mexico Press, 2023.

Carreño, Alberto María. *El arzobispo de México Excmo. Sr. Don Pascual Díaz y el conflicto religioso.* Mexico City, 1932.
Ellis, John. *Eye-Deep in Hell: Trench Warfare in World War One.* Baltimore: Johns Hopkins University Press, 1976.
González, Fernando M. *Marcial Maciel. Los Legionarios de Cristo: testimonios y documentos inéditos.* Mexico City: Tusquets, 2006.
Greene, Graham. *The Lawless Roads.* 1939. London: Penguin, 1991.
———. *The Power and the Glory.* 1940. London: Penguin, 1991.
Jenkins, Philip. *The New Anti-Catholicism: The Last Acceptable Prejudice.* New York: Oxford University Press, 2004.
Krauze, Enrique. *Mexico, Biography of Power: A History of Modern Mexico, 1810–1996.* New York: HarperPerennial, 1998.
Macías, Carlos. *Plutarco Elías Calles: pensamiento política y social, antología (1913–1936).* Mexico City: Fondo de Cultura Económica, 1988.
Meyer, Jean. *La cristiada.* 3 vols. Mexico City: Siglo XXI, 1973–1974.
Monteón, Michael C. "The Child Is Father of the Man: Personality and Politics in Revolutionary Mexico." *Journal of Iberian and Latin American Studies* 10, no. 1 (2004): 43–61.
O'Brien, Elizabeth. *Surgery and Salvation: The Roots of Reproductive Injustice in Mexico, 1770–1940.* Chapel Hill: University of North Carolina Press, 2023.
Olimón Nolasco, Manuel. *Servidor fiel: el cardenal Adolfo Suárez Rivera (1927–2008).* Mexico City: Miguel Ángel Porrúa, 2013.
Rémond, René. *L'anticléricalisme en France, de 1815 à nos jours.* Paris: Fayard, 1976.
Savarino, Franco, and Andrea Mutolo, eds. *El anticlericalismo en México.* Mexico City: Miguel Ángel Porrúa, 2008.
Solares, Ignacio. *El jefe máximo.* Mexico City: Alfaguara, 1991.
Voekel, Pamela. "Peeing on the Palace: Bodily Resistance to Bourbon Reforms in Mexico City." *Journal of Historical Sociology* 5, no. 2 (1992): 183–208.
Weis, Robert. *For Christ and Country: Militant Catholic Youth in Post-Revolutionary Mexico.* Cambridge: Cambridge University Press, 2019.

Glossary

agraristas. Supporters of land reform, often organized in militant struggles against large landowners.

anti-Catholicism. Opposition to the worldview, beliefs, and practices of the Catholic Church, its clergy, and its faithful.

anticlericalism. Opposition to religious authority in political or social matters.

Bloque de Jóvenes Revolucionarios. Block of Revolutionary Youth, Organization of leftist, ardently anticlerical youth and young adults started by admirers of Tomás Garrido Canabal of Tabasco that spread across Mexico.

Cardenista. A supporter of the president Lázaro Cárdenas (1934–1940) (n.); something or someone related to the Cárdenas (adj.).

Comité Nacional de Lucha contra el Alcoholismo, CNLCA. National Committee of the Struggle Against Alcoholism (1929–1940). Changed names several times throughout the 1930s; the main federal body organizing the anti-alcohol campaign; many of its key leaders were also strongly anti-Catholic.

Confederación Regional Obrera Mexicana, CROM. Mexican Regional Workers Confederation founded in 1918; Mexico's leading national labor confederation until the mid-1930s.

Constitutionalism. The political faction led by Venustiano Carranza during the Mexican Revolution.

cristero/a. A supporter of the Cristero War (1926–1929) (n.); something or someone related to the Cristero War (adj.).

defanaticization. Also: defanatization. Term used in campaign to eradicate beliefs and practices of Catholicism (and at times other Christian denominations) considered backward, immoral, and irrational.

de la Huerta Rebellion. The rebellion against the Mexican government in 1923–1924, which took the name of former Minister of Finance Adolfo de la Huerta, one of its leaders.

delahuertista. Having to do with the de la Huerta Rebellion (adj.); or a person associated with it (n.).

ejidos. During the revolutionary era, the landholding structure created by collective land grants made by the federal government to peasant communities.

encyclical. A papal letter sent to all bishops of the Roman Catholic Church.

episcopate. The bishops of a nation or region as a collective.

Escuela Magnético Espiritual de la Comuna Universal, EMECU. Magnetic Spiritual School of the Universal Commune. The largest spiritist organization in Latin America during the 1920s and 1930s.

Garridismo. The Socialist political movement in the state of Tabasco in the 1920s and 1930s led by Tomás Garrido Canabal.

Iglesia Católica Apostólica Mexicana, ICAM. Mexican Catholic Apostolic Church. An independent Catholic church condemned as schismatic by the Roman Catholic Church.

iconoclasm. The rejection or destruction of religious images.

indigenismo. Indigenism: ideology valorizing the Indigenous cultures in Mexico's past as the source of national identity while encouraging the acculturation of Indigenous people in the present.

irreligion. Opposition to religion in general.

jefe máximo. Former president Plutarco Elías Calles as the "supreme chief of the Mexican Revolution," without a formal role but as an important arbiter of political life.

ley de cultos. Anticlerical regulations passed by states to enforce Article 130 of the constitution.

ligas de resistencia. "Resistance leagues": local organizations that operated as hybrids between labor unions, mutual aid societies, and community organizations, and collectively constituted the mass popular bases of statewide political parties in some Mexican states in the 1920s and 1930s.

Liga Central. The statewide organizing body of ligas de resistencia.

Maximato. Time during which Calles was considered the *jefe máximo* (1928–1935).

Partido Nacional Revolucionario, PNR. National Revolutionary Party; the ruling party founded by Calles and others after Obregón's assassination.

Partido Radical de Tabasco, PRT. Tabasco Radical Party.

Partido Socialista del Sureste, PSS. Socialist Party of the Southeast (Yucatán).

quemasantos. Literally "saint burning," ritual bonfires where religious icons were incinerated.

rationalist education. Model of education emphasizing learning-by-doing (action pedagogy), instilling a collectivist as opposed to individualist mentality, and a rigorously scientific view of the world.

scientism. Belief that the scientific method is the only source of truth.

Secretaría de Gobernación. Mexico's interior ministry, which, unlike the US Department of the Interior, oversees electoral processes and carries out domestic surveillance.

Secretaría de Educación Pública, SEP. Ministry of Public Education.

Secretaría de Salubridad Pública, SSP. Ministry of Public Health.

Contributors

Jürgen Buchenau is the Dowd Term Chair of Capitalism Studies and professor of history and Latin American Studies at UNC Charlotte. He received his PhD from UNC-Chapel Hill and has authored and edited eleven previous books, including *Plutarco Elías Calles and the Mexican Revolution*, winner of the Alfred B. Thomas Book Award of the Southeastern Council of Latin American Studies; *Mexico's Once and Future Revolution: Social Upheaval and the Challenge of Rule since the Late Nineteenth Century* (with Gilbert M. Joseph); and *The Sonoran Dynasty in Mexico: Revolution, Reforms, and Repression*. His research has been funded by the National Endowment of the Humanities and the American Philosophical Society. He is currently Editor-in-Chief of *The Latin Americanist* as well as editor of the book series "The Americas in the World" published by the University of New Mexico Press.

Matthew Butler is an associate professor of history at the University of Texas at Austin. He received his PhD in history at the University of Bristol. He is a noted authority on popular Catholicism in Mexico. He is the author of *Mexico's Spiritual Reconquest: Indigenous Catholics and Father Pérez's Revolutionary Church* (University of New Mexico Press, 2023) and *Popular Piety and Political Identity in Mexico's Cristero Rebellion: Michoacán, 1927–1929* (Oxford University Press/The British Academy, 2004. Reprinted, 2014) and editor of the book that inspired this volume, *Faith and Impiety in Revolutionary Mexico* (Palgrave, 2007), as well as four other edited volumes.

David S. Dalton is the Ruth G. Shaw Humanities Fellow, associate professor of Spanish and Latin American Studies, and director of Latin American Studies at UNC Charlotte. His research theorizes the interface of science, technology, and the body and how this contributes to racial and gender hierarchies in Mexico and throughout Latin America. He is the author of *Mestizo Modernity: Race, Technology, and the Body in Postrevolutionary Mexico* (University of Florida Press, 2018) and *Robo Sacer: Necroliberalism and Cyborg Resistance in Mexican and Chicanx Dystopias* (Vanderbilt University Press, 2023). He has also edited several books and special editions in journals. These include: *Imagining Latinidad: Digital Diasporas and Public Engagement Among Latin American Migrants* (Brill 2023); *Healthcare in Latin America: History, Society, Culture* (University of Florida Press, 2022);

El cine de luchadores (*Revista de Literatura Contemporánea Mexicana* 2021); and *The Transatlantic Undead: Zombies in Hispanic and Luso-Brazilian Literatures* (*Alambique* 2018). He has written some thirty articles and book chapters on different aspects of Mexican and Latin American Studies.

Ben Fallaw is a professor of Latin American Studies at Colby College. Recent books include *State Formation in the Liberal Era: Capitalisms and Claims of Citizenship in Mexico and Peru* (with David Nugent), *Religion and State Formation in Postrevolutionary Mexico*, and *Forced Marches: Soldiers and Military Caciques in Modern Mexico* (with Terry Rugeley). His research has been supported by the Mellon Foundation, the American Council of Learned Societies, and the National Endowment for the Humanities. Currently he is completing an ethnobiography of Yucatecan politician Bartolomé García Correa entitled "Between the Maya and the Mexican Revolution."

Héctor Jaimes is a professor of Latin American literature and culture at North Carolina State University. His areas of expertise are Mexican studies (literature and the arts) and the Latin American essay. He is the author of *Filosofía del muralismo mexicano: Orozco, Rivera y Siqueiros* (2012) and *La reescritura de la historia en el ensayo hispanoamericano* (2001). He has edited *Mario Bellatin y las formas de la escritura* (2020), *The Mexican Crack Writers: History and Criticism* (2017), *Tu hija Frida: Cartas a mamá* (2016), *Fundación del muralismo mexicano: Textos inéditos de David Alfaro Siqueiros* (2012), and *Octavio Paz: La dimensión estética del ensayo* (2004). He is currently working on a book about contemporary Mexican authors.

Rebecca Janzen is a McCausland Fellow and professor of Spanish and comparative literature at the University of South Carolina in Columbia. A scholar of gender, disability, and religious studies in Mexican literature and culture, her research focuses on excluded populations in Mexico. Her first book, *The National Body in Mexican Literature: Collective Challenges to Biopolitical Control* (Palgrave Macmillan, 2015), explored images of disability and illness in twentieth-century texts. Her second book, *Liminal Sovereignty: Mennonites and Mormons in Mexican Culture* (SUNY, 2018), focused on religious minorities. *Unholy Trinity: State, Church and Film in Mexico* (SUNY, 2021) deals with film and religion in Mexico, and *Unlawful Violence: Law and Cultural Production in 21st Century Mexico* (Vanderbilt, 2022) is about human rights, law, and literature. The Plett Foundation, the Kreider Fellowship at Elizabethtown College, the C. Henry Smith Peace Trust, and the Newberry Library in Chicago have supported her research.

Sarah Osten is an associate professor of history and the director of the Latin American and Caribbean Studies Program at the University of Vermont. Her research focuses on modern Mexico and particularly on the changing and heterogeneous meanings of "revolution" in Mexican politics and society during the twentieth century, for both the state and its fiercest critics. Her first book, *The Mexican Revolution's Wake: The Making of a Political System, 1920–1929* (Cambridge, 2018), examined critical early precedents for the formation of Mexico's postrevolutionary political system established by Socialists in the southeastern states of Campeche, Chiapas, Tabasco, and Yucatán. She has also published research on political and state-sponsored violence, the political history of Chiapas, and women's suffrage in Mexico. She is currently writing a book about Mexican solidarity with Central American revolutions in the 1970s and 1980s.

Gretchen Pierce is an associate professor of history at Shippensburg University of Pennsylvania. She is an editor of the H-Net Community Commons H-LatAm network and also founded the academic research blog *Research Corner/Rincón del Investigador/Canto do Pesquisador*. Her research focuses on the intersections between the temperance movement, the state-building process, and the project of identity formation in revolutionary Mexico. She is the coeditor, with Áurea Toxqui, of *Alcohol in Latin America* (2014). She has also written chapters and articles in *Jahrbuch für Wirtschaftsgeschichte/ Economic History Yearbook* (2024); *Alcohol in Latin America; A Companion to Mexican History and Culture* (2011); and *The Social History of Alcohol and Drugs* (2009). She is currently working on a manuscript entitled "Altered States."

Elissa J. Rashkin is a research professor at the Centro de Estudios de la Cultura y la Comunicación, Universidad Veracruzana, Mexico. She is the author of *Soy de nación campesino. Representación y memoria en el agrarismo veracruzano*; *Women Filmmakers in Mexico* (also published as *Mujeres cineastas en México. El otro cine*); *The Stridentist Movement in Mexico* (also published as *La aventura estridentista. Historia cultural de una vanguardia*); *Atanasio D. Vázquez, fotógrafo de la posrevolución en Veracruz*; as well as articles on Mexican and international film, photography, literature, gender, and cultural history. She is the coeditor (with Ester Hernández Palacios) of *Luz rebelde. Mujeres y producción cultural en el México posrevolucionario* and current editor of the journal *Balajú, Revista de Cultura y Comunicación de la Universidad Veracruzana*.

Index

Page numbers in italic text indicate illustrations.

abortion, 115
Academia Juárez, 220
Acapulco, Mexico, 174
Acción Católica Mexicana ("Mexican Catholic Action"), 36
action pedagogy, 162
Actopan, Mexico, 169
Adelante (magazine), 139
aesthetics, 78, 82, 85, 192–93, 197–98, 204
Afro-Mexicans, 84
Against All Odds (Macías), 100
agency, women's, 109, 117n18, 119n33
Age of Revolution, 15n20
agnosticism, 80
agrarian reform, 37, 101, 142, 161, 168, 178, 216
agraristas (advocates for land reform), 30. *See also* land reform
Agua Prieta, Mexico, 25
Agua Prieta rebellion, 106
Aguilar Camín, Héctor, 23
Aguilar Sáenz, Manuel, 224
Alameda Park, Mexico City, 30
alcohol abuse. *See* anti-alcohol campaigns
Alcoholismo (Osuna), 141–42
El alcoholismo como plaga social (Alcoholism as a Social Plague), 143
alcohol use, Mennonites and Mormons, 218
Alemán Valdés, Miguel, 39

Allegory of the Virgin of Guadalupe (Revueltas), 191
Alva Guadarrama, Ramón, 197
Alvarado, Salvador, 4, 26, 50–55, 56, 67, 103
Amaro, Joaquín, 21, 31, 35, 245
American Birth Control League, 107–8
América Tropical (Tropical America) (Siqueiros), 194–95
Amerindians, 82–88, 91n33
AMLO (Andrés Manuel López Obrador), 243, 254n19
Anabaptism. *See* Mennonites
Anaheim, CA, 39
Angel of Independence, 30
Anreus, Alejandro, 194–95
anti-alcohol campaigns, 126–43; anti-Catholicism, 131–35, 247; defanatization, 54; Garrido's statute for Tabasco, 54; interrelations with anti-Catholic campaigns, 135–38; Masons and Protestants, 138–43; revolutionary, 128–31
anti-Catholicism, 1–11, 48–69, 70n2; all-encompassing definition, 238–41; anti-alcohol campaigns, 54, 131–37, 247; apex of, 30–35; of Calles, 21–25, 27, 29, 37–39; church-state focus, 237–38; conversion to Protestantism, 171;

cultural production, 10; denouement of, 36–40; education, 178–79; emotional lives of Mexican revolutionary anti-Catholics, 249–50; feminist activism, 99; Freemasonry, 23–25; fundamentalist, 240; of Gamio, 77–88; Garridista, 48–50, 62–66; in Greene's *The Power and the Glory*, 236–37; justification on scientific grounds, 157; Masons and Protestants, 138–43; Mennonites, 217–21, 247–48, 250; Mormons, 217–21, 247, 250; muralism, 193–95, 203–4; in pop psychology, 237; pragmatism, 245; religious minorities, 213–14, 216; religious separatism, 247–48; revolutionary governments, 7, 21, 30–35; roots of, 246–47; science/scientism, 158, 173–77, 248–49; sex, 246–47; since 1940, 241–44; southeastern Socialism, 67; southeastern Socialist parties and the governments, 53; subgenres of, 238–40
anticlericalism, 70n2; anti-alcohol campaigns, 126–27; as anti-Catholicism, 171; of Calles, 23–30, 33–35, 56, 167, 245, 248; Constitutionalists, 26–27; Constitution of 1917, 34–35; defined, 2; education, 178–79; "elite" anticlericalism, 2; feminist activism, 99; first wave of, 25–30; Freemasonry, 139; Garrido Canabal's political program, 51–52, 63; gendered reception of feminism, 99–115; ideology informing, 49; Knights of Guadalupe, 29–30; local anticlerical groups and science, 173–77; militant, 78–79; official policy, 4; opposition to hierarchy, 9; penal code reform, 6, 21, 34; Protestants, 140–42; revolutionary anti-Catholicism genre, 238–41; revolutionary anticlericalism, 4, 28, 30, 36, 158, 176, 178; revolutionary governments, 5; science and defanaticization in the federal classroom, 169–70; scientism, 157–58; scientistic, 161, 169, 179; and the SEP, 168; socialist education, 166; southeastern Socialist parties and the governments, 53; Tabascan-style scientific, 164–65; third wave of revolutionary, 36–37

anti-delahuertismo in Tabasco, 55–61
"Anti-Fanatic Hour" (radio program), 136
anti-Semitism, 7, 23
applied anthropology, 78, 84, 87–88, 89n5
archbishops, 5, 26, 33–34
Armstrong-Fumero, Fernando, 91n29
Article 3 of Constitution of 1917, 37, 164–67
Article 130 of the Constitution of 1917, 5, 33
artists' union, 195
Asad, Talal, 216
Asociación Católica de la Juventud Mexicana (Catholic Association of Mexican Youth), 28

Asociación Cristiana de Jóvenes, 140
Asociación de Temperancia (AT), 141
Asociación Nacional de Temperancia (ANT), 140–41
Aspects of Mexican Culture (Vasconcelos and Gamio), 79
assimilation, 77, 82, 85, 89n6
Atatürk, Kemal, 7
Ateneo de la Juventud Mexicana, 255n36
atheism, 80, 117n12, 161, 171, 237
authoritarianism, 62–66, 68, 159
Autonomous University of Chapingo, Mexico City, 200–204
Ávila Camacho, Manuel, 2, 6
Ávila de Rosado, Porfiria, 105

Báez Camacho, Gonzalo, 140
Baja California del Norte, 128
Bajío region, 9
Bantjes, Adrian, 4, 25, 49, 68, 159
baptisms, 176–77
Basave Benítez, Agustín, 90n15
Basilica of Our Lady of Guadalupe, 27, 157, 249
Bassols, Narciso, 178
Bastian, Jean-Pierre, 216
"bautizos socialistas" (socialist baptisms), 139
Belio C., Fabio, 170
Beltrán Castillo, Enrique, 157
Benemérito de las Américas, 220
Berber, Alfredo F., 177
birth control, 107–15, 246, 254n28
Black population of Mexico, 82
Bloque de Jóvenes Revolucionarios (BJR). *See* Red Shirts
Bolshevik Revolution, 7
Bonfil, Ramón G., 135

Book of Mormon, 217
Borah, William, 167
Borrego, Domingo, 162
Brading, David A., 79
Brandi, María A., 175
Brooklyn, NY, 107
Brown, Barbara Jones, 214
Buck, Sarah A., 111–12
Burgos Medina, Joaquín, 176
Burial of the Worker (Siqueiros), 194
Bustamante, Guadalupe, 126–27, 136

Call, Anson B., 225
Calles, Juan Bautista, 22
Calles, Plutarco Elías, 21–40; alcohol consumption, 128; anti-Catholicism, 30–40, 178, 241; anticlericalism, 4, 6, 22–30, 245, 248; anti-Delahuertismo in Tabasco, 55–61; church-state focus, 237; de la Huerta opposition to, 55–56; Departamento de Antropología, 86–87; emotional life of, 249–50; failure to Tabasconize federal schools, 165–67; Gamio and Vasconcelos, 79; laicism, 240; photograph of, 24, 32; pop psychology, 237; science of revolution in Tabasco, 159–61; southeastern Socialists, 67. *See also* Maximato
Calles, Rodolfo Elías, 36, 40, 137, 164
Calles Chacón, Hortensia Elías, 38, 39
Calles Law, 6, 21, 34, 238
Caloca Valle, Cayetano, 133
Camisas Rojas. *See* Red Shirts
Campeche, Mexico, 50, 52, 54, 61, 134, 169, 173
campesinos, 34, 52, 101

Campuzano, Plutarco Elías. *See* Calles, Plutarco Elías
Canada, 213, 218, 220
Cantón, Miguel, 162, 163–64
"Capilla riveriana" ("Riverian Chapel"), 204
Capistrán Garza, René, 34
capitalism, 65
Cárdenas, Lázaro, 6, 37, 51–52, 68, 129, 137, 159–61, 166, 174–79
Cardoso, Joaquín, 142
The Carnival of Ideologies (Clemente Orozco), 193
Caro, Leopoldo, 169
Carrancismo, 99–106
Carranza, Venustiano, 4, 23, 26, 27, 78–79, 90n18, 100–106, 118n26, 118n27, 118n28
Carrillo, Belisario, 60–61
Carrillo Puerto, Elvia, 108, 110, 113, 246
Carrillo Puerto, Felipe, 28, 52–54; anti-alcohol campaigns, 136–37; assassination of, 56–57, 67; de la Huerta revolt, 165; Delahuertismo, 245; grassroots anticlericalism, 176; rationalist school *(escuela racionalista)*, 162; systemic contempt, 240
Caruana, George, 33
Casa del Estudiante Indígena, 134
Catholic Church, 1–8; anti-delahuertismo in Tabasco, 55–61; apex of anti-Catholicism, 30–35; Carrancista ideologues, 101–3; Catholic hierarchy, 2–3, 9, 25–26, 30, 34, 35; counterrevolutionary forces, 61; denouement of anti-Catholicism, 36–40; feminist activism, 99; Gamio, 77–80; Garridista socialism, 54, 67–69; gendered anticlericalism, 100–115; influence and manipulation, 102–4; muralism, 197–204; postrevolutionary state, 215–21; Protestantism, 9–10, 140; public education, 85; public health, 127; pulque producers, 133; radical statement of Calles, 37; rebellion, 58; revolutionary government's conflict with, 21–22; social Catholicism, 25; socialist education, 62–64; Socialist reform, 49, 62–66; Spiritism, 39–40; state as check on the influence of the, 79; in the United States, 79
Catholicisms, other than Roman Catholic, 2, 8–9, 239
Celaya district of Guanajuato, 172
Central American countries, 6
central Mexico, 22–23
César Sandino, Augusto, 175
Cetina Gutiérrez, Rita, 109–10
Chagoyan, María Luisa, 140
Chapingo murals, 200–204
Chiapas, Mexico, 30, 36, 50, 52, 54, 56, 174–75, 182n51
Chihuahua, Mexico, 4, 22, 164, 219–20, 221–22, 224, 242–43, 247
"Christ the King" shrine, 28
Christus (Catholic publication), 142
church and state, 5–7, 9–10, 23, 34–35, 37, 80, 86, 194, 237–38
church buildings, 55, 63–64, 218–19, 251n12
churches turned into public schools, 62–64, 137

científicos, 89n5, 174, 240, 250
Civil Code of 1884, 105
Civil Code of 1928, 244
civil marriage, 3, 221
clergy and capitalism, 57, 65
clergy and Gamio, 79–81
"clericales" label, 138
El clericalismo en América a través de un continente, 113
CNLCA. *See* Comité Nacional de Lucha contra el Alcoholismo
Coahuila, 164
Coffey, Mary K., 203–4
Cohen, Theodore, 84
Colegio Aquiles Serdán, 142
Comalcalco, Mexico, 63–64
Comino (periodical), 140
Comisarenco Mirkin, Dina, 199
Comité Episcopal Mexicano, 249
Comité Nacional de Lucha contra el Alcoholismo (CNLCA), 126, 129–31, 133, 134–35, 139–43
Committees for the Defense of the Revolution, 53
Comte, Auguste, 82
Confederación de Trabajadores Mexicanos (Confederation of Mexican Workers; CTM), 241
Confederación Regional Obrera Mexicana (Mexican Regional Workers' Confederation; CROM), 9, 31, 37, 169, 238
Congress, 34, 37
Conservatives, 3, 25, 58, 114, 133, 161, 168
Constitutional Convention of 1916–1917, 27, 117n18, 129
Constitutionalism, 50, 118n26

Constitutionalists, 4, 25–27, 100–101, 244
constitutional reform of 1992, 241
Constitution of 1824, 3
Constitution of 1857, 3, 5, 216, 238
Constitution of 1917, 4–6, 8–9, 25–28, 33–35, 164–67, 203, 220, 238, 241
contraception. *See* birth control
Conventionists, 4
Corpus Christi church, 30
Cortina, Manuel, 170–71
Coss, Francisco, 26
Council of Ministers (Consejo de Ministros), 21, 30–31
Covid 19, 249
Craib, Raymond, 170
Craver, Samuel P., 140
Creation (Rivera), 191, 198–99, 247
Crespi, Tito, 29
Cristero Rebellion, 21, 36, 131
Cristeros (Catholic rebels), 6, 36, 58, 138
Cristero War (Cristiada), 6, 39, 67–69, 78, 203, 213
La Cristiada (Cristero Revolt), 34
Cristo Rey (weekly), 177
CROM. *See* Confederación Regional Obrera Mexicana (Mexican Regional Workers' Confederation)
Cruz, Ausencio C., 60–61, 166
Cubilete Hill, Guanajuato, 28
Cuernavaca, Mexico, 39, 194, 242
Cuervo, Tomás, 170
Cueto, Germán, 197
Cuitzeo, Michoacán, Mexico, 243
cultural production, 10
Cultural Sundays, 126, 133, 136–38
Curley, Robert, 25, 49, 59

Daniels, Josephus, 167
Dartmouth College, 10–11
de Cervantes, Aurora C., 175
defanaticization. *See* fanaticism
de Giuseppe, Massimo, 64, 72n31, 136
Delafield, Mrs. Lewis L., 107
de la Huerta, Adolfo, 26–29, 55–60
de la Huerta Rebellion, 28–29, 49, 55–56, 58–59, 60, 66–67, 165
delahuertismo, 55–61, 64, 67, 245–46
de la Luz Mena, José, 162
de la Madrid, Miguel, 241
Democratic Party, 167
Departamento de Antropología, 86–87, 90n18
de Sárraga, Belén, 113–14, 240
The Devil in the Church (Siqueiros), 194, 202
dialectics, 193, 199–204, 205–8, 246
Dialectics of Nature (Engels), 207
Diario de Yucatán (newspaper), 109
Díaz, Porfirio, 1, 3, 5, 23, 140, 166, 219
Díaz Ordaz, Gustavo, 173
Díaz y Barreto, Pascual, 31, 34, 57–58, 69, 239, 250
Diéguez, Manuel M., 4, 26
La Doctrina Carranza y el acercamiento indolatino (Galindo), 106
Dr. Atl, 101–2
Dream of a Sunday Afternoon in Alameda Central (Rivera), 198
Durango, Mexico, 222, 242–43, 247
Dyck, Andrea, 218

economic boycott of the LNDLR, 34
economic development, 6, 129, 135–36
economic nationalism, 50

education, 27, 77–88, 99–115, 135–36, 161–78, 191, 213, 220
Ehlers, Dolores and Adriana, 101
ejidos (communal lands), 171, 221–22
El Abogado Cristiano (periodical), 140–41
The Elements (Siqueiros), 191, 194
elite(s), 131–33, 165–66, 174, 215–16
Elizalde, José María, 9
El Niño Fidencio, 39
EMECU. *See* Escuela Magnético Espiritual de la Comuna Universal (Magnetic Spiritual School of the Universal Commune)
encyclicals, 25, 28, 35
Engels, Frederick, 207
Enns, Veronica, 218
Epic of the Mexican People (Rivera), 201
Episcopal Committee, 33–34
episcopate, 3, 5, 27, 28, 31–35, 36, 241
Escuela Magnético Espiritual de la Comuna Universal (Magnetic Spiritual School of the Universal Commune; EMECU), 175
España, David F., 139
Espinazo (Nuevo León), 39
Eugenia (Urzaiz), 1, 108
eugenics, 1, 82, 109–11, 119n38, 138–39, 157, 254n28
evangelicalism, 90n27
Excélsior (newspaper), 109
expulsion of priests, 5, 26–27, 33, 36, 136–37
expulsion of the Jesuits in 1767, 2, 35

Faith and Impiety in Revolutionary Mexico (Butler), 7–8
faith and science, 83

faith healing, 39, 251n11
family planning, 107–9
fanaticism, 26, 157–79; Amerindians, 86; defanaticization, 5–6, 36, 54, 90n27, 105, 119n33, 164–65, 168–73, 174–76; failure to Tabasconize federal schools, 165–67; Gamio, 77, 79–80; grassroots anti-Catholicism and science, 173–77; poverty, 134; problems caused by, 143; science and defanaticization in the federal classroom, 168–73; science of revolution in Tabsco, 159–62; SEP's attack on, 245; Tabasconizing state teachers, 163–65; Tabasco Socialists, 64; vice, 135–38
Father Pro, 239, 255n35
The Feast of Our Lord of Chalma (Leal), 191
Feast of the Holy Cross (Montenegro), 191
federal diputados, 166
Federalists, 3
federal schools/schoolteachers, 165–68, 171–73, 178–79, 185n122
federal teachers, 5, 161, 168–69, 171, 174–77, 185n122
Félix Flores, Ramón, 54
female sexuality, 99, 103, 105, 109, 112, 114–15
feminism, 99–115, 246; First Feminist Congress, 101–6; gendered reception of, 112–14; press criticism of, 112–13; reproductive rights *versus* the Church, 106–9; Second Feminist Congress, 106; working women's rights, 109–12

Fernández, Emilio "El Indio," 8
Fernández Aceves, María Teresa, 113
Ferrer Guardia, Francisco, 109–10
Filippi, Ernesto, 28
First Feminist Congress, 101–6, 246
Flores, Marcelino B., 226
Flores Magón brothers, 3
Folgarait, Leonard, 194
folk Catholicism, 8–10
Forjando patria (Gamio), 1, 78–80, 83–84, 248
Franco, Luis G., 141
Freemasonry, 23–25, 139, 174
From Porfirianism to the Revolution (Siqueiros), 199, 207–8
Frontera, Mexico, 63–64

Galindo, Hermila, 100–115, 116n4, 118n22, 118n26, 118n28, 118n29, 119n33, 246
Gamio, Manuel, 1, 76, 77–88, 91n33, 171, 240, 248, 250
García, Gabriel, 64
García Correa, Bartolomé, 164
García de la Cadena, Gumaro, 225–26
García Téllez, Ignacio, 139
Garridismo, 55, 58, 242
Garrido Canabal, Tomás, 48–69, 245; anti-Catholicism and authoritarianism, 62–66; anti-Catholicism and education, 178–79; anti-delahuertismo in Tabasco, 55–61; emotional life of, 250; failure to Tabasconize federal schools, 165–68; grassroots anti-Catholicism and science, 173–77; ICAM congregations, 9; interview to *Milwaukee Leader*, 48; photograph of, 160; polarizing politics,

70n3; Red Shirts, 68, 136, 167, 245; science of revolution in Tabasco, 159–62; southeastern Socialism, 48–55, 161, 169, 179; systemic contempt, 240; Tabasconizing state teachers, 163–65
Gastélum, Bernardo J., 87
G. Briseño, Elvira Serrato, 137–39
gendered anticlericalism, 99–115
The German Ideology (Marx), 209
Getty Foundation, 195
Gilbert, David, 3
Gillingham, Paul, 68
González, César, 103
González, Francisco Elías, 23
González, Pablo, 106
Gran Confederación Nacional Católica de Trabajo (Great National Catholic Labor Confederation), 28
Graniel, Eugenio, 63
Gran Logia Valle de México, 139
grassroots anti-Catholicism and science, 173–77
grassroots organizing, 28, 158, 167, 173–77
Great Apostasy (Talmage), 217
Greeley, Robin Adèle, 192
Greene, Graham, 236–41
Grito de Guadalajara, 167
Gruening, Ernest, 30
Guachochi, Chihuahua, Mexico, 242
Guadalajara, Mexico, 10, 33, 37, 142, 166, 167, 177
Guadalupanism, 9
Guadalupe-Hidalgo Treaty, 219
Guanajuato, Mexico, 170–72, 176–77
Guatemala, 6, 60, 87, 93n70
Guerrero, Mexico, 174, 182n51
Guerrero, Vicente, 30

Guerrero, Xavier, 195, 197
Gutiérrez y Olivares, Antonio, 134

Haberman, Roberto, 108–9
Hacia un México nuevo (Toward a New Mexico) (Gamio), 82
hammer and sickle symbol, 194–95
Harper, Kristin, 70n3, 161
Haus, Martha H., 225
Haya de la Torre, Raúl, 175
"Health Weeks," 176
Hernández, Epigmenio, 134
Hernández Aguilar, Jenaro, 172
Hidalgo, Mexico, 121n63, 169, 175
Hidalgo, Miguel, 30
high and low clergy, 31
Historia de las Américas series (Clemente Orozco), 10–11
historical materialism, 208
History of Morelos, Conquest and Revolution (Rivera), 194
History of Religion (Rivera), 194
Hombre en llamas series (Clemente Orozco), 10
Hospicio Cabañas, Guadalajara, 10
Huejutla, Hidalgo, 175
Huerta, Victoriano, 2, 4, 23, 25–26, 78, 128
hygiene, 78, 82, 137, 180n10, 216, 218, 249

Ibarra, Isaac M., 139
Ibarra, Luis, 142
ICAM. *See* Iglesia Católica Apostólica Mexicana
iconoclasm, 26, 49, 55, 165, 168, 169, 173, 178
identity formation, 54, 127, 128–29, 135

Iglesia Católica Apostólica Mexicana (ICAM), 2, 9–10, 29–30, 171
Iglesia Soledad de Santa Cruz, 29–30
images, biblical prohibition on, 218–19
images of Christ, 195
immigrants from the United States, 221–22
immigration, 214
Index Librorum Prohibitorum, 163
Indigenous Mexicans: anti-alcohol campaigns, 141, 144n15; anti-Catholicism, 244; cultural mestizaje, 173; ICAM congregations, 9, 30; indigenismo defined, 89n6; Indigenous cosmologies, 8; Indigenous/ethnic suffering, 194–95; literacy campaigns, 171; Mexico's faith history, 2–3; muralism, 10; science, 158; Tabasco Socialists, 64; temperance movement, 247; Vasconcelos/Gamio, 77–88, 92n52; Yaqui, 27, 134
indoctrination, religious, 101, 109
Inés de la Cruz, Sor Juana, 106
infectious diseases, 157
Instituto Juárez, 161
Interior Ministry (Secretaría de Gobernación), 159
interpenetration of opposites, 207–8
irreligion, 64, 100, 126–27, 135–38, 238, 240
Islam, 216
Islas Allende, Clemente, 131
Iturbide, Agustín, 30
Ivins, Anthony W., 217
Izamal, Mexico, 176
Izquierdas (newspaper), 131–33

Jacobins, 27
Jalisco, Mexico, 3–4, 25, 34, 56, 59, 164, 242
jefe máximo (supreme chief), 6, 36–37, 167, 250
El jefe máximo (Solares), 255n35
Jesuits, 2, 35, 243, 254n19
Jiménez de Lara, Arturo, 60–61
Jiutepec, Morelos, 242
José Rios, Juan, 57
Juárez, Benito, 3, 23, 63–64, 240
Juchipila, Zacatecas, 170
Judeo-Masonic conspiracy, 25

Kaminal Juyú, 87
Kellogg, Frank B., 31
Kennedy, Anne, 107–8
Knight, Alan, 25, 53, 58, 62–63, 68
Knights of Guadalupe, 29
Krauze, Enrique, 22–23

labor reform, 52–54
labor unions, 9, 131. *See also* ligas de resistencia
La Castañeda mental hospital, 142
Lagarde, Ernest, 31–35
laicism, 238, 240
Lamas, Manuel R., 137
Landeros Díaz, Lic. Agustín, 223
landholding and land use, 221–22
land reform, 52, 136, 159, 191, 220, 222
Laplace, Pierre-Simon, 171
La raza cósmica (Vasconcelos), 1, 78
Lateran Pacts, 35
Lau Jaiven, Ana, 112
laws of dialectics, 207–8
Lazcano, Francisco, 126–27, 131, 134, 139
Lear, John, 192–93

Legión Leal de Temperancia, 141
Legión Mexicana de Decencia, 142
Lemaître, Monique, 110
Lenin, Vladimir I., 7, 205
León, Mexico, 171
León Toral, José de, 34–35
Leyes de Reforma (Reform Laws), 3
Liberal Abraham González Club, Mexico City, 100
Liberals, 3, 140, 215–16, 237–38, 243
The Liberated Earth (La tierra fecunda) (Rivera), 204
liberation of women, 99–115, 170, 246
liberation of workers, 62, 65
licensing system for priests, 171, 238
Liga Antialcohólica Mexicana, 140
Liga Central, 53, 61, 63
Liga Nacional Defensora de la Libertad Religiosa (National League for the Defense of Religious Liberty, or LNDLR), 30, 33–34, 36, 239
ligas de resistencia, 52–53, 57, 59–61, 62, 65–66, 69
La limitación racional de la familia (Velázquez Bringa), 109–10
List Arzubide, Germán, 163–64, 177
literacy campaigns, 171
Llorente, Leonor, 39
Loge, Clara Steger, 105
Logia Psicológica Científica (Psychological-Scientific Lodge), 175
Logia Simbólica Cruzada Ideológica Femenina, 138
López, Fortino, 170
López de Santa Anna, Antonio, 23
Los Angeles, CA, 39, 194, 199

Machiavelli, Niccolò, 2, 8n8
Macías, Anna, 100
Macías, Carlos, 22
Madero, Francisco I., 3–4, 23–25, 39, 78, 113
Malpica Hernández, José, 161–62, 177
Man at Crossroads (Rivera), 205
"Manifesto of the Union of Mexican Workers, Technicians, Painters, and Sculptors," 197–204
The March of Humanity (Siqueiros), 199, 206–9
marriages, 219, 221
Martínez Assad, Carlos, 55, 58
Marxism/Marxist dialectics, 10, 193–95, 198, 199–203, 208–9, 246–47
Masonic lodges, 138, 139, 174
Masons, 126–27, 138–40
mass vaccination campaign, 176
materialist conception of history, 194–95, 209, 247
materialistic fundamentalism, 161–62
Maternity (Clemente Orozco), 191
Maximato, 36–37, 79, 90n17, 167, 179, 181n21
Maximilian, 3
Maya of Yucatán, 134–35
McConkie, Bruce R., 217
Medical Association, Tabasco, 176
Mennonites, 213–27; alcohol use, 218; alignment with postrevolutionary governments, 217–21; anti-Catholic beliefs, 217–21, 247–48, 250; Mexican federal government relationship with, 215–17; negative aspects of government's relationship with, 221–22
El Mensajero del Sagrado Corazón (Catholic publication), 142

Mérida, Carlos, 197
Mérida, Mexico, 103, 105, 109, 110, 246
mestizaje, 77–88, 89n6, 90n15, 173
mestizo modernity, 79, 85
mestizo nation, 8, 77, 82, 85
mestizophilia, 84, 248
Mexican Catholic Apostolic Church. *See* Iglesia Católica Apostólica Mexicana (ICAM)
Mexican citizenship and nationality, claims to, 214–15, 219, 223–27
Mexican Communist Party, 193–95, 203
Mexican federal government and religious minorities, 213–22
Mexican Knights Templar, 142
Mexican Revolution: anti-alcohol campaigns, 128–31; armed phase of, 158–59; economic and moral rehabilitation, 135; feminists of, 99–115; Garridista anti-Catholicism, 66; Garridista socialism, 50, 69; goals of the, 178; muralism, 193, 197, 201; positivism, 82, 250; sobriety promotion, 142–43; Urzaiz's *Eugenia*, 1
México, state of, 30
Mexico City, Mexico, 27, 29–30, 33, 68, 112–14, 131, 138, 165–68, 242
Meyer, Jean, 2, 5, 8
Meza Gutiérrez, José, 142–43
Meza Huacuja, Ivonne, 50
Michoacán, Mexico, 28–29, 34, 36, 119n33, 126, 134, 138, 182n51, 242–43
Mignolo, Walter, 89n6
The Milwaukee Leader (newspaper), 48, 50–52, 66

Los mitos (The Myths) (Siqueiros), 194–95
mobilization, 5–6, 36, 68, 115, 159
modernity, 1, 50, 78–79, 82, 85, 113, 201
modernization, 77–78, 135, 203
Molina Betancourt, Rafael, 168
Montenegro, Roberto, 191
Monteón, Michael, 23
moralism and women's rights, 104, 109, 115
morality, 54–55, 140, 176
Mora y del Río, José, 27, 31–33
Morelia, Michoacán, Mexico, 28–29, 33
Morelos, José María, 30
Moreno Chávez, José Alberto, 62
Mormons, 213–27; alcohol use, 218; alignment with postrevolutionary governments, 217–21; anti-Catholic beliefs, 217–21, 247, 250; Mexican federal government relationship with, 215–17; negative aspects of government's relationship with, 221–22; settler refugees to United States, 220; Taylor and Skousen's petitions for tax exemption, 222–27
Morones, Luis Napoleón, 21, 29–31, 32, 35, 39, 237, 245, 250n3
Morrow, Dwight, 36
Múgica, Francisco, 54–55, 67, 159, 162, 237, 240
La Mujer Moderna ("Modern Woman;" *Mujer Moderna*), 100–106
El Mundo Cristiano (periodical), 141
muralism, 10, 191–210, 246–47
murals. *See* muralism

El Nacional (newspaper), 166
National Cooperativist Party, 56, 246

National Palace, 201
naturalization certificates, 223–27
nature, forces of, 208
Navarro-Génie, Marco Aurelio, 175
negation of the negation, 207–8
neopositivism, 83–84, 89n5, 91n33
New Men, Women, and Children, 127, 129
Newton, Isaac, 170–71
New Workers School, New York City, 201, 205
non-Catholics, 9–10, 180n13, 214, 215–16, 226, 242, 252n15
Núñez Becerra, Fernanda, 112

Oaxaca, Mexico, 30, 56, 117n19, 121n63, 230n29
Obregón, Álvaro: anti-Catholic sentiments, 4; anticlericalism, 26–29; anticlerical provisions, 5; anti-delahuertismo in Tabasco, 55–59; anti-Semitic tropes, 23; appointment of Aarón Sáenz, 9; Calles, 31–35; and Galindo, 106; Gamio and Vasconcelos, 79; Garrido Canabal, 67; photograph, 32; social, legal, and political reforms, 191; War of the Winners, 4
O'Brien, Elizabeth, 244
Ochoa, José, 59
Ocosingo, Chiapas, Mexico, 174
Official Schools of Llano Largo and Colonia Madera, 224
organized labor, 50, 61
Oropeza Nájera, Roberto, 171–72
Orozco, José Clemente, 10–11, 191, 193, 197
Orozco y Jiménez, José Francisco, 31

Orrico de los Llanos, Miguel, 139
Ortiz Rubio, Pascual, 36, 165
Osorio, Elena, 105
Osuna, Andrés, 141–42
Otomí of Querétaro, 134–35

pagan Catholics, 80–81, 85, 91n28
painting ideology, 193, 198, 204
Pan-American Congress, 114
Pan-American Women's Conference, 112–14
Pani, Alberto J., 167
papacy, 2, 35, 237
parliamentary democracy, 3
Partido Católico Nacional (National Catholic Party), 3–4, 25
Partido Comunista Mexicano (PCM), 193
Partido Nacional Revolucionario (National Revolutionary Party; PNR), 35, 36–37, 52, 126, 137, 175
Partido Revolucionario Institucional (Institutional Revolutionary Party; PRI), 69, 161, 179
Partido Socialista Radical Tabasqueño (Tabasco Radical Socialist Party), 49–69
Patriarch Tikhon, 7
Pech, Crispín, 63
penal code reform, 6, 21, 34
Peña Nieto, Enrique, 243
Pérez, Arnulfo H., 166
Pérez Budar, José Joaquín, 9, 29–30, 239
Peronism, 70n3
Pew Research Center, 6
Pino Suárez, José María, 4
Pius XI (pope), 28
Plan of Agua Prieta, 4

pláticas (motivational talks delivered to communities), 169, 171
Platt of Zion, 220
PNR. *See* Partido Nacional Revolucionario (National Revolutionary Party)
political Catholics/Catholicism, 59, 133, 142, 246
political enfranchisement, 52–53
polygamy, 214–15, 219–20, 222, 226, 248
Popé, 2
popular Catholicism, 6, 8, 248–49
popular organizations, 27, 54, 137–38, 141
Porfirian positivists, 91n33, 157, 161, 174
Porfiriato, 78, 82, 91n33, 140, 216
Portes Gil, Emilio, 36, 131, 139, 142
Portrait of America (Rivera), 201, 205
Portrait of Mexico Today (Siqueiros), 207
Portrait of the Bourgeoisie (Siqueiros), 207–8
positivism, 25, 50, 82, 250
postrevolutionary state, 4–5, 68–69, 77, 85, 173–77, 178–79, 215–21
postrevolutionary state formation, 158–59, 172–73, 180n9, 237
poverty, 172
The Power and the Glory (Greene), 236–37
Practice of Irreligious Education (List Arzubide), 163–64, 177
pragmatism, 9, 27–28, 49, 78, 167, 217, 245
Pratt, Rey L., 217, 247
pre-Columbian religions, 10–11, 86
priests: anti-alcohol campaigns, 126–27, 131–35, 141–43; expulsion of, 5, 26–27, 33, 36, 136–37; Garrido Canabal's anti-Catholicism, 62; hygienic disputes, 248–49; licensing system, 238; penal code reform, 34; ratio of priests to inhabitants, 36; religious assaults and homicides, 243; religious services, 221; science and defanaticization in the federal classroom, 170–72; Socialist Party, 69; spiritism, 175; women and the power of the Church, 101. *See also* anticlericalism
Prieto Laurens, Jorge, 29, 56, 58, 246
Progreso, Yucatán, 175
progress, 215–17
prohibitionism, 7, 129, 137, 176, 218, 230n25, 246–47. *See also* anti-alcohol campaigns
propaganda, 131, 176–77
Protestants/Protestantism, 6, 9–10, 21–22, 79–80, 90n27, 140–43, 171, 215–17, 227, 247
public education, 62, 68, 85, 86–87, 99, 213, 220
Public Education Secretariat (Secretaría de Educación Pública), 216
public festivals, 135–36
public health, 127, 158, 172
public policy, 107
public schools, 216, 220
Puebla, Mexico, 30, 33, 182n51
Pueblo Revolt, 2
Puig Casauranc, Manuel, 87, 91n39, 135
pulque (fermented beverage), 133, 137

Quas Primas (In the First) (papal encyclical), 35
quemasantos (spectacular burnings of sacred items), 165, 168

Querétaro, Mexico, 4, 27, 134, 242

race and ethnicity in Mexico, Gamio's role in, 84
Racine, Karen, 23
radicalism(s), 56, 157, 167, 177, 246
Ramírez, J. T., 140
Ramírez, Luis, 169
Randall, Carlos, 40
rationalist education, 105, 159, 163–65, 166–67, 168–70, 173, 178–79
rationalist school *(escuela racionalista)*, 162
Ray, Guy W., 137
reactionary press, 108–9
Redención (newspaper), 161
Red Shirts, 68, 136, 167, 245
Reform War, 3
religion: alternative science to debunk, 175; Feminist Congress, 105–6; Gamio's view of Mexican Catholicism, 79–81; Liberal governments supported, 216; muralism, 191–95, 198–99; rationalist education, 166–67; role of in public life, 213; Tabasco Socialists, 62–66; Vasconcelos/Gamio dialectic, 84–86; vice, 135–38
religiosity, 62–64, 112, 113, 135, 172–73
religious assaults and homicides, 243
religious education, 214, 220
religious festivals, 127, 134, 143
religious freedom, 213, 220
religious minorities. *See* Mennonites; Mormons
religious practices, 64–66
religious question, 166
religious separatism, 247
religious services, 219, 221
removals of immigrants from the United States, 221
Rempel, Peter, 218
reproductive medicine, 244
reproductive rights, 106–9, 115
Rerum Novarum, 25
Restorationists, 10
revolutionary anti-Catholicism, 1, 4, 7, 227, 239, 243, 247
revolutionary anticlericalism, 4, 28, 30, 36, 158, 176, 178
revolutionary-era murals, 191
revolutionary festivals, 216, 219
revolutionary ideals, 50, 219, 222
revolutionary intellectuals, 90n15, 161, 164, 169–70, 176–77, 178, 216
revolutionary reformism, 48, 59, 63, 65, 70n3
Revueltas, Fermín, 191, 197
Reyes Larios, Hipólito, 115
Ridgeway, Stan, 161
Rivera, Diego, 10–11, 191–210; *Creation*, 191, 198–99, 247; dialectics, 205–6; *Dream of a Sunday Afternoon in Alameda Central*, 198; *Epic of the Mexican People*, 201; *History of Morelos, Conquest and Revolution*, 194; *History of Religion*, 194; *The Liberated Earth (La tierra fecunda)*, 204; *Man at Crossroads*, 205; *Muralist Manifesto*, 197–204; *Portrait of America*, 201, 205; *Symbols of the New Regime or the Allegory of Hardship of the Laborer and the Peasant or Symbols of the New Order*, 196; *Vaccination*, 15n39

Rivera, Norberto, 249
Rockefeller, John D., 205
Rockefeller Center, New York City, 205
Rodríguez, Abelardo L., 37, 128–29
Rodríguez, Cristóbal, 157, 240
Rodríguez, N., 137
Rodríguez Lozano, Rubén, 173
Rome, 2, 34, 134, 237, 241, 247
Roosevelt, Franklin Delano, 167
Rosicrucianism, 203
Rublee, Juliet Barrett, 107–8
Ruiz y Flores, Leopoldo, 31, 34
Rumbos Nuevos (magazine), 113
Ryskamp, George, 214

"Sábados Rojos, Sábados Burgueses (Red Saturdays, Bourgeois Saturdays)" (Caloca Valle), 132, 133
Sabbatarianism, 244
Sáenz, Aarón, 9–10, 240
Sáenz, Moisés, 10, 140–41, 240
saints, 55, 137, 140
Saínz Arenas, Rafael, 175–76
Saltillo, Mexico, 242
Salvatierra, Guanajuato, 174
"Sánchez Filmador," 112–14
Sánchez Prado, Ignacio M., 89n5
Sánchez Vázquez, Adolfo, 198
Sanger, Margaret, 107–8, 111
San Luis Gonzaga in Iztacalco, Mexico City, 242
San Luis Potosí, 166, 242
Santa María Magdalena church, Sonora, 242
Santiaguito church, Guanajuato, 242
schools, 62–64, 137

science: anti-Catholicism, 248; defanaticization in the federal classroom, 168–73; grassroots anti-Catholicism, 173–76, 178–79; scientific education, 5, 77–78, 80–81, 85, 86–88, 157, 166, 178–79; Tabasconization, 163–66; Vasconcelos/Gamio dialectic, 82–83
scientism, 157–59, 170, 172, 248–49
scientistic anticlericalism, 161, 169, 179
Second Cristiada, 36, 142, 171, 178
Second Feminist Congress, 106
Second Vatican Council, 195
Secretaría de Educación Pública (Department of Public Education; SEP), 178–79; anti-alcohol campaigns, 126–27; Catholic violations of anticlerical legislation, 159; Departamento de Antropología, 86–87; failure to Tabasconize federal schools, 165–68; fanaticism, 245; List's methods, 163; muralism, 199–201, 203–4; science and defanaticization in the federal classroom, 168–73; scientism, 249; spiritists, 174; Vasconcelos/Gamio Dialectic, 85
Secretaría de Salubridad Pública (Department of Public Health; SSP), 127, 129, 133
secular education, 77, 79, 105, 119n33
secularism/secularization, 26, 81, 86, 213, 216
La Señorita Etcétera (Vela), 113–14

SEP. *See* Secretaría de Educación Pública (Department of Public Education)
Serra, Junípero, 243
sex education, 105, 112
sexual education, 171
sexual instinct, 104–14, 246
sexuality, 100–115, 246–47
Sheffield, James R., 31
Simpson, Eyler, 171
"El Sindicato" ("The Syndicate") (Siqueiros), 200
Sindicato Femenil of Tiripetio, Michoacán, 126, 138
Siqueiros, David Alfaro, 191–210; *América Tropical (Tropical America)*, 194–95; *Burial of the Worker*, 194; *The Devil in the Church*, 194, 202; dialectics, 206–9; *The Elements*, 191, 194; *The March of Humanity*, 199, 206–9; *Los mitos (The Myths)*, 194–95; Muralist Manifesto, 197–204; *From Porfirianism to the Revolution*, 199, 207–8; *Portrait of Mexico Today*, 207; *Portrait of the Bourgeoisie*, 207–8; "El Sindicato" ("The Syndicate"), 200
Siurob Ramírez, José, 133–35
Skousen, Daniel, 214–15, 222–27, 248
Skousen, Sarah S., 215
Skousen, Smith H., 225
smallpox inoculations, 15n39, 176
Smith, Stephanie J., 105
sobriety, promotion of, 140–43
social and economic justice, 50, 52, 62, 65
social Catholicism, 25
Social Gospel, 140
Socialism, southeastern: anti-Catholicism, 67; anti-delahuertismo in Tabasco, 55–61; Garridista socialism, 48–55, 161, 169, 179; post-revolutionary political system, 69; religious fanaticism, 64–65
socialist education, 37, 62–64, 68, 134, 166, 168–69, 172, 178, 245
Socialist Party of the Southeast, 53–54
Socialist Saturdays, 171
Solares, Ignacio, 255n35
Sonora, Mexico, 22–27, 36, 129–31, 134, 135–38, 141–42, 164, 220–21, 242, 245
Soriano, Cesáreo, 26
Spiritism, 39–40, 171, 174–75, 249
SSP. *See* Secretaría de Salubridad Pública (Department of Public Health)
state-building, 54, 127, 128–29
state governments, 26–27, 50, 55, 58, 60, 67, 136
state-level policies, 4, 33, 36, 129, 137, 247
St. Catherine's Military School, Anaheim, CA, 39
superstitions, 169–73
Swarthout, Kelly R., 78, 83, 85
symbols, 191–95, 197–99
Symbols of the New Regime or the Allegory of Hardship of the Laborer and the Peasant or Symbols of the New Order (Rivera), 196
Syndicate of Technical Workers, Painters, and Sculptors (Sindicato de Obreros Técnicos, Pintores y Escultores), 194

Tabasco, Mexico, 48–69; anti-alcohol campaigns, 129, 136; anti-Catholicism, 242; anticlericalism, 245; failure to Tabasconize federal schools, 165–68; Garrido Canabal, 48; grassroots anti-Catholicism and science, 173–77; science and defanaticization in the federal classroom, 168–73; science of revolution in, 159–62; Tabasconization, 157–79
Tabasco Socialists. *See* Partido Socialista Radical Tabasqueño (Tabasco Radical Socialist Party)
Talmage, James, 217
tax exemption petitions, 222–27
Taylor, Ernest, 215, 223–24
Taylor, Ernesto L., 226
Taylor, Harvey, 214–15, 219, 222–27, 248
teachers, 135–38, 139–41, 161–62, 163–65, 166, 168–73, 174–77
Tejeda, Adalberto, 21, 31–35, 32, 245
temperance. *See* anti-alcohol campaigns
temporal issues, role of the Church in, 81
Teotihuacán, Mexico, 77, 91n28
Tepeyac, Mexico, 165, 239
Threlkeld, Megan, 114
Tixkokob, Yucatán, 175
Tomóchic rebellion, 22
Toro, Alfonso, 241
traditionalists, 168
Trincado, Joaquín, 175
truancy strikes, 172
true Catholics, 80–81
Turkey, 7

Turley, Isaac, 225
Tuxtla, Chiapas, Mexico, 175

Ubi Arcano Dei Consilio (By the Inscrutable Counsel of God), 28
unbelief, 2, 8, 127, 237, 238, 242
Unificando la campaña antialcohólica (Lazcano and Portes Gil), 126, 130
Unión de Damas Católicas Mexicanas (Union of Mexican Catholic Ladies), 28
Unión Femenina Católica Mexicana de Clases Trabajadoras, 142
unionization, 178, 195
United States: anti-Catholicism in the, 7; exile in the, 56, 58, 87; immigrants from, 219; Mexican Catholicism compared to US Catholic Church, 79; Mormon settler refugees to, 220; obligations to US capitalists, 31; against polygamy, 220; religious minorities associated with, 213–27; religious question, 167; reproductive rights, 107–8
El Universal (newspaper), 33–34, 161
El Universal Ilustrado (newspaper), 112–13
el Universo sin Dios (Malpica Hernández), 161, 177
urban and rural working classes, 52, 128, 137
Urías Horcasitas, Beatriz, 87, 92n68, 174
Urrea, Teresa, 22
Urzaiz, Eduardo, 1, 108
utilitarian Catholics, 80–88

vaccination, 176–77
Vaccination (Rivera), 15n39
Valdespino y Díaz, Ignacio, 25–26
Valenzuela, Gilberto, 31
Valles Ruiz, Rosa María, 102
La Vanguardia (newspaper), 101–6
vasconcelismo, 246
Vasconcelos, José, 1, 26, 36, 78–79, 82, 85–88, 191–94, 199, 248
Vatican City, 35
Vatican Council, 237–38
Vela, Arqueles, 113–14
Velázquez Bringas, Esperanza, 109–12, 113, 114–15, 120n42, 246, 254n28
Veracruz, Mexico, 30, 36, 56, 58, 100–101, 121n63, 182n51, 242
Vidal, Carlos A., 54
Villa, Pancho, 4, 100
Villahermosa, Mexico, 56–57, 245
Villarreal, Antonio, 26
Virgin of Guadalupe, 9–10, 56, 165, 216, 238, 245
Voekel, Pamela, 15n20, 252n16
V. y Sánchez Martínez, Salvador, 177

War of the Winners, 4
Wars of Independence, 15n20
water concessions, 222–24, 248
Wechsler, James, 205
Weis, Robert, 35
The Woman Rebel (magazine), 107
women, 99–115; agency, 109, 117n18, 119n33; anti-alcohol campaigns, 136–38, 140, 247; anticlericals, 246; consciousness-raising, 101–5; Galindo, 100–106; gendered reception of feminism and anticlericalism, 112–14; lay organizations, 6; moralism, 104, 109, 115; political enfranchisement, 52; reproductive rights *versus* the Church, 106–9; Sindicato Femenil of Tiripetio, Michoacán, 126–27; Spiritist circles, 40; suffrage, 102, 105, 120n53; working women's rights, 109–12
Word of Wisdom, 218
workers' rights, 52, 69, 168
working-class individuals, 127, 128, 137
World War I, 220

Xalapa, Veracruz, 242

Yaqui, 27, 134
Yeaworth, Ivy V., 140
Yucatán, Mexico: anti-alcohol campaign, 129; anti-Catholic movement, 176; Feminist Congresses, 103, 106, 246; grassroots anticlericalism, 176; List's curriculum, 163–64, 169; Maya of Yucatán, religious ritual using alcohol, 134; profanations in, 242; radical feminist activity, 108; rationalist schooling in, 162; reproductive rights, 106–9; southeastern Socialism, 50, 52–54; spiritists, 175; temperance and the anti-Catholic movements in, 136
Yucatec women, 110–12

Zapata, Emiliano, 4, 78, 100–101

www.ingramcontent.com/pod-product-compliance
Lightning Source LLC
Chambersburg PA
CBHW020943230426
43666CB00005B/143